Praise for *Investigative Ethics: Ethics for Police Detectives and Criminal Investigators*

"Liberally illustrated with challenging cases, this volume marshals and discusses the many ethical problems encountered by police investigators. In an area that tends to be governed by pragmatic considerations, it provides an important check on the desire and pressure for results."
John Kleinig, John Jay College of Criminal Justice

"Rarely has the publication of a work exploring modern crime investigation shown such a thorough grasp of the myriad challenges, many of them ethical, facing tenacious investigators."
Sir Dan Crompton, Former UK Police Chief and HM Inspector of Police

"*Investigative Ethics* is applied philosophy of the best sort. Its thoughtful analysis of foundational issues in police ethics—at once sophisticated and accessible—will provide a valuable resource for philosophers, legal academics, and police practitioners."
Stuart Green, Rutgers Law School

"*Investigative Ethics* makes a valuable contribution to the growing body of critical and informed literature on criminal investigative practice. While aimed at police detectives and criminal investigators, it has much to offer professional administrative investigators. Highly recommended."
Nigel Savidge, Lead Integrity Specialist, Asian Development Bank

T0341676

Investigative Ethics
Ethics for Police Detectives and Criminal Investigators

Seumas Miller and Ian A. Gordon OBE QPM

WILEY Blackwell

This edition first published 2014
© 2014 Seumas Miller and Ian A. Gordon

Registered Office
John Wiley & Sons Ltd, The Atrium, Southern Gate, Chichester, West Sussex, PO19 8SQ, UK

Editorial Offices
350 Main Street, Malden, MA 02148-5020, USA
9600 Garsington Road, Oxford, OX4 2DQ, UK
The Atrium, Southern Gate, Chichester, West Sussex, PO19 8SQ, UK

For details of our global editorial offices, for customer services, and for information about
how to apply for permission to reuse the copyright material in this book please see our
website at www.wiley.com/wiley-blackwell.

The right of Seumas Miller and Ian A. Gordon to be identified as the authors of this work
has been asserted in accordance with the UK Copyright, Designs and Patents Act 1988.

Library of Congress Cataloging-in-Publication Data applied for

Hardback ISBN: 978-1-4051-5772-8
Paperback ISBN: 978-1-4051-5773-5

A catalogue record for this book is available from the British Library.

Cover image: Magnifying glass © Jiri Hera / Shutterstock; Justice blindfolded © kanvag /
Shutterstock.
Cover design by RBDA

Set in 10/12 pt SabonLTStd Roman by Toppan Best-set Premedia Limited

1   2014

In memory of John Blackler APM (1933–2010) a former
police officer in the New South Wales Police

Contents

Acknowledgments

We wish to thank Andrew Alexandra, Dan Crompton, Michael Davis, Clive Harfield, and John Kleinig for comments on earlier versions of chapters in this book.

Earlier versions of some of the material in this book appeared in the following publications authored or co-authored by Seumas Miller:

The Moral Foundations of Social Institutions: A Philosophical Study, New York: Cambridge University Press, 2010; *Terrorism and Counterterrorism: Ethics and Liberal Democracy*, Oxford: Blackwell Publishing, 2009; *Police Ethics* (2nd edn), Sydney: Allen and Unwin, 2006; Winchester: Waterside Press, 2006 (co-authored with John Blackler and Andrew Alexandra); *Ethical Issues in Policing*, Aldershot: Ashgate, 2005 (co-authored with John Blackler); *Police Ethics: Case Studies* (vols. 1–3), Wagga Wagga: Charles Sturt University and NSW Police, 2000 (co-authored with John Blacker); *Police Ethics*, Keon Press, 1995 (co-authored with John Blackler); *Issues in Police Ethics,* Keon Press, 1996; Privacy and the internet, *Australian Computer Journal*, 29, 1997; Authority, discretion and accountability: The case of policing, in C. Sampford, N. Preston and C. Bois (eds), *Public Sector Ethics: Finding and Implementing Values*, London: Routledge, 1998; Corruption and anti-corruption in the profession of policing, *Professional Ethics*, 6.3/4, 1998; Corruption, in Edward N. Zalta (ed.), *Stanford Encyclopaedia of Philosophy*, Fall 2005 Edition; Torture, in Edward N. Zalta (ed.), *Stanford Encyclopaedia of Philosophy*, Spring 2006 Edition; Integrity systems and professional reporting in police organisations, *Criminal Justice Ethics*, 29, 2010; The fatal police shooting of Jean Charles de Menezes: Is anyone responsible? (co-authored with Ian Gordon), in Simon Bronitt, Miriam Gani, and Saskia Hufnagel (eds), *Shooting to Kill: Socio-legal Perspectives on the Use of Lethal Force*, Oxford: Hart Publishing, 2012; Police detectives, criminal investigations and collective responsibility, *Criminal Justice Ethics*, 33, 2014.

Introduction
Ethics and the Role of the Investigator

This book is an applied philosophical study of some of the main ethical issues that arise in the context of investigations of crime by police detectives. As such, it is not a general guide to best practice in police investigations, so it will not provide novice investigators with technical expertise.[1] Nor is it a contribution to ethical theory *per se* – although it does offer philosophical theories of various aspects of criminal investigations, for example, knowledge as the defining occupational end of detectives, and the collective moral responsibility of detectives, prosecutors, jurors, and others for the outcomes of trials in the context of what we refer to as the "chain of moral responsibility." It will not, therefore, enable novice philosophers to become advanced ethical theorists either.[2] Rather it occupies the conceptual space where ethics or morality and police investigations intersect, and it attempts to shed intellectual light on some of the practical ethical problems in that space. Accordingly, if the book succeeds, it will assist police investigators to have a greater understanding of the ethical underpinnings of their work, and to reflect more profitably on the ethical issues that arise in the course of it. Moreover, it might coax more philosophers to seriously engage with criminal investigators and the complex and important ethical and philosophical problems that their work gives rise to.

While the book is serviceable as a text both for graduate and advanced undergraduate students and for police detectives, non-police crime and corruption investigators, and other criminal justice practitioners, it does offer an array of novel arguments, ethical analyses, and philosophical perspectives. This was inevitable given the paucity of scholarly work in investigative ethics and given, also, the intellectual complexity of many of the issues. We

Investigative Ethics: Ethics for Police Detectives and Criminal Investigators, First Edition.
Seumas Miller and Ian A. Gordon.
© 2014 Seumas Miller and Ian A. Gordon. Published 2014 by John Wiley & Sons, Ltd.

leave it to others to judge whether or not the content of the book is sometimes illuminating rather than merely novel.

Investigation

Combating crime and corruption and enforcing the criminal law involves conducting criminal investigations. The categories of crime in question include crimes against the person such as homicide, rape, and assault (Chapter 5), and property crimes such as theft, burglary, and fraud (Chapter 6). Terrorism (Chapter 7) is a crime that is typically a crime against the person (detonating a bomb in a crowded train and thereby murdering innocent passengers), a property crime (destruction of the train carriage) and a political crime (committed with the intent of undermining the authority of the state). "Corruption" (Chapter 8), on the other hand, is a generic term that covers a wide range of moral offenses that are not always crimes, that is, legal offenses. (For the distinction and relation between the law and morality, see Chapter 1.) These offenses include bribery, nepotism, cheating, and abuse of authority. Our discussion in Chapter 8 focuses on police corruption.

In contemporary settings, the investigative capacity typically resides with the police service and, for major crimes, criminal investigation units within the police service. However, large public and private sector organizations often have their own investigative units, for example, fraud units, and in many jurisdictions bodies with the specific responsibility to deal with corruption have been established, for example, independent commissions against corruption.

Criminal investigators require knowledge (e.g., of the law), skills (e.g., how to conduct interviews), and experience (e.g., of efficiently and effectively conducting a successful investigation leading to prosecution). They also have to have legal powers, such as the power to question witnesses and suspects.

The various specialist areas within criminal investigation, like homicide, drugs, and terrorism, all require the exercise of generic investigative skills that are transferable from one area to another. However, each of these areas also requires a degree of specialized knowledge – for example, knowledge, on the part of drug investigators, of specific drugs and their means of production and distribution. Moreover, with the advent of computers, the growth of transnational organized crime, and so on, there is a greater need for specialized knowledge. Increasingly, therefore, investigators are required to undertake formal training and education programs.

The ethical issues that arise for criminal investigators are manifold. They include: investigative independence (Chapter 4); the use of criminals as informants (Chapter 9); deception and the infringement of privacy rights in surveillance operations (Chapter 10), profiling (Chapter 5), undercover operations (Chapter 11) and the use of traps or "sting" operations (Chapter 11); and the use of deception and/or coercion in interviewing (Chapter 12).

Prior to the nineteenth century, law enforcement agencies had no detectives as such. Indeed, in the United Kingdom, the United States, and elsewhere people were deeply suspicious of the notion of a detective, or at least of those people who undertook some of the kinds of work associated with the modern detective. These early forerunners of the detective were, for the most part, entrepreneurs working for themselves, and they undertook a variety of forms of investigative work. They functioned as informants for the public police service, thief takers (a kind of bounty hunter), and agents provocateurs (who infiltrated and trapped suspects, including underground political groups).

The public, the government, and the ordinary police were understandably unhappy with these private entrepreneurs who often used dubious methods for private, or even political, interests. At the same time it was acknowledged that they played an important investigative role or roles.

Accordingly, in the second half of the nineteenth century in England – partly at the instigation of Richard Mayne, who was (jointly with Charles Rowan) the first commissioner of the Metropolitan Police,[3] a new vocational role was carved out, namely, the role of the detective. Moreover, it was a role destined to attract an enormous amount of attention from writers and film-makers. The image of the modern detective, far from that of his or her contemptible forerunners, is one of glamour and mystique. Indeed, even in reality detectives have often come to see themselves as an elite group within police services. Investigative agencies, such as the Federal Bureau of Investigation (FBI) in the United States, are known worldwide and have been the subject of numerous films, TV series, and the like.[4]

Here it is important to resist stereotypes and self-serving images, and focus on what the role of detectives ought to be, both within the police organization and within the wider criminal justice system. Note also that we are distinguishing between the *de facto* role and the role as it ought to be. (On these matters of occupational role see Chapters 1 and 2.)

There are a host of questions about the optimal forms of organization for police services. This has led to various institutional design initiatives. Thus there has been, and there continues to be, restructuring of criminal investigations departments/bureaux for purposes of specialization (e.g., into organized crime units), decentralization, a strengthening of the investigative capacity of patrol police (e.g., team policing) and (at times) a reinforcement of accountability (e.g., breaking up perceived powerful and/or corrupt detective groups). The desirability or undesirability of particular organizational changes is not our concern here. Suffice it to state the obvious. The best organizational structures and mechanisms of cooperation are those that facilitate the purposes of, in this case, criminal investigations. Restructuring ought not to be simply the vehicle of some internal or external factional or political interest.

Particular organizational structures and cultures can either facilitate or impede police work, including criminal investigations work. For example, an "us–them" mentality can set police management against operational police, patrol police against detectives, and so on, thereby obstructing effective policing.

Again, the need for, and the dangers of, police discretion are things that organizational structures and mechanisms must accommodate. Curtailing discretion can simply disempower police. On the other hand, wide discretionary powers, especially in a context in which there is a lack of accountability in respect of their use, can be a recipe for disaster in high-risk areas, for example, corruption in drug investigations work.

In addition to the utility of particular forms of organization for criminal investigations within the police service, there is the question of the role and organization of criminal investigations in the larger context of the criminal justice system.

Principles of justice are inevitably imperfectly embodied in specific criminal justice systems and in the actual practices of criminal investigators. Arguably, the current criminal justice systems in the United States, United Kingdom, Australia, and elsewhere are in need of significant redesign in a number of respects. For one thing, certain kinds of crime, including in the drug and fraud area, are not being adequately combated. For another, incarceration rates over the past few decades appear to have risen inexorably in, for example, the United States, and yet the prisons in question do not seem to be having the required level of rehabilitative effect on offenders. Public concern in relation to the efficacy of contemporary criminal justice systems is manifest in the more focused criticism often directed at the adversarial character of criminal justice systems in the English-speaking world in particular.

Lustgarten gives this characterization of the adversarial system as it operates in the United Kingdom.[5]

> The English police operate in the context of an adversarial not an inquisitorial system. . . . In practical terms, this means a system in which the trial is of much greater importance. . . .The trial is governed by rules erecting relatively high evidentiary barriers to conviction: in the adversary system, 'there is a greater divergence between what the police actually know and what can be introduced as evidence at trial.'[6] Moreover, the verdict of that trial is reached by persons without legal training who, unlike mixed continental tribunals, need not give reasons for their decision. Thus the English police take an avowedly partisan stance in a system in which partisan contest is supposed to

produce truth. And the evidentiary barriers reinforce bureaucratic and resource imperatives of avoiding trials in the vast majority of cases by producing guilty pleas. . . . This gives the English police substantially greater incentive to seek a confession from the suspect; more generally and ominously, it would seem to be a constant pressure leading them to overstep their powers against those they 'know' are guilty.

This adversarial system impacts on investigative attitudes and practices. Specifically, it may well be that there is – and many have claimed that this is, in fact, the case[7] – a tendency to forego even-handed, objective inquiry into the truth in favor of simply gathering evidence to establish guilt within the rules of the system. Even-handed, evidence-based testing for truth is a matter for the court, it is held. By contrast, the detective's job is, on this view, to "win" by ensuring the prosecutor has a sufficiently strong case to guarantee a conviction. Whether or not this tendency exists is in the end an empirical matter and needs to be settled on the basis of empirical evidence, rather than a priori judgments.[8]

In the United States, in particular, the picture is somewhat complicated by the large proportion of cases that are settled by plea bargaining: "winning" might now consist quite often in ensuring a conviction for a lesser charge or for only some of the offenses a suspect has been charged with.

The more general point to be made here is that investigation, including criminal investigation, takes place in particular institutional contexts, and those contexts shape and influence investigative attitudes and practices and, indeed, the likelihood or even possibility of successful investigations. The former point has already been made in relation to institutional structures within a jurisdiction, for example, the adversarial system in the United Kingdom. The latter point is obvious in relation to institutional resources; other things being equal, an under-resourced fraud squad, for example, is unlikely to have the same degree of success as a well-resourced one. But the point is also relevant to investigation units operating in transjurisdictional, and especially transnational, settings. If the tax avoidance, bribery, fraud, drug production/selling and so on in question is transnational, and conducted on a massive financial scale by powerful corporations or criminal organizations in cahoots with corrupt governments, then the best efforts of even well-motivated, relatively well-resourced, highly competent, state-based investigators may well be doomed from the start (Chapter 6).

A recent specific exemplification of this problem is that involving Prime Minister Tony Blair's interference with the UK Serious Fraud Office's criminal investigation into the British aerospace (BAE Systems) arms bribery scandal (Chapter 4).[9] More generally, consider the 'dirty money' that continues to flow from the exploitation of mineral resources in impoverished African states notwithstanding the enactment of various counteractive international agreements, for example, in relation to "conflict diamonds"; or the international money-laundering activities of drug cartels, such as the Mexican-based cartels. The latter evidently used the multinational bank HSBC for this purpose over a 10-year period resulting in a US\$1.9 billion fine for HSBC for failing to have in place effective anti-money-laundering measures and for failing to conduct due diligence on some of its account holders. However, the drug cartels continue to launder their money and, as for HSBC, it retained its license to operate having in effect been deemed "too big to fail."[10]

Outside police organizations investigators operate within both the private and public spheres. In the public sphere they are attached mainly to government bureaus such as welfare agencies, but also to tax offices, finance departments, defense departments, and so on. In the private sector investigators are attached to such industries as insurance, banking, law, debt collection, security, stockbroking, and many more. Indeed, we might say that investigators are required in any situation where an individual is in a position to engage in unlawful conduct or to unjustly gain some advantage over someone else. Of course, typically this will involve gaining some material advantage over another, as is the case where a person defrauds or blackmails another person or organization. However, investigators may also be needed where the issue is not material gain, such as illicit monetary gain, or not just that kind of gain. There are cases, for example, of sexual harassment or of bullying in the work place that come under this heading.

Investigators must tailor their activities to the needs of the institution that they serve, for example, a police organization or (more broadly) the criminal justice system. However, these institutions are quite diverse. Obviously an investigator within a large corporation will not only be motivated by his or her specific occupational function within the institution – to see to it that it functions properly in this regard, that its employees, for example, comply with the law – but the investigator will also probably recognize the reputational interests of that corporation. Or in the government sphere an investigator in, say, the social welfare area will recognize not just the needs of a disadvantaged citizen but also the need to insulate public funds from unscrupulous "welfare" claimants.

A further point to be made here is that, in the context of the Global Financial Crisis (GFC) and its aftermath of large government debt, the financial constraints on police organizations and other public agencies responsible for investigating criminal conduct are severe, and the process already underway in many jurisdictions in the United States, the United Kingdom and elsewhere of subcontracting elements of this function out to the private sector is likely to accelerate. This may well exacerbate the problem mentioned above of tensions between investigative ends and organizational goals.[11]

Ideally, members of occupations such as investigators should internalize the fundamental ends that define, or at least ought to define, their particular ongoing task. In the case of criminal investigators, as will be argued in Chapter 2, the fundamental defining end is the truth – or at least knowledge in the sense of justified, true, stated belief. Moreover, the knowledge in question – the who, what, when, where, how, and why of a crime – is not simply the defining end of investigative activity, it is the regulative ideal,[12] indeed the morally desirable end, that investigators morally *ought* to be aiming at. An investigator who abandons the pursuit of the truth in relation to some crime in favor of, for example, "framing" a suspect whom he or she despises, corrupts the investigative process by undermining its fundamental moral purpose, namely, to determine the truth.

This process of internalization of defining occupational ends may only be implicit. These ends can guide the actions of investigators even though investigators are not explicitly aware that they do. Most important, they must identify with these defining ends. That is, their self-worth must come to depend in part on their capacity to realize them. The good teacher is one who not only has a capacity to impart knowledge but who also suffers a loss in self-esteem when he or she fails to exercise this capacity successfully. Similarly, the good investigator is one who not only has a capacity to detect illegal activity but also suffers a loss in self-esteem if he or she fails to do so.

Practitioners are defined, in part, not only by the end at which their efforts ought to be directed, but also by the characteristic activities that members of their occupation engage in, or ought to engage in.[13] When members of an occupation habitually engage in these desirable activities in the service of the proper ends of that occupation, they are said to possess the virtues of that occupation. Accordingly, investigators need to have the virtues of a commitment to truth, capacity for systematic reasoning, suspiciousness, a capacity to win the trust of people from different walks of life, and so on.

Naturally, the possession of investigative virtues and/or vices is in part dependent on features of the operational and institutional investigative environment. Such features include organizational goals, for example, to reduce crime, and the subcultural attitudes and values within which the investigator works, for example, a results-driven, "bend-the-rules" mentality.

On the one hand, investigators can be in a difficult position by virtue of being, for example, under-resourced agencies confronting well-resourced corporate organizations. Moreover, in the case of investigators employed by some large corporations, in particular, there can be issues of investigative independence. To what extent is investigative independence compromised, for example, when the subject of their investigation is a very senior person within the organization that employs them? Nor is the issue of investigative independence restricted to commercial organizations; political interference in publically funded police organizations is a very real and ongoing concern in many jurisdictions (see Chapter 4).

On the other hand, investigators and the agencies they work for are often in a very powerful position. They have access to an enormous amount of personal information, which could potentially be used to violate the privacy of citizens and employees (Chapters 3 and 10). Indeed, developments in information and communication technology have enabled a degree of access that is at times morally problematic. Consider, in this connection, the recent revelations concerning the collection by the US National Security Agency of the daily call records of millions of customers of Verizon and other telecommunication providers (see Case Study 3.2.3 in Chapter 3.)

By virtue of their crucial role in the effective handling of serious criminality, investigators are sometimes subject to significant pressures to engage in unethical conduct themselves. Accordingly, it is very important to have accountability mechanisms in relation to investigators and their agencies. Thus investigative offenses should be set down in legislation, there should be an independent authority with powers to investigate investigators in relation to serious criminality, and the provision of specific penalties (such as the loss of pension entitlements and other benefits, or even imprisonment), for investigators found to be corrupt.

As with most occupations, success or failure can impact positively or negatively on the dispositions and behavior of investigators, and these dispositions and behaviors can in turn impact on the likelihood of investigations succeeding or failing. Other things being equal, a well-trained and experienced investigator who is supported by his or her community (e.g., through the provision of information), employing organization and superiors (e.g., through the provision of adequate resources), is more likely to succeed and, therefore, less likely to develop dispositions or behaviors that are inimical to success. That said, notoriously in the history of policing there have been elite detective units that have bent or broken the rules, seen themselves as above the law, and ultimately engaged in serious and ongoing corruption (Chapter 8).

Obviously, investigators rely on victims, work colleagues of offenders, and ordinary citizens to report crime. However, there are other sources of information in relation to criminality that investigators can use to assist them in their task. The advent of computers has seen the capacity to record and track financial transactions accurately and speedily increase on an unprecedented scale. Countries such as Australia have stringent and elaborate arrangements for controlling the operation of accounts in financial institutions, as well as requirements for reporting cash transactions over a certain limit, identifying and reporting suspicious transactions, and monitoring all overseas money transactions. These provide an invaluable source of information that can be used to detect corruption and assist in its prosecution. As is the case with many of the mechanisms for dealing with criminality, transaction analysis is a very beneficial tool, but it comes at a moral cost: it impinges upon the privacy of members of the community. For transaction analysis involves vast amounts of information on citizens' financial activities being recorded and transmitted to enforcement agencies. We consider these important privacy issues in Chapter 3 and, especially, Chapter 10.

Ethics and Morality

Ethics or morality is about what actions an individual person or member of an occupation ought to do, and it is about what kind of character he or she ought to have. It is also about what features the organizations that employ members of specific occupations ought to have and, at a more fundamental level, what organizations there ought to be. These latter questions, or sets of questions, pertain to what might be referred to as institutional ethics, as opposed to the ethics of individual behavior and attitudes outside institutional contexts. Our concern in this monograph is principally with institutional ethics and, in particular, with the ethics of a specific occupational group, namely, criminal investigators. No doubt institutional ethics in this sense is directly or indirectly concerned with the behavior and attitudes of individual human beings; however, it is with the behavior and attitudes of individual human beings *qua criminal investigators* that we are principally occupied.[14]

Thus far we have used the terms "ethics" and "morality" interchangeably. However, sometimes ethics is distinguished from morality in the philosophical literature. One way of making the distinction is as follows. Morality is about minimum standards of behavior and attitude. Do not kill the innocent; do not tell lies; do not steal; do not commit fraud. These are all minimum standards of behavior; they are moral principles. Ethics – on this way of thinking – is a wider notion. Ethics involves ideals and aspirations; it goes beyond minimum standards. An investigator who was competent, and was not negligent might not be engaged in immoral behavior. Nevertheless, such an investigator might not be a good investigator. To be a good investigator implies doing more than merely complying with minimum standards. For example, a good investigator would be *scrupulous* in the gathering of evidence and *persistent* in the pursuit of the truth; a good investigator is not simply an investigator who is not negligent.

Henceforth, we will distinguish compliance with minimum standards (which we will normally refer to as morality) from ethics in the wider sense of a field of value that also embraces notions of what is good and worth aspiring to, that is, ideals as well as minimum standards.

In thinking and reasoning about moral or ethical questions there are a number of key concepts, distinctions, and theoretical standpoints that are typically deployed. We will now introduce some of the more important of these.[15]

First, we need to distinguish between actions, habits, and attitudes. Actions are morally right (whether morally required or morally permissible), for example, arresting an offender; or morally wrong, for example, punishing the innocent; or neither, for example, drinking a cup of coffee. Here we need to distinguish between actions and their consequences. Arresting a suspect is an action that might have good consequences, for example, if the suspect is actually the offender, or bad consequences, for example, if the suspect turns out to be innocent.

Some actions are morally significant by virtue of complying or failing to comply with minimum moral standards, for example, refraining from stealing from one's employer or from murdering one's business competitor. Others are undertaken in conformity with ideals or aspirations – for example, engaging in unpaid voluntary work for charitable organizations, or not taking advantage of one's competitor when they are in an unfortunate situation due to bad luck.

Notwithstanding the distinction between minimum moral standards and ideals, the boundary between these is blurred: there is a considerable gray area. Moreover, it is important to note that attending only to minimum standards – and especially being a "rule addict" and eschewing ideals – is an ultimately unsustainable position. Rule addicts will tend to lose sight of the underlying principles and values, including the ideals, that inform even the rules embodying minimum standards; ultimately this is corrosive of conformity to minimum standards, as well as of the realization of ideals.

Habits are dispositions to action that are typically performed by a person. For example, Winston Churchill evidently had the habit of smoking cigars. Habits include virtues, such as courage, honesty, and determination, as well as vices, such as cowardice, corruption, and dishonesty. However, virtues (and for that matter vices) are more than just habits since, for example, virtues are ethically good habits practiced for good reasons, whereas this is not necessarily the case with habits. Winston Churchill was said to be a courageous leader because he frequently, indeed habitually, made hard decisions in the service of his country. In the 1990s the New South Wales police officer "Chook" Fowler was said to be corrupt because he consistently, indeed habitually, engaged in illegal activity to enrich himself (Chapter 11, Case Study 11.2.1, Chook Fowler and "Crotch-Cam"). Some habits are neither virtues nor vices. For example, the habit of having a coffee after one's meal would not normally be regarded as either a virtue or a vice.

Once again, vices tend to call for moral condemnation: people who are corrupt or dishonest fail to meet minimum standards. On the other hand, persons possessed of virtues tend to be seen as ethical: they have dispositions to do what is good. They do more than merely avoid wrongdoing. However, once again there is a gray area here between minimum standards and ideals.

As noted above, the key property of virtues and vices is that they are elements of character: they are to do with what a person is (and, therefore, what a person regularly, or at least reliably, does), as opposed to what a person might do on some particular occasion as a one-off, that is, as an "out of character" action. Clearly character, and thus virtues and vices, is of central importance in ethics, including institutional and, specifically, occupational ethics.

Affective attitudes, including feelings, sensations of pain and pleasure, and emotions, are not actions as such; nor are they habits or merely dispositions to act. A person can obey all the rules, even do so as a matter of habit, and yet have a "bad attitude," at least in the short or medium term. Of course, in the long term this inconsistency is much less likely, since emotions, including attitudes, tend to influence dispositions and actions.

As with actions and habits, affective attitudes can be classified into those that are by and large good, such as a caring or sympathetic or sensitive attitude, and those that are for the most part morally wrong, such as an attitude of hatred or contempt. Naturally, some attitudes would not normally be regarded as either good or morally wrong, for example, the attitude or feeling of excitement generated at the thought of being paid a large salary. Moreover, there is a gray area here between morally problematic attitudes, such as hatred, and attitudes that one ought ideally to have, but that one ought not to suffer moral condemnation for not readily experiencing, for example, friendliness.

In contemporary moral philosophy a threefold distinction is often made between so-called deontological, consequentialist, and virtue-based theories of morality.[16] Deontological theories emphasize the intrinsic moral properties of an action as opposed to its consequences: for example, an act of lying is morally wrong and ought not to be performed even if it has good consequences in some settings. Deontological theories are also typically defined, in part, by recourse to the so-called formal principle of universalizability in one or other of its variants, such as "Act only on a principle if you could will that everyone act on that principle." By contrast, according to consequentialist theories such as utilitarianism, what matters morally are the consequences of actions rather than any inherent properties they might have, for example, "An action is right if it maximizes the greatest happiness of the greatest number and wrong if it does not" (principle of utility). Finally, according to virtue-based theories an action is right or wrong if it is the action which a virtuous person would perform. Deontological theories are associated with Immanuel Kant, consequentialist theories with J. S. Mill, and virtue-based theories with Aristotle.[17]

While there is a need to maintain the threefold distinction between actions, habits (including vices and virtues), and the consequences of actions, the construction of competing moral theories which give pride of place to one or other of these conceptual categories at the expense of the others is questionable.

Moreover, we suggest that the application of any of these theories to the behavior and attitudes of individual role occupants independently of adequate normative theories of the occupation(s) in question and the institutional settings in play is likely to yield impoverished and/or misleading results.[18] Hence our insistence in this volume and elsewhere on the provision of appropriate occupational and institutional normative theories, for instance, the normative theory of policing (Chapter 1).

As will become evident in the chapters below, we tend to favor teleological normative theories of social institutions, including police organizations, and of occupational roles, including the role of criminal investigator. Teleological theories give pride of place to the telos[19] or point or aims of actions and organizations. According to such theories, the identification of the virtues definitive of an occupational group will crucially depend on the aims of that occupation. If, as we will argue in Chapter 2, the fundamental aim of criminal investigators ought to be truth or, more precisely, knowledge, then many of the virtues of investigators will turn out to be *epistemic* or knowledge-based[20] virtues such as accuracy and logical thinking.

Here we note that, although teleological and consequentialist normative theories are often conflated, they ought not to be. According to consequentialism, the rightness or wrongness of actions, procedures, or policies is logically dependent only on their outcomes and, therefore, is not logically dependent on whether or not they were intended or otherwise aimed at. The arguments for and against consequentialism in its various permutations have a long history and are detailed and complex: far too detailed and complex to revisit here.[21] Rather, we simply record our view that consequentialism is committed to the implausible view that an action is morally right or morally wrong by virtue of its consequences, even though those consequences might be unknown and unknowable. This collapses the distinction between harmful actions and morally wrong actions (and also the parallel distinction between beneficial actions and morally right actions), and puts the moral rightness and wrongness of many actions beyond the epistemic reach of the moral agents who perform those actions. For the harmful or beneficial consequences of human actions over the long term, and even the short term, are quite often unknowable by the agents who perform the actions, either at the time of their performance or at any future time. Consider a police officer whose quick action saves the life of a child trapped in a crashed and burning car. Suppose the child grows up to be an armed robber who shoots dead two bank employees during the course of a hold-up gone wrong. It is true that what the police officer did was a causally necessary condition for these future harmful acts; if the police officer had not saved the child the future deaths would not have happened. And perhaps, with the benefit of hindsight, the officer might even regret his action. Nevertheless, the claim that it was also morally wrong for the police officer to save the child's life is implausible; yet consequentialism seems committed to just this claim.

By contrast, according to teleological theories, the intentions and, in particular, the outcomes aimed at, the *ends*, are in part *definitive* of the rightness or wrongness of actions, procedures, and policies – and, indeed, of social institutions themselves. On this kind of view the outcome of an action cannot be morally significant – as opposed to good or evil in some more general sense – unless it was in fact intended, or could have been intended (or was, or could have been, otherwise aimed at or known about).

In relation to the alleged conflict between deontological theories and virtue-based theories, we see only a degree of congruence. We doubt that we can account for the moral rightness of an action simply in terms of its being one that a virtuous person would perform; for the notion of a virtuous person will itself be in part determined by recourse to a notion of morally right action (virtuous persons are persons who (at least) habitually perform morally right actions). On the other hand, the fact that someone habitually performs morally right actions does not necessarily make them virtuous in the required sense, since they might do so for the wrong reasons. So virtues are not reducible to right actions.

As will also become apparent in the chapters below, our own favored account of normative ethical theory is a species of *moral pluralism*. We see little prospect of the nontrivial accommodation of, for example, moral rights within virtue theory (or vice versa). In our view the distinctions between, say, intrinsically right action, virtues, and morally significant consequences are just that: conceptual and morally relevant distinctions that need to be respected as basic, rather than set against one another in the service of a monistic ethical theory that seeks to privilege one of these conceptual categories at the expense of the others.

Moreover, the moral pluralism that we have in mind is substantive, as opposed to formalist, in character. By this we simply mean that purely formal or otherwise highly abstract principles, such as the principle of universalizability and the principle of utility maximization, have a relatively minor role to play in theoretical and practical ethics, and, certainly, in individual and collective moral or ethical decision making.

Is there, for example, a viable criminal justice system anywhere in which the principle of utility is taken to override the principle of convicting the guilty and ensuring the innocent go free, utilitarian philosophers such as Jeremy Bentham notwithstanding? And in relation to policing as an institution, ought the principle of utility to override the principle of objective investigation, if and when they conflict? Arguably, a commitment to a principle of utility is part of the problem with some police organizations. For example, in maximizing clear-up rates and so-called stakeholder satisfaction police departments sometimes tolerate "bending the rules" in investigations and thereby abnegate their institutional responsibilities as protectors of the moral rights of citizens, notably suspects.

What of the principle of universalizability: does it provide much-needed guidance in the kinds of institutional contexts in question? No doubt the principle of universalizability has a contribution to make, but evidently it is a limited one. It appears to be little more than a consistency test, and, as such, it offers only very limited guidance to moral agents, including police investigators, seeking to know what they ought to do or not do. Moral decision making relies heavily on substantive principles; purely formal ones are largely impotent.

Having provided a brief introductory overview of criminal investigations and morality/ethics, let us now turn to a detailed consideration of the issues. We begin with the relationship between law, morality, and criminal investigations (Chapter 1).

We note that Chapters 1 and 2 are principally concerned with underlying philosophical issues (e.g., the relation between law and morality, normative theories of policing and of the occupation of criminal investigator), as opposed to more practical ethical problems. We regard these underlying philosophical issues as being of fundamental importance, especially given the tendency of criminal investigators to simply take the criminal law as a given not to be questioned. By contrast with this tendency, we want to insist that criminal investigators are under an obligation to reflect on the moral basis of the criminal law. After all, criminal investigators contribute significantly to the enforcement of the criminal law and, therefore, their work often has profound moral consequences, both for those who are the victims of crime and for those who suffer severe punishment, such as incarceration, as a consequence of being convicted of breaches of the criminal law. Surely, therefore, investigators ought to be able to provide themselves with good and decisive reasons for the enforcement of the criminal law in general and, for that matter, of particular criminal laws.

That said, the book has been written so that those readers who might on occasion simply wish to consider particular practical ethical issues faced by investigators, and bypass these more fundamental philosophical issues, can skip the first two chapters and go straight to Chapter 3, or whatever chapter deals with the issues of particular interest to them.

Notes

1 For a useful such guide in the US context see Michael F. Brown (2001) *Criminal Investigation: Law and Practice* (2nd edn), Boston: Butterworth and Heineman, and in the UK context, Peter Stelfox (2009) *Criminal Investigation: An Introduction to Principles and Practice*, Cullompton, Devon: Willan Publishing. For an earlier empirical description of detectives at work, see Richard V. Ericson (1981) *Making Crime: Detectives at Work*, Toronto: Butterworths. For a set of more recent "rich descriptions" of detectives at work, see Robert Jackall (2005) *Street Stories: The World of Police Detectives*, Cambridge, MA: Harvard University Press.

2 For a useful introduction to ethics see A. C. Ewing (1953) *Ethics*, London: Macmillan, and in relation to more recent ethical theory see Bernard Gert (2004) *Common Morality: Deciding What to Do*, Oxford: Oxford University Press.

3 T. A. Critchley (1967) *A History of Police in England and Wales 900–1966*, London: Constable, p. 51.

4 Regarding the history of the FBI see Tim Weiner (2013) *Enemies: A History of the FBI*, New York: Random House.

5 Laurence Lustgarten (1986) *The Governance of Police*, London: Sweet and Maxwell, p. 2.

6 M. Damaska (1975) Structures of Authority and Comparative Criminal Procedure, *Yale Law Journal*, 80, p. 523.

7 See, for example, Candace McCoy (1996) Police, prosecutors and discretion in investigation, in John Kleinig (ed.) *Handled with Discretion: Ethical Issues in Police Decision Making*, Lanham, Maryland: Rowman and Littlefield, pp. 159–178.

8 See Robert Jackall (1996) Response to McCoy, in Kleinig (1996), pp. 179–182.

9 See *Guardian* (n.d.), www.guardian.co.uk/baefiles.

10 See Aruna Viswanatha and Brett Wolf (2012) HSBC to pay $1.9 billion US fine in money-laundering case, December 11, 2012, http://uk.reuters.com/article/2012/12/11/us-hsbc-probe-idUSBRE8BA05M20121211.

11 See, for instance, J. Ayling, P. Grabosky, and C. Shearing (2009) *Lengthening the Arm of the Law: Enhancing Police Resources in the 21st Century*, Cambridge: Cambridge University Press.

12 Philosophers have long held truth, for example, to be a regulative ideal. Naturally, it is possible on occasion to fail to realize a regulative ideal, either intentionally or otherwise. For example, speakers fail to realize the regulative ideal of truth when they lie or make an honest error. As we will see in Chapter 2, some regulative ideals, notably truth, are internal to the actions which aim

at them, and, therefore, in performing those actions one necessarily aims at the ideal. Acts of judgement are a case in point. In performing an act of judgment one cannot aim at falsity; one must aim at truth. Of course one can aim at truth and yet fail to 'hit' truth; one can make an error of judgment.

13   See, for example, Andrew Alexandra and Seumas Miller (1996) Needs, moral self-consciousness and professional roles, *Professional Ethics*, 5, 1–2, pp. 43–61, Seumas Miller (2010a) *The Moral Foundations of Social Institutions: A Philosophical Study* New York: Cambridge University Press, Chapter 6, and Andrew Alexandra and Seumas Miller (2010) *Integrity Systems for Occupations*, Aldershot: Ashgate, Chapter 1.

14   For detailed discussion of these issues see Miller (2010), Chapters 1 (pp. 52–54), 3, and 6.

15   The view presented here is derived from Andrew Alexandra and Seumas Miller (2009) *Ethics in Practice: Moral Theory and the Professions*, Sydney: UNSW Press, Chapter 1.

16   A further distinction is between objectivist and relativist – also referred to as subjectivist – theories. The latter, at least in their unsophisticated forms, are not influential among academic philosophers, although they have supporters elsewhere in the humanities and social sciences. See Alexandra and Miller (2009, Chapter 2) for standard criticism of relativist theories and an outline of the distinction between relativism and objectivism.

17   Aristotle *Nicomachean Ethics*, Immanuel Kant *Groundwork of the Metaphysic of Morals*, John Stuart Mill *Utilitarianism*. There are, of course, other theoretical positions, for example, contractualism. Moreover, the historical antecedents of contemporary theories are both complex and a source of controversy. For example, the tendency to render Kant exclusively, or at least predominantly, by recourse to some version of the principle of universalizability (roughly speaking, impartialism) arguably ignores the teleological aspect of his account, for example, as expressed in his principle of the kingdom of ends. See H. J. Paton's translation and analysis of Kant's *Groundwork of the Metaphysic of Morals*, entitled, *The Moral Law*, London: Hutchinson, 1948.

18   See Miller (2010). See also Seumas Miller (2009) Research in applied ethics: problems and perspectives, *Philosophia*, 37.2, pp. 185–201.

19   "Telos" is the ancient Greek word for point or purpose or aim.

20   "Episteme" is the ancient Greek word for knowledge. Epistemology is the philosophical theory of knowledge.

21   For useful discussions of consequentialism and its problems see Samuel Scheffler (ed.) (1988) *Consequentialism and Its Critics*, Oxford: Oxford University Press.

1

Law, Morality, and Policing

At the core of criminal investigations is the criminal law; criminal investigators play a key role in the enforcement of the criminal law. Accordingly, it is important in a book concerned with ethical or moral issues in criminal investigations to provide some theoretical understanding of the source, nature, and function of the criminal law, not the least because, as noted in the introduction, the outcome of criminal investigations often has profound moral consequences for victims and suspects alike.

Since the theory or philosophy of criminal law is a large area of academic inquiry in its own right, this chapter will necessarily be introductory and somewhat selective in its focus. Topics covered in this chapter include the relationship between the criminal law and morality, and the extent to which the criminal law has an objective basis. The objective basis in question pertains not only to the objectivity or otherwise of the moral principles the criminal law typically enshrines (as in the case of laws proscribing murder), but also to objectivity more broadly construed (such as the objectivity or otherwise of the scientific theory underpinning recent developments in DNA research). As will become clear, it is important for criminal investigators to attend to the question of the objectivity or otherwise of the criminal law, since they are a critical element of the system of its enforcement. Should criminal investigators be enforcing the criminal law if it has no objective basis? Arguably, not. But if it does have an objective basis, what is it?

Criminal laws, like other laws, are enacted by a legislature. Moreover, in a democracy, by virtue of being laws passed by the duly elected representatives of the polity, criminal laws, like other laws, reflect the will of the citizenry.[1]

Investigative Ethics: Ethics for Police Detectives and Criminal Investigators, First Edition.
Seumas Miller and Ian A. Gordon.
© 2014 Seumas Miller and Ian A. Gordon. Published 2014 by John Wiley & Sons, Ltd.

However, it is often held that criminal laws, unlike many other laws, not only reflect the will of the legislators, and those who elect them, but also embody core socially accepted *moral norms* of the community. Here we need to draw attention to two sets of distinctions. The first distinction is between *subjective* social morality and *objective* morality. Subjective social morality is simply whatever putative moral principles and values the members of some social group happen to believe in and comply with: the social morality of contemporary western society is one instance of this; that of cannibalistic tribes in Papua and New Guinea is another. Objective morality is the structure of moral principles and values that the members of a given society *ought to* believe in and comply with because it is *objectively correct*.

Here we note that the notion of objectivity pertains to the truth/falsity or correctness/incorrectness of judgments, beliefs, claims, statements, principles, theories, and the like, and stands in contrast with the notion of subjectivity (or relativism). Roughly speaking, subjectivism or relativism holds that there is no truth or correctness to be had in relation to some class of judgments, claims, and so on. Such classes of statements might include moral statements, empirical statements, and mathematical statements.[2] As we will see, some social scientists, for example, reject the objectivity of moral statements, but accept the objectivity of empirical statements made by scientists.

The notion of objective morality is problematic and we return to it below.[3] Suffice it to say here that many widely held moral beliefs, albeit not necessarily all such beliefs, are susceptible to rational analysis and justification with respect to their truth and falsity. Consequently, the behavior which they imply is objectively correct or incorrect. Consider, for example, the widely held moral belief that parents ought to provide for the health, education, and emotional needs of their children, and ought not to physically, sexually, and in other ways abuse them. Evidently this *moral* belief is based in part on a second and *factual* belief, namely, that if parents neglect their children's needs, and physically, sexually (and in other ways) abuse them instead, then (other things being equal[4]) these children will suffer severe physical and/or mental harm.

This second belief is true and rationally well-founded. It is an objective fact that untreated children's diseases cause severe physical and, ultimately, mental harm; and the same point can be made with respect to the severe physical and/or mental harm done to children when their other needs are not met or they are physically or sexually abused. Moreover, the truth of the second (factual) belief provides rational support for the first (moral) belief and, therefore, has behavioral implications. Specifically, taken in conjunction with the general proposition that (other things being equal) one ought to prevent severe harm being caused and ought to avoid causing severe harm, the second (factual) belief implies that children *ought* to be provided with an elementary education and with medicine when suffering from a disease, and *ought not* to be physically or sexually abused. It follows that the widely held belief that (other things being equal) parents ought to provide for at least some of the principal needs of their children and refrain from abusing them is a true belief, and behavior performed in accordance with this belief is morally correct behavior.

The second distinction is between the descriptive claim that criminal laws *in fact* embody core socially accepted moral norms of a community (its basic social morality) and a related normative one, namely, that they *ought to* do so. Certainly, there are many criminal laws that embody widely held moral attitudes, for example, laws against murder, assault, and theft, and it is agreed on all hands that such socially accepted moral principles do play a central role in the criminal law.

However, in the light of these two sets of distinctions we can now differentiate between two *normative* claims that are sometimes conflated. The first of these is the one just mentioned, namely, that the criminal law ought to embody (subjective) social morality. The second helps itself to the notion of objective morality and states that the criminal law ought to embody *objective* morality.

These preliminary remarks suggest that the relationship between the criminal law and morality is a complex one and warrants further exploration.

1.1   Criminal Law and Morality

As we have seen, the criminal law and morality are closely related. Indeed, many people conflate the criminal law and morality – they think that every act of compliance with a criminal law is morally right, and every act that is morally right is an act of compliance with the criminal law. So, if A assaults B without justification, then A's act is both unlawful and immoral. And if C bribes D to win a large government contract, then this act of bribery is both unlawful and immoral. Moreover, it is held that what makes such acts immoral is the fact that they are unlawful, rather than the other way around. This view is particularly common among people whose task it is to make or uphold the criminal law, such as lawyers and police officers. It is, however, a view that should be resisted: first, because law and morality are not the same thing and, second, because law to some extent reflects morality rather than the reverse.

Law and morality are not the same thing. Laws have properties that moral principles and values do not necessarily have. Thus, for something to be a law, whether it be a criminal law or some other kind of law, it must have certain institutional properties not necessarily possessed by moral principles and values. For example, laws are enacted by some institutional authority (e.g., a parliament), in accordance with some valid institutional process (e.g., the legislative processes of the Australian parliament), and laws typically have an explicit formulation in a specified location (e.g., a law that is an explicit directive in the English language in the statute books of the Australian parliament).

The criminal law to a considerable extent reflects morality rather than the reverse. Certain acts are made unlawful – specifically, count as breaches of criminal codes – because they are regarded by the community as being serious forms of immorality; that is, the criminal law reflects (subjective) social morality. Thus murder, rape, and assault are unlawful, at least in part, because they are regarded as profoundly immoral. Again, bribery is unlawful because it is regarded as a serious moral infraction.

Further, at least some of these criminal laws not only reflect *subjective* social morality, they also reflect *objective* morality. Presumably, murder is a case in point.

We note that bribery is not unlawful in some jurisdictions; and, indeed, was not unlawful in many jurisdictions prior to the 1977 US Foreign Corrupt Practices Act that set in train a raft of anti-bribery legislation in various jurisdictions. If bribery is not unlawful in a particular jurisdiction, this might be because it is not regarded as a serious moral wrong there, but rather as a practice that facilitates commerce or as a legitimate form of gift-giving or some such.[5] On the other hand, it could be argued that bribery in commercial dealings is, objectively speaking, a serious moral wrong because – let us assume – it actually undermines free and fair competition in the economic sphere and, as a consequence, does great economic harm. If so, then enacting laws against bribery would reflect objective morality, but not necessarily subjective social morality.

Because law and morality – specifically, objective morality – are conceptually distinct notions, we find that not all laws are morally right. This is probably most clear in the case of repressive states such as Nazi Germany or South Africa in the apartheid era. In these states laws were enacted that discriminated against people on racial grounds. For example, blacks could not vote or own property. These regimes passed many laws that were valid qua laws, that is, passed by the legislature according to the proper procedures, yet were morally abhorrent. We also find that not all morally good actions are legally enforced and, indeed, not all morally good actions should be legally enforced. Parents should be kind to their children, but there is no law to this effect – nor should there be.

So law and objective morality are not the same thing; nor, for that matter, are law and subjective social morality the same thing. From this it follows that sometimes the requirements of law and morality can pull us in opposite directions. This potential conflict between the criminal law, on the one hand, and social morality and/or objective morality, on the other, raises issues of profound importance. Consider the laws prohibiting voluntary euthanasia or ones instigating mandatory sentencing of juveniles for minor crimes. Should doctors engage in voluntary euthanasia in some cases, for example where terminally ill patients are suffering great pain, especially if there is a widespread view in the community that they should? There is evidence that some doctors do just this, and in violation of the law. What of judges, lawyers, and police in relation to crimes that they know are subject to mandatory sentencing? Should police officers on occasion turn a blind eye to an offense subject to mandatory sentencing, if they know that the outcome of making an arrest in such an instance will be far worse for all concerned, including the community? More generally, should police themselves on occasion breach the law for the greater good? Consider in this connection Case Study 1.2.1 below, The "Granny Killer," in which – according to the author of the case study – the detectives confront the option of breaking the law against trespass in order to avert the possibility of someone being murdered.

Notwithstanding the fact that law and morality are not necessarily the same thing, it is nevertheless true – at least in the case of the criminal law – that law and morality often coincide. Here we have in mind the coincidence not only between the criminal law and subjective social morality, but also between the criminal law and objective morality. For example, there are laws against theft, fraud, assault, and murder, and theft, fraud, assault, and murder are both widely believed to be morally wrong and morally wrong as a matter of objective truth.

This coincidence or overlap between much of the criminal law and central moral principles suggests that an important purpose of the criminal law is to maintain a community's minimum moral standards.[6] Naturally, some of these are contentious and, as society undergoes change, some of these hitherto socially accepted moral norms change too – for example, moral attitudes in relation to homosexuality have changed. However, there is evidently a core of widely accepted moral norms that there is reason to believe will never change or ought not to change, for example, the right to life and physical security, and freedom of thought and speech; presumably, these are in part constitutive of objective morality. But how do we demarcate those moral norms that ought to be criminalized and do so on an objective basis?

One historically important attempt within the liberal tradition to delimit on an objective basis the sphere of moral norms that ought to be enshrined in the criminal law does so by recourse to the principle not to harm others. Key proponents of this view are J. S. Mill and Joel Feinberg.[7] Here it is assumed, with some plausibility, that the notion of harm can be objectively specified – physical harm certainly can be, as can some forms of psychological harm. Thus a form of behavior, on this view, ought to be criminalized only if it consists in harming others and, specifically, seriously harming others and doing so deliberately (or at least recklessly or negligently).[8] Naturally, others (e.g., professional boxers) might consent to being harmed, or the harming in question might be morally justified, as in the case of harming in self-defense. If so, then the harming in question presumably ought not to be criminalized. So let us restrict the "Don't harm others" principle to acts of moral wrongdoing that consist of seriously harming (nonconsenting) others, albeit we cannot here embark on the project of specifying what counts as serious harm or the circumstances under which inflicting serious harm might be morally justified.[9]

This view has been subjected to various criticisms including the need to criminalize behavior that consists in failing to assist others who are suffering severe deprivations (as opposed to harming them), for example, behavior that consists in failing to pay taxes the purpose of which is to provide medical and other welfare benefits to the needy.[10] In short, the criminal law should attend not simply to the serious causing of harm but also to omissions in respect of serious deprivations.

Accordingly, another way to delimit the sphere of moral norms that ought to be enshrined in the criminal law is by recourse to the notion of moral rights with respect to serious harms and deprivations, specifically so-called basic moral rights.[11] Basic rights are those moral rights the enjoyment of which is necessary if ordinary humans are to be able to exercise their basic liberties and satisfy their basic needs in a social setting. Basic rights would include the right to physical security, food, water, shelter, essential medical assistance, elementary education, access to work opportunities that enable people to provide for themselves and their children, freedom of movement, thought, communication, and of association with others.

Notice that the moral rights in question include many enshrined in human rights legislation and like legal documents, notably the Universal Declaration of Human Rights. Here we need to stress the above-described distinction between the moral and the legal and, in this instance, between moral rights and legal rights. Although something might be a legal right and, indeed referred to as a legal *human* right – for example, in some legal instruments workers have what is referred to in these documents as a *human right* to a paid holiday[12] – it is a further question as to whether such a thing is in fact a moral right. Moreover, as will become evident below, there is a distinction to be made within moral rights between human (moral) rights – moral rights one has qua human being, such as the moral right not to be tortured – and institutional (moral) rights – moral rights one has in part by virtue of institutional arrangements, such as the right to a fair trial.[13]

Notice further that the rights in question are not restricted to rights not to be harmed by others; they include rights to assistance of various kinds when one is suffering severe deprivations, for example, rights to food when one is starving. Notice further that the rights in question can plausibly be given an objective basis in terms of the notion of harm (as we saw in relation to the "Don't harm others" principle) and also the notion of the basic needs of a human being in a social setting. This can be done notwithstanding the vagueness of the boundary between basic and nonbasic; after all, there is a distinction between black and white notwithstanding the existence of grayness. The idea here would be that behavior that consists in the violation of basic moral rights ought to be criminalized. In so far as the violation of basic rights typically involves harming someone, then this conception captures a central moral intuition of the earlier "Don't harm others" view. However, it is wider than this in that it includes rights to assistance when one is suffering severe deprivations.[14]

This rights-based view will be open to criticism from those who object for a variety of reasons to positive rights and, especially, to the enforcement of positive rights. Elsewhere Miller has elaborated a normative theory of institutions which tries to deal with this kind of objection.[15]

This rights-based view can also be criticized for setting the standard for criminality too low; surely there is behavior above and beyond that which violates basic rights, which ought to be criminalized. For example, should not the willful destruction or damaging of cultural objects, such as ancient cave paintings, be criminalized? Evidently, the notion of a moral right in play here needs to be extended to include moral rights above and beyond basic rights.[16]

On the other hand, if this view is adjusted so that it includes all moral rights, then it can be criticized for setting the standard for criminality too high. Arguably, there are some moral rights, violations of which ought not to be criminalized: specifically, those moral rights whose violation does not consist in causing serious harm and/or does not entail serious deprivation. Perhaps, under a university's rules governing a series of public lectures on controversial topics, the main speaker has a right of reply to his or her commentators/critics. Suppose a particular speaker agrees (informally) to do a public lecture only on condition that he or she can exercise this right of reply, and the right of reply is a standard institutional, and thus moral, right in the forums in question. Suppose, further, that the chairperson arbitrarily refuses to allow the speaker to exercise their right of reply. Surely we would not want to criminalize such a minor rights violation.

What criterion ought we to use to adjudicate between moral rights the violations of which ought to be criminalized and those for which this is not the case? We have already helped ourselves to the notion of rights violations that consist of causing serious harm and/or entail serious deprivations.

Accordingly, the question becomes: What criterion can be used to demarcate rights violations involving serious harm or deprivation – violations that, therefore, warrant criminalization – from less serious ones (that do not warrant criminalization)?

Ultimately, the harms/deprivations in question will have to be subject to scrutiny on a case by case basis. However, one candidate general criterion is morally justifiable enforcement (understood as coercive enforcement).[17] If the violations of a right are regarded as sufficiently egregious to warrant coercive enforcement, then the right in question is, at least *prima facie*, of sufficient moral weight for violations of it to warrant criminalization.

Here there are three points to be made. First, the level of force that is morally justified is on a sliding scale depending on the moral weight that the right has. For example, the right to life justifies the use of lethal force in its enforcement, but minor property rights might only justify the use of nonlethal force in their enforcement.

Second, aggregated violations of a right might justify a high level of coercive enforcement even though one-off violations do not (e.g., the use of plastic baton rounds fired from a baton gun against a mob engaged in looting might be justified, but not such use against a one-off offender).

Third, an agent might perform an action that is not in itself a direct rights violation but is, nevertheless, an action that the agent knows, or should know, will indirectly cause harmful or other rights violations (e.g., provoking others to commit unjustified violence). Various acts which cause damage to institutions evidently fit into this category (see Section 1.5 below). Use of coercive force in relation to such indirectly harmful actions might well be morally justified.

Here we note the distinction between moral rights and other kinds of moral or ethical consideration.

An obvious contrast here is between behavior in compliance with rights and behavior expressive of virtue. Kind or generous behavior is an expression of the virtue of kindness or generosity. One person does not necessarily have a moral *right* to another person's kindness or generosity, notwithstanding that it is a good thing to be kind or generous.

Another contrast is between moral rights and intended or otherwise aimed at good outcomes. Perhaps it is a bad thing not to assist one's profligate friend with his rental payments; a bad thing because the friend will be forced to seek accommodation with his aging parents who already live in cramped quarters. But surely one's friend does not have a moral *right* to such financial assistance.

We have distinguished between basic moral rights and (in effect) nonbasic moral rights. A further distinction, which cuts across this one, is between human rights and institutional rights (some basic rights are human rights but some are evidently institutional rights, e.g., the right to receive elementary school education).

Human rights are moral rights that individuals possess solely by virtue of properties they have as human beings, for instance, the right to life and the right to freedom of thought.[18]

Institutional (moral) rights are moral rights that individuals possess in part by virtue of rights-generating properties that they have as human beings, and in part by virtue of their membership of a community or morally legitimate institution, or their occupancy of a morally legitimate institutional role defined by specific moral purposes. Thus the right to vote is an institutional right, since it exists in part by virtue of possession of the rights-generating property of autonomy, and in part by virtue of membership of a political community. Again, the right, indeed duty, to arrest and charge someone for assault is a moral right and duty possessed by police officers that is not necessarily possessed by ordinary citizens in the same circumstances. This institutional right and duty is derived from the moral purpose that defines the role of a police officer, namely, to protect the rights of citizens and, in this particular case, to protect the human right of the victim not to be assaulted.

Moreover, we are assuming the following properties of moral rights.[19] First, moral rights generate concomitant duties on others: A's right to life , for example, generates a duty on the part of B not to kill A. Second, human rights and some, but perhaps not all, institutional moral rights, are justifiably enforceable: A has a right not to be assaulted by B, and if B assaults or attempts to assault A, then B can legitimately be prevented from assaulting A by means of coercion.[20] An example of a justifiably enforceable institutional moral right is the right to vote; it ought to be a criminal offense to prevent someone from exercising their right to vote. Again, it ought to be a criminal offense to commit perjury in a court of law, even in a civil case in which the matter in dispute involves no criminal behavior. Arguably, the underpinning moral rights in play here are those of the citizenry with respect to those who appear before their courts. Third, bearers of human rights, in particular, do not necessarily have to assert a given human right in order for them to possess it, and for the right to be violated: for instance, an infant may have a right to life even though it does not have the ability to assert it (or, for that matter, to waive it).

Above, we distinguished between law and morality (and within morality between moral rights and other moral phenomena). Moreover, we have argued that the criminal laws can usefully be understood as embodying justifiably enforceable moral rights not to be seriously harmed or suffer serious needs-based deprivations, and that the latter moral rights are objective in character. It follows that we have provided, at least in principle, an objective basis for the content of much of the criminal law.[21] However, this is not the end of the matter, since the criminal law has various other dimensions (e.g., a semantic dimension in so far as laws need to framed in a language and interpreted), and relies for its application on nonlegal considerations (e.g., testimonial evidence), and these, it might be argued, being necessarily subjective in character continue to threaten any claim that the criminal law is objective, even in principle. Accordingly, we need to discuss further the (alleged) subjectivity of the criminal law, notably in relation to so-called facts, and in the light of the important distinction made by the courts between law and fact. Given the already established relation between criminal law and morality, this will in turn raise the question of the distinction between morality and fact. Before engaging in this discussion, we present some case studies that might help to illuminate these matters in a policing context and illustrate, in particular, the centrality of human and other moral rights to criminal investigation and the disparate attitudes of criminal investigators to such violations, that is, to breaches of criminal law, on the one hand, and to their own breaches of criminal procedures (in the investigation of breaches of criminal law) on the other. We begin within a case study involving a serial murderer, the so-called "Granny Killer."

1.2   Case Studies

Case Study 1.2.1   The Granny Killer

Ritualistic offender behaviors, that were his signature, marked the 1 March 1989 murder of an 84-year-old woman. Signature behaviors that reappeared in many of the thirteen subsequent vicious and brazen daylight attacks on elderly women in populous areas of Sydney's North Shore in the late 1980s and early 1990s. Attacks resulting in five murders, eight assaults, indecent assaults and robberies—committed by an offender tagged by the media the 'Granny Killer'.

The investigation was conducted, first, by the North Region Homicide Squad, then the North Shore Murders Task Force—eventually to number 70 police—assembled, on 3 November 1989, following the second of two murders of elderly women, perpetrated consecutively on 2 and 3 November.

John Wayne Glover, a husky, 58-year-old Mosman salesman, seemingly happily married father of two girls, first made it onto the 470-names-long Task Force suspect list when he came to police attention following a suspected indecent assault on 11 January 1990 on an elderly female patient in a Greenwich private hospital. Glover was placed under covert police surveillance.

At 1026 hrs on 19 March 1990, Glover, who purchased a bottle of whisky from a Mosman bottle shop, was observed by police who followed him from his home to enter, with the ease of long familiarity, a property in Pindari Road, Beauty Point. The door opened and they heard the sound of a woman's voice before the door was shut. Glover was inside the home of Joan Sinclair, a 60-year-old divorcee, with whom he had, for some years, conducted a liaison.

As the autumn day stretched out, unease overtook the surveillance team. Task Force members traveled from their Chatswood office to Mosman Police Station, to await developments. Enquiries indicated the Pindari Street house was owned by Joan Sinclair—still police hesitated to call at the house. They claimed that they worried that 'they would have been up for unlawful entry' if they had tried to enter the property uninvited. But uppermost in their minds seems to have been the fear of tipping their hand to Glover. According to one Task Force member, 'all that mattered to me, to all of us, was catching Glover'.

The Task Force commander is reported as saying, 'With nothing to connect Glover to a single murder, we had to have a legitimate reason to speak to him . . . If he knew he was a suspect, he may never have put a foot out of line again and the Granny killings could well have remained unsolved'.[22]

At 1520 hrs a teacher from the local school brought Joan Sinclair's grandchildren—whom she had failed to collect after school—to her home. Finding the gate locked, she left a note indicating that the children were next door with a neighbor.

At 1800 hrs, two uniformed police were ordered to knock on the door, with the excuse that neighbors were complaining about a dog barking.[23] Unable to gain entry through the locked front gate, they climbed a neighbor's fence. Peering in through the French doors at the rear of the darkened house, they could detect no sign of life—but saw a bloody hammer, the Granny Killer's weapon of choice, lying in plain sight. Their report brought Task Force officers to the scene in minutes.

Entering, Joan Sinclair's body was discovered, exhibiting, postmortem, the serial killer;'s ritualistic, signature behaviors; she appeared to have been dead at least six hours. The effect of the discovery of this needless murder—and its implications—upon the Task Force officers was crushing. Glover was located, partly conscious in a tepid

(Continued)

bath, a whisky bottle and empty phials lying nearby indicating a suicide attempt. The police strove to preserve his life, a senior detective reputedly saying, 'I was obsessed by a feeling that we had to save him to stand trial. If he died, all the other murders would remain unsolved even though we knew he was our man'.[24]

Glover recovered, to stand trial. This was the Granny Killer's sixth and final murder and police were now in possession of the evidence necessary to secure his conviction.

(Extract from John Blackler's case study, The Granny Killer, in John Blackler and Seumas Miller (2000) *Police Ethics (vol. 2): Case Studies for Police Investigators*, Wagga Wagga: Charles Sturt University and NSW Police Service, pp. 15–16)

Case Study 1.2.2   Two Models of Criminal Process

A prominent professor of law has concluded that there are two prevalent models of criminal process in the Unites States, the 'due process' model and the 'crime control' model.[25] The due process model views the criminal process as conforming to the rule of law. It is a model stressing the possibilities of human error, especially the frailty of authority under pressure. Above all, it is a model emphasizing *legal* guilt over *factual* guilt. Thus an accused is held to be guilty if, and only if, the factual determinations made against him have been presented in a procedurally regular fashion by lawfully constituted authorities acting within duly allocated competences . . .

The crime control model, by contrast, emphasizes *factual* guilt. Its chief principle is efficiency through rational administration or 'the system's capacity to apprehend, try, convict, and dispose of a high proportion of criminal offenders whose offenses became known.'[26] This model stresses social control over individual justice. Its operative norms are those of a productive enterprise; its success is gauged by a high rate of apprehension and conviction in the context of mass administration of the criminal law.[27]

The police officer views criminal procedure with the *administrative biases of a craftsman,* a prejudice contradictory to due process of law. That is, the policeman tends to emphasize his own expertness and specialized abilities to make judgments about the measures to be applied to apprehended 'criminals', as well as the ability to estimate accurately the guilt or innocence of suspects. He sees himself as a craftsman, at his best, a master of his trade. As such, he feels he ought to be free to employ the techniques of his trade, and that the system ought to provide regulations contributing to his freedom to improvise, rather than constricting it . . . Like other doers, he tends to be resentful of critics who measure his value by abstract principles rather than the 'reality' of the world he knows and lives and sees.

To further understand the consequences of his 'craftsman' bias, it must be understood that he draws a moral distinction between criminal law and criminal procedure . . . The distinction is drawn somewhat as follows; the substantive law of crimes is intended to control the behaviour of persons who wilfully injure persons or property, or who engage in behaviours eventually having such a consequence, as the use of narcotics. Criminal procedure, by contrast, is intended to control authorities, not criminals. As such, it does not fall into the same moral class of constraints as substantive criminal law. If a policeman were himself to use narcotics, or to steal, or to assault, *outside the line of duty*, much the same standards would be applied to him by other policemen as to the ordinary citizen. When, however, the issue concerns the policeman's freedom to carry out his *duties*, another *moral* realm is entered.[28]

(Extract from John Blackler's case study, Two Models of Criminal Process, in John Blackler and Seumas Miller (2000) *Police Ethics (vol. 1): Case Studies in Street Policing*, Wagga Wagga: Charles Sturt University and NSW Police Service, pp. 154–155)

1.3   Law, Morality, and Facts

Thus far we have explored the relation between the criminal law and morality, including the extent to which the moral principles typically enshrined in the criminal law are objective and, therefore, the extent to which the criminal law might have an objective basis. A good deal of our discussions has centered on the notions of moral rights, harms, and severe deprivations as potential sources of objectivity in this regard. It is now time to bring in other dimensions of the criminal law, notably the relations between laws and facts (so-called), albeit once again with an eye to the objectivity or otherwise of the criminal law.

Before turning to the relation between laws and facts, we note the distinction made in Case Study 1.2.2 above between substantive and procedural criminal law. To an extent procedural criminal law functions as a means to facilitate the upholding of substantive criminal law and, therefore, one can understand the disparate attitudes of investigators to these bodies of law. If *x* is merely a means to *y* then one might abandon *x* if and when it ceases to be an effective means to *y*. However, this attitude is morally problematic in so far as criminal procedure is not merely a means to an end (substantive law) but embodies *moral* rights, notably the moral rights of suspects, such as to be free from unreasonable searches and seizures. We return to the issue of rights of suspects in later chapters.

The distinction between fact and law is a familiar one made in a variety of criminal justice contexts. Thus in jury trials juries are supposed to adjudicate on questions of fact, judges on questions of law (and give direction to juries to enable the latter to arrive at their final verdicts). Of course in one sense the existence of a law is itself a fact of sorts and so perhaps the distinction is really between legal and nonlegal facts.

Here we need to distinguish further between, on the one hand, a legal fact in the sense of a law or other legal instrument that actually exists (as opposed to, for example, an imaginary law or one that some person falsely believes to exist) and, on the other hand, a state of affairs that is not in itself a law (or other legal instrument), but is specified, or otherwise referred to, by a law, for example, lawful or unlawful behavior. What, then, is this distinction?

On the one hand there are particular (as opposed to general), concrete (as opposed to abstract) facts. An example is the fact (let us suppose) that John J. Jones III is driving his red Ford Fiesta with license number ABC123 at 55 mph. in the built-up area of downtown Boston on Monday, January 1, 2012 at 11a.m. On the other hand, there is the content of laws, including with respect to driving motor vehicles. Consider, for example, a law that states that car-drivers ought to drive under 60 mph. in built-up areas.

The first point to notice is that the form of this law is normative (as opposed to descriptive). Accordingly, it does not just describe or refer to some fact or facts with respect to driving behavior; it prescribes or proscribes certain forms of driving behavior.

The second point is that the content of this law refers not simply to a particular, concrete fact, such as the one mentioned above involving John J. Jones III. Rather, the content of the law is general and abstract. As such it refers to a whole set of potential concrete facts involving different drivers, cars, locations, and times.

The third point is that the law divides this set of potential concrete facts into two categories, namely, lawful states of affairs and unlawful ones, depending on whether the drivers in question are driving above or below 60 mph.

If the content of a law is able to categorize particular, concrete facts in this manner, then it must do so in large part, if not wholly,[29] by way of the semantic meaning of this law in a particular language, such as English. Notice that the same facts could be referred to by a law in French as by one in English. This raises the question of the interpretation of laws: what is the precise meaning of the law (in some language) in some specific context of application?

This is a complex issue that cannot be dealt with in any detail here. Suffice it to say that, although there is some room for vagueness in respect of the meaning of given laws, there needs to be a verifiable fact of the matter in relation to what any given law states and, in particular, what the legislators who enacted the law *intended* it to mean; that is, there must be verifiable semantic and associated psychological facts.[30] The associated psychological facts in question include *intended* meanings, for instance, the meaning intended by the legislators when they enacted the law. For, if this were not so, then citizens would not have a common and correct understanding of the content of laws and, therefore, could not reasonably be expected to comply with the law. So, on pain of the citizenry not being able to comply with the law, there must be legal facts in the sense of objectively verifiable interpretations of the law, and such interpretations are, in turn, dependent on verifiable semantic and associated psychological facts (notably the intended meanings of the legislators).

Notice that for the same reason there must also be objectively true statements of logic or reason. For, if the citizenry is to be able to comply with the law, then each citizen must not only be able to understand the meaning of given laws, each must be able to apply the law to him or herself on particular occasions. Such application involves a process of deduction or logical inference-making, albeit often of a quite straightforward kind. Here is an example: (i) the law prescribes that persons with a blood alcohol level above 0.5 do not drive; (ii) I now have a blood alcohol level above 0.5; therefore, (iii) the law prescribes that I do not drive at this time. So, on pain of the citizenry not being able to comply with the law, there must be objectively true statements of logic and, specifically, logical inferences that are objectively true (or objectively false).

Thus far in this section we have discussed the distinction between laws and fact, yet seen that laws are in a range of important ways themselves factual. Let us now turn more directly to a consideration of the notion of a fact.

Facts are often contrasted with theories. Facts are also contrasted with values – moral values, in particular. What is this contrast or set of contrasts? Roughly speaking, factual statements supposedly describe independently existing states of affairs that are, at least in principle, verifiable (and/or falsifiable); these states of affairs exist independently of anyone's judgment, belief, or statement that they exist or do not exist. Accordingly, a factual statement is objectively true (if the state of affairs exists) or false (if it does not). The paradigm cases are statements about ordinary, middle-sized, physical objects and their causal relations with one another, for example, the gun discharged a single bullet which entered the head of the victim killing him instantly. Such states of affairs obtain (or do not obtain) quite independently of whether or not anyone judges, believes, or states – let alone desires or hopes – that they obtain (or do not obtain). Indeed, the truth or falsity of any such judgment, belief, or statement itself depends on the obtaining (or not obtaining) of the state of affairs in question.

Earlier we distinguished between objectivism and subjectivism with respect to truth and falsehood. If someone holds that a class of statements is objectively true or objectively false, then that person is an objectivist with respect to that class of statements. Subjectivists hold the contrary view, namely, that with respect to a given class of statements there is no objective truth or falsehood.[31] So most people are objectivists with respect to statements about the ordinary physical world. Moreover, we have seen reason to hold that moral beliefs can be provided with an objective basis, for instance, by recourse to the notion of harm and/or of needs-based moral rights. Accordingly, moral beliefs can be held to be true or false, and the behavior they prescribe or proscribe, objectively correct or incorrect. That said, many people, especially social scientists, claim to be subjectivists with respect to moral beliefs and statements of moral value.

We cannot pursue these philosophical issues in any detail here.[32] Nevertheless, it is important to understand what is potentially at stake for criminal investigations in these controversies between objectivists and subjectivists. If subjectivism with respect to facts about the ordinary physical world were true, then, presumably, investigators could simply make it up as they go along; there would be no fact of the matter for them to discover. Criminal investigation would simply be a species of "creative writing"; the distinction between fact and fiction would have been extinguished. Perhaps this obvious "downside" of subjectivism with respect to facts about the physical world explains why its advocates are few and far between. What is perhaps less obvious is that subjectivism with respect to theories (theory subjectivism), and ultimately moral value claims (moral subjectivism), is also problematic.

Theoretical claims are likely to be regarded as objectively true to the extent that they are based on, for example, objectively true empirical claims, such as observational ones, about the ordinary physical world. So scientific theories in relation to DNA, for example, are at least in large part based on empirical evidence.

More generally, if there are physical *and* psychological statements of fact (e.g., with respect to human intentions and beliefs), and if there are logically valid processes of reasoning (as we saw above), then there is no barrier to there being objectively verifiable theories, namely, theoretical claims that are derivable from physical and psychological facts on the basis of principles of logical reasoning (including not only deduction but also induction).[33] If so, then subjectivism with respect to theoretical statements is false, and objectivism is true.

Of course, subjectivism with respect to theoretical claims, but not observational claims, seeks to sever the connection between the theoretical and the empirical and thereby undermine the objectivity of theoretical claims. If it were to succeed, there would be profound implications for criminal investigations. For example, the use of DNA evidence by investigators and courts would no longer be tenable, if the scientific theories upon which this use is based were no longer regarded as being objectively true.

In the last section we outlined some candidates for providing an objective basis for the criminal law, namely, the notions of harm and that of needs-based deprivations (in so far as these harms and needs-based deprivations are ones that generate enforceable moral rights). We are not going to revisit those arguments here. Rather we conclude this section by pointing to the implications of moral subjectivism for criminal investigations, given the relationship between the criminal law and moral principles outlined in the last section. Specifically, moral subjectivism threatens to undermine the authority of criminal law by undermining the objectivity of the moral principles upon which the criminal law is based.

If, for example, the moral principle that it is wrong to kill the innocent is not objectively true, indeed, no more true than the contrary principle that it is morally right to kill the innocent, then the legitimacy of the law prohibiting the killing of the innocent is called into question. Now consider penal sanctions such as imprisonment. Here we reiterate and amplify a point made above. Unlike many social rules, an individual's noncompliance with the criminal law is intended by the community to lead ultimately to bad consequences for that individual, notably loss of freedom. It is surely problematic, to say the least, to hand out a lengthy prison sentence for noncompliance with a law proscribing some form of behavior unless there is an objective basis for enacting that law in the first place. If there is no objective basis for believing the behavior in question to be morally unacceptable, how can we reasonably take away someone's freedom for engaging in that behavior? Fortunately, as we saw above, there are objective bases, for example, the behavior in question is extremely and verifiably harmful, and to this extent we can justifiably enact laws proscribing such behavior and apply sanctions to those who breach these laws.

1.4 A Normative Theory of Policing

Thus far we have distinguished between law and morality, and have discussed the relationship between, in particular, the criminal law and moral principles. In doing so we have offered some candidate objective bases for criminal law and, therefore, criminal investigations, namely, harms and needs-based deprivations which generate enforceable moral rights. We now need to situate criminal investigations – criminal investigations undertaken by police investigators, in particular – within the larger context of police organizations. Accordingly, let us now turn to a consideration of the role of the police, including the role of police investigators, with respect to the criminal law (and, therefore, with respect to those moral principles that are and ought to be embodied in criminal law).

On the account proffered above, the criminal law exists to protect certain moral rights, and therefore, arguably, the central and most important moral purpose of police work is to protect these same moral rights, albeit the pursuit of this purpose ought to be constrained by the law.[34] So, while police institutions have other important purposes that might not directly involve the protection of moral rights – to enforce the adjudications of courts in relation to disputes between citizens, to settle disputes between citizens on the streets, or to ensure good order more generally and so on – these may well turn out either to be derived from the more fundamental purpose of protecting moral rights or to be (nonderivative) secondary purposes. Thus, laws against speeding derive in part from the moral right to life, and the restoring of order at a football match ultimately, in large part, derives from moral rights to the protection of persons and of property. On the other hand, service of summonses to assist the courts is presumably a secondary purpose of policing.[35]

This conception of policing is a teleological one; it is a conception in terms of the ends or goals of policing.[36] Moreover, it is a teleological conception according to which the most important end or purpose of policing is the protection of moral rights.

On this view, while police ought to have as a fundamental purpose the protection of moral rights, their efforts in this regard ought to be constrained by the law. In so far as the law is a constraint – at least in democratic states – then our view accommodates "consent" as a criterion of legitimacy for the police role.[37] However, on our view legality, and therefore consent, is only one consideration, for we are insisting that police work, including police investigations, ought to be guided by moral considerations – namely, moral rights – and not simply by legal ones. This enables us to avoid the problems besetting theories of policing cast purely in terms of law enforcement, or protection of the State, or even peace-keeping.[38] Such theories are faced with the obvious problem posed by authoritarian states, or sometimes even democratic states, that enact laws that violate human rights – human rights being, as we saw above, a species of moral rights. Police officers in authoritarian states simultaneously violate human rights and abrogate their primary professional responsibility as police officers to protect human rights.

Further, we reiterate that, on the view that we are advocating, police engaged in the protection of moral rights ought to be constrained by the law, or at least ought to be constrained by laws that embody the will of the community in the sense that (i) the procedures for generating these laws (e.g., a democratically-elected legislature) are more or less universally accepted by the community, and (ii) the content of the laws are at least in large part accepted by the community (e.g., they embody general policies with majority electoral support or reflect the community's moral beliefs).[39] So we are in part advocating a broadly contractarian moral constraint on policing, namely the consent of citizens; although by our lights consent is not the *raison d'être* for policing, rather it provides an additional (albeit necessary) condition for the moral legitimacy of police work. Moreover, we are refraining from providing police with a license to pursue their (possibly only individually) subjective view of what counts as an enforceable moral right. What counts as an enforceable moral right is an objective matter. Nevertheless, some particular person or group has to specify what are to be taken to be enforceable moral rights and what are not to be so taken; and, in our view, ultimately this is a decision for the community to make by way of its laws and its democratically elected government. Here we take it that, in a properly constituted democracy, the law embodies the will of the community in the sense adumbrated above. Moreover, we can further distinguish between local, regional, and national communities, especially in states that have subnational elected bodies such as local councils. This enables us to give substance to notions of community-based policing or partnerships between police and local communities. For at the subnational level, and especially the local level, it becomes feasible for police to consult and work with communities to address law enforcement issues in a consensual manner.[40]

There is a further point to be made here. The law concretizes moral rights and the principles governing their enforcement, including human rights as well as institutional moral rights. To this extent, the law is very helpful in terms of guiding police officers and citizens in relation to the way that abstract moral rights and principles apply to specific circumstances. For example, there is a human right to life that can be overridden in accordance with certain moral principles, such as self-defense or defense of the lives of others. However, it is the laws governing the use of deadly force by police officers that provide an explicit and concrete formulation of these moral rights and principles, and thereby prescribe what is to be done or not done by police officers in specific circumstances.

In short, in our view police ought to act principally to protect certain moral rights, those moral rights ought to be enshrined in the law, and the law ought to reflect the will of the community. Should any of these conditions fail to obtain, then there will be problems. If the law and objective (justifiably enforceable) moral rights come apart, or if the law and the will of the community come apart, or if objective moral rights and the will of the community come apart, then the police may well be faced with moral dilemmas. There are no neat and easy solutions to all such problems. Clearly, if the law and/or the citizenry require the police to *violate* moral rights, or at least not to uphold them (e.g., health and safety legislation forbidding personnel to put themselves at risk to save the lives of others under some circumstances), then the law and/or the citizenry will be at odds with the fundamental purpose of policing. Accordingly, depending on the circumstances, the police may well be obliged to disobey the law and/or the will of the community. On the other hand, what is the appropriate police response to a citizen violating someone else's objective moral right in a community in which the right is not as a matter of fact enshrined in the law, and the right is not supported by the community? Consider, in this connection, women's rights to (say) education under an extremist fundamentalist religious regime such as the former Taliban regime in Afghanistan.[41] Under such circumstances, an issue arises as to whether police are morally obliged *qua* police officers to *enforce* respect for the moral right in question. Again, we suggest that they may well be obliged to intervene to enforce respect for such a moral right.

Normatively speaking then, the protection of fundamental moral rights – specifically those *justifiably enforceable* moral rights enshrined in the criminal law – is the central and most important purpose of police work, including police investigations. As it happens, there is increasing recourse to human rights legislation, in particular, in the decisions of domestic as well as international courts. For example, in accordance with the European Human Rights Convention and its enabling UK legislation, the Human Rights Act of 1998, police in the UK are now *explicitly* required to comply with the principle of reasonable use of force and this principle is enshrined in their use of firearms guidelines.

Recourse to human rights legislation is an interesting development. However, it must also be pointed out that the criminal law in many, if not most, jurisdictions already, in effect, constitutes human rights legislation. Laws proscribing murder, rape, assault, and so on, are essentially laws that protect human rights, as are longstanding domestic laws governing the rights of suspects, for instance, with respect to police use of force. So, for example, prior to the above-mentioned UK Human Rights Act of 1998, there was an understanding and (at least) implicit commitment of UK police to the principle of the reasonable use of force.

We also note that whatever the historical importance of the "Statist" conception of human rights – human rights as protections of the individual against the State – such a conception is inadequate as a *general* account of human rights. As laws against murder, rape, assault, and so on illustrate, human rights in particular, and moral rights more generally, also exist to protect individual citizens from their fellow citizens, and individual citizens from organizations other than the organizations of the State.

1.5   Criminal Investigations

Thus far in this chapter we have (i) provided an account of the relationship between, in particular, the criminal law and moral principles according to which the criminal law and, therefore, criminal investigations, have a normative basis in objectively correct moral principles – a key candidate here being justifiably enforceable, moral rights not to be harmed and to be assisted in respect of needs-based deprivations; and (ii) situated criminal investigations within the larger context of a normative theory of police organizations according to which policing is the protection of justifiably enforceable, legally enshrined moral rights. In what remains of this chapter, and in the light of (i) and (ii), we now need to sketch in general terms the purposes of, and the constraints on, criminal investigations undertaken by police investigators and to do so in the context of the traditional distinction between reactive and preventive criminal justice mechanisms and in the light of the above-adumbrated normative theory of policing. This sketch functions as a preliminary to the more detailed treatments in the following chapters of specific moral issues confronting police investigators.

As is obvious and has already been stated, combating crime and enforcing the criminal law involve conducting criminal investigations. Of course, criminal investigations are not the only way to combat crime. Indeed, they are arguably less effective in the long run than various preventative measures. Perhaps reducing levels of drug addiction is one such preventative measure in relation to burglaries. Whether or not this is so, criminal investigations are a necessary means of combating crime. More generally, there is a need for both reactive measures (e.g., the rape victim's report of the crime should be followed by an investigation), as well as preventative measures (e.g., locked doors and high fences). Moreover, reactive measures, including criminal investigations, need to be integrated with preventative measures.

As just mentioned, criminal investigation is often a reactive mechanism; typically, an investigation is triggered when a crime is reported or a complaint made.[42] However, the distinction between reactive and preventative mechanisms is somewhat artificial, and the likelihood of being the subject of a criminal investigation is an important deterrent. Moreover, so-called proactive, intelligence-based investigations ideally precede any actual offense, or at least the major crime in prospect. Further, many reactive investigations are also preventative in so far as the offender is likely to continue to offend if not apprehended. The "Granny Killer" is a case in point (see Case Study 1.2.1 above). This is perhaps most evident in terrorism investigations in which a principal aim is to save lives (see Chapter 7). So criminal investigations are preventative as well as being reactive.

A further point is that sometimes a choice has to be made between reactive-driven actions and prevention-driven ones. On occasion, such a choice can take the form of an acute moral dilemma. In the above-described "Granny Killer" case, for example, there was a reactive-driven non-intervention prior to enough evidence being gathered to convict the "Granny Killer" for past crimes; alternatively, there was the prevention-driven intervention to forestall a (possibly) imminent crime (the murder of Joan Sinclair). Of course, non-intervention might be, in the long run, preventative (as well as reactive), given that, once imprisoned, the "Granny Killer" would not be able to commit these crimes. Such choices are often the result of a process which involves both the calculation of the probable outcomes of the available actions (including inaction) and the weighing of the moral costs and benefits attendant upon those outcomes.

The reactive way of dealing with crime is perhaps the one that first comes to mind. The logic is direct: the activity is defined as one that is not acceptable (e.g., unlawful); an individual engages in that activity and, as a direct result, an investigation is conducted; the individual, if found guilty, is punished in some way. The rationale for the reactive response for dealing with criminality is threefold: offenders are held to account for their actions; offenders get their just deserts; and potential offenders are deterred from future offenses.

Reactive mechanisms for dealing with crime are fundamentally linear: setting out a series of offenses (usually in legislation or regulations), waiting for an individual to transgress, then investigating, adjudicating, and finally taking punitive action. The criminal justice system in many jurisdictions largely consists of reactive institutional mechanisms. As noted above, these systems are also preventative mechanisms by virtue of their deterrence role; however, the adequacy of this deterrence role is typically dependent on their effectiveness *qua* reactive mechanisms, that is, their success in detecting, investigating, and prosecuting offenders.

As already noted, reactive mechanisms, and criminal investigations in particular, are a necessary part of any feasible criminal justice system.

Sometimes, however, if too much reliance is placed on them the weaknesses of the reactive approach are made manifest.

One obvious weakness is the passivity of the approach; by the time the investigators swing into action, the damage has been already done. An obvious example of this is terrorist acts, such as those committed by suicide bombers. While it is important to investigate a suicide bombing after it occurs, it is far more important to prevent its occurrence, albeit preventative measures give rise to their own problems (see Chapter 7). Another problem stems from the fact that unlawful behavior such as bribery and drug dealing is often secretive, and so may never be discovered.

Yet a further problem stems from the inadequacy of the resources to investigate and successfully prosecute; investigation and prosecution are resource-intensive. Consider in this connection the crime of fraud. Fraud is widespread in modern economies, yet police and other agencies simply do not have the resources to investigate adequately all the reports of fraud brought to their attention. Moreover, in all probability an even greater number of cases simply do not come to attention as a result of decisions on the part of banks, credit card providers, and the like not to report them. Yet if the chances of being caught or complained about are relatively slight due to underresourcing and/or underreporting, then the deterrent effect is undermined, which, in turn, means that there are an even larger number of offenses and offenders for investigators to deal with (see also Chapter 6).

Of course, the effectiveness of a reactive approach requires that significant detection mechanisms and applicable sanctions are available. If so then those who engage in criminal behavior have good reason to believe that (i) they will be caught and (ii) they will be appropriately, perhaps severely, punished. The punishment might include a lengthy term of imprisonment. Offenders might also attract moral sanctions emanating from work colleagues, the community, and from significant others, such as friends and relatives. Moral sanctions may be considerably less effective than punishment in the case of, for example, members of criminal families.

Criminal investigations typically rely on a number of sources of information. One of the most important is victims, albeit this is often absent in the case of some crimes such as so-called "victimless" crimes like drug selling. It is necessarily absent in the case of murder. Other important sources of information are citizens who may witness crime and neighbors or fellow-workers who may report crime or suspicious activity to police or to their superiors.

Criminal conduct embraces a wide variety of activities ranging from serious criminal offenses, such as murder and major fraud, through to minor offenses, such as minor assaults and shoplifting. The latter may warrant interventions of a nonpunitive kind, for example, cautions, counseling, especially in the case of first offenders and juveniles. Our concern in this book is principally with serious criminal offenses, although we note that minor criminality, for instance, minor welfare benefit fraud, if engaged in by large numbers of people may in aggregate do great financial and other harm and, as such, warrant significant attention from criminal investigators. Finally, we note that the criminal justice system – and criminal investigations in particular – represents the most salient and sophisticated, reactive institutional response to combating serious crime.

Almost every jurisdiction has criminal laws against self-evident forms of serious immorality by members of the community, such as murder, assault, rape, fraud, theft, offering or soliciting bribes, or abusing the power of a public office.

While it is common for criminal laws to be consolidated into a criminal code, it is almost universal that legislation dealing with particular areas of activity, like the regulation of companies and corporations, will also consist in part of criminal offense provisions. In essence, these provisions will be dealing with criminality of a particular type and conducted in a specific context, for example, abuse of office, bribery, theft, fraud (as opposed to, say, murder, assault, rape).

In relation to the purposes of criminal investigations, in general terms – and in keeping with the normative account of policing proffered above – the investigation should be in the service of protecting justifiably enforceable, legally enshrined moral rights. Clearly homicide and rape investigations satisfy this desideratum. On the other hand, the investigation by police of dissidents for unlawful political activity in the context of an authoritarian state, such as China, may well not satisfy it. Nor might the keeping of files by organizations such as the UK's MI5 on the activities of leading members of the Labour Party during a Tory government's period of office.

In the light of the normative account of policing adumbrated above, evidently there is a public interest in criminal investigations in the service of the protection of justifiably enforced, legally enshrined moral rights. For violations of such rights, that is, criminal acts, are at one level acts in defiance of the community and, specifically, the state. Accordingly, there is legitimate public interest in criminal investigations, notwithstanding the fact that the wrongdoing in question might, in large part, consist only in harm done to one individual person, as in a case of assault.

On the other hand, there is also legitimate public interest in investigations of crimes in which there is no direct rights violation of any particular individual person. An example of police wrongdoing that needs to be investigated because it is in the public interest to do so, even though the wrongdoing in question does not necessarily violate any individual's rights is police corruption, for example, police officers accepting bribes (see Chapter 8). Here there is direct damage to an institution, namely a police organization, rather than to an individual person or persons. However, the institution in question exists, as we have seen, to protect justifiably enforced, legally enshrined moral rights. Accordingly, such corruption indirectly harms individual persons and, in so doing, results in infringements of their moral rights. Likewise, acts that damage institutions with respect to which individuals have property rights, such as stealing from a bank or defrauding a mining corporation, can indirectly cause harm to, for example, depositors or share-holders, and the harm in question can constitute an infringement of their moral rights, specifically, their property rights. So the investigation of crimes that consist of damage to institutions may well ultimately serve the protection of the rights of individual human beings; or at least, this is so in so far as those institutions exist to protect moral rights (e.g., police organizations), or are, at least in part, the objects of the property rights of individual human beings (e.g., private sector businesses). Nor are these the only kinds of case. Consider willful damage to public sector institutions – other than security agencies – which exist to fulfill purposes the non-fulfillment of which would consist in infringements of a moral right. Many schools and hospitals fall into this category, since, arguably, schools exist to provide for the aggregate needs-based right to education and hospitals to provide for the aggregate needs-based right to health care. If so, then an arson attack on a school or the theft of drugs from a hospital has untoward moral rights implications; other things being equal, such crimes, at least if conducted on a large scale, lead to a reduction in the fulfillment of moral rights. Accordingly, investigations of such crimes indirectly contributes to the protection of moral rights.[43]

In relation to the constraints on criminal investigations and, again, speaking in general terms, the investigation ought itself to be lawful and morally permissible. This raises a host of moral questions in relation to the process of investigation, for example, regarding suspect's rights. Many of these questions will be taken up in subsequent chapters. It also raises moral questions in relation to the investigator. For example, the investigator ought to have been properly authorized to undertake the investigation, so that it is not simply, for example, an unauthorized investigation embarked upon for personal reasons. Here we note that an investigation might be lawful and even morally permissible considered on its own terms, that is *qua* investigation, but the particular investigator might still not have been authorized to undertake it. This raises the important question of who ought to be entitled to authorize a criminal investigation.

A further constraint on criminal investigations is resources, a constraint which is especially salient in the post–GFC period of austerity in many jurisdictions in the United States, United Kingdom, and Europe. This constraint has moral significance given the implication that some crimes (e.g., minor property crimes) will not be able to be investigated or at least not be able to be thoroughly investigated. In the context of scarce resources priorities need to be determined in relation to investigations. These priorities ought to determined by a variety of criteria including not only the seriousness of the crime and the likelihood that it might be resolved if investigated, but also by a variety of corporate priorities. For example, there might be a need to focus on crime reduction, targeting, say, organized crime, rather than on fear of crime, ensuring, say, a visible police presence in areas of petty crime, notwithstanding greater public concern with the latter.

An important corporate priority, albeit one sometimes not explicitly prioritized, is organizational reputation. To what extent is organizational reputation factored in explicitly and given reasonable, but not overriding or unreasonable, weight? Certainly, police chiefs and commanders benchmark their forces against other forces in part on the basis of organizational reputation. To this extent reputation is an implicit criterion in "performance measurement."

Investigations should be conducted within budget and use the appropriate number of personnel (avoiding undermanning or overmanning). More generally, the resources used should be appropriate to the investigations: there should, for example, be appropriate use of resource-intensive intrusive surveillance methods. Here it is important to distinguish the budget set aside for an investigation and the budget available for conducting all investigations over the budgetary period in question. The budget for a specific investigation might be adequate even though the overall budget for investigations is not – and vice versa. We note that a large number of high-profile investigations can quickly destroy a budget, even one thought originally to be adequate.

The larger context for the efficient and effective use of public resources by investigators is the overall quantum of resources made available to the police organization by government. Naturally, appropriate resourcing of investigations cannot be achieved, absent the existence of adequate resources within the police organization, or at least within the investigative division of the police organization. Accordingly, an issue arises in relation to the system for allocating scarce resources within the police organization as a whole, and within the criminal investigations department itself.

Notes

1   At least ideally or by the lights of the standard theory of representative democracy, according to which, although the law *directly* reflects the will of the legislators, it *indirectly* reflects the will of the citizenry who elected the legislators to govern in accordance with *their* (the citizenry's) will and, for that matter, *their* (the citizenry's) interest. In practice, of course, many laws are in part

reflective of powerful sectional interest groups who successfully lobby, or are otherwise able to influence, democratically elected governments. For example, perhaps laws, or at least regulations, in the area of white collar crime have historically been less stringent than they ought to be. Moreover, laws undergo change as a result of moral progress. For example, pollution and health and safety infringements were formerly breaches of civil or administrative, rather than criminal, law.

2   For a sustained philosophical defense of objectivity in relation to these various categories of propositions see Thomas Nagel (1997) *The Last Word*, Oxford: Oxford University Press.

3   The subjective social morality/objective morality distinction is related to, but is not the same as, the so-called positive morality/critical morality distinction. Subjective social morality is roughly the same as positive morality; but critical morality is the structure of moral principles and so forth that a society uses to critique its prior beliefs and behavior. However, critical morality is not necessarily objective in character; moreover, some elements of positive morality will be elements of objective morality (namely those that are objectively correct).

4   Obviously, other things might not be equal. For example, other relatives or the state might provide for their needs, if the parents do not.

5   There is an important conceptual and normative issue as to what counts as bribery. See Stuart P. Green (2010) *Lying, Cheating and Stealing: A Moral Theory of White Collar Crime*, Oxford: Oxford University Press, Chapter 16, Bribery.

6   Patrick Devlin (1968) *The Enforcement of Morals*, Oxford: Oxford University Press.

7   John Stuart Mill *On Liberty* (any edition) and Joel Feinberg (1987) *Harm to Others: The Moral Limits of the Criminal Law*, Oxford: Oxford University Press.

8   Roughly speaking – and other things being equal – one's action is morally wrong if one intentionally harms another (and one's intention is under one's control), or one knowingly causes harm to another (and could have done otherwise), or one unknowingly causes harm to another, could have done otherwise, and should have known that one's action would cause the harm in question. For a detailed recent account of causation and responsibility in the law and morality see Michael S. Moore (2009) *Causation and Responsibility: An Essay in Law, Morals and Metaphysics*, Oxford: Oxford University Press. On the more specific notion of collective moral responsibility see Seumas Miller (2006) Collective moral responsibility: an individualist account, in Peter A. French (ed.) *Midwest Studies in Philosophy*, 30, pp.176–193. See also the discussion in Chapter 7, Section 7.6 in relation to terrorism.

9   But see Feinberg (1987).

10 Taxes typically provide for goods to which the citizenry have basic rights and goods to which they do not. On the view under consideration, there would presumably be a different moral justification for the enforcement of taxes to provide for goods in respect of which the citizens did not have basic rights, that is, to levy taxes above and beyond those required to ensure basic rights are respected.

11   Henry Shue (1984) *Basic Rights*, Princeton: Princeton University Press.

12   See, for example, Article 24 of the Universal Declaration of Human Rights.

13   The terminology used to refer to these various categories of legal and moral rights can be confusing. For a recent account of this issue see James W. Nickel (2007) *Making Sense of Human Rights* (2nd edn), Oxford: Blackwell Publishing, Chapter 1. Some legal rights and duties are also moral rights and duties but were not moral rights and duties prior to being legal rights and duties; to this extent the law "creates" morality. Such legal rights and duties are a species of institutional (moral) rights and duties. See discussion below.

14   Or at least rights to such assistance when it can be relatively easily provided.

15   See Miller (2010a).

16   Another important set of rights sometimes neglected are the rights of future generations. These rights are highly germane in relation to laws enacted to protect the environment.

17   See Seumas Miller and John Blackler (2005) *Ethical Issues in Policing*, Aldershot: Ashgate, Chapter 4.

18   The intuitive idea is that there are certain properties that individual human beings possess that are at least in part constitutive of their humanity. Naturally, there is room for dispute as to what these properties are; indeed, some putative properties might be criteria rather than defining properties. Moreover, while some putative properties, such as the capacity to reason, are more salient than others, such as the capacity for bodily movement, we do not have a worked-out theory to offer. However, the main point to stress here is that the properties in question are ones that are held to have *moral* value, for example, individual autonomy or life. This conception is consistent with a view of human beings as essentially social animals. See Seumas Miller (2003) Individual autonomy and sociality, in F. Schmitt (ed.), *Socialising Metaphysics: The Nature of Social Reality*, Lanham, MD: Rowman and Littlefield.

19   Typically, a distinction is made between claim rights (e.g., one's right to one's own body) and liberty rights (e.g., a right to sit on a park bench in a public area). If A has a claim right to x then B has no right to x and, indeed, B has a duty to refrain from taking x (or otherwise interfering with A's enjoyment of x). If A has a liberty right to y then B may well also have a liberty right to y. But perhaps B has a duty to refrain from preventing A from exercising A's right to y (other than incidentally by B exercising B's right to y).

20   Note that we are here asserting a *normative* conceptual connection between *human* rights and enforcement. We are not making the more familiar (and controversial) claim that for something to be a moral right, it must be able to be enforced. Here it is also useful to distinguish between different orders of rights and duties. For example, the right to life gives rise to the duty not to kill, but also the duty to protect someone from being killed.

21   Or at least for much of the substantive, as opposed to, procedural criminal law. See Sections 1.2.2 and 1.3 below.

22   L. Writer, S. Barrett, and A. Bouda (1992) *Garden of Evil: The Granny Killer's Reign of Terror*, Sydney: Ironbark, p. 147.

23   W. Brown (ed.) (1995) *Australian Crime*, Sydney: Book Company International, p. 240.

24 See Writer, Barrett, and Bouda (1992).
25 H. L. Packer (1964) Two models of criminal process, *University of Pennsylvania Law Review*, 113, November, pp. 1–68.
26 See Packer (1964), p. 10.
27 Jerome Skolnick (1977) *Justice without Trial; Law Enforcement in Democratic Society* (2nd edn), New York: Macmillan, pp. 196–197.
28 Skolnick (1977), p. 196–197
29 No doubt the legal context, including other laws, plays a role here.
30 Some of the complexities here are as follows. Words and sentences have meaning in a language to some extent independently of any given speaker's *use* of those words and sentences. Moreover, context to some extent determines meaning. The precise relationship between so-called "speaker-meaning" and "sentence-meaning" is a matter of dispute between philosophers of language. See, for example, Paul Grice (1968) Utterer's meaning, sentence meaning and word meaning, *Foundations of Language*, 4. Further, there is a dispute among legal theorists as to the degree of importance that ought to be attached to the original legislator's intended meaning (leaving aside questions of speaker-meaning versus sentence-meaning). Some theorists hold that legislation needs to be "reinterpreted" in the light of contemporary circumstances, notably in respect of its current relevance. Nevertheless, the original and, for that matter, current meaning of the legislation is in large part dependent on the original legislator's intention. It should also be noted that deviation from that intended meaning for the purposes of ensuring the current relevance of the legislation – whatever one thinks of the merits of such a process – is something above and beyond interpreting the original meaning. See, for example, Ronald Dworkin (1998) *Law's Empire*, Oxford: Hart Publishing.
31 Those who reject objective truth and falsehood are also referred to as relativists; we are using the terms subjectivism and relativism more or less interchangeably to refer to those who reject objective truth. It is important, however, to distinguish between subjectivists (relativists) and skeptics. Skeptics do not necessarily deny the existence of objective truth; rather they deny that we could *know* that we ever possessed objective truths. Some subjectivists (relativists) hold that there are *no* statements, including statements about the physical world and mathematical statements such as that $2 + 2 = 4$, that are objectively true (or objectively false). This view is implausible not the least because it is evidently self-refuting. It is self-refuting because the very statement of this view cannot – according to this view itself – be objectively true (or objectively false) on pain of contradiction. If the statement of this view is objectively true then it contradicts itself; it turns out that there is, after all, at least one objectively true statement, namely, the statement that there are no objective truths. On the other hand, if the statement of this view is not objectively true then there is no need to pay any attention to it; it is not, after all, making the objectively true statement that there are no objective truths.
32 As already noted, the terms "subjectivism" and "relativism" are often used interchangeably but there is a need to distinguish individualist from collectivist forms, such as cultural relativism. Moreover, sometimes subjectivism is used to refer to an individualist (rather than a collectivist) doctrine – and vice versa for

relativism. For an introductory discussion of moral subjectivism (i.e., moral relativism) see in particular Alexandra and Miller (2009), Chapter 2. For a general defense of objectivism see Nagel (1997).

33   Theoretical claims in the sphere of criminal justice are, we take it, typically not deductively derivable from factual statements or, at least, not thus derivable in any nontrivial sense. Rather the argumentative form that such derivations take is typically that of evidential weight, including the weight of inductive evidence. Nor do such theoretical claims make use of so-called theoretical entities in the sense that that term has in the natural sciences, e.g., statements with respect to non-observable, subatomic particles. Theorists of a behaviorist bent have on occasion sought to present statements about mental states as theoretical in this sense but this ignores introspection as a legitimate mode of access and, therefore, flies in the face of common sense and of the law.

34   Earlier versions of this normative account appeared in Miller (2010a), Chapter 9, Miller and Blackler (2005), Chapter 1, Seumas Miller, John Blackler, and Andrew Alexandra (2006) *Police Ethics* (2nd edn), Sydney: Allen and Unwin, Chapter 3, and Seumas Miller and John Blackler (1995) *Police Ethics*, Wagga Wagga, Keon Press, Chapter 3.

35   Naturally, we acknowledge that many laws do not derive from moral rights, and also that those that do often do not do so in any straightforward manner.

36   Miller has elaborated a teleological account of institutions in his 2001 work *Social Action: A Teleological Account*, New York: Cambridge University Press, Chapter 6 and also in *The Moral Foundations of Social Institutions* (2010). See especially Chapter 9 on policing as an institution.

37   We acknowledge that in common law countries the law reflects tradition, and therefore perhaps "consent" in another sense. See John Kleinig (1996) *The Ethics of Policing*, Cambridge: Cambridge University Press, Chapter 2.

38   See Kleinig (1996), Chapter 2. For a different kind of account in terms of the use of coercive force see Egon Bittner (1980) *The Functions of the Police in Modern Society*, Cambridge, MA: Oelgeschlager, Gunn, and Hain, 1980. See also Peter Neyroud and Alan Beckley (2001) *Policing, Ethics and Human Rights*, Cullompton, Devon: Willan Publishing, Chapter 2.

39   Here we are assuming that large fragments of a legal system can consist of immoral laws, and yet the system remain recognizably a legal system. See Dworkin (1998), p. 101. We are also assuming that, for a legal system to express the admittedly problematic notion of the will of the community, it is at least necessary that the overwhelming majority of the community (not just a simple majority) support the content of the system of laws taken as a whole – even if there are a small number of individual laws they do not support – and support the procedures for generating laws, for example, a democratically elected legislature, see Miller (2001), pp. 141–151. Finally, we are assuming that the fact that a party or candidate or policy or law secured (directly or directly) a majority vote is an important (but not necessarily decisive) consideration in its favor, and a consideration above and beyond the moral weight to be given to the existence of a consensus in relation to the value to be attached to voting as a procedure.

40 Moreover, community-based policing might reconstitute itself as problem-based policing, and thereby be more effective. See Herman Goldstein (1990) *Problem-Oriented Policing*, New York: McGraw-Hill, and Team Policing, in Steven G. Brandl and David E. Barlow (eds) (1996) *Classics of Policing*, Cincinnati, OH: Anderson Publishing Co., p. 86f.

41 Regarding the role of the religious police of the Taliban in the Department of the Promotion of Virtue and Prevention of Vice, see Ahmed Rashid (2001) *Taliban: The Story of the Afghan Warlords*, London: Pan Books, Chapter 8.

42 An earlier version of the material in this section appeared in Seumas Miller, Peter Roberts, and Edward Spence (2005) *Corruption and Anti-corruption; A Study in Applied Philosophy*, Saddle River, NJ: Prentice Hall, Chapter 7.

43 See Miller (2010a) for a general normative theory of social institutions which lends support to this claim.

2

Knowledge, Evidence, and the Aims of Investigation

In the last chapter we outlined and discussed the following related propositions: (i) the criminal law and, therefore, criminal investigations, can be provided with a relatively narrowly circumscribed and objective basis by recourse to, in particular, justifiably enforceable moral rights not to be harmed and to assistance in relation to needs-based deprivations; (ii) policing has, as its fundamental purpose, the protection of justifiably enforceable, *legally enshrined* moral rights; and (iii) criminal investigation is undertaken ultimately in order to protect justifiably enforceable, legally enshrined moral rights. However, the precise role, or roles, that criminal investigation has, or ought to have, in relation to this larger purpose is in need of further specification. It will turn out that the investigative role is essentially an epistemic or knowledge-focused role; that is, that the principal role of detectives is to acquire knowledge with respect to the who, what, when, where, how, and why of crimes (and, therefore, knowledge of moral rights violations and violators (offenders) – given our normative rights-based accounts of criminal law and of police organizations). It will further turn out that the exercise of this epistemic role is itself but one stage in an extended institutional process involving other interlocking institutional roles (e.g., prosecutors, judges, jury members, correctional officers) and stages, notably the criminal trial.

Here we note that the crimes in question could have already taken place, in which case the response of the investigators is essentially reactive. Alternatively, although the substantive crime of particular interest might not have taken place, an investigation has been triggered by suspicious activity or lesser criminal activity or the like. In the latter kind of case the

Investigative Ethics: Ethics for Police Detectives and Criminal Investigators, First Edition.
Seumas Miller and Ian A. Gordon.
© 2014 Seumas Miller and Ian A. Gordon. Published 2014 by John Wiley & Sons, Ltd.

investigation is proactive or preventive in character. Consider in this connection an investigation in relation to terrorist activity in which the principal aim is to prevent a terrorist bombing by means of a proactive investigation. (See the discussion of reactive and preventive policing in Chapter 1, Section 1.5 and of the investigation of terrorism in Chapter 7.)

If, as we argue in the first section below, the investigator's role is essentially an epistemic or knowledge-focused one, then there is a need to provide an analysis of knowledge: the thing the investigator is principally aiming at or, at least, ought to be aiming at. This is a deep and longstanding philosophical issue, the details of which lie outside the purview of this work; nevertheless, it is one we need to address to some degree. Here there is a threefold distinction between so-called knowledge-how, knowledge-by-acquaintance and propositional knowledge. Although we begin in the opening section with an elaboration of this threefold distinction, it is propositional knowledge that is of most interest to us and we provide a basic analysis of propositional knowledge as (roughly) justified true belief expressed in sentences of a language. Propositional knowledge is of the greatest interest since the knowledge which criminal investigators pursue, and hopefully attain, needs to be rendered in a form suitable for use in a court of law, that is as explicitly linguistically expressed knowledge (expressed not only orally but also in writing, e.g., in documents).

In the second section we present two case studies to illustrate, among other things, what is morally at stake in criminal investigations. In the third section we elaborate on the nature and form of the explanations/justifications that criminal investigators must necessarily provide for their knowledge claims, and in the fourth section we address the question of the moral responsibility of investigators and do so in the light of their essentially epistemic role. In the final section we address issues of investigator accountability.

2.1   Knowledge and the Aims of Investigation

At the outset it is important to make the following distinctions in relation to knowledge. There is knowledge in the sense of *knowledge-by-acquaintance*. That is, knowing someone or something. For example, if two strangers have a face-to-face conversation, then there is direct (physical and psychological) experience of one another; there is, therefore, knowledge-by-acquaintance. Note that one can be said to have knowledge-by-acquaintance of, say, x at a time, t, even though one is not necessarily in a face-to-face encounter with x at t; however, if so then the knowledge-by-acquaintance of x in question would presuppose at least one face-to-face encounter with x in the past.

Such knowledge-by-acquaintance can have greater or lesser breadth (roughly, the extent or quantity of knowledge) and depth (roughly, the centrality or importance of knowledge).[1] Thus a man has knowledge-by-acquaintance of his wife of many years, and this knowledge has considerable breadth and depth as a consequence of the detailed background knowledge (based in large part on past encounters) that the man brings to bear on any particular face-to-face encounter with her. In a brief face-to-face conversation with her he will notice much, and things of importance, that would be missed by a stranger. On the other hand, if the stranger is a well-trained police officer, then he might notice things about her that her husband would miss and that might be important to the officer's investigation. So the police officer's knowledge-by-acquaintance might also have depth, albeit in relation to a single issue.

In addition to knowledge-by-acquaintance there is so-called *knowing-how*. To know how to do something, for example, how to ride a bike or how to interview a suspect, is, in essence, to possess a skill. Naturally, knowledge-how typically goes hand-in-glove with knowledge-by-acquaintance. Knowing how to ride a bike, for example, presupposes direct experience of bikes (knowledge-by-acquaintance), knowing how to interview a suspect presupposes direct experience of suspects (knowledge-by-acquaintance), and so on. Moreover, knowledge-how facilitates knowledge-by-acquaintance. Thus an experienced and competent police interviewer (someone with a high degree of knowledge how to interview) may well quickly come to know a witness (knowledge-by-acquaintance) at a level of depth which a novice interviewer would struggle to attain because, for example, the novice is unable to make the witness feel at ease.

Finally, there is so-called *propositional knowledge*. This is knowledge that some state of affairs obtains. Propositional knowledge is expressed in language by sentences with a subject and a predicate. For example, suppose a detective knows that the fingerprints found on a knife at the crime scene were those of the suspect. Here there is trace material found at the crime scene, namely, the fingerprints on the knife, and this trace has been caused by the suspect handling said knife. The investigator has propositional knowledge of this state of affairs if he or she knows it and has expressed this knowledge in a sentence (or sentences) of a language.

Note that, although propositional knowledge is expressed in language, it is not necessarily expressed in a form accessible to others. Thus, the detective might know that Jones is the murderer and express this thought to himself in a sentence, but the detective does not necessarily utter this sentence for others to hear it; he does not necessarily assert or *make a statement* (in the ordinary commonsense meaning of that term, as opposed to its meaning in criminal justice contexts, e.g., the witness statement) expressing his propositional knowledge. (Henceforth we will indicate that a statement is a formal statement made in a criminal justice context and available as testimonial evidence in a court of law by the use of the upper case, namely "Statement".) A statement in the commonsense meaning of that term (and, for that matter in the formal criminal justice sense) is something that is outwardly expressed; it is said out loud or put in writing, and does not merely remain in the realm of inner thought.

Propositional knowledge goes hand-in-glove with both knowledge-by-acquaintance and knowledge-how. Much knowledge-by-acquaintance is translated into explicit thought and, as such, is expressed in language (to oneself and, very often, also to others). Thus a woman sees a tall young man in a dark suit with squint eyes assaulting a small old man, and the tall man bumps into her as he runs from the scene of his crime shouting at her as he goes to get out of his way. He then gets into a blue Ford Fiesta and drives off. The woman has knowledge-by-acquaintance of the tall man, the old man, and of the assault and the getaway car; she is a witness to a crime. Moreover, the witness translates that knowledge-by-acquaintance into propositional knowledge: firstly, by reflecting on who and what she has seen, heard, and otherwise experienced and, secondly, by writing it down in the form of a witness Statement.

On the other hand, propositional knowledge can facilitate, and give direction to, knowledge-by-acquaintance. Suppose the witness upon seeing the assault makes an explicit judgment that it is indeed an assault ('My God, he is assaulting the poor man'). She now has propositional knowledge of the event. Suppose further that she then makes a deliberate decision to try as best she can to see what the tall man looks like (i.e., to enhance her knowledge-by-acquaintance of him) and also to watch in which direction and by what means he is making his getaway (i.e., her propositional knowledge that he is an offender is giving direction to her intentions with respect to her knowledge-by-acquaintance of his movements).

Clearly investigators need to have all three sorts of knowledge. They need to verify certain claims by direct observation (knowledge-by-acquaintance). They need to know how to do various things, including how to take evidence, interview a witness, and so on (knowing-how). They also have to have, and to be able to obtain, propositional knowledge. Indeed, most of what they end up putting into print, for example, an investigator's report, is propositional knowledge (expressed in statements).

We suggest that the fundamental *point* of criminal investigation is knowledge and, more specifically, propositional knowledge expressed in statements – since such knowledge needs to be communicated to others and not left in the head of the investigator. In short, criminal investigators *ought* to have the acquisition of knowledge as their principal aim or end. Accordingly, a necessary condition for being a good investigator is that one aims at knowledge. So an otherwise highly skilled investigator who did not have knowledge with respect to crimes and their perpetrators as his *overriding* aim, but rather (say) a desire to have a very high clear-up or conviction rate, would not be a good investigator. For example, the highly skilled investigator who, nevertheless, ignores counterevidence when forced to choose between getting to the truth of the matter (and, thereby, coming to have knowledge) and securing convictions is not a good investigator (see case studies below).

It has been suggested[2] that the aim of investigation and, therefore, of investigators is not knowledge (or even truth[3]) but is rather simply to gather evidence (both inculpatory and exculpatory) and let the courts worry about knowledge or the truth of the matter.[4] However, this suggestion misunderstands the relationship between evidence and truth. Rational evidence gathering is necessarily guided by truth. The truth of the matter at issue – whether or not the suspect committed the crime, for example – is what good and decisive evidence is evidence for; so truth seeking gives direction to evidence gathering. It follows that an investigator who was not aiming at the truth of the matter, for example, with respect to who killed John Doe's wife, would not know, or even care to know, what counted as evidence and what did not, and would not seek to unearth as much and as good evidence as possible. Of course, it is not up to the investigator to make the final adjudication with respect to the legal guilt of a suspect, but that is a different (albeit related) matter to which we return below.[5]

It goes without saying that the pursuit of knowledge with respect to criminal acts and their perpetrators is constrained by the law; this much is acknowledged in the general normative account of policing outlined in Chapter 1. Moreover, knowledge is not the only aim of criminal investigation; criminal investigation has other additional aims, and ought to have them. Such purposes include bringing offenders to justice, crime prevention, intelligence gathering, protection of witnesses, asset recovery, ensuring reasonable clear-up and conviction rates (as we saw above), and so on. However, our claim is that these are secondary purposes for investigators by virtue of being, for example, derived purposes, or larger institutional purposes from which the investigator's primary purpose is itself derived. Crime prevention is an instance of the latter; intelligence gathering is an instance of the former. Moreover, some of these secondary purposes, such as witness protection, are both derived purposes and ends-in-themselves. Witness protection is a derived purpose in so far as it is done in order to enable the truth to be uncovered and an offender to be brought to justice. But witnesses also have a nonderived inherent moral right to be protected from violence, intimidation and so on; they have this in common with everyone else, whether they be a witness or not.

Here we need to emphasize the distinction between factual guilt and legal guilt. It is the investigator's role to arrive at knowledge in respect of whether or not a suspect is factually guilty and, if so, to recommend that the suspect be prosecuted (or otherwise to present this knowledge to the relevant prosecuting authority). But factual guilt is not legal guilt.

Legal guilt is, of course, a matter for the courts to determine. Naturally, a suspect ought to be found legally guilty only if he or she in fact committed the crime (i.e., is factually guilty); but, to reiterate, legal guilt is not a matter for the investigator to determine.

It is sometimes suggested that there is no such thing as factual guilt, but only legal guilt. However, surely someone who in fact committed (say) an act of murder (by deliberately, unnecessarily, and unlawfully killing a person), and yet is pronounced in the relevant court of law to be innocent, is *in point of fact* – the formal verdict notwithstanding – guilty of murder by virtue of having intentionally killed the person in question and done so in breach of the law. Courts of law can and do pronounce on the guilt or innocence of those who come before them, but they cannot (and, therefore, do not) magically change the past. If, as a matter of fact, in 2012 A intentionally killed B in breach of the law (i.e., A is factually guilty) then a court sitting in 2013 cannot change that fact. Accordingly, if the court in question pronounces A to be innocent then the court has made a mistake.

In all this there is a kind of institutional division of labor and separation of roles that involves each type of institutional actor – investigator, prosecutor, judge, jury, and so forth – making a contribution to the further end of identifying and appropriately punishing the guilty and exonerating the innocent. However, unlike many institutional arrangements, the criminal justice process is predicated on strict adherence on the part of institutional actors to the separation of roles on pain of compromising this further end.

We emphasize that this separation of roles is consistent with all of these actors despite their diverse and separate roles having a common further aim; agents can have a common aim and yet it be a requirement that each is to make a different and distinct contribution and not perform the tasks assigned to the others, and all this in the service of that common aim.

In respect of this separation of roles, the relationship between the institutional actors, including investigators, in the criminal justice process is *unlike* that which holds between a manager, a waiter, and a barman in a small pub. There is no reason why, for example, the manager and the waiter might not assist the barman in doing his job of pouring beers during a rush period or even stand in his place when he is called away. But there is good reason why the prosecutor should not also be the judge or the investigator the jury; in an adversarial system any such conflation of roles would constitute a structural conflict of interest and, as such, would be likely to undermine the administration of justice.[6]

Institutional arrangements such as this, in which there is a separation of roles (and associated responsibilities) but, nevertheless, a common further end, involve what Miller has referred to elsewhere as a "chain of institutional and moral responsibility."[7]

In chains of institutional and moral responsibility all the participants aim (or should be aiming) at the further end in addition to undertaking their own roles (and, therefore, aiming at the end definitive of their own particular role). Moreover, all the participants (at least, in principle) share in the *collective responsibility* (of which more below, but see Chapter 7, Section 7.6 for an analysis) for achieving that further end (or for failing to do so).[8] Let us work with the example of Peter Sutcliffe, the Yorkshire Ripper, who was ultimately convicted of 13 counts of murder (most of the victims being prostitutes working in Yorkshire in the United Kingdom – see Chapter 5, Case Study 5.2.1.)

The detectives involved were collectively (in the sense of jointly) morally responsible for gathering and analyzing the evidence that identified Peter Sutcliffe as the Yorkshire Ripper; they acquired the required knowledge of Sutcliffe's *factual* guilt and, thereby, realized the collective end[9] (in the sense of a common end pursued by each individual detective) of their institutional role as detectives. On the other hand, members of the court and, in particular, the members of the jury were (collectively) morally responsible for finding Sutcliffe *legally* guilty and, thereby, realized the (collective) end of their institutional roles as jury members. So far so good; but what was the ultimate end that was realized by the detectives *and* the members of the jury (as well as the other actors involved in the institutional process, e.g., the judge)?

Presumably the end in question is for the factually guilty to be found legally guilty (and the factually innocent not to be found legally guilty[10]) and this is an end (a collective end) that is realized by the detectives working jointly with the members of the jury (and the other relevant institutional actors). It is not an end that the detective could achieve on their own; they can only arrive at knowledge of factual guilt. But equally it is not an end that the members of the jury could realize on their own; for they rely on the knowledge provided by the detectives.[11]

Notwithstanding this above-described mandatory separation of roles (in the context of a chain of institutional and moral responsibility), detectives have been known to try to preempt the outcome of the criminal justice process, for example, by "loading up" suspects who they believe are guilty and deserving of severe punishment, rather than remaining within the confines of their designated role of evidence gathering in the service of truth and being content to rely on prosecutors, judges, and juries to undertake their different (albeit, ultimately interlocking) roles in relation to assessing the case against suspects, determining guilt, passing sentence, and so on. (In this connection see the case studies below, 2.2.1, The Birmingham Six and 2.2.2, The Harry Blackburn Investigation.)

As mentioned above, propositional knowledge is at least true belief expressed in a language; and the knowledge[12] pursued by investigators is true, *stated* (outwardly expressed) belief. Indeed, since the knowledge aimed at by criminal investigators not only has to be communicated to some others, fellow investigators, for example, it ultimately has to become a matter of common knowledge in a public legal setting, then this aimed-at knowledge is knowledge expressed in statements and in accordance with various institutional protocols, for example, in the context of a brief of evidence.

If knowledge is at least true belief then an existing state of affairs, for instance, a dead body, is not a matter of knowledge until it, so to speak, "enters the head" of someone, that is to say, becomes the content of a belief. However, in order for a belief to be knowledge it must be a *true* belief; falsehoods are not knowledge. If someone believes that the world is flat or that $2 + 2 = 5$ then that person has a false belief and, therefore, does not have knowledge. So knowledge is at least true belief. But what is truth?

Roughly speaking, a belief or statement is true if and only if the world is as the belief or statement holds it to be.[13] Thus the belief or statement that snow is white is true if snow is in fact white and, indeed, only if in fact snow is white; again, the belief or statement that this blood sample is that of Jones is true if and only if it is in fact that of Jones. To this extent the so-called correspondence theory of truth is acceptable, indeed trivially true.

Moreover, beliefs, judgments, statements, assertions, and the like have truth as their point; a statement, judgment, or belief ought to aim at the truth and, if it turns out to be false, then it is defective qua statement, judgment, belief. Or, to put things slightly differently, these states or acts "aim at" reality, and are successful – that is, true – in so far as reality is as they hold it to be. Consider a detective's evidence-based judgment that a suspect robbed the bank. In making this judgment the detective is aiming at reality; trying to get it right in relation to whether the suspect *in reality* committed the crime. If it turns out that the suspect was in fact overseas on the date in question and, therefore, could not have committed the crime, then the detective's judgment will have failed; it will have turned out to be a *false* judgment. So judgments, statements are truth-aiming; they are teleological phenomena. Truth is what judgments, statements, assertions, beliefs, and the like aim at, or at least *ought* to aim at (given that there are liars and loose talkers who do not in fact aim at truth), and it is the property possessed by judgments, statements, assertions, beliefs, and the like when reality is as they hold it to be.

Truth is attained by the investigator when he or she has a true belief that (say) Peter Sutcliffe is the Yorkshire Ripper. However, truth in the sense of true belief is not sufficient. The investigator needs to be able to justify his or her true belief by recourse to evidence. Moreover, this justification must consist in reasons, namely, good and decisive reasons; a bad reason is an unacceptable justification and a good reason is not necessarily sufficient to warrant true belief (there might be, for example, a countervailing good reason not to hold that belief). Typically, there will be a set of good reasons which, cumulatively, should constitute a decisive reason for the investigator's true belief.

Accordingly, the investigator has as a goal *justified* true belief. But justified true belief is knowledge. So knowledge is the goal of the investigator; specifically, propositional knowledge expressed in statements.

We note that if knowledge is expressed in statements – specifically, in written form – then it is possible for it to be to be stored in libraries, databases, and the like and, thereby, available for access by multiple users. Indeed, if further rendered into an electronic form and stored in large databases then the possibility of combining, cross-tabulating and so on different items of knowledge is made possible; something of enormous significance for intelligence-based investigation (see Chapter 3).

We also note that what might count as a good and decisive reason for a belief outside a formal legal setting might not count for one within the courtroom setting in particular. For example, some forms of evidence are not admissible in a court of law because they were gathered unlawfully. The notion of knowledge relies on justification in its ordinary, nonlegal sense.

In summation, the investigator has as his or her goal – or, at least, *ought to* have – knowledge in the following sense (and using the above example): (i) the investigator believes Sutcliffe is the Yorkshire Ripper; (ii) it is true that Sutcliffe is the Yorkshire Ripper; (iii) the investigator has a justification (which constitutes a good and decisive set of reasons) for believing Sutcliffe is the Yorkshire Ripper, for example, Sutcliffe has the motive, the ability, the opportunity and there is physical evidence of his presence at the various crime scenes; (iv) the investigator has expressed the proposition that Sutcliffe is the Yorkshire Ripper in a statement (or statements).

Why does the investigator need a rational justification?[14] Why is not the truth (true belief or true statement) sufficient? (Notice that true beliefs and true statements are not quite the same thing, and not simply because a true statement is an overt expression of a true belief. For someone could make a true statement without actually believing it. We return to this issue below.)

So why is there a need for a rational justification? For one thing, speaking generally, beliefs need to be grounded in reasons if they are to be rationally held beliefs, as opposed to irrational or nonrational ones. Here, reasons are the means by which we reliably determine which beliefs are true and which are false. An irrational person might accidentally possess true beliefs. But, as Plato famously argued centuries ago in the *Theaetetus* and elsewhere, accidental true beliefs do not constitute knowledge. For example, taking a hallucinogenic drug might cause you to believe that Fred is dangerous, and Fred might in fact be dangerous. But your true belief that Fred is dangerous would not thereby constitute knowledge. This is because hallucinogenic drugs are not a reliable method (we are assuming) for arriving at the truth.[15]

For another thing, institutionally speaking, the investigator needs to be able to justify his or her beliefs, his or her statements, to others – especially to the courts of law – and to do so by means of the provision of good and decisive reasons. Sutcliffe cannot be convicted simply on the basis of the investigator's – or anyone else's – belief or statement that he is guilty, even if the belief or statement happens to be a true one. To this extent our institutions, including the criminal justice system, embody a general principle of rationality; not only in respect of the investigator's role but also, crucially, in respect of the roles of the judge and of the jury, who also ought to have rational justifications for their adjudications. Moreover, this principle of rationality underpins the principle of justice – the latter being the *raison d'être* for the criminal justice system. For this principle of rationality – the provision of good and decisive reasons – provides the assurance to the community that the innocent are going free and the guilty are being punished, that is, the assurance that justice is being done. For graphic real-life illustrations of the importance of evidence in relation to both determining the truth of the matter and providing assurance to the community that this is so we present the following two case studies.

2.2 Case Studies

Case Study 2.2.1   The Birmingham Six

On 21st November 1974, two public houses in Birmingham were bombed by the IRA. Twenty-one people were killed. Six men were charged with the largest number of murders in British history and in June 1976 they were tried in Lancaster. The trial lasted 45 days. The evidence against the six men consisted of forensic evidence and the written confessions of four of the men. There was also circumstantial evidence about associations with known IRA people. The admissibility of the confessions was disputed by the defense on the basis that they had been beaten out of the defendants. The judge allowed the confessions to go before the jury. All six defendants were convicted. On Thursday 14 March 1991, the Birmingham Six won their freedom.

(Continued)

In March 1990 the Home Secretary had ordered a new inquiry into the case after representations from the men's solicitors in which the forensic police evidence was challenged. Following the inquiry of Sir John May into the wrongful conviction in the Maguire case (May, 1990), which was closely linked to the Guildford Four case,[16] the credibility of the forensic science techniques used in the Birmingham Six case was totally demolished. In August 1990, the Home Secretary referred the case back to the Court of Appeal after the police inquiry had, quite independently, found discrepancies in the police interview record of one of the men. It seemed that the police had fabricated documentary evidence against the six men. The Director of Public Prosecutions could no longer rely on either the forensic or the police evidence that convicted the six men in 1975. The Court of Appeal heard the case at the beginning of 1991 and quashed the convictions of the six men.

(Extract from Seumas Miller, John Blackler, and Andrew Alexandra (2006) *Police Ethics* (2nd edn), Sydney: Allen and Unwin, p. 243)[17]

Case Study 2.2.2   The Harry Blackburn Investigation

On the evening of July 24th, 1989, 59-year-old, recently retired police superintendent Harry Blackburn was paraded before the media on his way to the Sydney Police Centre to be charged and processed into the criminal justice system, accused of being a violent serial sex offender with crimes spanning a period of 20 years. At the subsequent televised press conference, an assistant police commissioner congratulated Detective Chief Inspector Jim Thornthwaite, publicly acknowledged as head of the Blackburn investigation team, for his and his team's efforts.

The prejudicial effect of the 'media walk' – the press conference – even the import of the charges and the subsequent media beat-up, was profound and persuasive of guilt, the entire stage-managed process purposive of generating favourable publicity for the police organisation; a sub-text, a response to public concerns about police corruption, visible proof of the capacity and willingness of the police to pursue and prosecute their own, even the most highly placed, for wrongdoing. In this climate, there was a wide and instant public presumption of guilt. *It seemed everybody needed Harry Blackburn to be guilty.*

In this self-congratulatory atmosphere, Detective Sergeant Phil Minkley, field commander of the investigating unit, celebrated the success with his fellow investigators. The celebrations continued, and in the early hours of the following morning, Minkley and his brother-in-law and fellow investigator, Constable First Class Kevin Paull, were on their way home when the vehicle crashed.

This incident was something of a metaphor for the entire dubiously conducted investigation; who was actually the driver of the vehicle at the time of the collision remains still a matter of contention. Minkley was seriously injured, and unable to complete the closing phases of the investigation. Closure of the police case against Blackburn, the task of 'putting the brief together', was then handed over to Inspector Clive Small; Thornthwaite went on leave.

Closer acquaintance with the Blackburn investigation caused Small to experience doubts – and soon turned his involvement into a review of the conduct of the investigation itself. It was learned that as long ago as 1970, Jim Thornthwaite, then a Detective Constable First Class, was struck by the similarity of the physical description of a rapist operating in Sydney's southern suburbs to that of Sergeant Third Class Harry Blackburn, stationed at Kogarah police station, in that same area. Thornthwaite conveyed his suspicions to the investigating police, but there is no record that Blackburn was ever formally the subject of an investigation.

By 1985, at the time of the beginning of a further series of violent sexual attacks in the southern suburbs, Blackburn had been promoted to Superintendent in charge of the Physical Evidence Section, and Thornthwaite, now a Detective Senior Sergeant, was officer-in-charge of the Tactical Intelligence Unit, part of the State Intelligence Group. Thornthwaite, who had named Blackburn to investigators several times over the years as a suspect in other sexual attacks, was now, by virtue of his position, able to have Blackburn followed and photographed.

The attacks continued, and Thornthwaite called in Minkley and Paull, investigators of a 1988 attack – part of the same series – and conveyed his suspicions to them. On January 6th, 1989, a witness (later described as an 'idiot') was interviewed by Minkley and Paull, and in questionable circumstances, identified a photograph of Blackburn as the offender – despite the fact that the attacker had been masked.

On this slight evidence, Thornthwaite advised the officer-in-charge of the Tactical Intelligence Group that Blackburn had been

(*Continued*)

positively identified as the attacker. The police commissioner when informed, directed the investigation, tagged 'Operation Photo', to continue; because of its sensitivity, a special covert system of command – direct to the Commissioner's Office, with liaison through the Commissioner's chief of staff, and administrative coordination through the police Legal Services Branch – was established. The Director of Public Prosecutions was requested to assist police with legal advice; adequate physical and other resources were guaranteed the investigating team.

Within the investigation, a system of *'mindlock'* began to operate; facts fitting the investigative hypothesis were accepted without adequate testing, those contradicting the hypothesis were dismissed; Division of Forensic Medicine DNA evidence eliminating Blackburn was discredited, fingerprint evidence absolving Blackburn was ignored, and other factual inconsistencies were disregarded.

Witnesses were extensively prompted, and there was a perceptible loss of investigatorial objectivity. There is evidence Minkley viewed the investigation as a vehicle for self-promotion, portraying to peers the guarantee of adequate resourcing as a means of obtaining whatever he asked for, even extending to a trip to Greece for himself and Paull to show a victim Blackburn's photograph – the victim did not identify Blackburn.

Operation Photo became a runaway train, a casebook example of how not to conduct a criminal investigation. Ostensibly under Thornthwaite's direction, investigators incompetently and unilaterally pursued unsupported and unproductive avenues of inquiry. Forensic evidence was largely disregarded, and this disregard concealed within their reports by investigators, who in their dealings with the DPP were less than frank. Based on their misinterpretation of the 'evidence', the team received approval, in a special sitting of the Supreme Court, to search and even plant a listening device in Blackburn's home (and typically for Operation Photo, the opportunity was taken to steal a better, private photograph of Blackburn, to show to witnesses). Thornthwaite was promoted to Detective Chief Inspector and the team was on a 'high' as the investigation moved towards Blackburn's arrest.

Clive Small's review of Operation Photo disturbed him:

It is clear that at a very early stage he had grave reservations about the validity of the brief, and asked some very pointed questions of the investigating police. He found evidence of clear incompetence and perhaps even of deception. Inspector Small recommended an approach to the Director of Public Prosecutions for all charges to be withdrawn. This must have caused shock waves throughout the police hierarchy, and may have even got through to the government ranks. This was just prior to or on 25th September, 1989. It appears that from the time that Inspector Small started to express his doubts regarding the brief and ask awkward questions, there was a word of mouth campaign against him.[18]

Clive Small had to fly in the face of the collective wisdom of the police hierarchy, the media, and the general public. The royal commission showed there was no substance at all in the case against Blackburn. The operation had been one massive stuff-up from beginning to end. It was partly a failure in command and control, partly a failure on the part of senior officers, partly a failure of some of the key investigators – in particular Minkley, the most dominating personality in the initial investigation, who could have swung its course in quite another direction.[19]

The DPP declined to proceed with the prosecution; on October 11th, 1989, at the 302 Castlereagh Street Local Court, no evidence was offered, and the Magistrate dismissed all charges against Harry Blackburn, with costs. Media pressure subsequently forced the government to appoint Mr. Justice Lee as a Royal Commissioner to inquire into the matter. There was to be compensation ultimately – but there was to the last, neither admission, nor apology on the part of the police executive, themselves seemingly the victims of mindlock. They were instead now stubbornly going over the retired Superintendent's entire, 41-year record of worthy service with a fine tooth comb, seeking some evidence, any evidence, of wrong-doing.

Everybody needed Harry Blackburn to be guilty – the problem was, he was innocent. Victim of a 20-year-long *idée fixe* – of malice, of mindlock, of a disregard for forensic evidence, of men's ambition, of political expediency – destruction of the blameless Blackburn, and the fate of other actors, can form no part of our interest here. Instead, Commissioner Lee's comments:

> Mr. Small has done all that any man could have done to get the senior police to recognise the appalling predicament in which Mr. Blackburn had been placed at the hands of the investigating police, but the senior police clung blindly and tenaciously to the hope that Mr. Small might be wrong, and they did so, it seems, without either really acquainting themselves with the fine print in the evidence in the brief, or treating the evidence with objectivity, as every competent investigator into crime knows he must do.

(Continued)

– but then, how could they forgive somebody they had harmed so egregiously?

(Extract from John Blackler's case study, Harry the Hat, Thornthwaite, and Minkley, in John Blackler and Seumas Miller (2000) *Police Ethics (vol. 2): Case Studies for Police Detectives*, Wagga Wagga: Charles Sturt University and NSW Police Service, pp. 135–138)

2.3   Explanation and Justification: Good and Decisive Reasons

There are typically two sorts of justification in play in a criminal investigation and subsequent court hearing and, hence, two sorts of reasons. First, there are justifications offered for various *beliefs*. For example, there is the justification for the *belief* that the accused committed the crime (or did not do so). Such justifications are comprised of reasons for believing and include, but are not exhausted by, the evidence that typically figures among these reasons. Relevant forms of evidence include physical evidence, such as objects (e.g., weapons, tools, stolen property), electronic data (e.g., visual images provided by CCTV cameras), traces (e.g., fingerprints, tool marks), DNA samples (e.g., blood samples), testimony, and documents.[20] The provision of a justification for a belief is sometimes referred to as theoretical reasoning by philosophers.

Second, there are justifications offered for various *actions*. For example, there is the justification for the *action* prescribed by the court, namely, that the offender be punished by a term of imprisonment (or in the case that the accused is found to be innocent, that he or she be set free). Such justifications consist of reasons for acting. The provision of a justification for action is sometimes referred to by philosophers as practical reasoning.

These two modes of justification – and thus forms of reasoning, theoretical and practical – are interconnected in criminal investigations in a manner to be explained below.

Naturally, the reasons someone actually has for believing some proposition might not be good reasons, in other words, the reasons the person has are not the ones the person *ought* to have if he or she is to have the belief in question. Thus, a detective might believe that a suspect is the offender because of a "gut feeling." But "gut feelings," even if sometimes suggestive of lines of inquiry, do not constitute evidence: they are not, that is, in themselves good reasons, let alone decisive reasons, for true beliefs. Justified true beliefs are based on good reasons – reasons such that if one has them then (other things being equal) one *ought* to believe the propositions in question. For example, DNA evidence might be a good reason to believe that the accused was present at the scene of the crime. Thus DNA evidence *justifies* the belief, and does not merely provide a reason for it. By contrast, a "gut feeling" might provide a reason of sorts (a mere reason) for one's belief but it does not justify it.

When it comes to criminal actions, and the investigation thereof, the reasons in play can be quite complex and hence arises the possibility of having a set of reasons which have a certain weight, albeit they are not – taken in combination – good reasons, let alone decisive reasons. The case studies described above (2.2.1, The Birmingham Six and 2.2.2, The Harry Blackburn Investigation) illustrate this point. In both of these cases the investigators had *some* relevant reasons to believe that the persons they suspected had committed the crimes, but these reasons were far from sufficient. The cases also illustrate the dangers mentioned above of using evidence as a means to demonstrate one's prior beliefs or prejudices rather than being open-minded and allowing the evidence to dictate one's beliefs.

As with reasons for beliefs, the reasons someone actually has for performing some action might not be good reasons, that is to say that the reasons the person has are not ones the person *ought* to have if he or she is to perform the action in question. Thus a husband might intentionally kill his wife for the reason that she has engaged in adultery. But revenge is not a good reason, let alone a decisive reason, for murder. Justified actions are based on good reasons, that is, reasons such that if one has them then (other things being equal) one ought to perform the action in question. For example, self-defense might be a good reason for the intentional killing of another person. So self-defense can justify an act of intentional killing and does not merely provide a reason for it. By contrast, revenge provides a mere reason for intentional killing and does not justify it.[21]

We have distinguished between reasons for belief and reasons for action (theoretical and practical reasoning) and in both cases we have distinguished *justifying* reasons from mere reasons. However, there are three further sets of distinctions that need to be made before we proceed.

First, in relation to justification for actions, in particular, we can distinguish moral or legal justifications from rational justifications in general. Self-interest, for example, might provide a good and decisive reason for action, but self-interest is not necessarily a legal or moral justification. For example, it may well be in one's self-interest to engage in tax evasion if one can get away with it or to apply for promotion in the police service if one is eligible. But self-interest is not necessarily a moral or legal justification for action.

Second, in relation to practical reasoning, we need to distinguish justification from explanation. The above-mentioned husband with the adulterous wife was not justified in killing her; revenge does not *justify* murder. On the other hand, the motive of revenge may well *explain* the husband's murderous action. Such an explanation is a rational explanation in so far as it explains by recourse to the husband's reasons for his action, notwithstanding that these reasons do not justify (morally or legally) his action.

Third, in relation to the explanations of outcomes we need to distinguish rational explanations from causal explanations. Rational explanations, as we have just seen, invoke a person's reasons for his or her action, for example, revenge. Causal explanations invoke the causes of some outcome.

Importantly, causes are not necessarily reasons, although in some cases they might be – the motive of revenge, for instance, might be both a reason and a cause. An example of a cause that is not also a reason is a lightning strike which causes a bushfire. Causes occur outside the sphere of human action (as well as within it), whereas reasons pertain only to human action.

Criminal investigation frequently involves the provision of complex structures of both rational explanation (e.g., provision of motives) and causal explanation (e.g., plunging the knife into the victim's neck caused blood spatters on the wall).

Notice that, from the perspective of an external standpoint such as that of the observer or investigator, a reason for action can also function as a reason for belief, albeit indirectly. Suppose an investigator knows that a suspect has a motive to commit a crime (and also had the opportunity, ability, means, etc.), in other words, the investigator knows that the suspect had a reason to commit the crime. In such a case the investigator – *as an external observer/investigator of someone else's action* – now has a reason to *believe* that the person in question might have committed the crime. Alternatively, if the investigator knows that the suspect lacked such a motive, then the investigator has a reason to doubt that the suspect committed the crime.

So, for the person with a motive, that motive can function as a reason for his or her criminal action. But for the investigator the fact that the person being investigated had that motive can be a reason for believing that they performed the crime in question. Accordingly, the suspect's practical reasoning can figure in the investigator's theoretical reasoning. Let us work through the above-mentioned example.

Assume that our investigator believes that John Doe engaged in the following process of practical reasoning: I strongly desire to kill Jane for having an affair and have no countervailing stronger desire; I can do so by stabbing her with this carving knife; therefore, I will stab her to death (and he does so).

The investigator now engages in the following process of theoretical reasoning from his own belief premises (beliefs 1, 2, and 3) to his concluding belief (belief 4):

1. Investigator's belief 1: John Doe strongly desired to kill his wife (motive);
2. Investigator's belief 2: John Doe was in the house at the time that Jane Doe was killed (opportunity);
3. Investigator's belief 3: John Doe is a strong man and his fingerprints are on the knife used to kill his wife (ability and means);
4. Investigator's conclusion (belief 4): John Doe killed his wife by stabbing her.

To reiterate, the reasoning engaged in by the criminal investigator ought to terminate in knowledge of the who, what, where, when, how, and why of the crime. So, viewed from this perspective, the investigator's overall chain of reasoning is, as we have seen, theoretical reasoning; reasoning that justifies (a) true belief(s) or true statement(s). Moreover, the reasoning in question is justificatory in so far as it seeks to provide good and decisive reasons for *believing* the conclusion of the investigator, in the above example, that John Doe murdered his wife by stabbing her and did so out of revenge.

Nevertheless, the content of the investigator's knowledge typically refers, in part, to an intentional action, namely, the crime that has been committed and, as such, implies a process of practical reasoning on the part of the offender. In this respect crimes are different from unintended accidents; in the latter, but not the former, the person who caused the bad outcome would typically have no reason for causing it – it being unintended. Indeed, many crimes involve not simply an intention to commit the crime but also a prior and extended process of premeditation, for example, of planning.

The offender's process of reasoning could be very simple and attenuated (as in unpremeditated crimes, e.g., he hit her in a fit of rage), or complex and protracted (as in premeditated crimes, e.g., a complex fraud).

Moreover, the offender's reasons are not necessarily or even typically *justificatory* of his or her actions – John's motive of revenge does not legally or morally justify his killing his wife and he may well not suggest that it did; rather, these reasons are *explanatory* of the actions. At any rate, the investigator is essentially only interested in the offender's practical reasoning in so far as it assists him or her in explaining the offender's action and, therefore, in working out the who, what, and so on of the crime. Whether or not the offender's action was morally and/or legally justified and, in particular, whether or not the reasons the offender had for his or her action legally justified that action is essentially a matter for the court, not the investigator, to determine.[22]

Whether simple or complex, the key elements in the practical reasoning of an offender involved in the commission of a crime mirror the key elements in the explanation provided by the criminal investigator of the specifics of the offender and the offense. In both cases these elements typically include: (i) the offender's *motive* (or other end), such as revenge for his wife's infidelity, (ii) the availability of *the means*, for instance, a carving knife, (iii) the offender's *ability* – he must, for example, have sufficient strength to stab his wife to death; (iv) the *opportunity* – he must have been alone with her at the time and in the room in which the murder took place. Naturally, from the perspective of the offender's practical reasoning as well as the investigator's explanation of what took place, the offender has to *believe* he or she has the means, the ability and the opportunity.

On the other hand, the investigator's explanation will typically help itself to evidence that the offender might not be aware of. For example, the investigator might conclude that the offender stabbed his wife in part on the basis of DNA evidence from a trace of the offender's skin found in the fingernail of the victim when she scratched his face while attempting to defend herself.

2.4   Knowledge, Certainty, and Evidential Standards

Thus far we have spoken somewhat loosely of the investigator's justification in terms of an informal notion of good and decisive reasons. We have, it is true, invoked notions of evidence, for instance, physical evidence, such as DNA, and testimonial evidence, and of deductive and inductive inference, as well as of inferences based on schemata of practical rationality. Nevertheless, the informal notion of good and decisive reasons needs to be replaced by some more determinate notions. After all, the investigator's conclusion (with respect to the offender and the offense) ought to rely, not on his or her justificatory standards – however exemplary they might be – but rather on a determinate, explicit, stable, and legally accepted justificatory standard or set of standards, such as compliance with legal principles of evidence, compliance with certain generally accepted principles of practical and theoretical reasoning (e.g., deduction, induction).

Here we need to pay particular attention to the justification for beliefs – as opposed to justification for action – and, specifically, to legally admissible forms of evidence.[23]

We begin by offering a few general remarks on the nature of evidence. Consider the following state of affairs: a set of fingerprints on a knife known to have been used to commit an assault. The fingerprints are evidence. The fingerprints are evidence that a second state of affairs obtains, namely, that Joe, whose fingerprints match those found on the knife, assaulted the victim, Fred. So evidence is a state of affairs from which an inference can be drawn to a second state of affairs. Often inferences are made from one proposition to another: "Joe assaulted the victim" is inferred from "Joe's fingerprints are on the knife used to assault the victim." Certainly investigators' reports are couched in propositional format, that is to say that they consist of sentences which are for the most part statements. However, a state of affairs is not as such a proposition; rather, propositions represent states of affairs (among other things). So, in order for an inference to be drawn between propositions, the relevant states of affairs must be represented in propositional form. For example, the detective's veridical visual experience of a body lying on the ground in a pool of blood needs to be represented in propositional form, for example, in the English language. Moreover, if the detective is to make inferences the propositions in question need to be expressed in (say) English *inwardly to himself* ("There is a body lying in a pool of blood right before my eyes"), at least in the first instance. Naturally, once the proposition has been expressed inwardly to himself it can be expressed outwardly to others. In fact, of course, the inward and outward expression of the proposition can be simultaneous, as when the detective comes upon the body in question and spontaneously utters the sentence in question to his colleague as much as to himself.

One important evidential relation is that of causation. The victim's blood on the suspect's knife, for example, is evidence that the suspect is the murderer of the victim, since the blood is the effect of a cause, namely, the causal event of the suspect stabbing the victim. So evidence can pertain not only to states of affairs, but also to the causes of states of affairs.

Knowledge acquired by investigators has multiple sources. Some of the most important include knowledge based on physical evidence, for example, fingerprints and skin samples, knowledge derived by inductive and deductive reasoning, and knowledge based on testimony such as eyewitness reports.[24] In relation to testimony, we can distinguish the testimony of ordinary citizens from that of so-called expert witnesses, for example, psychologists.

In recent times the range of physical evidence available to investigators has widened due to scientific advances such as DNA testing, developments in computer forensics, images provided by CCTV cameras, and so forth. These scientific advances have led to a tendency to downplay testimony in favor of physical evidence. However, it is important to stress that even physical evidence is defeasible and, as such, is capable of misleading investigators. For example, physical evidence is subject to human intervention – specifically, tampering – and to other kinds of contamination and degradation, hence the importance of ensuring the integrity of the chain of evidence. The possibility of tampering, of course, raises ethical questions as well as epistemic questions (questions with respect to knowledge or degree of certainty).

Here we need to distinguish between knowledge and so-called intelligence on the one hand, and knowledge and certainty on the other.

Knowledge is also to be distinguished from intelligence in the sense of "information" – including unsubstantiated reports, hearsay, and the like

– that is gathered by investigators. Intelligence in this sense is more likely to be true than accidentally true beliefs – and much more likely to be true than lies or ideology. However, intelligence is often unconfirmed; much intelligence is at best *prima facie* true. Intelligence may have some evidential backing, but even so this backing might not be sufficiently strong to warrant its being believed. Or in some cases intelligence is knowledge in its own right, but is not legally admissible as evidence. Hearsay (roughly, a report by someone of what someone else said) is a case in point.[25]

We will return to the issue of intelligence and its uses in the next chapter. For now let us define intelligence as stated propositions that might shed light on some actual or potential investigation; propositions that are linguistically expressed in (usually written down) statements and stored in a database or elsewhere.

It is also important to distinguish between knowledge and certainty. As we have seen, knowledge is justified, true, stated belief. However, knowledge in this sense is something less than certainty.

If someone has *absolute* certainty with respect to some belief then he or she cannot be mistaken about it. Naturally, the belief in question must be a true one for which the believer has good evidence. But truth is not sufficient for certainty; without evidence one cannot be certain of one's beliefs, even if they happen to be true. Indeed, as we saw above, without evidence we do not have knowledge, let alone certainty. Moreover, good evidence is not sufficient for certainty. Scientists used to believe that all swans were white, based on the evidence that all known swans were white. Then black swans were discovered in Western Australia and the belief was falsified. Nor is truth based on good evidence sufficient for certainty, albeit perhaps it is sufficient for knowledge. An investigator might believe on the basis of good evidence that Sutcliffe is the Yorkshire Ripper and this might, in fact, be true. So arguably the investigator *knows* that Sutcliffe is the Yorkshire Ripper. But, of course, the evidence that the investigator has is defeasible; it is *possible* that the evidence is flawed in some respect, for example, that Sutcliffe made a false confession, or indeed in many respects. Indeed, even if the evidence is not flawed in any respect, it is a logical possibility that Sutcliffe is not in fact the Yorkshire Ripper notwithstanding that all the evidence indicates that he is the Yorkshire Ripper. For the evidence is in large part inductive evidence as was the evidence for the proposition that all swans were white – as opposed to deductive evidence, such as that $2 + 2 = 4$. So the evidence stops short of being a deductive proof. Therefore, notwithstanding the fact that the belief that Sutcliffe is the Yorkshire Ripper might well be based on good evidence (i.e., is a justified belief), it remains a possibility, however remote, that Sutcliffe is not the Yorkshire Ripper. So the investigator does not have *absolute* certainty.

The possibility of error in most, if not all, areas of inquiry has led philosophers to try to identify at least some beliefs about which most rational adults, including investigators, cannot be mistaken. Candidates include simple logical truths, for example, it is not the case that Sutcliffe is the Yorkshire Ripper *and* that Sutcliffe is not the Yorkshire Ripper, or propositions with a probability of one, for example, the thrown six-sided dice will either turn out to be 1, 2, 3, 4, 5 or 6. Another historically important candidate for beliefs about which one cannot be mistaken is beliefs about one's present mental state such as a state of severe pain, for instance, I cannot be mistaken about my belief that I have a severe headache. Whether or not one accepts any or all of these candidates for absolute certainty is potentially important in the assessment of evidence in some criminal justice contexts, including ones that might in the future come to rely in part on emerging technology such as brain images to determine, for example, mental states or mental illness. For if one cannot be mistaken about many of one's present mental states then the evidence of brain scans might be regarded as less reliable for certain purposes than the evidence of (sincere) first-person reports of mental states.[26]

Notwithstanding these philosophical claims regarding certainty, it remains true that there is very little that investigators could not be mistaken about. Accordingly, the issue of degrees of certainty comes to the fore. In criminal justice contexts there are various somewhat vague notions in play, which purport to capture various degrees of rational certainty and uncertainty. These vary somewhat from one national jurisdiction to another. They include suspicion, reasonable suspicion, probable cause, on the balance of probabilities, and beyond reasonable doubt.

The notion of certainty that has been under discussion is rational certainty. It should be distinguished from merely psychological certainty. A psychotic who holds the entirely irrational belief that a harmless person is trying to kill him, nevertheless, might be psychologically certain of this falsehood. Rational certainty, by contrast, is the possession of reasons that provide grounds for believing that there is a very high probability that (say) Sutcliffe is the Yorkshire Ripper. Psychological certainty (one's de facto psychological state of certainty) should, but often does not, mirror rational certainty (the psychological state of certainty one rationally *ought* to be in, given the evidence).

Roughly speaking, rational certainty exists on a continuum and the degree of psychological certainty one has ought to mirror this continuum and, in particular, reflect the degree of evidence for the belief in question. At one end of the spectrum there is no certainty or even belief. Thus, an investigator might have a suspicion based on knowledge of the suspect's motive; however, motive is far from sufficient to justify the belief that the suspect is guilty, let alone the certainty that the suspect is guilty (or to meet the "beyond reasonable doubt" standard required for criminal convictions). The investigator's knowledge that the suspect had the ability and opportunity, as well as the motive, would justify a higher level of suspicion – perhaps reasonable suspicion. But it may not justify arresting the suspect. On the other, motive, ability and opportunity, coupled with an eyewitness report (testimony) of his presence at the scene of the crime might be sufficient to justify an arrest, albeit not a conviction.

There are important ethical issues here. For example, in relation to serious crimes for which penalties are severe, the degree of certainty of guilt needs to be high (e.g., beyond reasonable doubt) for a conviction to be justified. There are also difficult theoretical issues concerning knowledge (sometimes referred to as epistemological issues). For example, how are we to understand the notion of "beyond reasonable doubt" or that of "on the balance of probabilities"?

In summation, knowledge ought to be the primary goal of criminal investigators, and here knowledge can be regarded as true, stated belief for which there is a justification in the sense of good and decisive reasons. Moreover, a justification in this sense would include evidence from direct observation, the testimony of reliable sources, and physical evidence.

Further, the content of cognitive states, including but not restricted to beliefs, can be held with different degrees of rational certainty, depending on the nature of the evidence in question. Roughly speaking, a higher degree of certainty is required the further one goes along the investigative and prosecutorial process; a process that commences with an investigation based only on reasonable suspicion and terminates in an adjudication of guilt or innocence based on the standard of being beyond reasonable doubt.

2.5   Knowledge and Moral Responsibility

In Section 2.1 above, we introduced the notion of a chain of institutional and moral responsibility, and the moral responsibility investigators have with respect to the further end of the criminal justice process, namely, that the factually guilty be found legally guilty (and the factually innocent not be found legally guilty). In this section we focus on the moral responsibility of investigators with respect to, so to speak, the proximate end of determining factual guilt or innocence.

Of course, it is only from the perspective of the larger institutional process that this end is merely proximate. If, on the other hand, we focus more narrowly on the principal role of the investigator then matters are somewhat different. For the principal, indeed defining, role of the investigator is, as we have argued above, knowledge (propositional knowledge expressed in statements) and, in particular, knowledge with respect to factual guilt (or innocence). Moreover, by the lights of our overarching normative theory of the criminal law and of criminal investigators (elaborated in Chapter 1), even this further collective end of criminal investigators (jointly aimed at with members of juries and others in the chain of institutional and moral responsibility) that the factually guilty be found legally guilty (and the factually innocent not be found legally guilty), serves in turn the larger purpose of the protection of justifiably enforceable, moral rights not to be harmed and to receive assistance in relation to needs-based deprivations.

Given that the primary aim of the criminal investigator is knowledge (of the who, what, where, when, how, and why of a crime) a very important moral question arises as to the investigator's moral responsibility in this regard. Is, for example, an investigator morally responsible for failing to acquire such knowledge and, therefore, morally blameworthy? Conversely, is an investigator who succeeds in acquiring such knowledge morally praiseworthy?

Certainly the outcomes of criminal investigations have great moral significance, both for victims as well as suspects and, indeed, for society at large, given that – as we saw in Chapter 1 – crime is typically a moral as well as a legal offense. Accordingly, in so far as investigators are responsible for these outcomes, then they can be held morally responsible. But are they responsible?

An important difference between actions and beliefs, even beliefs about actions, for example, A believes that A ought to do x, is that actions can often be done at will, whereas this is not so for belief acquisition. Moreover, this contrast can lead to a sharp division between questions of morality and questions of knowledge. Morality, it might be held, pertains only to actions (and habits) for which one can be held responsible, whereas belief acquisition – and, therefore, knowledge acquisition – not being under one's control can have no intrinsic moral dimension. To be sure, knowledge involves principles of rationality, for instance, in relation to good and bad evidence for one's beliefs, but such principles do not include – on this view – any specifically moral principles. If this view is correct, then it seems that criminal investigators are not morally responsible when they acquire knowledge of crimes and not morally responsible, either, when they fail to do so.

However, it is doubtful that morality pertains only to actions for which one can be held responsible. Bad character traits such as racial hatred, a violent temper, and pedophilia for which one is not necessarily responsible are, nevertheless, moral deficiencies. Consider, for example, someone raised in a racist society, or a pedophile who was himself routinely subject to sexual abuse as a child and developed pedophilia as a consequence. Indeed, lack of autonomy and, therefore, of the ability to act with moral responsibility is itself a moral deficiency, notwithstanding that one might not be responsible for this lack, for example, if one was raised as a slave or became a drug addict in one's mother's womb.

More important for our purposes here, this contrast between actions and beliefs in relation to their being freely acquired should not be over-stated. First, beliefs are often acquired after a process of investigation and the decision to investigate is a voluntary decision to act, for which an investigator can, obviously, be held morally responsible. For example, the belief that Sutcliffe is the Yorkshire Ripper could not have been acquired if detectives had not decided to investigate the murders of Yorkshire prostitutes. That is, without this act of will – to conduct an investigation – the detectives would simply not have had any belief with respect to the identity of the Yorkshire Ripper; they would have remained in a state of ignorance. Moreover, given the moral significance of identifying the Yorkshire Ripper, deciding to remain in ignorance would have been morally culpable.

Of course, in the case of the Yorkshire Ripper it was obvious that an investigation needed to be undertaken; the situation was far being a moral dilemma. Nevertheless, a decision still had to be made to investigate – whether by the investigators themselves or their superiors – and as such it was a decision to acquire morally significant knowledge rather than to remain in ignorance. That is, it was a decision for which the investigators were morally responsible (albeit, they were neither blameworthy nor praise-worthy for making this decision).

By contrast with the Ripper case, there are many situations in which it is far from clear whether or not an investigation ought to be conducted. Perhaps resources are stretched; perhaps it is not obvious that a crime has been committed, notwithstanding a claim to this effect by a member of the public. Case Study 5.2.2, Jeffrey Dahmer and Police Discriminatory Behavior, in Chapter 5 illustrates the tragic consequences of a failure to investigate; and, in particular, of willfully and culpably ignoring information provided by members of the public.

Decisions to investigate typically involve discretionary moral judgments. For example, an investigator might decide to investigate one serious crime rather than a number of less serious ones in a context in which limited resources prevent him or her from investigating all of the crimes in question. Here "serious" might refer in part to the degree of harm involved in the crime and, hence, the degree of moral significance in play. Indeed, on some occasions such judgments can be to the effect that an investigation into a crime ought not to be conducted, because the morally bad consequences of doing so heavily outweigh the morally good ones. Consider a minor assault on a man committed by his juvenile son in the overall context of a family in which the son is angry with his father because the father regularly beats the mother (who is, nevertheless, not prepared to come forward to the police).

So, moral responsibility is involved in decisions to investigate and the latter are, in effect, decisions to come to have beliefs. However, the contrast between belief formation and action is too sharply drawn in a second and, indeed, a third respect relevant to the ascription of moral responsibility.

Belief formation often results from investigations that comply with the rational principles that govern, or ought to govern, knowledge acquisition, for instance, principles of evidence gathering with respect to physical evidence and the testimony of witnesses.[27] But compliance with such principles is freely chosen; detectives decide to gather, for example, blood samples from a crime scene and have their DNA analyzed with a view to determining whether or not a suspect was present. Accordingly, whether or not the investigator's suspicion transforms into a belief that the suspect is indeed the offender is in part dependent on the investigator's freely chosen actions of complying with epistemic principles. So, once again belief formation is dependent on prior freely chosen actions. However, in this case it is not simply that the detectives will come to have some belief or other in relation to a matter, such as who the Yorkshire Ripper is, but rather that a specific belief or its negation will be formed, such as that Sutcliffe is the Yorkshire Ripper (or that he is not). Again, which belief they come to have is highly morally significant; so it matters a great deal whether their belief is a true one or not and this in turn depends on the quality of their decisions with respect to evidence gathering and the like.

The third respect in which belief formation is analogous to action is as follows. Beliefs are often the terminal point of an act of judgment and acts of judgment are often freely performed. For example, the belief that Sutcliffe was the Yorkshire Ripper was formed as a result of the detectives' judgment that, on the basis of the evidence gathered, he was the Yorkshire Ripper. Naturally, their judgment was not freely made in the sense that they could make any old judgment that they felt like making, including a judgment that was completely inconsistent with the evidence. But freely performed judgments are not to be identified with capricious or irrational judgments. And in this respect judgments are akin to actions in general; an action that is "compelled" by reason does not thereby cease to be a freely chosen action. Suppose a police officer uses a Taser gun on an armed offender in self-defense – and could not have done otherwise, if he was to preserve his own life. Here the police officer has acted freely, notwithstanding that "he had no other choice" rationally speaking; that is, his action was fully rationally justified and the alternative (to allow himself to be killed) was without rational justification (assuming Taser guns are a form of nonlethal force).

The upshot of this discussion of the belief formation of investigators is that investigators can be held morally responsible for the outcomes of their investigations. As already stated, the outcomes of these investigations are morally significant for victims, suspects, and the wider community. Moreover, investigators are responsible, in part, for these outcomes in so far as they are responsible for their investigation and its particular outcome, namely, an epistemic outcome, namely justified true, stated belief (or at least this ought to be the outcome). There are several aspects of an investigation that an investigator is responsible for, and with respect to each aspect there is the possibility of success or failure. Speaking generally, an investigator is responsible for failing to arrive at, or succeeding in arriving at, knowledge. Moreover, there are a variety of explanations for such failure. The investigator's failure could be the result of failing to commence the investigation, failing to aim at knowledge (once the investigation has commenced), inadequate evidence gathering, invalid inference making and/or lack of judgment. Conversely, his or her success would typically result from pursuing knowledge of the who, what, where, when, how, and why of the crime, engaging in careful and comprehensive evidence gathering, valid inference making, and exercising good judgment.

As it happens, many investigations involve joint action on the part of more than one investigator and other contributors, for example, analysts. This raises the important moral question of the collective moral responsibility of investigators. We return to this issue in Chapter 7. Here we note that an investigator can do all that can be reasonably expected of him or her only to have some other contributor fail to discharge adequately their responsibilities. For example, an investigator might conduct a first-rate investigation and brief of evidence, only to have an incompetent prosecuting lawyer undo the good work when the case goes to trial.

2.6   Evidence-based Investigation: Quality and Accountability

In the light of the above account of the point of investigations as the acquisition of knowledge in the sense of justified, true, stated belief, we can now make a few general points in relation to the criteria of quality of evidence-based investigations – the epistemic quality, so to speak – and the means to hold investigators to account in this regard.[28] Here we have in mind not the, so to speak, institutional mechanisms of accountability, such as supervisors, oversight bodies and, for that matter, external institutions such as the media, but rather the criteria that need to be applied to try to ensure quality and, therefore, to enable institutional mechanisms of accountability to do their job.

Investigations should be well planned. All the aspects of the investigation are clearly identified – who did what, when, where, how and why. On the basis of the aspects identified and the information/evidence available, an investigative plan is to be formulated, including in relation to avenues of inquiry, additional information/evidence to be gathered, witnesses to be interviewed, and task allocation.

The plan is to some extent a dynamic process given that new lines of inquiry suggest themselves, new evidence comes to light, and so on. Nevertheless, at any particular stage of its development the plan – in the form that it exists at that stage – is adhered to. Audits of investigators' reports are a performance indicator in relation to the quality of investigation plans.

Open-mindedness is essential if the outcomes of investigations are not to be predetermined. Open-mindedness consists in having the discovery of the truth – or, at least, knowledge – as the ultimate aim of an investigation, and allowing the evidence to settle the question of what is or is not the truth. While open-mindedness is an attitudinal state it is one that has a number of behavioral manifestations in investigations, including identifying and exploring all appropriate avenues of inquiry, interviewing all relevant witnesses, and gathering all relevant physical evidence (including exculpatory as well as inculpatory evidence). Auditing procedures can be developed to reflect these behavioral indicators of a lack of open-mindedness. Surveys of witnesses might also provide an indicator.

All information and evidence gathered should be subjected to a thorough scrutiny. The information/evidence provided from the crime scene, from witnesses, and so on, including unsubstantiated as well as substantiated claims, needs to be identified and verified (or at least its degree of likelihood established). Additional information/evidence required by the investigative plan must be sought and verified. Additional information and evidence should be integrated into the investigative plan as it evolves.

Information provided that is not germane to the investigation might, nevertheless, constitute intelligence and should be forwarded to the relevant agency. We note that information that is germane to the investigation includes information germane to the defense case, for example, information that might exonerate a suspect.

The independent case audit is an important indicator of the thoroughness of the treatment of information/evidence. Judicial comments on briefs and reviews of failed prosecutions are other indicators.

There needs to be comprehensive recording and preservation of all information and evidence. Appropriate access to electronic and other data systems is provided to the investigator, and the information/evidence gathered and the information-gathering tasks undertaken (in chronological and logical order) are accurately and adequately recorded on the system(s). Quality of recorded data can be assessed in part by way of auditing the database.

Moreover, the security of all information and evidence is also important. Adequate security of information and evidence must be provided and relevant procedures followed, for example, confidentiality is not breached, physical evidence is secured, the chain of evidence assured.

Process audits will determine the existence or otherwise of such procedures; such process audits are an indicator of whether or not information/evidence security is actually even taken seriously.

Case audits can provide evidence of compliance or noncompliance with these procedures; such case audits are an indicator of the actual degree of information/evidence security in the context of the existence of procedures.

In the final analysis, the aim of any investigation is, or ought to be, that it unearths the evidence-based truth in relation to the matter under investigation, i.e., the point of investigations is knowledge. There is a sense in which all the other indicators of the quality of an investigation are, or ought to be, governed by this consideration. Accordingly, it is of fundamental and overriding importance that the proximate conclusions of an investigation are identical with the truth of the matter, or as much of the truth of the matter as it is possible to unearth. How do we know that the investigation has unearthed the truth? Quite simply, on the basis of evidence. Hence the importance of evidence, be it physical, the testimony of witnesses, or whatever other forms are available; hence also, our description of the fundamental aim of investigations as evidence-based true belief.

On the other hand, the investigator's response to the truths unearthed in terms of recommendations made, for instance, that a suspect should be prosecuted, needs to take into account a range of considerations including the degree of certainty possessed in relation to the "truths" in question and the degree of seriousness of any infringements of law or regulation. Accordingly, the investigators' final recommendation might need to help itself to more than merely evidentiary considerations; nevertheless, a good and decisive justification for the recommendation needs to be provided.

The general point to be made is that to have any point investigations need to yield results, but the only results worth having are *justified* results. Audits of investigators' reports are an important indicator here. Performance can also be judged here in terms of successful prosecutions and judicial comments on briefs.

Our final point concerns the desirability of a professional approach to presentation. It is of fundamental importance for an investigator to make an evidence-based recommendation, but it is also of great importance that the evidence is presented in a logical and luminous manner. More generally, investigative reports, plans, correspondence, and so on need to be presented in a clear, concise, and complete manner. Audits of, for example, investigators' reports, or complaints files as a whole, in relation to completeness are a performance indicator here.

Notes

1 Knowledge-by-acquaintance apparently also admits of degrees – consider, for example, talking to someone on the other side of a wall – and has vague boundaries – consider, for example, talking to someone on the phone.
2 See, for example, Stelfox (2009), p. 118.
3 The aim is understanding in the sense of a structure of mutually supporting "items" of knowledge comprising the who, what, where, when, how, why, etc. of the crime.
4 The investigator in aiming at knowledge is also aiming at truth – but truth for which he or she has good and decisive evidence. Otherwise the investigator might discover the truth without knowing that he or she has done so.
5 In many jurisdictions it is not up to the investigator to decide whether or not a suspect he has charged with a serious offense should go to trial; this being a matter for the prosecuting authority.
6 On conflicts of interests see Seumas Miller, Peter Roberts, and Edward Spence (2005) *Corruption and Anti-corruption; A Study in Applied Philosophy,* Saddle River, NJ: Prentice Hall, Chapter 3.
7 See Seumas Miller (2014) Police Detectives, *Criminal Investigations and Moral Responsibility Criminal Justice Ethics,* 33.
8 On collective responsibility see Seumas Miller (2001b) Collective responsibility, *Public Affairs Quarterly,* 15.1, pp. 65–82 and (2006) Collective moral responsibility: an individualist account, in Peter A. French (ed.), *Midwest Studies in Philosophy,* 30, pp. 176–193.
9 On collective ends see Seumas Miller (1992) Joint action, *Philosophical Papers,* 21.3, pp. 275–299 and (1995) Intentions, ends and joint action, *Philosophical Papers,* 24.1, pp. 51–67. See also Miller (2001b), Chapter 2 and (2010a), Chapter 1.
10 Assuming there are only two possible verdicts, guilty and innocent; which is not the case in some jurisdictions, for example, Scotland.
11 Chains of institutional and moral responsibility consist of a process in which the completion of one stage institutionally triggers the commencement of the next stage, so that, for instance, arrest is followed by the suspect being either charged or released within a specified time-frame.
12 Sometimes, for the sake of brevity, we use the term "knowledge" to mean propositional knowledge, as opposed to knowledge in general. However, the context should make this clear.
13 There are various complications here. For example, there are approximations to the truth. Moreover, philosophical theorizing on truth is longstanding and complex. See, for example, George Pitcher (ed.) (1964) *Truth,* Saddle River, NJ: Prentice Hall.

14   Note that a rational justification for a belief in this sense should not be assimilated to a rational justification for an action, let alone a moral justification of an action or the more technical notion of a legal justification for the performance of some unlawful act. See Section 2.3 below.

15   Notoriously, justified true belief is not a sufficient definition of knowledge because subject to so-called Gettier counterexamples. See Edmund Gettier (1963) Is justified true belief knowledge? *Analysis*, 23, pp. 121–123. Thus, a detective might believe truly that Sutcliffe is the Yorkshire Ripper and have a good reason for believing this, for example, a witness testified to seeing Sutcliffe raping a victim. However, if the witness was lying we would be disinclined to regard the detective as having knowledge that Sutcliffe was the Yorkshire Ripper. One means to handle these is to add an excluder clause to the effect that the justification itself does not rely on any false beliefs.

16   This was an infamous related UK case involving a miscarriage of injustice. See, for example, Gerry Conlon (1991) *Proved Innocent: The Story of Gerry Conlon and the Guildford Four*, London: Penguin.

17   This case study was written by John Blackler and originally appeared in precursors to this 2006 monograph, namely, the first Allen and Unwin edition (1997) and a prior work, *Police Ethics*, published in 1995 by Keon Press.

18   Frank Davis (1990) *Blackburn; A Forensic Disaster*, Sydney: Harry the Hat Publications, p. 39.

19   Malcolm Brown and Paul Wilson (1992) *Justice and Nightmares; Success and Failures of Forensic Science in Australian and New Zealand*, Kensington, NSW: University of NSW Press, p. 213.

20   For a useful introduction to evidence in criminal justice contexts see Christopher Allen (2008) *Practical Guide to Evidence*, London: Routledge-Cavendish. For discussion of some of the main methods of forensic detection see, Joe Nickell and John F. Fischer (1999) *Crime Science: Methods of Forensic Detection*, Lexington, Kentucky: University of Kentucky Press. For a somewhat skeptical discussion of many of these methods see Erica Beecher-Monas (2007) *Evaluating Scientific Evidence: An Interdisciplinary Framework for Intellectual Due Process*, Cambridge: Cambridge University Press, Chapter 5.

21   What counts as a good reason or, conversely, a bad reason is a complex and difficult matter that we cannot delve further into here. Obviously, the law to some extent adjudicates here; some reasons are, for example, regarded in law as mitigating, if not justifying.

22   Naturally, the investigator needs to be aware of, in particular, any legal justification or at least legal defense that a suspect might have for performing an action. For this might absolve the suspect of having committed any crime, or at the very least mitigate it, and, if this is obvious, then perhaps the matter should not be pursued any further. If it is not obvious then the investigator may well have to exercise his or her discretionary judgment.

23   For detail on these issues see Allen (2008) and Alan Leaver (1997) *Investigating Crime*, Sydney: Law Book Company.

24   The reliability of eyewitness reports has been questioned by recent researchers as in Gary Wells and Elizabeth Olson (2003) Eyewitness testimony, *Annual Review of Psychology*, 54, pp. 277–295. However, there are a myriad complica-

tions here. One important issue is the relationship between the eyewitness and the persons involved in the incident in question. It is one thing to question the reliability of an eyewitness who has never seen (say) the offender before; it is an entirely different matter if the offender is known to the witness.

25 In most jurisdictions hearsay evidence is admissible under certain restricted circumstances.

26 One purpose of brain images is, of course, to try to determine sincerity. This does not vitiate the more general point. On the general issue here see Walter Sinnott-Armstrong, Adina Roskies, Teneille Brown, and Emily Murphy (2008) Brain images as legal evidence, *Episteme*, 5, pp. 359–373.

27 Philosophers refer to such principles as epistemic principles – derived from the Greek word, "episteme," meaning knowledge.

28 Much of the material in this section is extracted from Seumas Miller (2010b) What makes a good internal affairs investigation? *Criminal Justice Ethics*, 29.1, pp. 30–41.

3

Intelligence and Intelligence Gathering

As we saw in Chapter 1, crimes are typically harmful violations of moral rights and, therefore, justice dictates that offenders be brought to book – and also that those wrongly suspected go free. In the last chapter our focus was on the principal aims of the investigator (normatively speaking, i.e., the aims that the investigator *ought* to have): roughly speaking, evidence-based knowledge of the who, what, where, when, how, and why of the crime. This aim was seen to be morally significant in the light of both the inculpatory and exculpatory nature of such knowledge (or alleged knowledge).

In order to realize this aim of evidence-based knowledge of a crime, the criminal investigator relies heavily on something that might fall well short of evidence-based knowledge and that might never be put before a court of law, namely, intelligence.[1] In this chapter we provide an account of intelligence, its various types and uses in criminal investigations, and the moral issues that can arise. In Chapter 5 we provide a more detailed account of the use of intelligence in a major murder or like inquiry. In Chapter 10 we consider in more detail one of the more important moral issues that can arise from intelligence gathering, and surveillance and monitoring more generally, namely, the privacy issue.

3.1 Intelligence

Intelligence, as we saw above, can best be thought of as propositional in form, expressed in a language and stored somewhere, for example, in a

Investigative Ethics: Ethics for Police Detectives and Criminal Investigators, First Edition.
Seumas Miller and Ian A. Gordon.
© 2014 Seumas Miller and Ian A. Gordon. Published 2014 by John Wiley & Sons, Ltd.

detective's notebook or in a police organization's data bank. Intelligence, therefore, consists of statements stored in some information storage system.[2]

Information and intelligence are closely related concepts. Both can be thought of as statements stored in some information system. Moreover, both information and intelligence, as we will use the terms, are either true or false, but neither is necessarily true. Finally, neither information nor intelligence necessarily has a good and decisive justification. Accordingly, neither information nor intelligence is necessarily knowledge. On the other hand, a piece of information or of intelligence might be true and might have a good and decisive justification, which is to say that *some* information and *some* intelligence is knowledge.

Notwithstanding that information and intelligence are closely related concepts, they are not the same thing; specifically, intelligence is information, but information is not necessarily intelligence. In the context of criminal investigations, intelligence is information that is utilized, actually or potentially: (i) to facilitate the outcome of specific criminal investigations (e.g., to identify and apprehend the Yorkshire Ripper); (ii) in the day-to-day tasking and deployment of an organization's subunits (e.g., a local police station or local area command unit) in response to crimes of particular types in particular locations (e.g., violence at closing time outside certain late night venues on weekends) – this is what is known as tactical intelligence; or (iii) in the long-term planning of the organization's deployment of resources and its strategic response to crime trends (e.g., home-grown terrorism), which is known as strategic intelligence.

Information used as intelligence can be gathered from the public (e.g., multiple reports of suspected drug dealing at a certain location), from victims of crime and witnesses to crime; it can be collected in the course of routine police work (e.g., information provided by street police regarding the movements of a known offender), deliberately sought out by an investigator pursuing a line of inquiry (e.g., the modus operandi of a particular house burglar), or collected by the law enforcement organization as a matter of policy (e.g., all international financial transactions in excess of $10,000).

Victim and witness information can be accessed from a number of sources, including police reports of crimes or other incidents, child abuse case files, domestic violence reports, and hate crime cases. All police forces should establish processes to ensure that victim and witness information is captured for intelligence evaluation as appropriate.

Prior to its use as intelligence, information received should be evaluated for its intelligence worth. Some information will be discarded as being worthless qua intelligence. Information judged to have some potential intelligence worth can be evaluated according to different criteria, including the likelihood that it is true, its importance (assuming it is true), and (relatedly) the reliability of its source. Police forces and other investigatory agencies typically use a standard assessment form to record and evaluate information, for instance, with respect to its likely accuracy and the reliability of its source, and to assess any risk to the source of that information.

In criminal investigations, an intelligence system is: (i) a system of information input, storage, and retrieval; (ii) that enables information stored in different parts of the system to be processed in various ways (e.g., cross-referencing a suspect's name with the names of offenders and known associates of relevant offenders); (iii) and that can be utilized to facilitate criminal investigations (e.g., to identify crime hotspots). As such, it should hold accurate, up-to-date, and relevant information that is easy to input, process, and retrieve. Moreover, the system should be secure, so as to ensure there is no unauthorized access.

Once evaluated and stored in a secure database, information is available for research and analysis, as well as ad hoc retrieval by investigators requiring answers to particular questions. Analysis is here to be understood as the development of the intelligence into a package that identifies critical links between incidents, between suspects and their associates, and between suspects and incidents, to better understand patterns of crime, incidents, and behavior (of suspects and offenders). The product, "the intelligence package," is used by the organization to plan and direct subsequent operations. The intelligence package may feature in the organization's strategic or tactical tasking and coordination group meetings, where priorities are identified and decisions made on the deployment of resources. A later review of the tactics employed will provide any learning points from the operation, and these will help to build "organizational memory" of criminality in the organization's sphere of activity.

Since 2002, police forces and other investigatory agencies in the United Kingdom have been encouraged to adopt the National Intelligence Model (NIM).[3] This model has been replicated, at least in part, in forces throughout the world, including in Europe and Australia. Intelligence-led policing, in any jurisdiction, requires four intelligence products:

1. *Strategic assessments*: These give an overview of the long-term crime trends and issues in the jurisdiction in question. This assessment is used to set the control strategy and its intelligence requirements;
2. *Tactical assessments*: These identify the shorter-term issues and any intelligence requirements additional to those provided for in the relevant strategic assessment.
3. *Target profiles*: These provide detailed information about either a person (e.g., a suspect or victim) or a group of people (e.g., a criminal organization or vulnerable group). They do so in the context of control strategy priorities or immediate high-risk issues such as a terrorist attack.

4. *Problem profiles*: These provide detailed information about: (a) existing and emerging crime or incident patterns; (b) priority locations in terms of crime or other incidents (e.g., accident zones); and (c) other identified high-risk issues.

Crime Pattern Analysis (CPA) is a generic term for a number of related analytical processes, notably crime or incident series identification, crime trend analysis, hot spot analysis, and general profile analysis.

Crime series identification typically takes place when it is suspected that one offender or group of offenders is responsible for a number of crimes. The series can be identified in a number of ways, for example, by the same or similar method of committing the crime (modus operandi) or by forensic links such as fingerprints or DNA. Early identification of a "series" is particularly relevant in murder cases, where the offender may commit crimes across a number of police forces.

Crime trend identification tracks the trajectory of the incidence of offenses over time. It is important for police managers and investigators to have knowledge of the crime rates over time in the specific categories of crime that they are engaged in combating. For one thing, such knowledge enables the appropriate allocation of investigative and other resources. For another, it facilitates the evaluation of the efficacy of the strategies and tactics being used by police to combat crime.

Hotspot analysis identifies when, where, and how offenses are being committed. It is especially useful in relation to high-volume crime categories such as housebreaking and property theft.

General profile analysis yields detailed knowledge of suspects, victims, vulnerable individuals, organizations and groups, and criminal organizations, thereby giving direction to investigators in respect of their lines of inquiry, evidence gathering, and the like.

Notwithstanding the utility of CPA for police managers and investigators in relation to actual crime, it important to remember that the actual quantum and seriousness of crime do not necessarily equate with the public's view of the threats posed by crime to their safety and well-being. For example, the level of fear of crime among the elderly might be very high, notwithstanding that the actual levels of crime are quite low. In devising an intelligence-based control strategy and tactics for combating crime, the astute local commander will take into consideration the results of community consultation, representations from community leaders, local councillors, and his or her postbag.

In the United States in the post–9/11 period there has been a complete overhaul of the intelligence models uses in criminal investigations and, indeed, of the laws governing the gathering, analysis, and dissemination of such intelligence – and related intelligence, notably that gathered for national security purposes. Such legislation has included the controversial USA Patriot Act originally introduced by President George W. Bush in 2001 (see Case Study 10.2.1, USA Patriot Act, in Chapter 10.). A major concern in relation to the post–9/11 intelligence-gathering initiative has been the collection and storage of vast amounts of information about ordinary citizens in the absence of particularized reasonable suspicion (of which more below in Case Studies 3.2.2 on the Swift controversy and 3.2.3 on the Verizon controversy).

A number of these changes in the United States have focused on the need for intelligence-based policing in the context of interagency cooperation and the establishment of the so-called Department of Home Security. However, an important illustration of what has taken place in the United States at the level of the individual institution is the transformation of the FBI into an intelligence-driven organization, or at least into an organization with a considerably larger intelligence capacity.[4] For example, prior to 9/11 there were approximately 1000 intelligence analysts (IAs) in the FBI. Now there are triple that number and these intelligence analysts work right alongside the agents. The intelligence function, including the gathering, analyzing, and dissemination of information, is now centralized under the Directorate of Intelligence (DI). The DI, established in 2005, is a key component of the FBI's National Security Branch and manages all Bureau intelligence activities.

A central purpose of such intelligence-based models is to ensure that the delivery of police services, including crime prevention and detection, is optimally informed by high-quality intelligence.

The amount of information collected and analyzed by an intelligence-based information system will be vast and may include data on persons who have no connection with criminality or other wrongdoing. Much of this data will be on the public record but some might not be, potentially giving rise to a range of privacy issues – notably, as mentioned above, in the United States post 9/11.[5] However, in addition to the general kinds and sources of information mentioned above there are the following more specialized kinds and sources.

Technical intelligence

So-called technical intelligence gathering relates to information gained from covert surveillance, eavesdropping, CCTV footage, and the like. Typically, a central unit with dedicated IT systems manages covert operations and the gathering of technical intelligence. This will be expanded upon below in the chapters on covert operations (Chapters 10 and 11, in particular).

Financial intelligence

Organized crime is big business and can generate large amounts of cash that need to be legitimized (money laundering) and then invested in some other way. Financial investigations are often very document-intensive and involve records such as bank accounts, real estate files, and motor vehicle records, which point to the movement of money. Any record that pertains to or shows the paper trail of events involving money is important. The major goal in a financial investigation is to identify and document the movement of money. The link between where the money comes from, who gets it, when it is received, and where it is stored or deposited, can provide proof of criminal activity.

For example, the Australian Transaction Reports and Analysis Centre (AUSTRAC) works collaboratively with Australian industries and businesses in their compliance with legislation to counter money-laundering and the financing of terrorism.

The Financial Crimes Enforcement Network (FinCEN) brings together law enforcement, financial, and regulatory communities as part of its mission to safeguard the US financial system from abuses. Dealing primarily with intelligence and information, FinCEN focuses its efforts on identifying and tracking such activities as terrorist financing and money laundering. The Network's primary responsibilities include administering the Bank Secrecy Act; supporting law enforcement, intelligence, and regulatory agencies with data sharing and analysis; and building global cooperation with counterpart financial intelligence units. FinCEN is a Bureau in the Treasury Department's Office of Terrorism and Financial Intelligence.

Having described the nature of intelligence and outlined its various categories and uses in criminal justice investigations it is now time to provide some concrete cases studies involving the use (or under-use or misuse) of intelligence and the moral implications thereof.

3.2 Case Studies

Case Study 3.2.1 The Soham Investigation

The murder of Holly Wells and Jessica Chapman at Soham in August 2002 and the subsequent inquiry report by Sir Michael Bichard, had a profound and far-reaching effect on the way the UK Police Service gathers, manages, uses, and shares information. In July 2005, as a

(Continued)

direct result of the Bichard inquiry, the Home Secretary issued a statutory Code of Practice on the Management of Police Information (MOPI).

Whilst common usage of NIM (National Intelligence Model)[6] will improve the opportunity to share intelligence between police forces and agencies, previous failure to share information has regularly contributed to putting members of the public at risk. In the Soham case, two young schoolgirls were murdered, and their killer was found to be their school caretaker – Ian Huntley. The murder investigation eventually discovered that another police force and a social services department held highly relevant information showing a history of sexual offending by Huntley against under age girls. This information had not been disclosed when Huntley had been vetted for the role of caretaker; if it had been disclosed he would not have been appointed. Nor was it disclosed during the murder investigation until a witness came forward and informed the police.

A critical finding in the Bichard Report was:

> One of the key failings was the inability of Humberside Police and Social Services to identify Huntley's behaviour pattern remotely soon enough. That was because both viewed each case in isolation and because Social Services failed to share information effectively with the police.
>
> It was also because, as the Humberside Chief Constable admitted in his evidence, there were 'systemic and corporate' failures in the way in which Humberside Police managed their intelligence systems.[7]

The Soham case occurred whilst the NIM was being implemented in police forces and other agencies. NIM can improve effectiveness by having standardized processes and common language but it is weakened, in England and Wales, by the lack of a national intelligence database – each force has a stand-alone system. Bichard severely criticized this gap and also reported a lack of clear, national guidance for the police about information management – the way in which information is recorded (and reviewed, retained, or deleted). The Bichard Inquiry Report recommended the creation of a national intelligence system for England and Wales and the introduction of the PLX system, which flags that intelligence is held about someone by particular UK police forces.

In the past there has been reluctance by some organizations to share their data with the police (and other legitimate investigatory agencies); for example medical and social services data on individuals. Sadly there are cases of child abuse and deaths (e.g., Victoria Climbie and others) where the lack of information being shared has, in the subsequent enquiry, been strongly criticized. There has been considerable pressure on such organizations to create protocols between agencies to facilitate this exchange and deal with issues of "patient confidentiality" etc.

The Soham case highlights the importance of making full use of information from external sources such as the local community and partner agencies, which in turn can help identify the most appropriate strategy and tactical options to reassure the public, improve quality of life, reduce crime and the fear of crime, and enforce the law. This is not only relevant to minor crime; a report by Her Majesty's Inspectorate of Constabulary (HMIC) talks about an emerging view that a "bottom-up" approach to gathering intelligence on serious threats from organized crime offers the best way of assessing the market and tackling the social harms associated with it. A vigorous bottom-up approach could, in fact, complement work done at a national level and provide a much more accurate picture of both the spread of this criminality and police impact in disrupting or disabling it. Neighborhood policing, properly linked in and tasked, must be part of the solution, offering the prospect of significantly enhancing intelligence on these issues. The report states community intelligence is under developed.

Case Study 3.2.2   The Terrorist Finance Tracking Program and SWIFT Controversy

The events related to this . . . controversy came to light with a *New York Times* article on June 23, 2006, in which it was revealed that, not long after 9/11, the CIA, through the US Treasury Department, secretly put (via administrative subpoena)[8] pressure on a Belgian cooperative – SWIFT – that routes 11 million international financial transactions per day (amounting to USD 6 trillion) to give it access to its records.[9] The US government claimed that the emergency powers granted by Congress soon after 9/11 allowed it to do so and that it was not prevented from doing so by "American laws restricting government access to private financial records because the cooperative was considered a messaging service, not a bank or financial institution."[10]

(*Continued*)

Exactly what was looked at is not known, though US authorities have naturally argued that the data reviewed was limited and that they focused on terrorism, not tax fraud or drug trafficking. It appears that the primary tool used on the subpoenaed data was "link analysis," whereby those who had suspected ties then had all wired financial transfers in which they were involved tracked. It was claimed that the analyses had yielded positive results (though this has been disputed).[11]

When the US actions were made public (initially by a whistle-blower), the Belgian government immediately protested, and a European Parliament resolution (7/7/2006) alleged that "the SWIFT transfers were undertaken without regard to legal process . . . and . . . without any legal basis or authority." Although the Belgian Privacy Protection Commission sympathized with the United States' concern about terrorism and security, it argued that the requests were not focused on individuals suspected of terrorist activities and involved the transfer of massive amounts of data. Moreover, SWIFT was not a mere "messenger" but a "controller" in the processing of personal data. It concluded that European law with respect to personal data was more stringent than US law with respect to "the principle of proportionality, the limited retention period, the principle of transparency, the requirement for independent control and an adequate protection level."[12] SWIFT had, furthermore, failed to get assurances that were required under European law with respect to data of the kind involved.[13] Talks were subsequently commenced to try to work out a common framework for the sharing of data.

(Extract from John Kleinig, Peter Mameli, Seumas Miller, Douglas Salane, and Edwina Schwartz (2011) *Security and Privacy: Global Standards for Ethical Identity Management in Contemporary Liberal Democratic States*, Canberra: ANU e-Press, pp. 83–84)

Case Study 3.2.3   Verizon

A top secret court order obtained by the *Guardian* reveals the large-scale collection by the National Security Agency of the call records of millions of Verizon customers, daily, since April. The court order doesn't allow the NSA to collect any information whatsoever on the contents of phone calls, or even to obtain any names or addresses of customers.

What's covered instead is known as "metadata": the phone number of every caller and recipient; the unique serial number of the phones involved; the time and duration of each phone call; and potentially the location of each of the participants when the call happened.

All of this information is being collected on millions of calls every day – every conversation taking place within the United States, or between the United States and a foreign country is collected.

The government has long argued that this information isn't private or personal. It is, they say, the equivalent of looking at the envelope of a letter: what's written on the outside is simple, functional information that's essentially already public. That forms the basis of collection: because it's not personal information, but rather "transactional" or "business" data, there's no need to show probable cause to collect it. Collection is also helped by the fact this information is already disclosed by callers to their carriers – because your phone number is shared with your provider, you're not treating it as private.

But that is not a view shared by privacy advocates. Groups such as the Electronic Frontier Foundation say that by knowing who an individual speaks to, and when, and for how long, intelligence agencies can build up a detailed picture of that person, their social network, and more. Collecting information on where people are during the calls colors in that picture even further.

The primary purpose of large-scale databases such as the NSA's call records is generally said to be data-mining: rather than examining individuals, algorithms are used to find patterns of unusual activity that may mark terrorism or criminal conspiracies. However, collection and storage of this information gives government a power it's previously lacked: easy and retroactive surveillance. If authorities become interested in an individual at a later stage, and obtain their number, officials can look back through the data and gather their movements, social network, and more – possibly for several years (although the secret court order only allows for three months of data collection).

(Extract from James Ball (2013), www.guardian.co.uk, Thursday, June 6)

3.3 The Uses and Misuses of Intelligence

As argued in Chapter 2, the ultimate aim of the investigator to provide evidence-based knowledge of crimes is morally significant in the light of both the inculpatory and exculpatory nature of such knowledge (or alleged knowledge). For the same reason, intelligence gathering, evaluation, and use is morally significant, albeit less so in the light of its having a less direct bearing on the outcomes of criminal investigations than legally admissible evidence *per se*. If the intelligence relied on is correct, then this can be highly morally significant by virtue of its role in solving crimes and, therefore, in securing justice for victims and suspects alike. On the other hand, if intelligence is unavailable or incorrect, then this can also be highly morally significant, but for the opposite reason: the rights violations of victims go unaddressed, offenders go unpunished, or, perhaps even worse, the innocent are punished for crimes they did not commit. The above-described Soham case study illustrates the moral significance for criminal investigations of high-quality intelligence: quite literally, lives may depend on it.

Accordingly, the goal of maximizing the quantum and quality of intelligence, and the legitimate use thereof, is something of a moral imperative, as is the requirement to discard or otherwise avoid using incorrect intelligence. Importantly, these moral imperatives apply to a range of personnel, including police managers and analysts as well as investigators, in other words, all those personnel who contribute to the design, maintenance, and use of the intelligence system.

The legitimate moral purposes of intelligence gathering, processing, and accessing can be undermined if investigators, for example, collect and utilize intelligence for inculpatory purposes only. This is an aspect of the problem we encountered in the last chapter of criminal investigators who lose sight of their institutional role as knowledge seekers in favor of securing prosecutions of those they believe to be guilty.

Moreover, intelligence gathering, processing, and accessing can be undertaken for morally unacceptable purposes, including to further some private purpose (e.g., using a police database to find out details about an attractive girl one wants to befriend) or, in extreme cases, to serve a criminal end (e.g., accessing the confidential details of a current criminal investigation in order to thwart it.)

While the significance of an adequate quantum of high-quality intelligence is obvious in the case of criminal investigations, this is not its only purpose. In policing as elsewhere, intelligence also has utility in the performance management of staff, including criminal investigators. Crime statistics, statistics pertaining to the incidence of police use of their powers, for example, vehicle and person searches and the like, are indirectly relevant to the ultimate ends of policing and of criminal investigation in particular. After all, if the performance of investigators is not well managed then this has implications for the detection and prevention of crime. However, overuse of such statistics can be counterproductive; indeed it can tend to foster unlawful and/or unethical practices. For example, detectives can end up focusing on the number of drug busts, rather than their quality, in order to ensure they "meet their quota" and engage in artificial inflation of statistics by, for example, arresting minor well-known users for no purpose other than to meet their numerical targets.[14] Clearly, crime statistics and, indeed, intelligence gathering more generally, are simply a means to an end, not an end-in-itself. If it becomes an end-in-itself, or merely a tool in the hands of managers and politicians to exercise control over their subordinates, then this is misuse and, as noted, can lead to officers manufacturing statistical outcomes or even breaking the law, for example, by conducting illegal searches to meet numerical targets.

While it is important to ensure that intelligence-gathering, -processing, and -accessing activities are not undertaken for unlawful or morally illegitimate purposes, it is also important to realize that there are constraints on all such activity, even if it is intended to be undertaken for morally legitimate purposes. Specifically, there is a moral right to privacy.

3.4 Right to Privacy

Privacy is an important moral right and one enshrined in human rights and other legislation. However, the right to privacy is not absolute; the right to privacy can be overridden under certain circumstances. In relation to the gathering, processing, or accessing of data and/or intercepting of communications by law enforcement agencies that involve an infringement of privacy, a balance has to be struck, based, in part, on a principle of proportionality between the rights of citizens – including suspects – to privacy and confidentiality on the one hand, and the rights of actual and potential victims to protection from serious crime on the other.

Moreover, the state of technology at a given point in time to some extent determines the possibility of striking the appropriate balance at that time. For example, the current availability to the general public of very secure computer systems and of high-level encryption products can make accessing data and/or intercepting communications on the Internet by law enforcement agencies extremely difficult and expensive. On the other hand, recent claims in the international press[15] that the documents provided by Edward J. Snowden, the NSA contractor, reveal that the NSA has since circa 2000 been covertly collaborating with technology companies in the United States to build entry points into their products to enable the NSA to access messages before they are encrypted is cause for concern on a number of counts. Given the practice is covert and was abandoned by government in the face of public opposition in the 1990s, there is both an issue of accountability and an issue of legitimacy. (We discuss the substantive privacy issue in Chapter 10.)

A further point here is that the notion of striking a balance, in so far as it implies trade-offs between privacy rights and other moral rights, is sometimes morally problematic in that a trade-off is not necessarily required. For example, more efficient and effective use of available information, information technology systems, and information-gathering agencies might be sufficient for investigative requirements and have the virtue of not infringing the privacy rights of ordinary citizens not suspected of any crime.[16] By contrast, the alternative policy – evidently favored by the administration of President George W. Bush in the United States – of collecting and storing a vast amount of new information about ordinary citizens might actually be relatively inefficient and ineffective from an investigative perspective and might also bring with it the twin vices of infringing privacy rights and undermining the community trust in investigative agencies vital for the success of criminal investigations in the long term. See Case Study 3.2.3 on Verizon above.

That said, at times there is a need for trade-offs and, therefore, for striking a balance. In striking this balance in relation to gathering, processing, and accessing databases a number of principles need to be kept in mind. These principles apply to information to which a person has a right to privacy. Such data might include details in relation to their health, their finances, and their private life. (The nature and extent of the right to privacy is discussed in Chapter 10.) Naturally, much of the information in intelligence databases is not private in this sense, for example, a person's name, occupation, citizenship and marital status are matters of public knowledge. However, with respect to information to which a person has a moral right to privacy the following general principles apply.

First, data gathering, processing, and/or accessing is by definition an infringement of the right to privacy and, therefore, there is a presumption against it. This presumption can be overridden by other very weighty moral considerations – especially the need to protect other moral rights – or by exceptional circumstances, such as might obtain in wartime. But the presumption cannot be overridden by a blanket appeal to the common good or to the general need for security. For example, there must be at least a reasonable suspicion[17] that the person whose privacy is to be infringed has committed, or intends to commit, a serious crime – or is implicated in a serious crime – and that the resulting information is likely to substantially further the investigation under way in relation to that crime. Moreover, the law enforcement officials must be subject to stringent accountability requirements, including the issuing of warrants in circumstances in which the justification provided is independently adjudicated.

An increasingly important issue in relation to privacy is the integration and sharing of different sets of information available to different government agencies – including those for law enforcement. This is morally problematic in that, as we have seen, there is a presumption against the gathering of personal information about citizens by government officials, including law enforcement personnel. This presumption can be overridden in relation to specific kinds of information required for specific legitimate purposes, such as tax gathering or the investigation of someone reasonably suspected of engaging in serious criminal activity. But information gathered for one purpose should not be made available for another purpose, unless a specific case can be made out for doing so.

This latter problem is illustrated in Case Study 3.2.3 above on the Verizon controversy. While privacy laws tend to focus on the content of phone calls, emails, and the like, the Verizon episode draws our attention to so-called metadata, for example, the unique phone number/email address of caller/recipient, the time of calls and their duration, and the location of caller/recipient. Such metadata, while collected to facilitate the communication purposes of callers/recipients and their telecommunication providers and consented to for this purpose, also enables the nonconsensual construction of a detailed description of a person's activities, associates, movements, and so on, especially when combined with financial and other data. The availability to security agencies of such descriptions is surely an infringement of privacy and, therefore, needs justification – notably by reference to the moral and legal principle of reasonable suspicion (or probable cause in the United States).

An important aspect of this general problem has arisen in recent years in intelligence gathering for the purpose of combating terrorism. On the one hand, combating terrorism is a matter for domestically focused law enforcement agencies such as the FBI and, therefore, intelligence gathering is, or ought to be, constrained by morally based legal principles and subject to accountability mechanisms built into the criminal justice system. On the other hand, combating terrorism – notably international terrorism – is a matter for externally focused national security agencies such as the CIA and, as such, intelligence gathering is not, and perhaps ought not to be, subject to the same stringent moral and legal constraints and accountability mechanisms. However, post 9/11 the lines between domestic law enforcement intelligence gathering and foreign intelligence gathering have become blurred, notably in the legal sphere. For example, under the provisions of the above-mentioned Patriot Act law enforcement agencies were, arguably, subject only to the wiretap provisions of the Foreign Intelligence Surveillance Act (FISA) and not to the normal judicial controls operating in the criminal justice system.[18] Nor is the blurring restricted to the legal sphere. Whatever the moral principles governing intelligence gathering in domestic law enforcement, they surely differ to some degree from those governing foreign intelligence gathering. However, the phenomenon of international terrorist groups who perpetrate terrorist attacks on domestic soil muddies the waters and, as a result, the specification of appropriate moral principles for the collection of intelligence in relation to such groups is problematic, as it is in other areas of counterterrorism.[19]

Consider in this connection the recent PRISM controversy in the United States. The NSA's PRISM project involves agreements between the NSA and various US-based internet companies (Google, Facebook, Skype, etc.) to enable the NSA to monitor online communications of non-US citizens based overseas. Evidently the NSA can directly access these companies' systems. Now, according to the FISA Amendments Act of 2008: (i) the monitoring or gathering of data from foreigners outside the United States by NSA is approved; (ii) however, data gathered but found not to be relevant to the foreign-intelligence-gathering purpose of, say, counterterrorism must not be retained; (iii) there is no probable cause/reasonable suspicion requirement unless the person whose privacy is being infringed is a US citizen. Accordingly, the issue arises of the rights to privacy of non-US citizens, notably citizens of liberal democratic states allied with the United States, such as EU citizens. This problem is especially acute given the United States' stated commitment to the universal moral and human rights constitutive of liberal democracy, of which freedom – and, therefore, to some extent privacy – is a core element.

The moral issues raised by the integration and sharing of different sets of information available to different government agencies is not simply a problem for isolated individuals whose rights might be infringed; the problem is potentially a societal one. One of the purposes of privacy law is to deny, as far as possible, the formation of linkages between statutory bodies, and thereby to prevent such linkages enabling the coming into being of a "Big Brother" system of invasive inquiry and social control of the kind that existed in Eastern Europe under communism.[20] Accordingly, organizational "Chinese walls" are supposed to separate the investigators employed by one of the several different organs of government from the investigators employed by another of these organs. Limited contact across the statutory barriers may only be made – or denied – at the highest level and for good reason; and such contact is to take place in a parsimoniously sanctioned and limited manner following stringent protocols.

Another issue here is the relationship between public-sector investigators and private-sector investigators. Is the erasing of the line between police investigations and investigations in the private sector problematic? The problem here is the possibly disparate and conflicting commitments of investigators in the two spheres.[21] The ends of police investigators ought clearly to be driven by the public interest in law enforcement and protection of the individual rights of citizens. By contrast, private investigators must aim at the organizational interests of the corporation that employs them, possibly to the exclusion of the interests of the public at large. And there is the very real question of the independence of investigators operating under the control of the management of an organization in the private sphere.

A further set of moral issues pertains to the private sector vis-à-vis the individual citizen. Arguably, the threat to individual privacy, and in relation to the balance of informational power, comes not only from the state but also from the private sector's data-gathering activities. In the United States, for example, there are few limits on private sector data-gathering activities.[22]

3.5 Confidentiality and Security

As we have just seen, it is agreed on all hands, and enshrined in legislation, including in Europe in human rights legislation, that privacy is an important moral right, indeed a human right. What is perhaps not so often stressed, at least outside policing circles, is the moral importance that attaches to confidentiality.

Moreover, the nature of the relationship between privacy and confidentiality is not well understood. After all, in policing at least, the information to be kept confidential is quite often information arrived at by infringing someone's privacy, for example, that of a suspect. However, there is a close relationship between privacy and professional confidentiality. We discuss this further in Chapter 10.

In policing, there is an imperative not to compromise investigations by disclosing confidential information. The duty to keep confidences so as not to compromise investigations is based on a number of different considerations. It is, in part, based on the need to ensure that offenders do not escape justice – a tip-off to an offender can, for example, undermine a police investigation. It is also, in part, based on the need to ensure that witnesses and/or informants are protected. However, the ultimate and central moral basis for the principle of confidentiality in the context of police investigations is the moral rights of victims, or potential victims. If confidentiality in criminal investigations is breached, then citizens can have no guarantee that their rights – their legally enshrined, justifiably enforceable, moral rights – will be protected; rather, offenders will be able to offend with impunity.

In the light of the moral importance of protecting confidentiality and, thereby, ensuring investigations are not compromised and the rights of victims, witnesses, and informants are protected, the security of intelligence databases is critically important.

Yet, as we have seen, the quantum and quality of the information in these databases needs to be maximized as does their utilization by investigators. This need to generate greater amounts of at least potentially sensitive intelligence and to provide officers from multiple jurisdictions with access to it, stands in some tension with the need for information security (in addition to privacy and other constraints mentioned earlier). Here the solution is not necessarily to reduce intelligence gathering and accessing because of security concerns, but rather to increase security and (relatedly) accountability.

National databases are essential if all information and intelligence is to be available to investigating officers, but they require a rigorous monitoring and security policy if misuse is to be prevented. A significant threat to any organization is the loss of confidential information from its database for whatever reason. Information held by the police is extremely valuable to criminals and they are prepared to pay for access to it. The integrity of any intelligence database, demands a secure infrastructure (where effective vetting is paramount) to:

- counter disclosure of information to unauthorized persons;
- provide physical security policies and procedures;
- provide technical security policies and procedures;
- manage information (including in relation to covert surveillance activities);
- provide protocols with partner agencies for information access and exchange.

Additional safeguards can be put in place for higher levels in the system where the most confidential data is stored and access is limited to a few authorized persons. Audit trails from the information accessed back to the inquirer are subject to monitoring and the reason for access taken up with the inquirer. Where it is suspected that inappropriate access is occurring, covert monitoring of activity can be implemented.

Police services and other agencies generally have a strategic plan for their organization, based on information they have gathered, their resources and the expectations of stakeholders inside and outside their organization. What is not always produced is a Strategic Threat Assessment (STA). Such an assessment identifies the factors that may negatively impact on the fulfillment of the strategic plan and provide for the means to counter these factors. The STA is not limited to corruption issues alone – it can identify a variety of threats to the organization and so allow risk assessment and early intervention to occur.

Notes

1   Two recent introductions to the theory of criminal intelligence gathering, analysis, and using are Patrick F. Walsh (2011) *Intelligence and Intelligence Analysis*, London: Routledge, and Jerry H. Ratcliffe (ed.) (2009) *Strategic Thinking in Criminal Intelligence*, Sydney: Federation Press.

2 For a discussion of some of the philosophical and ethical issues that arise in relation to such systems see Seumas Miller (2008) Collective responsibility and information and communication technology, in J. van den Hoven and J. Weckert (eds) *Moral Philosophy and Information Technology*, New York: Cambridge University Press, pp. 226–250. See also Miller (2010a), Chapter 11.

3 National Centre for Policing Excellence (2005) *Guidance on the National Intelligence Model*, http://whereismydata.files.wordpress.com/2009/01/national-intelligence-model-20051.pdf

4 See Weiner (2013).

5 For discussion of these issues in the United States, Europe, India, and Australia see John Kleinig, Peter Mameli, Seumas Miller, Douglas Salane, and Edwina Schwartz (2011) *Security and Privacy: Global Standards for Ethical Identity Management in Contemporary Liberal Democratic States*, Canberra: ANU e-Press.

6 See Brian Flood and Roger Gaspar (2009) Strategic aspects of the UK National Intelligence Model, in Ratcliffe (2009).

7 M. Bichard (2004) *Bichard Inquiry Report* dera.ioe.ac.uk/6394/1/report.pdf p. 89 and p. 77.

8 Unlike other subpoenas, administrative subpoenas do not have to be reviewed by judges or juries. They are issued under the International Emergency Economic Powers Act, 1977.

9 Eric Lichtblau and James Risen (2006) Bank data is sifted by US in secret to block terror, *New York Times*, June 23, A1.

10 Stuart Levey, Under Secretary, Terrorism and Financial Intelligence, US Treasury. This was backed up by reference to *US v. Miller*, 425 US 435 (1976).

11 The claim is that it was helpful in the tracking of Hambali, the Indonesian leader of the al Qaeda-related terrorist organization, Jemaah Islamiyah. Other suggestions about its usefulness were reported in the original *New York Times* and *Wall Street Journal* articles.

12 Royaume de la Belgique, Commission de la Protection de la Vie Privée (2006) Summary of the Opinion on the Transfer of Personal Data by SCRL SWIFT Following the UST (OFAC) Subpoenas, https://www.aclu.org/files/images/asset_upload_file96_26942.pdf. See also Dan Bilefsky (2006), Data transfer broke rules, report says, *New York Times*, September 28.

13 Embarrassed, SWIFT tried to wriggle out of the rebuke by claiming that because it had offices in the United States, it was required to obey the subpoenas.

14 See, for example, John A. Eterno and Eli B. Silverman (2012) *The Crime Numbers Game: Management by Manipulation*, CRC Press, and Seumas Miller (forthcoming) *Analysis of Focus Groups and In-depth Interviews of NSW Police Officers*, Report for NSW Police.

15 Nicole Perlroth, Jeff Larson, and Scott Shane (2013) Files show N.S.A. foiling encryption, *International Herald Tribune* September 7, p. 1.

16 This claim has been made with respect to the FBI and other US security agencies in relation to the 9/11 Al Qaeda terrorists who flew planes into the Twin Towers and the Pentagon.

17   The more intrusive and sustained the infringement of the right to privacy, the higher the standard of evidence that ought to be required in relation to reasonable suspicion, such as probable cause, or even good and decisive reasons.

18   In fact, under the Bush Administration there were numerous warrantless interceptions of electronic and other communications in breach of both FISA and the normal provisions of the criminal justice system. See John Kleinig et al. (2011), pp. 39–40.

19   In relation to other areas see, for example, Seumas Miller (2009) *Terrorism and Counter-terrorism: Ethics and Liberal Democracy*, New York: Blackwell, Chapters 4 and 5.

20   See, for instance, Stanley Cohen (1985) *Visions of Social Control: Crime, Punishment and Classification*, Cambridge: Polity Press.

21   See, for instance, Les Johnston (1992) *The Rebirth of Private Policing*, London: Routledge.

22   See Kleinig et al. (2011), Chapter 2.

4

Investigative Independence

We argued in Chapter 1 that criminal investigation is undertaken ultimately in order to protect justifiably enforceable, legally enshrined moral rights, and in Chapter 2 that criminal investigators have, or ought to have, as their principal role to acquire knowledge with respect to the who, what, when, where, how, and why of crimes (and, therefore, knowledge of moral rights violations and violators (offenders)).

However, as we have seen in Chapters 2 and 3, there are a range of genuine difficulties in acquisition of this knowledge (e.g., lack of evidence, inadequate intelligence, false testimony, flawed reasoning) and, of course, there are moral constraints on investigations, notably suspects' rights (see Chapters 7, 10, 11, and 12).

In this chapter we discuss a major problem confronted by investigators, both at an individual and an institutional level, namely, the problem of investigative independence.

Sometimes the "position" from which a person makes a claim can undermine the possibility or likelihood that the claim being made is a true one. For example, if an investigator is the brother of the suspect, then the investigator's claim that the suspect is innocent will rightly be taken with a grain of salt. In such cases we say that they have not been made from an objective standpoint and, therefore, might well be false. This raises the issue of the independence of investigators.

Evidently, police detectives need to have a considerable degree of operational autonomy, if they are properly to discharge their functions of investigating crime. This is partly a matter of efficiency and effectiveness; the police are, or should be, not simply competent practitioners but (so to

Investigative Ethics: Ethics for Police Detectives and Criminal Investigators, First Edition.
Seumas Miller and Ian A. Gordon.
© 2014 Seumas Miller and Ian A. Gordon. Published 2014 by John Wiley & Sons, Ltd.

speak) the experts. It is also in part a matter of the need for institutional independence. Politicians, for example, need to be subject not only to an independently adjudicated law, but also to an independently enforced law. If a powerful politician, or powerful group of politicians, acts unlawfully, the police must investigate, arrest, and charge them. In order to ensure that the police effectively carry out these investigative tasks in relation to government, the police need to have a substantial degree of institutionally based independence from government. Naturally, what must go hand in glove with independence is accountability; police must be held accountable for the exercise of their independence.

In short, there are four interconnected notions: (i) operational autonomy; (ii) competence (indeed, expertise); (iii) institutional independence; (iv) accountability.

An important complicating factor in relation to this four-way nexus is the need for police organizations to be responsive to government; after all, government will have, and needs to have, security policies and it is a function of police organizations to implement these policies. The point to be made here is that this need for responsiveness to government is in some tension with the need for operational autonomy and police independence.

If independence is a key requirement for police investigators and police organizations then it is presumably also a requirement for investigators in other sectors. In recent times there has been a rebirth of private policing, most prominently in the security arena but also in the investigations area. For example, in the important area of fraud investigation, many corporations are employing their own investigators. The increase in the numbers of non-police investigators raises some important ethical issues in relation to investigative independence.

On the one hand, specialized non-police investigators may be better placed than police investigators to investigate cases where complex organizational and technical issues are involved. Also, this growth in non-police investigators reflects the inability of police resources to cover all areas. On the other hand, non-police investigators may well be less accountable than public police. Specifically, there is the possible conflict of interest that can arise for the non-police investigator when the interests of the employing private company or corporation are held to be of greater importance than those of bringing the wrong doer to justice. This situation is particularly acute when the investigator reports directly to the manager of a company.

4.1   Police Independence

The extent to which an institution – as distinct from an individual member of an institution – ought to have independence from government turns in large part on the function of that institution, and the extent to which it is necessary for that institution to have independence in order to properly carry out its function(s) or end(s). For example, the judiciary needs a high level of independence from the legislature and the executive, if it is to properly carry out its specialized tasks of interpreting and applying the law.[1]

Institutional independence needs to be seen in the context of the so-called "separation of powers." Specifically, the executive, the legislature, and the judiciary ought to be kept separate; otherwise too much power is concentrated in the hands of a unitary state agency. It is highly dangerous for those who make laws also to be the ones who apply those laws. Politicians, for example, need to be subject to laws adjudicated by judges who are institutionally independent of politicians, on pain of undue influence on judicial processes and outcomes.

Historically, the proper extent of independence of one institution from another has been problematic, and is in any case a matter of striking a balance between competing considerations. To what extent should the public service be independent of the government of the day? The public service exists to serve the public interest by implementing the policies of the government. So, on the one hand, the public service must be responsive to the elected government of the day. Yet, on the other hand, the public service must have a degree of independence in order to ensure that proposed policies are lawful and fully and accurately costed, and that presidents, prime ministers, cabinet ministers, and the like are provided with "frank and fearless" advice in relation to their policies.[2]

There is, inevitably, a tension arising from the sometimes disparate commitments of public servants to the policies, and therefore the interests, of the elected government of the day on the one hand, and to the public interest on the other. But this does not mean that this tension is not capable of more or less satisfactory resolution by striking a balance between these commitments when they come apart. Any attempt to resolve this tension once and for all is problematic. For here there are apparently only two options, neither of which is palatable. The public interest as interpreted by public servants might be allowed to override the directives of the government – resulting in a public service unresponsive to the elected government. Alternatively, the public service could be denied any latitude to provide bottom-up, independent input to government – resulting in a politically motivated, slavishly loyal public service that unhesitatingly implements policies it knows to be unjust, unworkable, not financially viable, unlawful, or otherwise against the public interest. Such a public service might even engage in cover-ups and improprieties on behalf of the government.

Although police services in contemporary liberal democracies are public-sector agencies, they provide a somewhat different kind of example.[3] Certainly, there is an important and difficult issue in relation to the institutional independence of the police. Evidently, police need to have a considerable degree of operational autonomy if they are properly to discharge their functions of upholding the law, maintaining the peace, and thereby securing the moral rights of citizens. This is partly a matter of efficiency and effectiveness; the police are, or should be, the experts. It is also in part a matter of the separation of powers doctrine mentioned above; politicians, for example, need to be subject not only to an independently adjudicated law, but also to an independently enforced law. If a powerful politician, or powerful group of politicians, acts unlawfully, appropriately authorized police must investigate, arrest, and charge them. In order to ensure that the police effectively carry out these tasks in relation to government, they need to have a substantial degree of independence from government.

Moreover, the police must not simply come to be the instrument of government policies, for the priority of the police is to serve the law, and on our account, to protect moral rights enshrined in the law. The police states of communist Eastern Europe, Nazi Germany, Iraq under Saddam Hussein, and the like, are testimony to the importance of a substantial degree of police independence from government in favor of serving legally enshrined moral rights. Indeed, police operational autonomy has, on occasion, been abridged by democratically elected governments in order, for example, to create and preserve a manageable level of public disorder from which the incumbent political party and their supporters may politically or materially benefit. This is evidently what happened in the 1970s in Queensland, Australia, during the premiership of John Bjelke-Petersen.[4] Among other things, Bjelke-Peterson ordered his police force to intervene forcibly against protesters exercising their democratic rights. The point to be made here is that the police ought not to be used for narrow political purposes. Such use is an infringement of the operational autonomy of the police. It is also an inappropriate function for the police to be performing; the police should be above politics, at least in this sense of politics.

Direct ministerial control of policing was eschewed in Mr. Justice Lusher's 1981 Report of the Commission to Inquire into New South Wales Police Administration:

> a distinction is to be drawn between the function of government in the administration of justice and possibly law enforcement on the one hand, and most, if not all, other areas of the government function. In the latter, whilst subject to the law in the broad sense, the area of policy and the views and intentions of the government of the day are necessarily reflected quite commonly and properly. The keeping of the peace, preventing of crime, and the detection of offenders and bringing them to justice are singularly related to the law and its application in practice, and the activity is governed by the law, to be carried out within it and always subject and answerable to it.[5]

Acknowledgment of the formally autonomous nature of policing has (largely) ensured its operational autonomy from direct party-political control in New South Wales. This convention, and the thread of legal reasoning that supports it, informed Mr. Justice Lusher's interpretation of Section 4 of the Police Regulation Act, 1899. The Lusher Report suggested the Commissioner of Police's governance of the NSW Police Force was "subject to the directions of the Minister", but such "direction" must not limit the Commissioner's unreviewable discretionary authority. The Report distinguished the Minister's authority from that of the NSW Police Commissioner as: "the responsibility [of the Minister for Police] for the provision of resources and for ensuring that police act efficiently and effectively and according to law from the responsibility of the police themselves for law enforcement."[6]

Justice Lusher's concept of police operational autonomy reflected the 1962 findings of the UK's Royal Commission on the Police:

> The duties which it is generally agreed in the evidence should be performed by chief constables unhampered by any kind of external control are not capable of precise definition, but they cover broadly what we referred to earlier as 'quasi-judicial' matters; that is, the enforcement of the criminal law in particular cases involving, for example, the pursuit of enquiries and decisions to arrest or prosecute . . .
>
> We entirely accept that it is in the public interest that a chief constable, when dealing with these quasi-judicial matters, should be free from the conventional processes of democratic control and influence.[7]

Were one to accept the concept of the "quasi-judicial" nature of policing, one might then agree with the notions of Lusher and others, that policing should stand to some extent separate from direct ministerial control in an analogous manner to the judiciary.[8] Here it is important to stress that this quasi-judicial nature of policing pertains to evidence gathering in relation to crimes, arrest of suspects, and the like. It does not pertain to the adjudication of cases; to this extent, it does not conflict with the judicial role.

The quasi-judicial character of policing importantly distinguished its function from that of the military and from agencies engaged in foreign intelligence gathering (espionage). The latter serve the national interest in the international arena – as opposed to upholding domestic law – and are, or ought to be, under the control of the country's political leadership, which in a democracy is the elected government of the day. Moreover, the constraints operative in ordinary law enforcement are substantially loosened in, for example, espionage activities directed at foreign authoritarian regimes or international terrorist groups, and reasonably so.

However, recent developments, notably counterterrorism initiatives in the United States, have blurred this institutional demarcation between domestic law enforcement and foreign espionage, and done so in ways that are potentially problematic, we suggest, for the institutional integrity of law enforcement agencies and their institutional independence of government, in particular.

In this connection let us consider the recent controversies surrounding the operations of the US-based security agency, the National Security Agency (NSA).

As noted in Chapter 3 (Section 3.4) the NSA's PRISM program involves agreements between NSA and various US-based Internet companies to enable NSA to monitor the online communications of non-US citizens based overseas.[9] However, there is no probable cause/reasonable suspicion requirement in relation to this monitoring/data gathering, unless the persons in question are US citizens.

So, with respect to its foreign intelligence gathering activities, the NSA is overreaching normal law enforcement powers with respect to ordinary citizens of liberal democratic allies of the United States not themselves suspected of any crime or anti-US activity. However, this activity is presumably not in breach of US laws and, indeed, one might regard it as predictable, given the nature and function foreign intelligence gathering (i.e., espionage) as opposed to law enforcement.

However, in addition to its foreign intelligence gathering activities, the NSA is an organization concerned with domestic law enforcement, for example, in relation to terrorism and, as the Verizon controversy has revealed (see Chapter 3, Case Study 3.2.3), the NSA has also arguably been violating the privacy of US citizens by engaging in large-scale collection of metadata. This domestic activity may well be in breach of US laws.

A further point in relation to PRISM is that the FISA court operates in secrecy, and there is a concern that it has crossed the line between making adjudications in relation to the lawfulness of actions (e.g., in the issuance of warrants) and interpreting the law in a manner that amounts to making the law. What is problematic about the latter form of activity on the part of FISA is that law is being made in secret, in other words, the law in question is not transparent to the citizenry (or, at the very least, it is not transparent to the citizenry whether or not there are such secret laws).

What are the implications of these various controversies surrounding the NSA for the institutional independence of police institutions? These controversies suggest that there has been a blurring of the law enforcement and the military/foreign intelligence gathering functions and associated legal/moral standards. Moreover, the question arises as to whether security organizations focused on counterterrorism and the like, such as the NSA, have become hybrid institutions. If so, there is a grave risk that the institutional integrity of law enforcement agencies, and their institutional independence of government and commitment to upholding the law (including, the protection of individual rights), in particular, have been compromised.

Certainly, the NSA's violation of the privacy rights of ordinary citizens in the United States and elsewhere suggests that this may well be the case.

Notwithstanding the acceptability of this notion of the quasi-judicial nature of policing, and the consequent need for a degree of police independence, the precise nature and extent of that required independence remains unclear. The 1994–1997 *Royal Commission into the New South Wales Police Service: Final Report*, vol. II, Chapter 3, pp. 243–245, concerned itself with the ministerial direction of the police. At Paragraph 3.26, it invoked a distinction between *policy* matters and *operational* matters, and indicated that the latter were the preserve of the police, the former of the Minister.

However, this distinction is problematic. It is, at the very least, an over-simplification to claim that policing can be divided into two parts, one designated "policy", the other "operations". The further notion that the part determined to be "policy" can be unproblematically handed to a political figure is doubtful. Laurence Lustgarten, writing from the British experience, points out the difficulties inherent in trying to make out this distinction:

> The precise pedigree of the distinction [policy/operations] is unclear. It breaks down entirely in relation to policing.
>
> More precisely some of the crucial "policy" decisions are about "operations." The method of policing, for example, will determine whether the force relies upon computerized information collected by various forms of pressure upon those at the edges of criminal involvement, leading to isolated "swoops" upon subjects but otherwise remaining aloof from the public, or an intensive commitment to street patrols leading to personal knowledge of most people in the area, involvement in community welfare projects, and coordination with other "care and control" agencies in crime prevention. The choice could be described as policy, but its concrete manifestations are in the day-to-day contact with the public – abrasive or supportive – and it is these which may produce dissatisfaction and demands for change. "Swamp 81" in Brixton is only the most spectacularly disastrous example;[10] public strip-searching, excessive force in dealing with youths congregating on the street, or attempts to gain access to the confidential school records of a particular pupil are more typical examples of causes of antagonism.
>
> The distinction becomes even less tenable when one examines the decision to set up a drug squad. This involves allocation of manpower and related resources that would otherwise be used in alternate ways. In other words, it represents a decision that drugs deserve greater or increased attention when compared to traffic control, burglary, or rape. It may also have serious consequences for relations with various groups within the community – innocent persons feel harassed by searches; women or householders who feel that the safety of the streets or their property is not receiving sufficient protection. The decision is highly controversial and a classic example of political choice. Yet it could equally well be categorized as "operational" – it merely involves re-assignment of a limited number of constables to particular duties.[11]

We have been discussing institutional independence in the context of the interface of police and the government of the day. Enough has been said by way of demonstrating that the notion of the police as simply the instrument of government is unsustainable. On the other hand, determining the precise nature and extent of police independence has turned out to be extremely difficult. We have emphasized the importance of maintaining a degree of police independence from government. However, it is equally important to point to the dangers of high levels of police independence. After all, the police are the coercive arm of the State and, historically, the abuse of their powers has been an ever-present threat. Specifically, the police institution as the coercive arm of the State does need to be subjected to (at least) the constraint and influence of the community via democratically elected bodies, notably the government of the day.

As is the case with the independence of other institutions, there is a need to strike a balance between, on the one hand, the independence of the police, and on the other hand, the need for: (i) community and government control of the police, and (ii) police accountability for their methods and actions.

4.2   Police Accountability

If an institution has substantial independence from other institutions, and if that institution has a very hierarchical structure, then those who occupy the upper echelons will have a relatively high degree of discretionary power. Military commanders, especially in time of war, are a case in point. Police Commissioners in times of emergency are a further case in point. But now consider the extraordinary powers possessed by police in authoritarian regimes, such as former Soviet Union. Indeed, the power of the one-time head of the secret police, Beria, became so great as to be thought to be a threat to the de facto head of state, Stalin.

Evidently the power of the police needs to be constrained, and there are a number of ways to achieve this. One way is to devolve police authority in a quasi-federated structure, as used to be the case in the United Kingdom,[12] where the police were, to an extent, a function of local government and there was no national police force as such. This accountability structure changed with the direct election of Police and Crime Commissioners (PCCs) in November 2012 when 41 new commissioners were elected to hold police forces (except the Metropolitan Police[13] and City of London Police[14]) to account across England and Wales. PCCs have the power to hire and fire chief constables and set police budgets and crime-fighting strategies, but the legitimacy of their mandate was questioned after only 15% of the public voted in the first elections. Elections for Police and Crime Commissioners did not take place in Scotland or Northern Ireland, where there are single police forces, as policing and justice powers are devolved to the Scottish Parliament and Northern Ireland Assembly.

Another way is to delimit their sphere of operational autonomy in favor of the policies, including policies in relation to police methods, of a democratically elected government; although, as we have seen, this can be counterproductive. A third, and much favored, method is to ensure accountability by way of oversight bodies, such as Ombudsmen, Police Boards, and the like.

Institutional independence stands in some tension with this highly desirable feature of institutions, accountability. Accountability is clearly a matter of great importance when it comes to institutions with great power, and especially institutions, such as the police and the military, that are possessed of near monopolistic powers of physical coercion in relation to their citizens.

The notion of accountability is not the same as, but yet should go hand in hand with, the notion of responsibility. Here we need first to distinguish some different senses of responsibility. Sometimes to say that someone is responsible for an action is to say that the person reasoned or deliberated concerning some action, then formed an intention to perform it, and finally acted on that intention and did so on the basis of those reasons. However, on other occasions what is meant by the expression "being responsible for an action" is that the person in question occupies a certain institutional role, and that the occupant of that role is the person who has the institutionally determined right and duty to decide what is to be done in relation to certain matters. If the matters in question include directing the actions of other agents, then the occupant of the role is not only responsible for what transpires, he or she is a person in authority. So being in authority is a species of being responsible in our second sense of that term. We will come back to the notion of authority later on in this chapter.

If a person is responsible in this second sense for some action or sphere of activity, then typically that person is, or at least ought to be, accountable for it. To say that someone is accountable in this sense is to say that he or she is able to be, or ought to be able to be, called to account for and made to justify the action or actions in question. Sometimes accountability brings with it liability, and an adverse judgment on the part of those to whom one is accountable can result in the infliction of punishment. Given the opportunity in policing for wrongdoing, and the historical tendency to corruption in police services, accountability is obviously of great importance.

The notion of accountability is complex. There are different kinds of accountability and different persons to whom one can be accountable. Personal accountability is accountability to oneself, and typically involves the provision of justifications to oneself for one's actions. With the possible exception of psychopaths, each of us has moral standards and values. There are some things we simply would not do, and there are other things we regard as so important we ought to do them even if it is not in our interest. Accountability is not to be equated with liability, but in formal institutional settings it typically implies liability, especially liability to punishment. In relation to personal accountability, if we fall short of our own moral standards and values, we suffer shame or remorse, or at the very least are disappointed with ourselves.

As members of a community or society, we are also accountable to others in a number of ways. Obviously we are legally accountable. Some of our actions are subject to legal scrutiny and judgment. Moreover, sanctions, including punishment in the form of imprisonment, can flow from adverse legal judgments. But we are also held morally accountable by other individuals and groups. Our actions are judged as unfair, weak, and so on by our friends, spouses, and the members of the community to which we belong. Moreover, adverse judgment is typically followed by expressed attitudes and actions that signal disapproval and even contempt. Such judgment making and expressed disapproval arguably constitute a process of holding individuals accountable. And while this process is informal and carries no legal sanctions, it is one that can powerfully influence our behavior.

As members of an institution, we are not only morally and legally accountable, we are, of course, administratively accountable, and in police institutions there is typically an elaborate array of institutional mechanisms to ensure accountability. In recent times, the number and kinds of these mechanisms have increased markedly, to the point where the costs, as well as the benefits, of accountability mechanisms are beginning to become an issue of concern. For example, the existence of a plethora of both internal and external administrative accountability mechanisms in Australian police services is a matter of concern to some Australian police.[15]

A particular problem for accountability procedures arises in institutional contexts. Obviously, a person ought to be held accountable for his or her own actions. However, in institutional contexts there are many actions, outcomes, and spheres of activity to which many different persons in fact contribute.

Because of the cooperative nature of activity in institutions, it is often unclear who is actually responsible for some untoward outcome, and the extent of their contribution to that outcome. This issue in moral philosophy is known as the "problem of many hands." An example that comes to mind in the recent history of policing is the investigation of former Police Superintendent Harry Blackburn of the New South Wales Police.[16] After a lengthy police investigation, Blackburn was falsely accused of being a sex offender (see Case Study 2.2.2 in Chapter 2 above). However, in the course of the investigation, hypotheses were accepted without adequate testing, evidence eliminating Blackburn as a suspect was discredited, witnesses were extensively prompted, and so on. The point of interest here is that these errors, acts of negligence, and so on, were not committed by one person, but by quite a large group of individuals, each of whom was supposedly being guided by their own judgment. So the question arises as to how moral responsibility is, as it were, to be parceled out. We return to this issue of collective responsibility in Chapter 7.[17] And, of course, there are the corresponding questions as to how accountability and liability are to be ascribed to these different individuals. Let us now turn to some cases studies illustrating police independence, or lack thereof, before proceeding with further discussion.

4.3 Case Studies

Case Study 4.3.1 BAE and the Serious Fraud Office

The *Guardian* newspaper publicised a series of allegations that British Aerospace (BAE) was using front companies and providing cash and treats for Saudis on an enormous scale. Robert Wardle, director of the UK's Serious Fraud Office (SFO), launched a full-scale investigation.

The SFO's key discovery was that as well as a £60 m Saudi slush fund, £1 bn may have gone into Swiss accounts linked, among others, to two intermediaries for the Saudi royals, Wafic Said and Mohammed Safadi. Prince Bandar, it was alleged, had also been directly collecting more than £100 m a year, paid quarterly into Riggs Bank in Washington and authorized by Deso, the UK ministry of defence's arms sales unit.

The SFO made formal requests to the Swiss authorities. By September 2006 the Swiss signalled that they were collecting up the bank records. But the Swiss also officially notified Said, as one of the account holders.

Mike Turner, BAE's chief executive, publicly claimed the Typhoon contract was in danger. MPs were warned constituency jobs were at stake. In November, Jack Straw, the leader of the Commons, whose Blackburn constituency is close to a BAE factory, pressed the supposedly independent attorney general [Lord Goldsmith] on this score. Under this pressure, Wardle offered to compromise. He would accept

(Continued)

from the BAE chairman, Dick Evans, a guilty plea on the relatively minor slush fund payments. In return the embarrassing Bandar, Said and Safadi inquiries would be dropped.. But this time BAE's supporters did not intend to make their previous mistakes and leave any room to manoeuvre. Bandar is thought to have intervened with Downing Street. That December Tony Blair called in Goldsmith and insisted that "national security" could be said to be at stake, rather than simply commercial interests. M16, however, refused to tell the OECD that they "agreed with [this] assessment". Blair's stance came down to a claim that the Saudis might stop sharing intelligence on al-Qaida. Its terrorists might then, in theory, be able to blow up Britons. Wardle was under great political pressure. The Prime Minister was telling him lives were at stake. The term of his four-year contract as SFO director had expired. Sitting on the attorney general's desk at that very moment was his application for a two-year extension. Wardle gave in and agreed to drop the Saudi investigation. He stated, and Goldsmith repeated to parliament, that "the rule of law" had been outweighed by a "wider public interest."

(Extract adapted from David Leigh and Rob Evans, *Guardian* newspaper, www.guardian.co.uk/baefiles)

Case Study 4.3.2   Special Agent Joseph Occhipinti

With seventy-eight awards or commendations for meritorious service, Special Agent Joseph Occhipinti was the most decorated federal agent in US history and Chief of the Anti-Smuggling Unit of the US Immigration Service for the New York Area. Occhipinti had been drawn into an NYPD investigation into the murder of a police officer. Officer Michael Buczek, with his partner, had responded to a routine service-call to an apartment and walked unknowingly into a drug rip-off. Buczek had been killed by a fleeing DR (Dominican Republic) criminal and inquiries soon revealed the drug rip-off which resulted in the policeman's murder was directed at a drug outlet in another apartment in that building. Little evidence was forthcoming from the Dominican immigrant community: "The essential problem, investigators discovered, was that a great many Dominicans think of themselves precisely, and only, as Dominicans."[18]

Occhipinti mounted 'Project *Bodega*'; accompanied sometimes by NYPD or DEA (Drug Enforcement Agency) officers, and working with three specially appointed DANY (District Attorney New York) officials, he raided fifty-five *bodegas* in all seeking illegal aliens, the foot soldiers of the drug trade. The raids resulted in arrests and convictions, and hauls of drugs, weapons, and cash. Occhipinti routinely reported several corrupt approaches he had received in the course of Project *Bodega* to the FBI's Corruption Unit.

There was an immediate response from the Heights claiming INS (Immigration and Naturalization Service, or '*Migra*' in DR slang) infringement of Dominican immigrants' civil liberties and illegal search and seizure. Complainants were a purposely formed 'Coalition for Community Concerns', whose membership included the complainant *bodega* owners, and the Dominican Merchants and Industrialists, a body formed in 1980 (and, typically, unconcerned with conditions in the Heights and previously involved in running candidates in elections in the Dominican Republic). The 'Mr Big-Enoughs' of the Heights were able to mobilize cash and clout sufficient to confront the intervention of local and US authorities into the Dominican drug trade's US beach-head.

Affrighted federal authorities cautioned Occhipinti to 'back off', but he determinedly continued to pursue his inquiries. The Dominicans received support from New York City's administration, long prone to patronage-politics and political and financial corruption.

New York's Democrat mayor David Dinkins, who owed his narrow 1980 election win to 70 per cent of the city's Hispanic vote, politicized Occhipinti's investigation, publicly branding it as a 'Republican-backed conspiracy'[19] on 3 April 1990 and demanding the INS shut Occhipinti's operations down. Responding to political pressure, DANY had already shut down the NYPD investigation into the murder of Officer Buczek, lest it expose further criminality in the Heights.

On 10 April 1990, Dennis De Leon, New York City's Human Rights Commissioner, announced an investigation into allegations of alleged violations of human rights, illegal arrests, and search and seizure—based on the *bodega* proprietors' complaints.

Unsupported allegations and political expediency effectively put a stop to Occhipinti's activities against the DR drug trade. But it wasn't enough; there must also be condign and deterrent revenge taken against Occhipinti on behalf of the Dominican drug traders, and justification had to be found for the actions of their political pawns.

(Continued)

There was support for the notion of an allegorical triumph of a Latino community over the hated *Migra*, albeit being a community permeated with criminality—and the sacrifice of an INS agent seemed a small price to pay if it would purchase the growing bloc of Hispanic votes and cash.

Possibly one of the most significant developments in the anti-corruption initiative had been the intrusion since the mid-1970s of the US government. The US Justice Department's stringently conducted investigations into corruption by local officials[20] was matched by their oversight of the operations of their own enforcement agencies. On 6 March 1991, the US Attorney's Office for the Southern District of New York made public the grand jury indictment on counts of having violated the human rights of twelve DR *bodega* owners—almost all of whom had serious criminal records.

The cases were referred to Federal District Court judge Constance Motley. Motley had powerful Democratic Party affiliations and ties to Mayor Dinkins, he of the 'Republican-backed conspiracy' theory. Motley herself had a quite extensive record for civil activism. Judge Motley's former law clerk, Jeh Johnson, was one of the US attorneys prosecuting the case against Occhipinti; nothing was being left to chance.

On 17 May 1991 on the eve of the trial, Occhipinti's lawyer asked to be excused, claiming he was suffering a nervous breakdown. Judge Motley refused to allow Occhipinti to obtain other counsel. Motley would not allow the defence to introduce the criminal records of the complainants—now federal prosecution witnesses—into evidence, the defence claiming a concerted criminal conspiracy based on perjured evidence. Former INS agent Occhipinti was convicted on 28 June 1991 on seventeen counts of civil rights violations and Judge Motley sentenced him to three years—and one month—imprisonment.

Drug importers, DR criminals and *bodega*-located drug dealers were cock-a-hoop, boasting openly of having procured perjury and engaging in conspiracy, and claiming to have 'fucked the *federales*'— which they certainly had. Occhipinti's supporters gathered evidence of the conspiracy: a convincing body of material from reputable sources accrued. When presented to the US Justice Department's Office of Professional Responsibility, however, it was dismissed.

Occhipinti appealed against his conviction and entertained some hope—Judge Motley's decisions were amongst the most overturned in the Southern District. Attempts were made to intimidate the court; a noisy Dominican demonstration took place on the US Court of Appeal steps, demonstrators broke into the court room during the appeal proceedings, and riots were threatened in New York, Washington and elsewhere if the court upheld Occhipinti's appeal—it was dismissed within the hour.

Judge Motley ordered Occhipinti's immediate arrest; heavily shackled, he was conveyed from New York, not to some 'Club Fed' institution, but to Oklahoma's El Reno Federal Penitentiary, a maximum security prison. After seven months imprisonment, the political purpose of his conviction having been served, US President George Bush commuted Occhipinti's sentence on 15 January 1993—significantly, not until immediately prior to Bush leaving office.

Occhipinti's supporters continued to investigate the criminal conspiracy leading to his conviction, but unfortunately the extent of the investigatorial-prosecutorial-judicial-political machinations will probably never be uncovered. After launching an investigation which appeared purposive only of discrediting the exculpatory evidence placed before it and reconfirming the result of their original investigation, the Federal Bureau of Investigation closed out the possibility of a review of the matter.

Patent, in this account, is the degree to which party politics in the United States is able to abridge the convention of the separation of powers, particularly in the federal arena. The destruction of INS agent Occhipinti seems, in retrospect, an affordable price for the administration to pay to bring in the Latino vote.

(Extract from John Blackler's case study, Special Agent Joseph Occhipinti, in John Blackler and Seumas Miller (2000c) *Police Ethics (vol. 3): Case Studies for Police Managers*, Wagga Wagga: Charles Sturt University and NSW Police Service, pp. 189–195.)

4.4   Independence of the Investigator

Our two case studies graphically illustrate political interference in criminal investigations, indeed interference of a kind which, in both cases, undermined the investigation entirely. In both cases the institutional independence of the investigative agency was called into question, given the nature of the interference. Evidently, the Serious Fraud Office in the United Kingdom and various investigative agencies in the United States (New York Police Department, Federal Drug Enforcement Agency, etc.) are very far from being immune from political interference to the point at which important criminal investigations can be shut down and criminal investigators themselves subjected to wrongful investigation and conviction as a consequent of trying to do their job.

Here we need to invoke the distinction made above between the independence of the investigative agency and the independence of the particular investigator. The former is largely a matter of institutional design. The latter is more an issue of the particular qualities of individual investigators. Having discussed and illustrated the former in some detail let us now concern ourselves with the latter.[21]

As mentioned above, self-evidently individual investigators need to be highly competent; they need to be experts. This is both a presupposition and a justification of their being granted investigative independence. Clearly they will not have high levels of competence if they have not done the necessary training (e.g., successfully undertaken an investigator's course), obtained the requisite experience (e.g., undertaken a reasonable number of relevant investigations), and possess the necessary aptitude (e.g., have displayed a capacity for logical thinking and open-mindedness) and demonstrable expertise (e.g., have *successfully* completed previous investigations). Accordingly, competence and performance indicators – for example, audits of the investigator's past investigator reports, briefs of evidence, ratios of successful to unsuccessful prosecutions, and so on – need to be developed to determine what counts as a competent investigator, and these should be applied to investigators in a systematic and objective manner.

It should also be noted that competence is to some extent relative to the *person* to be investigated. Presumably, other things being equal, a novice investigator should not be assigned the task of, for example, undertaking the investigation of a serious complaint made against another police officer who is a highly experienced investigator.

Again competence, or at least standards of investigative competence, is to some extent relative to investigative competence elsewhere within the organization and outside it. What processes are in place to attract high-quality investigators from other parts of the organization or from other organizations?

As we have stressed, the investigator needs to be, and to be seen to be, independent. There are at least three respects in which the independence of the investigator might be compromised:

1. Institutional independence both from government and other agencies and from a given police organizations, as in the case of police from a given police organization investigating large numbers of complaints of *systemic* police corruption in that organization. Some have argued that, in relation to serious police corruption (whether allegedly systemic or not) and other serious forms of criminality, the investigators should not

be members of the police organization whose members are under investigation.

2. Conflict of interest. Consider, for example, an investigator investigating an allegation against his relative. The notion of a conflict of interest involves one person, P1, being required to exercise judgment in relation to another person, P2 (e.g., P1 is investigating an allegation made by P3 against P2), and P1 has a special interest tending to interfere with P1's proper exercise of his/her judgment in relation to P2.[22] The special interest in question can be a personal interest, for instance, P2 is a relative, or a conflicting role interest, for instance, P2 is P1's immediate superior.

3. Bias. Consider, for example, an investigator investigating an allegation of corruption by a non-police complainant against another police officer. Strictly speaking, this is not necessarily a conflict of interest since the investigating officer might not have a *special interest* in the required sense. Indeed, one might reasonably expect police to resist any temptation to be unduly influenced by the fact that the person being investigated is merely a police officer in the same organization and not, for example, a friend. On the other hand, there might be a tendency for bias or, at least, the appearance thereof.

In relation to each of the above, performance indicators might be developed, such as the existence of a requirement to make conflict-of-interest disclosures (to avoid conflicts of interest) and case audits of police investigations in relation to conflicts of interest.

4.5   Accountability of Investigators

Investigators need to be held accountable for their investigations, including processes undertaken and the results delivered. Accordingly, they need to be able to withstand scrutiny from both internal and external agencies. A variety of such forms of scrutiny have been mentioned above, including audits and the like. An important dimension of accountability, indeed a presupposition of accountability, is transparency; what procedures are in place to ensure that investigative processes are transparent, including not only to internal and external oversight agencies but also to victims, witnesses, and suspects. (Naturally, the nature and level of transparency needs to be consistent with security and confidentiality requirements.)

A further point here is that the decisions and recommendations made by the investigator need to be justified in terms of reasons, and these reasons need to be adequately documented.

Accountability is operative at two levels (at least): (i) there is the accountability of the investigator in relation to a particular investigation considered in itself; and (ii) there is the accountability of the investigator in relation to his or her investigative performance over a period of time. The latter is susceptible to performance indicators not necessarily applicable to the former, for example, the number and ratio of investigations of a given investigator leading to prosecutions.

Investigation is a dynamic mode of activity, in part because those investigated seek to avoid investigation and/or subvert investigative techniques. Hence, the need to identify and implement best practice, including using the latest investigative tools, such as tools made available by forensic science, and to innovatively apply such practices and tools to the specific context in which the investigators are operating, for example, in the design of integrity tests. Hence a criterion of the quality of investigations is the extent to which they not only deploy best practice but are monitored with a view to improvement in light of new developments.

In addition, data needs to be collected in relation to investigations undertaken, including the number of investigations undertaken and finalized per annum, time taken to finalize investigations, the outcome in terms of decisions such as conviction rates, and the levels of satisfaction of victims, witnesses, and so on, since they provide an important picture of agency work and can be used to indicate areas of underperformance by investigators.

Notes

1   Earlier versions of the material in this section and the one following appeared in Seumas Miller (1998) Authority, discretion and accountability: The case of policing, in C. Sampford, N. Preston, and C. Bois (eds) *Public Sector Ethics: Finding and Implementing Values*, London: Routledge, pp. 37–53, and Seumas Miller and John Blackler (2005), Chapter 2.

2   For discussions of public service accountability in a range of different countries, see J. G. Jabbra and O. P. Dwivedi (1988) *Public Service Accountability: A Comparative Perspective*, West Hartford, CT: Kumarian Press.

3   For a useful introductory discussion of this issue, see Keith Bryett, Arch Harrison, and John Shaw (1994) Police and government in a democracy, in their *An Introduction to Policing* (vol. 2), Sydney: Butterworths, pp. 39–57.

4   Evan Whitton (1988) *The Hillbilly Dictator: Australia's Police State*, Sydney: BBC Books.

5   The Hon. Mr. Justice Lusher (1981) *Report of the Commission to Inquire into New South Wales Police Administration*, Sydney: NSW Government Printer, p. 680.

6   Lusher (1981), p. 183.

7   The Royal Commission on the Police (1962) *The Royal Commission on the Police: Cmnd. 1728: Final Report*, 1962, paras 87 and 88.

8   For a contrary view, see Lustgarten (1986), p. 24.

9   Claire Cain Miller (2013), Secret court ruling put tech companies in data bind, *New York Times*, June 13, 2013.
10   In 1981, Operation Swamp was undertaken in Brixton, London, by the Special Patrol Group of the London Metropolitan Police. It involved saturation policing, and riots ensued. It was the subject of *The Scarman Report*, see Scarman (1982).
11   See Lustgarten (1986), pp. 20–21.
12   Prior to November 2012 in England and Wales police were subject to central government via the Home Office, as well as to local government via the Police Authority. However, the authority of local government has been diluted by the 1995 requirement that the Police Authorities have a significant number of members nominated by the Home Secretary. See Peter Neyroud and Alan Beckley (2001), *Policing, Ethics and Human Rights*, Cullompton, Devon: Willan Publishing, p. 97.
13   The elected Mayor of London is the PCC.
14   The Court of Common Council undertakes the role of PCC.
15   For example, arguably the system for handling complaints against NSW police officers is unwieldy, resource-intensive, and ineffective. The complaints system involves a multiplicity of internal and external agencies, including the internal affairs department of the police, local area police commanders and various of their committees, as well as the independent bodies, the NSW Ombudsman, and the Police Integrity Board. There is evidence that too many complaints are investigated, and too many of these inadequately investigated – in other words, efficiency and effectiveness would require that there were fewer, but better-quality, investigations of complaints. See Seumas Miller, David Biles, Tracey Green, and Jerry Ratcliffe (2001) *Report on Drug-related Complaints Against the NSW Police* (Australian Research Council-funded SPIRT Grant), and Jerry Ratcliffe, David Biles, Tracey Green and Seumas Miller (2005) Drug related complaints against police: some findings from a New South Wales study, *Policing: An International Journal of Police Strategies and Management*, 28.1, pp. 69–83.
16   See Davis (1990).
17   See, for example, Miller (2006).
18   Robert Jackall (1997) *Wild Cowboys; Urban Marauders and the Forces of Order*, Cambridge, MA: Harvard University Press, p. 85.
19   See Jackall (1997), p. 94.
20   Frank Anechiarico and James B. Jacobs (1996) *The Pursuit of Absolute Integrity: How Corruption Control Makes Government Ineffective*, Chicago: University of Chicago Press, Pt. III, Chapter 7.
21   An earlier version of the material in this section and the following one appeared in Miller (2010b), pp. 30–41.
22   Definition taken from Michael Davis's (1988) entry on conflicts of interest in the *Encyclopaedia of Applied Ethics*, London: Academic Press, Volume 1, A–D, p. 590.

5

Crimes against the Person

Thus far in this book we have concerned ourselves with a number of central issues to do with the normative framework within which criminal investigations take place, namely, the relationship between the criminal law and morality, the epistemic or knowledge-focused role of investigators, the nature and ethico-normative dimension of evidence and of intelligence in criminal investigations, and the importance of the independence of investigative agencies and of individual investigators. In the next two chapters we focus attention on the two most salient generic forms of criminal investigations, namely, the investigation of crimes against the person (murder, rape, assault, and the like) and the investigation of property crimes (theft, fraud, and the like). In the six chapters that follow these two we shift gear somewhat and focus our attention on more specific moral or ethical issues. Some of these more specific issues typically arise only in particular kinds of criminal investigations, such as terrorism investigations or police corruption investigations; others, such as ethical issues in interviewing, arise in criminal investigations more generally.

In this chapter our focus is on the investigation of crimes against the person. Here it might be helpful to sketch the contours of a typical criminal investigation of a murder and to do so by way of working through a generic example.

It is important at the outset to determine what is at stake in undertaking any criminal investigation. Criminal investigations, as we have seen, are justified in general terms by the fact that they are investigations of crimes and crimes are, or ought to be, serious moral offenses. Moreover, the moral

Investigative Ethics: Ethics for Police Detectives and Criminal Investigators, First Edition.
Seumas Miller and Ian A. Gordon.
© 2014 Seumas Miller and Ian A. Gordon. Published 2014 by John Wiley & Sons, Ltd.

unacceptability of serious crimes against the person, unlike many property crimes, tends to be uncontroversial; the objective moral basis of such crimes in physical and psychological harms being readily perceptible. (We discuss some of the moral ambiguities of property crimes – including disputes about the limits of property rights – and their investigation, in the next chapter). Nevertheless, criminal investigations also need to be prioritized, if for no other reason than the limitations on available investigative resources. In the case of a murder investigation it is self-evident that what is at stake is of great moral significance and, therefore, such investigations need to be given a very high priority.

The right to life and, more specifically, the right not to be killed is the most basic of all human rights: life is, after all, a necessary condition for the enjoyment of all the other human rights and freedoms and, indeed, for the enjoyment of any benefit whatsoever. Moreover, in the case of serial murderers there is an ongoing threat to the lives of persons other than the past victim(s). In addition, of course, there is the trauma visited upon the family and friends of the murdered person, and the loss to the community in terms of the contribution that otherwise would have been made by this person.

The loss of life and its consequences for others is compounded in the case of murder by the fact that the victim's right to life has not only been infringed, as in the case of an accidental killing, but it has been violated; for murder involves the deliberate killing of a fellow human being, and doing so without adequate justification (by contrast, for example, with killing in self-defense).

For all these reasons the crime of murder and the imperative to apprehend and appropriately punish murderers and, thereby, bring a measure of justice to victims and deter would-be murderers, is and ought to be taken very seriously indeed. The seriousness of the crime of murder is reflected in the fact that in most jurisdictions it has no statute of limitations. Having spelled out, albeit briefly, what is morally at stake in a murder investigation, let us turn to our generic example to determine what are some of the other moral or ethical issues in play.

5.1 Anatomy of a Homicide Investigation

It is 8 a.m. on a Sunday morning (in any developed liberal democracy such as the United States, the United Kingdom, or Australia) when a woman rings the police to report that a man is lying seriously injured in a supermarket parking lot. She declines to give her details but the police call-taking system has recorded her mobile number. The call sets in motion a complex and structured investigation process. The priority for police officers arriving at the scene is saving life, but an ambulance team has arrived first and the paramedic states the man is dead, having been shot twice in the back of the head. This initial assessment of what has occurred can be a gray area; the paramedics will give life-saving treatment, which may impact on the preservation of the crime scene – but the priority must always be to save life. The body is left *in situ* and the police secure the scene. An officer assesses the situation and then informs the relevant police command and control unit in relation to what has occurred and what resources are needed. The unit will organize specialist resources such as investigators and crime-scene officers. The investigation is underway.

The scene is quickly becoming a hive of activity; an officer begins a log of events and people associated with the scene. The log is essential to retain knowledge of who was there and their role; equally important is ensuring that persons entering follow one route. Among other things, this knowledge will assist in isolating the fingerprints and/or DNA samples of those persons of interest to the investigation, such as possible suspects. This will be done in part by the elimination of those fingerprints and/or DNA samples which belong to those persons who have been at the crime scene according to the log but are not potential suspects, such as the victim. Time is of the essence, and it is vital to get details of people who are still at the scene when the police arrive. The parking lot is relatively quiet but vehicles are coming and going to use the cash-point machines on the supermarket building; consequently, the lot is sealed off from public use.

In this instance, there was no-one near the body when the ambulance team arrived, but if a suspect had been present then the suspect becomes another crime scene in which forensic integrity and continuity is crucial for the evidence chain. What takes place at the point in time when the crime scene is established has clear implications for the knowledge being pursued by the investigation. If, for example, procedures of evidence are not followed, then vital evidence may be missed, destroyed, or contaminated, thereby undermining the investigators' pursuit of knowledge of the crime and the offender. Moreover, whether or not procedures are correctly followed has implications for any later court proceedings above and beyond the conclusions the investigators arrive at. If, for example, correct procedures are not followed, then the evidence provided by the investigators to the court may be called into question simply on that basis – for example, if the chain of evidence is broken.

This is a suspicious death and a cordon to stop unauthorized entry into the scene and to minimize the likelihood of members of the public seeing the body is in place. Access is barred until the forensic crime team arrives to begin its investigation. That bar includes senior officers who may turn up to monitor progress; the manager of the crime scene should have absolute control of who enters that scene until the forensic team is finished and the senior investigating officer is satisfied the scene has been exhausted.

The victim is quickly identified as Smith, a known drug dealer linked to organized crime. Because of the type of injury the officers at the scene are talking about it being an execution. When a nearby black BMW car is found to be insecure with the keys in the ignition, a radio check identifies it as Smith's car. The car now becomes another crime scene.

A supervisor and detectives have arrived at the scene and are quickly followed by a reporter from the local newspaper. The officers are briefed on what has occurred and what action has been taken so far. The reporter is speaking to other officers at the scene looking for a "story."

One of the detectives visits the office of the supermarket to secure the closed circuit TV equipment that constantly monitors the parking areas around the supermarket. Meanwhile the reporter produces his mobile phone and begins to take pictures of the body, which is lying uncovered on the ground. A nearby police officer grabs the reporter's phone and refuses to give it back saying to the reporter that this is a murder scene and the victim's family has not been informed of his death. More generally, as with other information germane to a current murder investigation, information extractable from the crime scene, including that based on visually available physical evidence, may need to be kept confidential lest the investigation be compromised. The public's right to know is at this stage overridden by the requirements of an ongoing murder investigation, given (as we saw above) what is at stake.

In a homicide investigation (or any other complex investigation) a senior investigating officer (SIO)[1] will be appointed to lead the investigation; most major jurisdictions have officers specifically trained in homicide investigation, who will follow a set procedure.

At the outset of an investigation, the SIO will make an assessment and begin a written record in which he or she will detail their investigative strategy and identify and prioritize their main lines of inquiry. This record must accurately record all decisions by the SIO and the reasoning behind them. Ideally the investigation will be "intelligence–led" in the sense outlined in Chapter 3. This will help focus the strategic direction of the investigation, manage activity, and inform and direct staff during regular briefings.

The "golden hour" is a term used by investigators to highlight the importance of scene preservation from the outset; a time to assess and organize the extraction of information and exhibits whilst minimizing contamination or destruction of any evidence. It is the time to speak to persons in the vicinity, either as witnesses or as potential suspects. Written notes taken at the time may prove invaluable when comparing witness accounts at a later time in the incident room. The SIO should be in no rush to jump to conclusions about the case remembering that things are not always what they seem.

The arrival of the forensic examination team allows the scene to be covered and hidden from the public. The pathologist has also arrived and the detailed scientific examination begins. Forensic evidence can help any investigation but is of particular importance in homicide investigation, since the principal witness (the victim) cannot describe what occurred. The integrity of the evidence relies crucially on the integrity of the process of preserving evidence during its transmission from the place where it was obtained to the location where it is examined for evidential content. Forensic evidence, such as paint transfer, fingerprints, DNA, fibers transfer, and tool marks, is increasingly used to link crime scenes to each other as well as to suspects.

DNA has quickly become a major contributor to crime detection and new DNA techniques are constantly evolving, notwithstanding privacy concerns (see Chapter 3 and, especially, Chapter 10). For example, familial DNA can assist an investigator to identify an offender on the basis of the DNA of their family members. Familial DNA is a somewhat controversial process. For example, there are privacy concerns such as the possibility of the unwanted identification of the biological parents of a child being reared in another family. However, familial DNA can be an effective means to identify an offender. Familial searching is a deliberate search of a DNA database conducted for the purpose of potentially identifying close biological relatives to the unknown forensic profile obtained from crime-scene evidence. It is based on the concept that close relatives (siblings or parent/child) will have more genetic data in common than unrelated persons. Familial searching should only be performed if the comparison of the crime-scene DNA profile, with the known offender/arrestee DNA profiles, has not identified any matches. Moreover, in the United Kingdom it is required that a relative must already be in the database, for instance, because they have a prior conviction, or otherwise give their consent in order for the search to identify them as a potential relative of the crime scene profile.

The United Kingdom has been conducting familial searching of its National DNA Database (NDNAD) since 2003; has conducted about 200 familial searches where approximately 40 serious crimes have been solved. One example was the murder on Christmas Eve 2004 of Margaret Weir in Maryhill, the Glasgow area where she had lived. Margaret had been stabbed nine times in the face, throat, and chest in the early hours of the morning. A crime-scene profile was developed from skin found under her fingernail. Despite an intensive investigation and media coverage a suspect had not been identified, so a volunteer DNA sample session was held in the neighborhood. Several hundred samples were obtained and one volunteer profile showed a commonality with the original crime-scene profile, but it was not a match. The SIO redirected his inquiry to the family members of the volunteer and a suspect, Daniel Jebb, was identified; he did not live in the local area where the murder was committed and it was highly unlikely that he would have been otherwise traced. He had no previous criminal record. Jebb pleaded guilty to the murder.

Notwithstanding its importance in assisting investigators to identify offenders and provide evidence to convict them, DNA collection is controversial. Certainly, DNA matching is a much more useful method than, say, fingerprint matching: unlike fingerprints, removing all traces of DNA material is difficult. Moreover, DNA matching is a more reliable process than fingerprint matching. However, unlike fingerprints, DNA material contains a great deal of information about a person; it is, after all, a biological blueprint. Of course, investigators are not necessarily interested in this additional information. However, the concern is that governments might be – in particular, authoritarian governments with, for example, ambitions to engineer the characteristics of their populations. Perhaps such concerns ought to lead to vigilance with respect to governments and restricted access to DNA information rather than disallowing its availability to investigators of serious crimes.

In many jurisdictions when the victim is identified a police officer must be assigned to liaise with any relatives that the police consider may need support. These liaison officers typically retain a role as investigators since relatives are also a potential source of information. This dual role can be a difficult one requiring an ability to display sensitivity to the needs of distraught relatives while also ensuring that the requirements of the investigation are met, including in relation to information that relatives may be reluctant to divulge.

Homicide is an horrific crime and, as such, may generate fear in the local community. This fear should be addressed at the earliest opportunity. An impact assessment will be made and an action plan developed to help reassure the public. Normally, the SIO will manage the investigation and the police commander in the local area will deal with community needs and responses. In crime involving children or racial issues community tensions can quickly escalate.

The investigation of homicide (or any other major inquiry) is a team operation but one requiring a balance on the part of the SIO between being a good team leader receptive to the ideas of subordinates, and exercising, at times, a high degree of control. In most investigations an incident room will be set up as a focal point for the inquiry. Such an investigation generates an enormous volume of information and other data. The manual systems that were used in the past to access and evaluate this large volume of information found it hard to cope; the result was often a deficit of the good-quality, timely information required for the investigation to proceed efficiently and effectively. In the Yorkshire Ripper Inquiry (see Case Study 5.2.1 below) this contributed to a delay in identifying the offender in a situation in which delays could mean further loss of life. The offender was in the system but the data bank was too large to be efficiently and effectively searched by its cumbersome manual cross-referencing processes. As a result, the system was unable adequately to assist decision making in relation to generating and prioritizing the lines of inquiry necessary for identifying the offender.

The Yorkshire Ripper inquiry was the catalyst for major change to investigative procedures in the United Kingdom. Now complex investigations are conducted using modern technology and, in particular, using HOLMES 2 – Home Office Large Major Enquiry System 2. HOLMES 3 is being developed.

HOLMES 2 is used to:

- Collect and integrate vast amounts of information and other intelligence data;
- Process and prioritize information to help identify lines of inquiry;
- Manage the allocation and progress of tasks assigned to investigating officers;
- Synthesize otherwise disparate information through graphical representation;
- Produce documentation suitable for presentation in court.

HOLMES 2 has been developed as a single, computer-based information technology application for major investigations that is compatible with the information systems of all the UK police forces. HOLMES 2, as with any computer-based information system, relies on the quality of the data input, which is provided by trained staff who handle the large amounts of data which will be processed in a major inquiry. A typical major investigation produces many statements, intelligence items, descriptive forms, and other documents that require careful processing to ensure vital clues are not overlooked. This mass of information in text form can prove extremely difficult to analyze – the Ripper Inquiry, for example, had over 220,000 statements. HOLMES 2 has sophisticated analytical tools which can cross-reference the documents and create actions for investigators to complete. For example, if a witness statement mentions a blue car with the part registration 575, the system would identify that information as an action to be allocated to an investigator to trace the car. When that action was completed the result would be fed into HOLMES 2 and it would again cross-reference the database – so ensuring no lines of inquiry are left without an action or result. The HOLMES 2 manager can interrogate HOLMES 2 to get a list of incomplete actions for chasing up by investigators. HOLMES 2 has a facility that presents information graphically alongside the original documents, so users can easily identify important information and quickly link together key items.

Every person who is named in the inquiry is given a "nominal number," which is unique and allows that person to be tracked in the system.

Each homicide investigation is different; some, described as "domestic murders," are within the family and the suspect is readily identifiable. The integrity of the investigation and evidence gathering does not change, but they require fewer resources and may not be put onto a HOLMES 2 system. HOLMES 2 requires a sizeable staff of skilled operatives and is therefore used only on complex inquiries.

Whilst in overall command, the SIO will have a team of managers for subcategories of activity: activities emanating from the crime scene, tasks undertaken in the incident room, tasks using HOLMES 2 system (or an equivalent system outside the United Kingdom), house-to-house inquiries, and so on.

As we have seen, intelligence plays a crucial role in criminal investigations and major homicide investigations in particular. Accordingly, there is a need for an intelligence support function, including one relying on the intelligence system of the police service conducting the investigation being appropriately linked to national intelligence systems. Access to the intelligence provided by these interlinked systems may be required by surveillance teams and other specialist groups such as covert operations and search teams. Needless to say, the urgency of such intelligence in murder investigations is greatly heightened by the possibility of further killings.

Consider a scenario in which there have been a number of homicides committed in an area which spreads across three separate police jurisdictions. Suppose that these homicides are believed on the basis of the *modus operandi* to have been committed by one person or are otherwise linked. Suppose further that a witness reports seeing a vehicle near the location of one victim around the time of her death. The witness describes the vehicle as a silver small van and gave a partial registration mark. The SIO will consider the information and may prioritize a line of inquiry in the incident room to identify the vehicle and its owner/users. The inquiry would be created on HOLMES 2, and actions generated for the investigation. Specifically, the intelligence support function would be tasked to interrogate all relevant internal and external databases to identify the vehicle; the national vehicle licensing register being one. Meanwhile a search of data held in the HOLMES 2 system for the other homicides may reveal other sightings of a similar vehicle.

When the target vehicle is identified, its registration mark can be checked against other databases to establish and track any vehicle movements. Such databases include those derived from automatic number plate recognition, court databases for any fixed penalties or motoring offenses, and police service/national intelligence databases for recorded sightings. Where the victim crime scenes have closed-circuit TV systems in their locality, the latter would also be examined for any evidence of the vehicle. The collective information would then be fed into HOLMES 2 to conduct an analysis including cross-referencing with data already held. So a dossier of information will be built up concerning the potential suspect, that is, the vehicle's owner/user.

Today the SIO has access to a number of databases that can be used to help focus major inquiries. The Violent Criminal Apprehension Program (ViCAP) maintains the largest investigative repository of major violent crime cases in the United States and is available to all law enforcement agencies. It is designed to collect and analyze information about homicides, sexual assaults, missing persons, and other violent crimes involving unidentified human remains. Cases fitting these categories can be entered into the system by law enforcement officers and compared to other cases in an attempt to correlate and match possible connections. ViCAP has been a tool in solving many cases, including old cases and across wide geographical areas. ViCAP has been used to identify and track serial killers, where individual crimes may not otherwise have been linked.

In the United Kingdom the Violent and Sex Offender Register (ViSOR) is a database which records persons required to register with the Police under the Sexual Offences Act 2003: persons sentenced for more than 12 months for violent offenses, and persons not convicted but considered to be at risk of offending. Registration includes an annual confirmation of registration by the person attending a designated police station, details of all bank accounts, credit cards, passport details, and any foreign travel regardless of its duration, and registration of any addresses in the United Kingdom where they stay for more than seven days. The ViSOR database holds records of name and address, photographs, risk assessment, modus operandi (MO) of offenders, and an audit trail. It is linked to the prison and probation services and available to all police forces in the United Kingdom.

In the United States and other countries with a large multiplicity of sometimes overlapping jurisdictions, each with their own law enforcement agency, there is often a need for interagency cooperation, both with respect to information sharing, and sharing of expertise and other resources.

Fusion centers were created after 9/11 to address gaps in communication concerning potential criminal and terrorist activity between law enforcement agencies on the local, state and national level. One example comes from Tennessee. Jerri Powell,[2] special agent in charge of the Tennessee Bureau of Investigation (TBI) crime information unit and co-director of the fusion center, who said "the center connects and shares information between about 450 law enforcement agencies in the state. In addition to TBI, the center is staffed by representatives from the FBI, federal and state homeland security, the Bureau of Alcohol, Tobacco, Firearms, and Explosives, state probation and parole, the state correction department and metro Nashville police department. When an officer calls in and needs assistance on locating someone, or getting a piece of information, these analysts will help them," she said. "They will help prepare charts for them to go to court, they will help them with specialized investigative techniques." An instance of this occurred in Nashville, Tennessee[3] where a woman claiming to be an immigration agent called at a house of a mother and four-days-old baby. The phony agent attacked and stabbed the woman before abducting her baby. A joint investigation took place which involved expert facilities being made available to the local investigator, the integration of disparate intelligence gathering processes, and effective dissemination of relevant information to the investigator. Tracking the mother's movements prior to the attack led to the retrieval of CCTV footage that assisted in the identification of a vehicle and the person who had rented it. Subsequent analysis of the suspect's credit card showed her in the vicinity of the offense at the time. The suspect's movements across jurisdictions were tracked and an arrest was made within three days and the baby safely returned to its mother.

As mentioned above, the Yorkshire Ripper investigation was a major investigation of crimes against persons and served to illustrate a number of important facets of such investigations, notably the importance of efficient and effective criminal justice intelligence systems. That investigation is described in 5.2.1 below. The Jeffrey Dahmer case study graphically illustrates the dire consequences of, among other things, investigators failing to heed information provided by members of the public (see 5.2.2 below). The Robert Black case study (see 5.2.3 below) illustrates, among other things, types of evidence gathered by investigators of serious crimes against the person which although they do not include the direct evidence of eyewitness reports, confession or the like might, nevertheless, be sufficiently detailed and logically compelling to justify conviction in some cases.

5.2 Case Studies

Case Study 5.2.1   The Yorkshire Ripper

On the night of October 30th, Peter Sutcliffe struck down Wilma McCann, 26, a part-time prostitute, on a Leeds street with blows from a hammer. He dragged her onto a nearby playing field and, in a post mortem signature behaviour, stabbed her in the chest and

(Continued)

stomach with a Phillips-head screwdriver. This was, perhaps, the first of the 'Yorkshire Ripper' attacks – if one discounts – as the West Yorkshire police inexplicably did – other unsolved attacks including the death from head injuries and stab wounds to the abdomen of another prostitute, Joan Mary Harrison, in the nearby police jurisdiction of Preston on November 20th, 1975. The discovery on January 20th, 1976 of the body of a third mutilated prostitute, Emily Jackson, 42, at Leeds finally convinced the West Yorkshire Police they were dealing with a serial killer.

The McCann and Jackson murders were not – for a period of three years – connected with a series of other 1975–6 attacks on women in the West Yorkshire police jurisdiction.[4] On July 5th, 1975 at Keighley, Anna Rogulskyj, 36, was attacked; on August 15th at Halifax, Olive Smelt, 46, was attacked. Both women survived after extensive surgery. On May 9th, 1976 at Leeds, intellectually-challenged Marcella Claxton, 20, was attacked; her screams drove her attacker off. Then the attacks ceased.

There was a gap of 11 months between the Emily Jackson killing and the February 6th, 1977 murder of prostitute Irene Richardson, 28, at Leeds. On April 23rd, 1977, the body of prostitute Patricia 'Tina' Atkinson, 32, was discovered in her flat at Bradford, her body bearing the Yorkshire Ripper's signature mutilations. On June 25th, a shopgirl, Jane MacDonald, 16, was murdered at Leeds. On July 27th, an intoxicated Maureen Long, 30, accepted a lift in the cruising Peter Sutcliffe's car. Left for dead on wasteland, she survived with head and abdominal injuries.

On October 1st, 1977, Sutcliffe drove to Manchester to pick up prostitute Jean Jordan, 20, driving her to the Southern Cemetery where he killed her, then dragged her into the bushes. He was scared off and left a new five-pound note in the deceased's possession. Aware that the note, a part of his salary, could be traced from the bank, he returned to the scene eight days later; Jordan's body lay undiscovered in the bushes where he had left it, but Sutcliffe could not locate the note. Sutcliffe then mutilated Jordan's body with broken glass found near the scene. Jordan's body was finally discovered, and Sutcliffe's five-pound was also found.

Sutcliffe Interviewed

Police traced the note to a bank at Shipley, near Leeds. Thought to be part of a firm's payroll, about 5000 employees in nearby factories were interviewed by police:

Amongst the workers who were interviewed [twice] was a 31-year-old lorry driver named Peter Sutcliff, who worked at T. & W. Clark (Holdings) Ltd., and lived in a small detached house in Bradford . . . his wife Sonia was able to provide him with an alibi. The police apologized and left, and the Yorkshire Ripper was to go on murdering for three more years.[5]

On December 14th at Leeds, prostitute Marilyn Moore entered Sutcliffe's car. He struck her with a heavy metal object, fracturing her skull, but then drove off. She too survived surgery. On January 21st, 1978, Sutcliffe killed prostitute Yvonne Person at Bradford – her body was not discovered for two months. On January 31st at Huddersfield, Sutcliffe killed prostitute Helen Rytka, 18; she was the only victim with whom Sutcliffe is known to have had sexual intercourse.

After this, minimally the eighth Ripper murder, the West Yorkshire Police offered a cash reward for information leading to the killer's conviction, the Home Office having rejected a prior request by the Police Authority. The £10,000 reward was more than doubled by the *Yorkshire Post,* the *Yorkshire Evening Post,* and by public subscription.

On May 16th at Manchester, Sutcliffe killed prostitute Vera Millward, 41, the last prostitute victim of the Yorkshire Ripper. Much has been made of Sutcliffe's supposed compulsive hatred of prostitutes – it was a notion that Sutcliffe also promoted after his arrest,[6] part of an attempt to establish a defense of diminished responsibility. The reality is that Sutcliffe had already attacked 'straight' women and girls – and would do so again; none of his future attacks would be on prostitutes. Sutcliffe's attacks on prostitutes were directly explainable in terms of economic need, ensuring their availability at street level in the red-light districts, their willingness to enter his vehicle, and their preparedness to accompany him to private places. Sutcliffe simply victimized the most vulnerable women in society.

At that time, there were estimated to be 400 prostitutes working in Manchester, and about 200 in the Bradford, Huddersfield, and Leeds red-light districts. There was a movement of prostitutes from town to town encouraged by the 'moral enthusiasm'[7] of Chief Constable James Anderton of the Greater Manchester Police. Police tactics, alienating this element of society, are difficult to follow:

(*Continued*)

. . . illustrated by the statement made at the inquest into the death of the fourth Leeds murder victim, Chief Superintendent Hobson, head of the Leeds CID, told the inquest that in an effort to reduce prostitution in the Chapeltown area [of Leeds] in the twelve months prior to December 1978, 152 women had been arrested or re-arrested for, or reported for, prostitution, and a further 68 had been cautioned. These women were obviously drawn from the very section of the community of the greatest potential value as witnesses to the murders.[8]

Police activities seemed more directed to the highly visible suppression of prostitution than upon the apprehension of the murderer of prostitutes. After an absence of 11 months, Sutcliffe murdered clerk Josephine Whittaker, 19, at Halifax.

Parochialism

George Oldfield, Assistant Chief Constable of the West Yorkshire Police, had assumed overall command of the investigation following the June 25th, 1977 murder of 'respectable' 16 year-old Jane MacDonald.[9] Field command devolved upon Detective Superintendent Richard Holland, head of the 'Ripper Squad.' By early 1979, their lack of success became increasingly the subject of media comment; Nicola Tyler, writing in the London *Evening News* had this to say: 'Why don't they call in Scotland Yard? Many people feel if the police were on the ball, they would have caught him by now.'[10] London's Metropolitan Police CID – Scotland Yard – can respond to such requests for assistance from a provincial police force. Ronald Gregory, Chief Constable of the West Yorkshire Police, stated:

> There is no way I would call in Scotland Yard in this case. This is not to decry the Metropolitan Police in any way, because they are a very good force indeed. But a force the size of West Yorkshire [5000 men] has as much and probably more experience than Scotland Yard officers would have if they came to help. When I mentioned the notion of bringing in the 'Met' to Detective Superintendent Dick Holland, head of the Ripper Squad, he said it was a thoroughly insulting suggestion.[11]

An explanation for West Yorkshire's attitude was offered by the neighbouring Lancashire's Chief Constable, Albert Laugharne:

> Aid sought by a small force from a larger is a situation which, despite increasingly major incidents, may still be done somewhat reluctantly. It is done less often than ideally it ought to be, if the Chief Constable feels he thereby throws doubt on his self-sufficiency.[12]

Greater folly was yet to come; on June 26th, 1979, Oldfield held a bizarre conference at Wakefield, attended by media, and executives from West Yorkshire, Northumbria, Lancashire, and Manchester Police Forces. He revealed that a tape and letters, believed to be genuine, had been received from the Yorkshire Ripper. The letters were in fact a hoax:

> The 'I'm Jack' hoax letters and tape caused a great deal of confusion and time-wasting on the investigation. The tape that taunted and haunted the Ripper Squad arrived in the post at the West Yorkshire Police HQ on June 18th, 1979. It was immediately linked with three letters that came in during the previous three months. ACC George Oldfield and his boss, Ronald Gregory, weighed the evidence – and decided it was genuine. . . .[13]

> A man with a 'Geordie' accent taunted George Oldfield, the officer in charge of the case; these later proved to be false leads. The cassette caused police to direct enormous efforts to the Wearside area, and increased the murderer's sense of invulnerability.[14]

The hoaxer utterly destabilized the police investigation – and whilst police combed the Sunderland area for a supposed 'Geordie' Ripper, Yorkshireman Peter Sutcliffe killed student Barbara Leach, 20, at Halifax, on April 4th, 1979. Oldfield was ill and exhausted by the end of the 1979 summer. 'Project R', a massive and costly advertising campaign to solicit the public's assistance in identifying the spurious murderous Geordie, got underway without him.[15]

The Home Secretary intervened in 1980 to set up an advisory body of scientists and police under Scotland Yard's Commander Ron Harvey. They doubted the authenticity of the hoax letters and tape. Their computer model determined the 'centre of gravity' – or centre-point of the spread of West Riding crimes – to be North Bradford; the Ripper's home would be in the suburbs of Manningham or Shipley. The West Yorkshire Police were advised they would find that the offender lived in that area. Close enough – Sutcliffe lived in Heaton, a North Bradford suburb between Manningham and Shipley.[16]

On August 18th, 1980, Sutcliffe murdered clerk Marguerite Walls at Leeds, varying his *modus operandi* by strangling her with a rope. In October that year, he attacked Dr. Upadya Bananadra, 34, at Headingley, and in November, student Theresa Sykes, 19, at

(Continued)

Huddersfield; both survived. On November 17th, Sutcliffe murdered his last victim, student Jacqueline Hill, at Bradford.

Arrested

Peter Sutcliffe's January 2nd, 1981 arrest by Sheffield Police was prosaic and had nothing to do with detective work. Sutcliffe had picked up a prostitute Olive Reivers. Patrolling, Sergeant Bob Ring and PC Robert Hyde became suspicious of the number-plate on Sutcliffe's parked car. When spoken to, Sutcliffe gave police a false name. A radio check revealed the number-plate on Sutcliffe's car had been stolen from another vehicle. The unknowing police took the Yorkshire Ripper into custody.[17]

Sutcliffe then used the oldest trick in the book, asking to be allowed to relieve himself. The arresting police bought it, and moving with mock-modesty to bushes nearby, Sutcliffe deftly disposed of the hammer and screwdriver. Taken to Hammerton Road Police Station, he again used the ploy of asking to relieve himself and disposed of his knife in the cistern. A length of clothesline, however, was found in his pockets. In response to the West Yorkshire Police's request that they be advised of all men discovered in the company of prostitutes, the Sheffield officers contacted their West Yorkshire colleagues and advised them. The West Yorkshire Police thought they might like to interview Sheffield's prisoner. He was obligingly driven to Dewsbury police station the following day to be interviewed by the Ripper Squad. News of the impending interview with the Ripper Squad rang alarm bells in the minds of the Sheffield police officers; they hastened to the scene of their arrest of the suspect, and with more luck than they were entitled to, they recovered the Ripper's hammer and screwdriver from the bushes where he had relieved himself. A search of the toilet used by Sutcliffe at Hammerton Road police station located his knife concealed in the cistern. Confronted with this evidence, Sutcliffe admitted that he was the Yorkshire Ripper. Tried, he was convicted of 13 counts of murder and seven counts of attempted murder.

(Extract from a case study written by John Blackler in John Blackler and Seumas Miller (2000b) *Police Ethics (vol. 2): Case Studies for Police Investigators*, Wagga Wagga: Charles Sturt University and NSW Police Service, pp. 41–46.)

Case Study 5.2.2 Jeffrey Dahmer and Police
Discriminatory Behavior

Jeffrey Dahmer was white, 31 years old, and in steady employment.
He had served 10 months imprisonment for sexually abusing a male
child, and was currently on probation. He was also a sexual deviate,
child molester, and as later police investigations were to shockingly
reveal, a sadistic serial killer.

On 27 May 1991, Dahmer had lured 14 years old Laotian, Konerak
Sinthasomphone to his Milwaukee apartment. Dahmer had offered
the youngster money, if he would pose whilst Dahmer took photographs. In the apartment, Dahmer drugged the child, grossly sexually
abused him and sadistically subjected him to torture. Dahmer left the
apartment in the early hours of the morning to buy beer and, whilst
he was absent, the still disoriented Sinthasomphone escaped from the
apartment, running naked into the street.

Distressed, drugged, naked, bleeding from his rectum, the obviously brutalized boy's plight attracted the attention of two young,
African-American women, Sandra Smith and Nichole Childress. They
went to his assistance and waiting with him, called the 911 emergency
operator from a nearby public telephone, within a block of Dahmer's
apartment. The 911 operator dispatched both police and paramedics
to the scene.

In a nightmare scene, Dahmer had meanwhile returned; Smith and
Childress, convinced that Dahmer had brutalized the child, prevented
attempts by Dahmer to remove his victim from the scene,
Sinthasomphone clung to them, until the police arrived. What next
happened almost beggars belief: 'Sinthasomphone's distressed state
was sufficient to alarm the witnesses, but the officers – for whatever
reason – told paramedics they were not needed and dismissed them.
Despite having medical personnel available at the scene, police failed
to request even a quick check of the child to ensure he was not physically injured.

Apparently intent on handling the matter as they saw fit, MPD
officers refused to listen to information that bystanders were attempting to convey. Childress, Smith and others tried to tell officers that
Sinthasomphone was a juvenile, that they believed he was trying
desperately to escape from Dahmer, and that Dahmer had referred to
Sinthasomphone using several different names – signifying that the

(*Continued*)

two were neither friends, lovers nor close associates. Bystanders also attempted to tell the officers that Sinthasomphone was under the influence of drugs or alcohol, and that he had been assaulted and sexually abused. Witnesses later recounted that during the entire time MPD officers were at the scene, the child seemed to be fearful of Dahmer. In response, the police allegedly threatened to arrest Childress and Smith if they persisted in trying to provide them with information or if they continued to request that the police further investigate the incident. Police also threatened Smith and Childress with arrest if they tried to intervene to help the boy.'[18]

It was later alleged that Dahmer informed the Milwaukee police that Sinthasomephone was an adult, and that he and Dahmer were homosexual lovers and were having a tiff. The police accepted Dahmer's story and without inquiring further or seeking to know what the child's wishes were in the matter, actually delivered Sinthasomphone back to Dahmer's small apartment, then departed. The MPD officers apparently detected nothing amiss – Dahmer had killed and dismembered a child in the apartment only two days prior.

The door had scarcely shut on the departing MPD when Dahmer strangled Sinthasomphone to death and sodomized his body. He was probably dismembering the child's body, taking photographs as he went, when Mrs. Glenda Cleveland, a concerned citizen who had witnessed the scene in the street, telephoned the Milwaukee police to express her concern for the child's safety. She was assured by police that Sinthasomphone was in fact an adult, and that the matter was 'under control'. The police involved appeared to be convinced that what they had seen was nothing more than a homosexual lovers' tiff.

Back at District Three station house, the three policemen made their second mistake of the evening – they joked about the homosexual quarrel they had just broken up. But a tape recorder happened to be switched on, and when Dahmer was arrested two months later, and admitted to killing the Laotian boy, the tape was located and played on radio and television.

The story caused universal uproar. On 26 July, four days after Dahmer's arrest, the three policemen were suspended from duty with pay. Later, administrative charges were filed against them, but finally dismissed. Public anger was now transferred from Jeffrey Dahmer to the police department. Police chief Philip Arreola found himself assailed on all sides, subjected to harsh criticism from his own force for not supporting his own men (in the following month the Milwaukee Police Association passed a vote of no confidence in him), and from Milwaukee's blacks and Asians for racism.[19]

On their return to the police station, the Dahmer–Sinthasomphone incident had became the subject for ribald humour – but how police could so seriously have misread the episode remained a mystery. A number of explanations have since been advanced to account for the outrageous actions of the police, most located about a generalised MPD prejudice against minority groups such as homosexuals.

On 22 July 1991, a distraught young man, Tracey Edwards, attracted the attention of a cruising MPD police patrol vehicle. Handcuffs dangled from Edwards' wrist as he informed police that he had been held captive and attacked in Jeffrey Dahmer's apartment; he told police that Dahmer confessed that the plastic bags of human "meat" in the freezer were intended to be eaten. The threat to eat the heart of Tracey Edwards – the latest intended victim – had been no idle bluff.'[20]

Since their colleagues had returned Sinthasomphone to this apartment to be murdered, two months earlier, serial killer Dahmer had been needlessly at large. Making good use of his reprieve, Dahmer had sexually abused, tortured, murdered and dismembered another four young men.

(Extract from a case study written by John Blackler in John Blackler and Seumas Miller (2000b) *Police Ethics (vol. 2): Case Studies for Police Investigators*, Wagga Wagga: Charles Sturt University and NSW Police Service, pp. 60–63)

Case Study 5.2.3   Robert Black

In July 1990 a 6-year-old girl, Mandy Wilson, was abducted as she walked in her street in Stow (Scottish Borders). By a stroke of immense good fortune, a neighbor saw her walk towards a parked white van and he could see her feet under the open passenger door beside those of a man. The girl's feet vanished, the van drove off; the witness took the registration number and immediately called the police. The witness was describing the event to the girl's father (a police officer) when the van reappeared and was immediately stopped by the police. The father found his daughter bound, gagged, and stuffed in a sleeping bag behind the driver's seat. She was terrified and had already been sexually assaulted. Later medical evidence intimated the child would

(Continued)

likely have died within the hour due to the circumstances of her confinement.

The driver of the van was Robert Black, a delivery driver who traveled throughout the United Kingdom including Northern Ireland. Black appeared before the High Court in Scotland when, due to the circumstances of his arrest, he pleaded guilty and was sentenced to life imprisonment.

Black now became the main suspect for three previous cases, the murders of Susan Maxwell, Caroline Hogg, and Sarah Harper, there being evident similarity between the cases in terms of MO (modus operandi) and other factors; Black, however, declined to speak about the abductions and murders of the three girls. The Enquiry Team began a thorough and scrupulous examination of Black's movements and lifestyle between 1982 and 1990, where a key focus was on his job as a delivery driver. Using work records, including wage records and fuel receipts, they built up a picture of his movements and were able to place him in the vicinity of each abduction at the appropriate time and also where the bodies had been found – all in the Midlands of England. The Team also discovered an attempted abduction of a 15-year-old girl, which had failed because she had fought back and a friend had gone to her assistance. The witnesses' descriptions of the assailant were an exact match to Black.

There was no forensic evidence and no admission by Black – the case was built on the above-described circumstantial evidence linking the various murders to one another and to Black – but in April 1992 the Crown Prosecution Service elected to prosecute.

This was a unique case in UK criminal law. The defense argued there was no direct evidence to establish that Black had committed the offenses and argued that each murder should be treated separately. But the court allowed the murders to be presented as a series and allowed evidence from the earlier case relating to the abduction of Mandy Wilson and the attempted abduction of the 15-year-old. Black appeared at Newcastle upon Tyne Crown Court in April 1994, when the prosecution detailed the striking similarities between the murder cases and also the attempted abduction and the actual abduction of Mandy Wilson. The series of murders exhibited a common MO followed by Black, and Black was linked to each of them in terms of his movements.

Black was convicted of all the charges before the court and sentenced to life imprisonment on each one; there was a minimum term of 35 years recommended for each of the murders.

In October 2011 Black was further convicted of the abduction and murder in 1981, in County Down, Northern Ireland, of Jennifer Cardy, aged 9 years. This offense also relied on painstaking investigation of Black's work records and included testimony from Detective Chief Superintendent (retired) Roger Orr, SIO in the Mandy Wilson abduction, where he described Black's actions in that offense and in the Maxwell/Hogg/Harper murders. The prosecution alleged the evidence given by Mr Orr amounted to "a signature for Robert Black and that the case of Jennifer also bears that signature." It is strongly believed that Black may be responsible for a further twelve abduction and murders of young girls, in the United Kingdom, France and Holland. To date he has declined to assist any police enquiry.[21]

5.3 Moral Rights of Suspects and Moral Rights of Victims

When a potential suspect comes to the notice of the investigation team (as in the vehicle scenario above) but without any tangible evidence to approach or question that suspect, then the SIO has to decide on what action to take. As described above in the Granny Killer case study (Case Study 1.2.1 in Chapter 1), in 1989 in Sydney, Australia following a series of murders of elderly women, a potential suspect, John Glover, was identified, but the lack of substantive evidence prevented the police from approaching him for interview. Instead a covert surveillance operation was mounted.

Suspects – people who are only suspected of having committed a crime, but who have not been tried and found guilty – have not lost any of their moral rights, although some of them might be curtailed for limited periods, for example, a temporary loss of freedom when arrested. Naturally, under certain conditions, including reasonable grounds for suspicion of having committed a crime, suspects may legitimately be the objects of scrutiny by the police. Under further conditions, including the provision of actual evidence, suspects may have moral obligations to allow themselves to be subjected to the judgment of the courts to determine their guilt or innocence. But, prior to conviction for an offense , the moral rights of suspects are fundamentally the same as for ordinary citizens who are not suspects.

Suspects have a moral right to life, a right not to be tortured, a right to privacy etc. They have these rights simply by virtue of being human beings. However, there is a difference in the moral importance of these human rights. The right to privacy is not as important a moral right as the right to life; hence the moral acceptability of surveilling Glover.

Of course, as we have seen, the police and the criminal justice system do not simply exist to protect the rights of suspects. They exist to protect the rights of victims, who include not only the person who has been the direct target of the criminal act but also such others as members of that person's family and his or her friends, as well as those who may be terrorized by the crime and feel constrained in their activities (consider the impact of the activities of the Yorkshire Ripper, detailed in the case study above). They also exist to ensure that punishment is administered to offenders. Accordingly, if a suspect is known by the police to be guilty of a serious crime, then the police are obliged to do their utmost to apprehend the suspect and provide sufficient evidence for a successful prosecution.

However, there is, inevitably, a certain tension between these two moral requirements of the police – the requirement to respect the rights of suspects (including the duty to make available evidence that may assist a suspect) and the requirement to apprehend, and provide evidence to ensure the conviction of, offenders.

Consider an offender such as the aforementioned Yorkshire Ripper. Such a person constitutes an enormous threat to innocent people. If the police know the person is guilty, then is it necessarily morally wrong in this particular case to "knock this person around" a little or deceive them in the course of interrogation in order to guarantee a conviction and remove this threat? Part of the problem here is that police can think that they know suspects are guilty when in fact they are not. (For further discussion of ethical issues in interviews see Chapter 12.)

The need to balance the rights of suspects and those of victims is further exemplified by the case study (in Chapter 1) concerning the investigation of "Granny Killer," John Glover. As the discussion in Chapter 2 demonstrated, the proper moral ends of investigators can come into conflict. On the one hand, it was important to ensure that Glover was apprehended and convicted. Once suspected offenders are aware they are being surveilled, they may cease to commit any crimes and evidence for a conviction may never be forthcoming. On the other hand, as the Granny Killer episode demonstrated, too great a concentration on securing a conviction can put the lives of innocent people at risk.

In complex inquiries the SIO may require access to highly specialized teams who may be tasked for covert investigation of potential suspects. Whilst the SIO may set the tasks required through HOLMES 2, the confidential unit in the force will handle the authorization processes for such action. It is preferable for a sterile corridor to be in place between the inquiry team and covert operations in order to minimize disclosure of identities of undercover officers or informants.[22]

If, for example, the suspect for a homicide is in a "hard to reach" group such as a criminal gang, the SIO may wish to use covert means of gathering evidence against that suspect. This could be done by telephone interception of the suspect's phone or using an informant who is trusted within that group. The process for using informants and undercover operatives is detailed in Chapters 9 and 11, as are the various moral problems that their use gives rise to, notably their safety.[23]

Full details of the use of the informant and/or undercover operatives and their purpose should be recorded. Undercover operatives ought to be managed and controlled by officers outside the homicide investigation team. The intelligence gleaned would be managed and disseminated to the SIO from the specialist unit controlling the operative.

The use of undercover operatives, including surveillance teams, is expensive and in constant demand within large police services. The SIO will not have limitless resources for the inquiry and he or she will have to conform to their budget. Whilst every murder is a serious crime, the very nature of some – for example, multiple deaths, cross-border cases, cases involving children, and high-profile cases – will all bring different demands on the budget. The priority is to detect the crime and safeguard the public, but cost is an ever-present reality for the SIO. Whether to pursue a line of inquiry or not is a policy decision to be recorded. For example, full-time surveillance on a suspect may be the ideal option but the circumstances at the time, including cost, may not permit that option. This decision may be challenged in any later review but its recorded presence with reasons is a degree of protection. The SIO will have a number of hard decisions to make during the course of their investigation.[24]

The issue of resource constraints has recently come to the fore due to the reduction in police budgets in most areas of Europe, Australasia (perhaps less so), and the United States. The world global recession has "hit" many public service budgets, not least, that of the police.

A dilemma arises when there is a perceived requirement to reinvestigate a historic crime, which might be murder, serial rape, or alleged criminal acts committed by public officials or politicians. Where new evidence comes to light or crime scene exhibits lend themselves to advances in forensic technology (DNA, for example), then the costs of reinvestigation are justified. But, in this context of a reduction in resources, tensions arise when either politicians or lobby groups press for exhaustive reinvestigations against a background of little or no new evidence, or investigative "leads." Those tensions become acute when any section of the media adopts a campaigning role on behalf of one pressure group or another.

The police are entitled to take a long hard look at "value for money" considerations, the impact on contracting police budgets,[25] and so question if the likely outcome will justify what can be heavy expenditure over one, two years and more. Within this there are ethical, moral, practical, and financial dilemmas, made more acute if local community pressure is present.

Pressure for reopening an investigation (which might have been "closed" 10 or 15 years previously) is easy to support, but those supporting "the cause" do not have responsibility for dividing up the police financial cake, and resources applied to investigation "A" are not available for investigations "B," "C," or "D." Perhaps the answer to the dilemma when police say "No" to further investigations is for police to ensure transparency with respect to the reasons for their decision and to show courage in the face of political or media pressure. This in turn presupposes a degree of police independence of government, an issue discussed above in Chapter 4.

The investigation of serious offenses in general, and not just of murders, follows the model described above and will be intelligence-led. Unlike homicide inquiries, in other serious offenses against the person, the victim may be able to give an account of what has taken place although the trauma experienced, and fear, may impact on the level of cooperation with the investigator. This is known to occur in sexual offenses and, in particular, rape. Consequently, some police officers are specially trained to investigate cases involving vulnerable victims.

There is a moral obligation on the part of police officers and others to provide appropriate care for vulnerable victims such as rape victims. Accordingly, when a rape is reported it ought to be standard practice for the medical and forensic examination of the victim to be conducted in a purpose-built and secure rape suite, located elsewhere than in a police station. Specialist officers should undertake the interview of the victim, and it should be video-recorded; this allows later use in court proceedings where it may be too traumatic for the victim, for example, a child, to appear in person and give evidence. Officers ought to conduct early assessments to determine whether victims require special measures (protection, counseling, specialist medical treatment) and, where necessary, that early special measures meetings take place.

The investigation of rape generally involves a team of specialist officers with assistance from outside agencies, for example; specialist medical provision, social services, and rape counselors.

The investigating officer may want to involve the case prosecutor at the case-building stage to address issues around evidence and disclosure. Scrupulous care should be taken to avoid any cross contamination when gathering forensic evidence, especially when detaining a suspect; the victim may know the offender or be in a personal relationship. The investigation will consider all evidential sources and not be focused solely on the victim's statement. Evidential DNA samples can be cross-matched with samples held by the national databases.

Physical protection for the victim and their identity is an essential process in the investigation. The detention of a suspect for rape can attract media attention and increase the risk of victim identification. To protect the victim, it is important that the investigating officer has a strategy to deal with the media.

As already noted, in Chapter 12 we discuss the ethical issues arising from interviewing. Here we simply note that interviewing rape victims can be extremely difficult, given the high levels of trauma of the victim. As far as the suspect is concerned, evidence of bad character in rape cases is of particular importance, and evidence of bad character should be researched during the planning stages of the suspect interview.

The question of consent on the part of a victim of rape is a fundamental factor. The investigating officer will address issues of consent during the suspect interview. In the United Kingdom A is only guilty of the rape of B if: A acts intentionally; B does not consent to the act; *and* A does not reasonably believe that B consents. Deciding whether a belief is reasonable is to be determined having regard to all the circumstances, including any steps that A has taken to ascertain whether B consents. A will not have a reasonable belief in consent if A knows or believes that B has not consented or A is reckless, that is, does not care or is indifferent to whether or not B has consented.[26]

There is a legal and moral issue here as to whether or not the defense of a genuine though unreasonable mistaken belief that the victim consented ought to be allowed. If not, then A has the responsibility to ensure that B consents to the sexual activity at the time in question or, at least, that someone in A's position would reasonably believe that B had consented. It is, therefore, important for the police to ask A in interview what steps A took to satisfy themself that B had consented.

5.4 DNA and Forensics

DNA has proved to be a powerful tool in criminal investigations and there are now national databases in many countries around the world. Access to databases needs to be strictly controlled and police forces ought not to have direct access to data. This is partly an issue of privacy: the right to privacy of citizens with respect to their personal information (see Chapter 10). It is also, in part, a matter of ensuring the objectivity of DNA matching – and public confidence in this objectivity. This need for objectivity entails that the database authority be an independent body – including independent of law enforcement agencies and of government (see Chapter 4) – that informs police of matches. It is also desirable, and in many cases possible, to have a search conducted if there is reason to believe that DNA from a crime scene may belong to an offender who is from another country.

The right to privacy of those convicted of a serious crime is overridden by the rights of those threatened by the perpetrators of serious crimes;

accordingly, retention of the DNA profile of convicted murderers, rapists, and the like is evidently justified. Matters are less clear in the case of those convicted of minor crimes and those who are charged with a crime, serious or otherwise, but not convicted.

There are different practices in different jurisdictions. In England, for example, it had been the practice to retain the DNA profile of any person charged with a crime on the National DNA Database (NDNAD) even though they were not convicted of the offense.[27] There was a provision, however, where such a person could apply to the court for the profile to be removed. In Scotland, whilst the same rules apply to taking a DNA sample, the Scottish DNA database only retains profiles where the offender has been convicted or is likely to pose a significant threat to the public.

Arguably, the English option could lead to a significant number of murders, rapes, and serious assaults being detected by "cold case analysis" – where forensic samples from old cases (pre-DNA) have been examined for DNA trace and found to match with those on the database where the culprit does not have a conviction, only an arrest on suspicion of a crime.

On December 4, 2008 the European Court of Human Rights (ECHR) delivered its judgment in the case of S and Marper. They found the blanket policy in England and Wales of retaining indefinitely the DNA and finger-prints of those innocent of an offense was in breach of article 8 of the European Convention on Human Rights. The Protection of Freedoms Act 2012 has now modified the English model of DNA retention to restrict the scope of the DNA database and to give added protection to innocent people whose DNA has been retained. Once a person is arrested, even though not yet convicted, the Act allows him or her to be fingerprinted and a sample of his or her DNA to be taken. The fingerprints and DNA profile are then cross-matched with fingerprints and DNA samples stored in crime data-bases to check whether the arrested person is implicated in any of these crimes. If there is no match or an acquital, then the arrested person's DNA profile and fingerprints are deleted.

The DNA database has a volunteer section which houses profiles from mass screening of individuals. This is generally linked to a serious crime where every person living or visiting the area at the time of the crime is asked to give a DNA sample for elimination purposes – but it will also catch the offender if they give a sample. Equally, it can give rise to more scrutiny being given to those who refuse.

There is also a section of the database for police officers to volunteer a sample when they join a police force: to be used as elimination at subse-quent crime scenes where they may attend to investigate and leave a trace. Some police forces require this sample to be mandatory if the officer or staff member wishes to be a crime-scene examiner or the officer applies to be an investigator.

Forensic and other scientists can be useful sources of information and expertise for criminal investigators. Even if a forensic examination has not revealed evidence that could go before a court, nevertheless, the scientist may offer an opinion as to what has happened. This may lead to a positive line of inquiry and, for example, justify putting a suspect under covert investigation.

An important conceptual issue that has arisen in relation to the use of DNA as evidence is the degree of evidential weight that ought to attach to it. Sometimes claims like the following are made: "John Doe must be the murderer since the chances of John Doe not being the murderer are a million to one against because there is a DNA match between his blood and a blood sample found on the victim and the chances of someone else having the same DNA profile as John Doe are a million to one against." Here it is important, first, not to confuse the probability of someone else having the same DNA profile as John Doe with the probability that John Doe is the murderer; these are not the same thing. This being so, we need, second, to identify other evidential considerations in play, including ones to which probabilities might be assigned. There are a number of these, each of which introduces a degree of uncertainty (sometimes minor, sometimes major depending on the particular case) but which cumulatively greatly reduce the "million to one against" argument and might in some cases reduce the evidential weight in favor of the suspect being the offender to the point at which it does not reach the "beyond reasonable doubt" threshold. These considerations include the following:

1. There is a degree of uncertainty with respect to whether John Doe's blood got on the victim as a result of some innocent encounter or otherwise than as a result of him attacking the victim.
2. There is a degree of uncertainty with respect to the source of the two blood samples actually matched. Was, for example, the blood sample at the scene of the crime actually transported without incident and matched with John Doe's or was there a mix-up (given the thousands of such samples being taken, transported, and tested) – as has in fact happened in some jurisdictions.
3. There is a degree of uncertainty with respect to the matching of DNA samples; the certainty of the matching process is itself a matter of degree, for example, as a consequence of degraded samples.
4. There are important evidential considerations in play other than the DNA match which have to be given some weight and, as such, reduce the relative evidential weight to be attached to the DNA match. For example, did the suspect have a motive or an alibi? Is there another suspect with motive, opportunity, ability, and so on?

5. Statisticians have argued that in cases involving DNA evidence there is a need to take into account countervailing probabilities that the suspect is not in fact the offender, notably prior probabilities with respect to the size of the population of those persons who could have committed the crime.[28] If we assume that there are only 100,000 (including John Doe) who could have committed the crime because, say, it was committed on an isolated island in the middle of the ocean with 100,000 able-bodied adult inhabitants any one of whom had the opportunity and ability to commit the crime then, arguably, the initial statistical probability of it being John Doe is 100,000 to one against and this statistical improbability needs to be set against the million to one against his DNA being identical with someone else's (a consideration in favor of his being the murderer). The result is one million divided by 100,000, which gives the statistical likelihood (given only these two considerations) of his not being the murderer being reduced from one million to one against to ten to one against.

5.5   Profiling

Profiling of potential suspects for serious crimes has been the subject of extensive research in the United States, Europe, and Australia. Offender profiling involves making inferences from characteristics of offenses to characteristics of offenders, and thereby identifying the perpetrator of a particular crime or set of crimes. Of course, in a general sense, police investigators have always been engaged in this kind of inference making. However, contemporary criminology has sought to use a range of research methods and theories to enhance traditional police practice, including statistical analysis and psychological and psychoanalytic theory.

Many police services have access to crime analysts and specialist police staff who analyze crime according to specific criteria, for example, modus operandi, behavior exhibited by offender, and links to other crimes and offenders. Moreover, there are academics researching serious crime who make their findings available to police investigators.

The crimes that have involved the use of profiling have historically mainly been rape and serious sexual assaults and motiveless or sexually motivated murder cases. However, profiling is not restricted to these crimes.

This process is greatly facilitated by databases of offenders (rapists, pedophiles, etc.) and their modus operandi and psychological/behavioral profiles. Here, as elsewhere, the integration or linking of databases in different jurisdictions is also helpful.

Profiling has two main types. The first type involves developing a profile or set of characteristics of a category of persons, for instance, a typical police officer at risk of corruption, based on generalizations from the past behavior of persons belonging to this category. So a set of characteristics might be developed including such things as numbers of complaints, associating with known criminals, gambling habits, substance abuse, financial problems, and operating in a high-risk area such as drug law enforcement, and consolidated so as to constitute the profile of a typical police officer engaged in corruption. Once the profile is constructed, the internal affairs investigators can, at least in theory, monitor individuals with that profile in their preventative anti-corruption strategies.

The second type involves developing a profile or set of characteristics of a particular person known to have committed a crime but whose identity is unknown, for instance, the serial rapist who raped Mary, Betty, and Jane. The profile is based on generalizations from the modus operandi, past behavior, and so on of this person and/or like persons. Once the profile is constructed the police, say, can look for the particular person that fits the profile for the purpose of solving the crime(s) in question.

An important conceptual issue that arises at this point is the extent to which the construction of such profiles in the case of profiles of individuals, as opposed to categories of persons, needs to rely on evidence which is not simply generated by processes of generalization. Frederick Schauer in his influential book on the subject[29] downplays direct and apparently highly particular, nonstatistical, evidence-producing processes such as eyewitness accounts, arguing that they are both less reliable than statistical generalization, and in any case dependent on, and in part constituted by, processes of generalization.[30]

Here Schauer relies implicitly on two controversial philosophical standpoints, namely the Humean regularity theory of causation and indirect realism in relation to the external world.

According to the Scottish philosopher David Hume, causal relations between events are nothing more than constant conjunctions of events and, more specifically, there are no such things as a particular relation of causal necessity between two events or between a causal agent and the effect the agent produces. It follows that – *contra* common sense – a human agent cannot be directly aware of causing some outcome, such as the experience of effort and resistance that arises when one pushes a car uphill. Let us call the anti-Humean and commonsensical view "causal particularism." According to the regularity theory, but not causal particularism, to offer a causal explanation of some event is just to bring it under some generalization or set of generalizations. According to causal particularism – as we are defining this term – causal relations are particular relations of necessity and are, at least in some cases, able to be directly perceived.[31]

As we have seen, Schauer's view comprises the Humean regularity theory of causation and the view that causal relations cannot be directly perceived.

The latter is a species of what is referred to as indirect realism. We need to briefly discuss indirect realism, given that it has implications for the nature and reliability of important forms of evidence in criminal investigations, notably eyewitness accounts (as mentioned earlier).

According to indirect realism, and apparently to Schauer, we do not directly see, touch, or otherwise directly perceive the external world; rather we infer its existence from what we do directly "perceive," namely our sense data. Here it is important to note that direct realism is consistent with epistemological error, such as seeing a straight stick as bent in a glass of water. According to the direct realist, we can and do make perceptual errors; but the point is that in a normal setting when we get it right we do really and directly perceive the object (and not simply our own mental states produced by the object). So, for the direct realist, some observations are direct and thus in an important sense noninferential, whereas for Schauer – and all indirect realists – all observations are necessarily inferential. However, indirect realism is a controversial philosophical theory and one that Schauer, in particular, has not given us sufficient reason to accept.

In summation: the Humean regularity theory and its theoretical bed-fellow, indirect realism, are both highly controversial and are not, therefore, necessarily to be preferred to causal particularism and direct realism – the latter duo providing, at least in principle, stronger theoretical backing for the reliability of eyewitness reports and knowledge-by-acquaintance more generally (see Chapter 2 for an account of knowledge-by-acquaintance).

Recent developments in communications and information technology, including the creation and integration of large databases, and high-speed, long-distance accessing and communication of content, for instance, via the Internet, have enormously facilitated profiling in both its main forms.

However, the existence and possibility of widespread profiling has raised a host of ethical problems, including in relation to privacy and personal identity. These concerns mainly pertain to profiling in our first sense, that is, where a crime has not been committed. For example, in the case of police officers who are not known to have committed any crime, what is the justification for monitoring their behavior – other than for ordinary work performance purposes? Are police any different from ordinary citizens in this regard? We presumably would not accept profiling in this sense for the purposes of monitoring ordinary citizens. We discuss these privacy issues in Chapter 10.

Schauer's work can be viewed, at least in part, as an attempt to provide an antidote to many of the fears that have arisen in relation to the practice of profiling.

By Schauer's lights as an advocate of the morality of decisions based on generalizations, profiling is already an acceptable and ubiquitous practice. For example, he discusses the case of Sokolow who was searched by customs officials at an airport and found to possess drugs.[32] He was searched because he fitted the profile of a drug courier and this was taken to constitute reasonable grounds for suspicion. Sokolow argued in court that fitting a profile did not constitute reasonable grounds for suspicion, but he lost the case. Schauer claims that, "the issue is not about profiling at all, for profiling is inevitable" and "profiling is largely unobjectionable."[33]

Schauer's discussion of profiling is problematic in a number of respects. For one thing, his definition of profiling is very permissive; profiling, properly understood, is arguably a much narrower range of activities than Schauer's account would have us believe. For another, on many influential accounts of judgment he distorts the nature and function of *discretionary* judgment; discretionary judgment is not, many theorists would hold, simply personal, unscientific profiling. This is the case if causal particularism, for example, is correct. Finally, it could be argued that Schauer displays minimal understanding of the dangers of profiling in its appropriately delimited sense.

Notes

1 The SIO is the police officer responsible for directing a criminal investigation. He or she is also responsible for ensuring that proper procedures are in place for recording information and retaining records of information and other material in the investigation.
2 See Kristin Hall (2012) On operations of Tennessee's Fusion Center, http://blogs.knoxnews.com/humphrey/2012/02/on-operations-of-tennessees-fu.html.
3 See FBI (2012) http://www.fbi.gov/news/stories/2012/january/fusion_011712/fusion_011712
4 See *Real Life Crimes* (1993) *Peter Sutcliffe; the Yorkshire Ripper*, Real Life Crimes 5, London: Midsummer Books, p. 99.
5 See Colin Wilson and Damon Wilson (1992) *World Famous Serial Killers*, London: Magpie, p. 73.
6 See *Real Life Crimes* (1993), p. 107.
7 See N. Nicholson (1979) *The Yorkshire Ripper*, London: Star, p. 42 and p. 75.
8 See Nicholson (1979), p. 41.
9 See Nicholson (1979), p. 55.
10 See Nicholson (1979), p. 105.
11 See Nicholson (1979), p. 105.
12 See Nicholson (1979), p. 105.
13 See *Real Life Crimes* (1993), p. 103.
14 See Wilson and Wilson (1992), p. 73.
15 See Nicholson (1979), p. 107.
16 See *Real Life Crimes* (1993), pp. 104–105.
17 See Wilson and Wilson (1992), p. 75; Anonymous (1993), pp. 105–106.

18   See Victor E. Kappeler, Richard D. Sluder, and Geoffrey P. Alpert (1994) *Forces of Deviance; Understanding the Dark Side of Policing*, Prospects Heights, IL: Waveland Press, p. 182.
19   See Wilson and Wilson (1992), p. 106.
20   See Wilson and Wilson (1992), p. 104.
21   See Robert Black in *Murderpedia*, http://murderpedia.org/male.B/b/black -robert.htm (accessed January 14, 2013).
22   Now termed a CHIS or Covert Human Intelligence Source in the United Kingdom.
23   In the United Kingdom the SIO can obtain authority to have a CHIS tasked where the use is to detect crime and the use is proportionate to what is sought to be achieved.
24   These types of investigation invariably produce sensitive information where it is essential to protect sources from harm whilst meeting the rules of evidence. In most jurisdictions there is a legal requirement to share all evidence and ancillary information with the accused's defense to ensure fairness in the trial process. However, in many jurisdictions there is a process whereby an application can be made to the presiding judge to have sensitive information withheld. If this is not granted, then the prosecuting authority may well decide that the risk of disclosing the information is so great that the case should be withdrawn, with the consequence that the accused person walks free.
25   Forces in the United Kingdom are subject to heavy budget reductions. By 2014, UK police forces face a 20% reduction in real terms in their budgets. Transparency International UK (2012) *Report Benchmarking Police Integrity Programmes*, http://www.transparency.org.uk/our-work/publications/ 10-publications/473-benchmarking-police-integrity-programmes   (accessed September 27, 2013).
26   In England and Wales, the Sexual Offences Act 2003, Sections 1–4 (see United Kingdom Government, 2003) with similar provisions in the Sexual Offences (Scotland) Act 2009, Section 16.
27   This would not include minor offenses such as speeding but it would include driving under the influence of alcohol/drugs.
28   See Philip Dawid (2008) Statistics and the Law, in Andrew Bell, John Swenson-Wright, and Karin Tybjerg (eds), *Evidence*, Cambridge: Cambridge University Press, Chapter 6.
29   See Frederick Schauer (2003) *Profiles, Probabilities and Stereotypes*, Cambridge, MA: Belknap.
30   See Schauer (2003), p. 94.
31   See, for example, Rom Harre and E. H. Madden (1975) *Causal Powers*, Oxford: Blackwell. See also Michael S. Moore (2009) *Causation and Responsibility* Oxford: Oxford University Press, Chapters 19 and 20 for a sophisticated and somewhat different way of framing these issues.
32   See Schauer (2003), p. 172.
33   See Schauer (2003), p. 174.

6

Property Crime

6.1 Property Rights

Property crime includes burglary, theft, motor vehicle theft, arson, shoplifting, and vandalism.[1] It consists in the taking of money or property, or damage to property. It does not necessarily involve force, or threat of force, against a person, although sometimes it does, as in armed robbery, for example, in which case it is typically both a property crime and a crime against a person. Property crimes, which do not involve the use of force, typically involve either secrecy (e.g., burglary), or deception (e.g., fraud). We will discuss fraud in the last section of this chapter.

Some property crimes are high-value, low-volume crimes, for instance, the meticulously planned theft of a famous artwork, but many are low-value, high-volume crimes in which easily disposable goods, such as cash, electronics, or commonplace jewelry, are the target items. The motivations for property crimes are multiple, but they include the desire to be wealthy, the desire to avoid poverty, or simply the desire not to have to work for one's living. Many criminals are born into criminal families and for them crime can be, in effect, a way of life. In the case of high-volume crimes, such as house burglaries, the motivation is often drug addiction; the proceeds go to feed a drug habit.

What is morally wrong with property crime and why should it be a crime to steal from others (or defraud them, albeit fraud involves theft) or damage or destroy their property? The most obvious answer is the existence of one or other or both of the following two conditions: (i) people have *moral*

Investigative Ethics: Ethics for Police Detectives and Criminal Investigators, First Edition.
Seumas Miller and Ian A. Gordon.
© 2014 Seumas Miller and Ian A. Gordon. Published 2014 by John Wiley & Sons, Ltd.

rights to property – so theft and destruction of property is a rights violation; (ii) theft or destruction of property can *seriously harm people* by, for example, significantly reducing or even entirely removing their means of making a living, as through theft of someone's cattle or land. Arguably, if *both* of these conditions obtain, then the moral rights to property in question ought to be enshrined in the criminal law. Matters are less clear if only one of these conditions obtains.

As we have seen in earlier chapters, moral rights violation and harm causing are not the same thing and can come apart. It is not necessarily the case that violating someone's property rights harms them, for instance, someone might steal $10 from a billionaire without harming the billionaire and, indeed, without the billionaire ever becoming aware of it. Conversely, someone might be harmed when property to which they do not have a right is taken from them, for instance when squatters are removed from a house in which they are living without the owner's permission.

The nature and extent of property rights in the sense of moral rights to property (as opposed to legal ones) is a complex matter beyond the scope of this work. However, it is necessary to provide a brief overview since various different property rights are enshrined in the criminal law of different jurisdictions and criminal investigators enforce the criminal law. It is incumbent upon criminal investigators to have some understanding of the moral dimensions of the law that they enforce, including laws protecting property. Specifically, it may well be the case that criminal investigators are enforcing an unjust property law or fragment of the framework of property laws (indeed, conceivably the whole framework might be unjust). If so, then investigators need to be aware of this, especially given our normative theory which justifies policing in general, and criminal investigations in particular, on the basis of justifiably enforceable, legally enshrined moral rights.

The moral right to property is actually a bundle of moral rights – indeed, a set of such bundles, for example, the right to consume a loaf of bread, rights to use a motor vehicle and exclude others from using it, intellectual property rights, land rights – some of which are use rights, others exclusion rights, and still others transfer rights. None of these moral rights are *absolute* rights; arguably, there are no absolute moral rights – but, if there are, these are not among them. Moreover, each of these rights requires a justification, that is, the provision of some rational moral basis; and identifying this basis, or rather bases, reveals the moral defeasibility of property regimes. These use, exclusion, and transfer rights have three main kinds of moral basis.

The first kind of moral basis is, roughly speaking, "I or we found it first and there was no prior owner to it or no known prior owner." This is both a relatively weak moral basis (e.g., it is trumped by needs-based human rights), and a relatively rare one in relation to major forms of property ownership in modern settings given, for example, the geographical reach of the framework of nation-states and their property regimes. In relation to land ownership, and the resources (e.g., minerals) and products (e.g., farm products) dependent on land ownership, it is greatly overstated, at least at the national and institutional level. For example, European powers did not find America, Australia, Africa, and so on first, and then claim it for themselves in the absence of any prior owners – rather, in effect, they stole the various lands in question from indigenous peoples, notwithstanding statements of *terra nullius* and the like in various legal documents.

The other two moral bases are of much greater importance. They are natural (as opposed to institutional) moral rights, specifically *need* (e.g., the consumption of food/water to survive, the use of land to grow food for oneself and one's family), and *contribution to production of the good in question* – the philosopher John Locke's "mixing of one's labor" with material gives rise to a moral right to the resulting product (or part thereof).

Needs-based property rights and/or producer-based property rights are consistent with a variety of legal property regimes including collectivist or socialist property regimes as well as private property ones. Typically, property regimes are such that property rights, including access to the use of land and its products, use of manufactured goods, and intellectual property rights, are allocated in part on the basis of need, for example, welfare payments via taxation, and in part on the basis of productive contribution, for example, wages. Importantly, such allocation is also in part based on mutually agreed (e.g., by legal contract) transfer from one person or organization to another. The mechanisms of transfer include the market, for example, among buyers and sellers. Naturally, the transfer of property rights to a good, x, from one person, A, to another person, B, presupposes that A has the property rights to x in the first place.

From the fact that a person, A, might have produced something or, indeed, might otherwise own something, – A perhaps discovered the cure for HIV Aids or A owns the land through which a river runs – it simply does not follow that A can use or not use it as A sees fit, and exclude or not exclude others from it. For example, A does not have a moral right to pollute the river that runs through his or her land so that downstream users, B and C, become ill and die; nor does the fact that A has bought the arable land in question give A the moral right to infuse it with toxic substances and thereby render it unusable by future generations. Again, A morally ought not decide to hide his or her cure for HIV Aids from all others so that it is not available to save the lives of millions.

In fact, the legal basis of many, if not most, things to which people claim property ownership is transfer; as we saw above, A has a prior right to x and agrees to transfer his or her right to x to B (perhaps in return for B's payment of y). However, the moral (as opposed to legal) right to transfer x is far from unproblematic. Specifically, from the fact that A might have certain use and exclusion rights to something that A has produced, it does not follow that A has the right to transfer all those rights to B or C or that, if A does, the transferred rights have the same strength as they had when they attached to A as the originator of the product in question. For example, perhaps A morally ought not to be allowed to transfer his or her ownership rights to a so-called strategic national asset, such as a power grid, to would-be foreign buyers. Again, the author of a book transfers various economic rights to the publisher. However, there are certain rights that the author typically retains and ought to retain, for instance, the right to be known as the author and not to have the work altered by the publisher. Accordingly, there might be no good and decisive objection to a law that prevented someone from falsely claiming the authorship of a book, even if the actual author had agreed to this.

So much by way of an introduction to the notion of moral rights to property.[2] It will be evident that legal rights to property can diverge sharply from moral rights and this gives rise to acute problems of legitimacy and, as a result, moral dilemmas for law enforcement officials. For example, *should* a law enforcement officer in a corrupt authoritarian regime enforce the law in favor of an authoritarian leader and against impoverished citizens in a situation in which the leader has, in effect, stolen the wealth of these citizens, albeit without breaking any laws, for example, by promulgating laws confiscating land, resources, and so on and allocating these to himself and his relatives?

Naturally, law enforcement agencies in developed liberal democracies such as the United States, the United Kingdom, and Australia enforce the laws constitutive of their respective property regimes in the knowledge that these regimes enjoy a measure of moral legitimacy; liberal democracies led by elected politicians are not authoritarian regimes run by de facto criminals.[3] Doubtless, this is true. However, the distinction is not as clear cut as might appear, as the recent global financial crisis (GFC) has served to demonstrate (see Case Study 6.4.1, *Madoff's Ponzi Scheme and the GFC* below). The behavior of major financial institutions based in London or New York has generated a crisis of moral legitimacy in the financial system to the point where the property rights of bankers and other beneficiaries of that system, whether owners, investors, CEOs, or other managers, is being called into question by, for example, Wall St. protesters.[4] The creators and sellers of so-called toxic financial products may have a legal right to the profits they have made, but do they have a moral right to them?

A further point to be made here concerns the moral judgments on the part of governments and law enforcement agencies involved in choosing to investigate – and adequately resource such investigation of – one kind of crime or criminal rather than another. Evidently the investigation of white collar crime and criminals associated with the recent and ongoing GFC – notably various forms of fraud such as securities fraud – has not been pursued with the zeal and resources commensurate with the level of serious-ness, including harm done to home-owners, retirees with diminished savings, and financial institutions themselves.[5] (Again, see the case study below, *Madoff's Ponzi Scheme and the GFC.*)

At a more mundane level, and leaving aside questions of the moral legitimacy of particular property laws or regimes and moral problems arising from transjurisdictional anomalies, law enforcement agencies and criminal investigators in any given jurisdiction have limited resources – indeed, as we saw in Chapter 5 in relation to the post GFC austerity measures, decreasing resources – and need to allocate those resources on the basis of priorities. This is partly a matter of public policy and/or stra-tegic resource allocation at the level of the police organization: for instance, whether to allocate more resources to apprehending burglars than car thieves. But it is also a matter for individual investigators or, at least, individual investigative teams. For example, in accordance with a triage system, investigators might give priority to the most serious, solvable prop-erty crimes over the less serious and those unlikely to be solved (even if serious). However, this raises the question of what counts, or should count, as more or less serious. Is a high volume of minor crimes such as pick-pocketing, directly affecting a large number of elderly people in the community, less serious than a major property crime affecting only one organization, for instance, the theft of $10,000 from a multinational bank? Is the monetary value of the amount stolen the thing that ought to be given the greatest weight, or is it the harm done to the victim? The theft of an impoverished tradesman's tools might do much more harm, given its negative impact on the ability of the tradesman to earn a living and provide for his family, than the burglary of a billionaire's holiday home, notwithstanding that the monetary value of the latter was much greater than that of the former.

6.2 Property Crime

Unlike a murder victim, the victim of a property crime is available, at least in principle, to provide evidence in relation to the crime, for instance, the nature of the goods stolen, the where, when, and how of the crime. Unfortunately, property crimes are often done in secrecy and so, unlike, say, assaults, the victim is not able to identify the offender; moreover, there are often no witnesses to the crime. On the other hand, the item stolen is avail-able as evidence, if it can be retrieved. If, for example, the stolen item is found to be in the possession of person A, then this is (prima facie) evidence that A stole it or at least that A knows who stole it (since A presumably received it from this person).

The direct victim of a property crime is sometimes an organization, for example, a defrauded corporation. However, even in these cases the indirect victim – the ultimate victim, so to speak – is a person or persons, for example, the shareholders or the customers (corporate fraud), the bank's depositors (bank robbery), the community at large (tax evasion). This is so even if the precise amount of the property loss suffered by any individual person as a consequence of the crime cannot be specified because the impact of the crime is too indirect and diffuse, as when a corporation passes on the loss to its customers by way of increased charges.

For a number of reasons not all property crimes that are committed are actually reported to the police. These reasons include the following ones.

1. If the amount involved is trivial, or there is a belief, on the part of the victim, that the police would or could do nothing about it. This attitude often prevails in areas where there is a high volume of crime and the population has lost faith in the police being able to stop criminal activity.
2. Nonreporting may occur in areas of high minority ethnic populations, in particular those newly arrived in a country, who remember the attitude of the police in their former homeland who were perhaps lazy, indifferent, or corrupt, so they consider the police in their new country may be the same.
3. The offender is known to the victim and the victim wants to avoid creating a police record for that person, perhaps a relative or child of a close friend, neighbor, and so on.
4. The victim may want to personally deal with the matter whether by receiving restitution in the form of money or other favor from the offender or, more problematically, by imposing some form of retribution on the offender. Such retribution-seeking behavior may result in a more serious crime being committed (e.g., assault), particularly in cases where one criminal has stolen from another. Another scenario could include extortion, where the victim seeks to profit from the crime being committed by the offender getting, for example, sexual gratification or confidential information from the offender who now becomes a victim.
5. The victim is insured and simply makes a claim on their insurance policy.
6. A major area of nonreporting of crime is by financial institutions who are concerned about the reputational risk and, in any case, may protect themselves against losses from crime by, in effect, building in such losses as a business cost and, thereby, pass on the costs to their customers.

The morally problematic outcomes of not reporting crimes are multiple and include the following: (i) the harm done to the victim, for instance, the property loss, might go unaddressed – bearing in mind that the failure to report might not be a failure on the part of the ultimate victim(s), as in the case of an organization which fails to report crimes and simply passes on the loss to its customers; (ii) the offender might escape justice; (iii) further, and perhaps more serious, crimes might be perpetrated by the offender – bearing in mind that these victims might be persons other than those who were the victims of the original crime (and who failed to report it); (iv) other would-be offenders might be emboldened to commit crimes; (v) the criminal recording system might not be a (reasonably) accurate portrayal of criminal activity in a jurisdiction, which in turn may impede the efforts of the police to combat crime, for example, due to misallocation of police resources; (vi) the community might come to have the belief that the type of crime in question can be committed with impunity, which in turn may cause the members of the community to lose faith in the ability of the police to protect them and their property.

6.3   Investigation of Property Crimes

In cases where victims do contact the police, or crimes otherwise come to the attention of the police, an investigation typically takes place.[6] Traditional means of investigation involve an officer visiting the crime scene to take a detailed report of the crime and assess the scene to determine if a forensic specialist should examine it for fingerprints, forensic samples (e.g., blood), and any physical evidence (e.g., tools) left by the offender. Speed of enquiry is of the essence in order to ensure the recovery of scientific evidence such as trace materials on the offender's body, clothing, in vehicles, and so forth.

Enquiries would be made in the vicinity to find potential witnesses to the offense and, where available, local informants may be contacted for information. It is, however, not uncommon to find potential witnesses who are reluctant to speak to the police and even hold back or destroy important information to protect family, friends, and colleagues. There are a number of reasons for this lack of a willingness to be involved, but it can arise as a result of a previous personal experience as a witness or the reports of others who have come forward as witnesses. The court system in most countries is bureaucratic and typically regarded by those who come into contact with it, whether as offenders, victims, or witnesses, as insensitive to their needs and entitlements. For example, witnesses are often required to put themselves out by taking time off work and travelling to courts at some distance from their homes or workplaces, and yet the time taken off and the travel, meals, and other expenses incurred in being a witness are not adequately remunerated or, if they are, not in a timely fashion.

On occasions, the method by which a crime was committed (its modus operandi – MO) may be so unusual that it points to an offender who habitually uses that MO, for example, safe blowing in a very specific manner. If the investigator has such knowledge of MO or recovers it by interrogating an intelligence database or from an informant, then a path to a suspect could open up. For example, in recent years in Australia there has been a spate of thefts from the cash dispensing machines outside banks by means of explosive gas attacks (EGAs), which have involved (literally) blowing up the machine to enable the cash therein to be stolen. This EGA MO often caused collateral damage to the facade and inside of the building and put the lives and limbs of the offenders and others in the vicinity at risk. The MO relied on knowledge of a specific gas suitable for this purpose and the know-how to use it efficiently and effectively, and without harming those using it.

If the various lines of inquiry prove negative, it is usual for the crime to be quickly filed as undetected or unsolved. This decision would be made by the investigator, then generally endorsed by a supervisor. The crime report would be filed pending any further development in the future.

As noted above, investigation of property crimes is typically subjected to a triage process with respect to the extent of the investigation. Factors in play here include: solvability in the light of the available evidence and of witnesses, type and location of offense, value of item stolen/damaged, harm done to victim, whether or not the stolen item is dangerous, and so on.

Ideally, this process of prioritization should be unbiased and based on objective factors. However, in practice there will be occasions when public interest, media pressure, and, in some jurisdictions, political pressure may be brought to bear on decision making in this regard and sometimes this will be difficult, if not impossible, to ignore. Such influences might need to be accommodated to a degree in so far as the allocation of resources is concerned, for example. However, they need to be resisted in so far as they are attempts to interfere with the investigative process itself, for example, the determination of suspects or evidence gathering and evaluation. Naturally, the ability to resist depends in large part on the institutional independence of both the police organization and the investigator (see discussion in Chapter 4 above).

With the advent of computer databases and intelligence-based policing, there is the opportunity to use data gathered in relation to reported crimes to help investigators conduct their investigation. Crime pattern analysis will identify hotspots of offenses, MO, and times. This will allow preventative measures, such as saturation policing and providing target-hardening advice to property owners (e.g., gas suppression devices in the case of the explosive gas attacks on cash dispensing machines mentioned above), as well as tactical options for operations to catch the offender(s), such as covert observations, use of CCTV, trigger alarms to ensure rapid police response (e.g., in the course of the investigation of the explosive gas attacks it was determined that banks be required to install trigger alarms and to immediately notify police of suspect alarm activation), and tasking informants.

Some covert methods are subject to regulation in their use to preserve privacy in a community – in the United Kingdom, for example, such means are reserved for dealing with serious crime where other methods of investigation have failed or would be unlikely to succeed. Even the use of cameras in public has to be authorized by a senior officer, so, for example, there is widespread use of CCTV watching and recording of the public the product of which can be used by the police when investigating an offense. If, however, the same public cameras are to be used by the police in a pre-planned operation where the police will direct their use, then an authority would be required before such use.

The availability of forensic technology to investigators has greatly improved the evidential link between crime scenes and offenders. DNA evidence has been used to solve property crime in those countries with a database. It has been found that the collection and analysis of physical evidence, including DNA evidence, at crime scenes, not only improves the ability of investigators to identify, arrest, and prosecute offenders in crimes against the person, such as murder and rape, but also in property crimes.

The development of DNA evidence has allowed a more precise crime scene examination to be done and any samples of DNA found (e.g., blood, sweat, etc.) can be matched against the DNA database that most developed countries hold. This exercise is expensive and takes time so, until fairly recently, it was not generally used for volume crimes. The improvement in DNA processing has improved the time aspect, but the financial cost remains. DNA examination is usually prioritized on the basis of the seriousness of the offense, so that factor may still delay identification of a suspect in volume crime investigations. Success is also dependent on the offender actually being in the database at the time or being entered at some time in the future.

In some crime scenes partial samples are found – for instance, part of a fingerprint or a fraction of the DNA sequence required for positive identification. These bring difficulties for investigators; the evidence is insufficient for court but useful for gathering intelligence on the potential suspects with an added risk that it may lead the investigation down a wrong path. An experienced investigator would probably argue that the collation of partial material is important as intelligence and so the risk must be taken but managed.

Here it is important to point out that the reliability of various forms of forensic evidence and, indeed, of forensic expertise is a matter of controversy. There is little doubt that DNA evidence is backed by well-tested and fully accepted scientific theory, albeit the weight of such evidence is less than the public seems to think (see discussion in Chapter 5). However, the reliability of evidence in the form of fingerprints, shoeprints, tyreprints, toolmarks, firearms, bitemarks, and handwriting (often referred to as criminalistics) does not have anything like the same degree of scientific backing. Specifically, it is argued by some[7] that the claim of unique individualization, for example, that a person's fingerprint identifies a person to the exclusion of all other persons, is possibly false and, even if true, unknowable because untestable. Moreover, even if unique individualization is true, there is the problem of smudged, distorted, incomplete fingerprints that some expert has to bring to correct completion by the exercise of his or her imagination and judgment. In short, it is argued that criminalistics is not backed by well-tested, fully supported scientific theory. This is not to say that fingerprints, and the like do not afford evidence but rather that the weight to be accorded this evidence is, at the very least, a matter of controversy.

A corollary of this is that the formal and informal testimony of experts in criminalistics needs to be treated with some caution by investigators (and, of course, by courts).

Here, as elsewhere, investigators need to gather as much and as good evidence as possible. The weight of the totality of the available evidence (including both exculpatory and inculpatory evidence) is important and is, obviously, a function of the amounts and kinds of evidence, such as fingerprints, DNA, eyewitness reports, expert evidence, and so on. Indeed, it is only when an investigator has a sufficiently weighty quantum of evidence (again, including inculpatory and exculpatory evidence) that he or she can, with confidence, begin the process of weighing that evidence in the different sense of weighing the inculpatory against the exculpatory, and doing so by the appropriate standard, for example, by the standard of beyond reasonable doubt.

Time is an important factor in burglary and theft in relation to the property that has been stolen, as it can be devastating emotionally for a victim who has lost highly sentimental and irreplaceable possessions. Investigators will either visit secondhand dealers, antique dealers, or jewelers with details of property stolen, or circulate lists, or advise the victim to do so. Some police investigators have resorted to subterfuge to address volume crimes and set up "sting" operations. For example, police officers pose as secondhand dealers and open a shop where they buy suspect property from unsuspecting sellers (whether the original offender or not). The proceedings are covertly recorded, the sting is allowed to run for a length of time, then the suspected offenders are arrested and prosecuted. These tactics raise important issues of privacy and of entrapment which we discuss in later chapters (Chapters 10 and 11, respectively).

In recent times the police services in most countries have had a focus on improving procedures and practices in relation to evidence gathering. In the United Kingdom, for example, interviews of both suspects and witnesses are conducted using structured interview techniques, such as cognitive interview techniques. Investigators in many jurisdictions in the United States, United Kingdom and Australia now use audio and/or video to tape interviews of suspects. The ethical issues arising from interviewing are discussed in Chapter 12.

Whilst property crime does not generally involve force against a person, there have been incidents where the householder, in a burglary, for example, has used force against the offender causing injury and even death. In a recent incident in the United Kingdom, John Bennell, 27, from Hyde, Greater Manchester, died from a stab wound to the chest after four masked men tried to break in the back door of a terraced house in Salford. Mr. Bennell's father stood up for the right of householders to protect their property. He told *The Sun* newspaper: "I'd hope I'd have the guts to protect my property. I know things can get out of hand, but you're entitled to protect your property."

The incident comes after Prime Minister David Cameron vowed to bring in stronger measures to protect homeowners defending their property. "We will put beyond doubt that homeowners and small shopkeepers who use reasonable force to defend themselves or their properties will not be prosecuted,"[8] he said.

This is not a new idea; in the United Kingdom the law has always allowed the use of reasonable force. The problem is more with the intent of the householder and the means whereby they used force and how the prosecutor and then the courts interpret "reasonable." The issue for the public was that the householder, in some cases, ended up being prosecuted or sued by the offender because of the injury caused.

When a suspect for volume crimes, such as burglary, is arrested, they may admit responsibility for other similar offences. It is not good practice, in line with prosecution guidelines, to apply multiple similar charges to an offender when one or two substantive charges will suffice to evidence the offender's criminal actions. In the United Kingdom the other admitted offences can be listed on a schedule and put before the court for it to consider when sentencing the offender. The procedure is termed "taking into consideration" (TIC). There have been difficulties with this procedure; it can improve the detection rate for a police force and there have been instances where the offences admitted in this manner have been found to be false admissions; sometimes through forensic evidence identifying a different person as being responsible. Police services now engage in a more rigorous scrutiny of such admissions – if they use the TIC procedure at all. The fact that some courts increase the sentence for an offender, who has made numerous admissions, will also impact on such admissions being made.

The gathering of intelligence has always been a key tool for the police (or other agency) investigator and one that has been greatly enhanced by force and national intelligence databases. Intelligence-led policing is considered the most effective way to police an area and this has introduced much greater proactivity by the police to prevent the offense occurring in the first place and gathering intelligence to drive investigative operations for volume crimes such as burglary and theft of vehicles.

Intelligence is often gained by "stop and search" activity or by patrolling police officers moving on individuals who are congregating or behaving in a way that is below committing an offence but are doing so in an antisocial manner requiring some intervention. The criteria for police action is that a reasonable suspicion (or reasonable belief or probable cause) exists in the mind of the officer that the subject has, or is doing, something "suspicious" to justify being stopped and searched or moved on. "Reasonable" implies an objective decision, but it can be the case that subjectivity creeps in, based on appearance, ethnicity, previous knowledge, and so forth. This is a difficult area for officers; such activity is often a performance indicator for officers and policing areas, where the force and/or commanders will impose targets and compare numbers; so officers seek opportunities to meet the targets. Stop and search and intervention in antisocial behavior has taken place throughout policing history and resulted in the arrest of many criminals. It does, however, also create a database of persons searched or moved on, where there is no criminality identified. In some jurisdictions the performance target has resulted in stigmatization of persons (often juveniles) with a potential impact on their later lives – through employment checks and the like.

All forces should focus on educating the public with respect to measures to protect themselves and their property from crime. The term "target hardening" applies to physical means of securing houses, commercial premises, and vehicles using efficient locks, alarms, reinforced doors, and suchlike. This process has been particularly effective with theft of vehicles, where police organizations put pressure on vehicle manufacturers to improve the standard of security on their vehicles, bringing a reduction in thefts and driving away of modern cars. It did, however, have an adverse result where luxury vehicles targeted by thieves were stolen by force (carjacking), or by burglary of the home and theft of the keys for vehicles parked on driveways.

Where a spate of offenses are occurring in a police area, analysis of the crimes and their locations will identify hotspots which can be mapped out and overlaid with other intelligence, for example, addresses of known offenders and their associates. This would contribute to an intelligence package being compiled and used to devise a tactical plan to deal with the offenses. It may be that a prolific offender has recently been released from prison and has been sighted in the relevant areas, perhaps even in suspicious circumstances, but without sufficient evidence to arrest. That person would become a target, and the local police would focus on his or her movements including, if a specified tactic, an overt and determined process to stop them continuing the offenses. This tactic requires careful management to minimize invoking a justified (or even unjustified) complaint of harassment from the target.

A significant tool for the investigator is the growth of closed-circuit television (CCTV) coverage in cities and towns. It is the norm now that for much of the time a person's movements in an area may be recorded on a public or private CCTV system. Investigators will invariably check the footage of local camera systems around the scene. Widespread use of CCTV raises privacy concerns (see Chapter 10). A point to be made in relation to this is that there is presumably only a serious moral problem if there is ongoing monitoring of cameras. If footage is only accessed when there is evidence of a crime, then privacy concerns are to a considerable extent assuaged.

Any global entertainment event, such as the London 2012 Olympics, will attract a huge upsurge in the incidence of counterfeiting and piracy over a long period. Growth in new distribution routes and marketplaces like the Internet make intellectual property crime more attractive to organized criminals, who see intellectual property crime as low-risk and high-yield. It is also the case that a large and willing market exists in the public who are prepared to buy such articles knowing they are counterfeit.

In the United Kingdom when the police send a case to the Crown Prosecution Service (CPS) which has been investigated by a third party, or by the police assisted by a third party (for example the Federation Against Copyright Theft (FACT) or Federation Against Software Theft (FAST)), it is the CPS's duty to take over such police prosecutions (Section 3 of the Prosecution of Offences Act 1985). The investigation is conducted in the normal manner; specifically, such investigations must be independently managed and directed by the police. Third parties should have no involvement with the decision-making process and no guarantees should be given regarding the charge and conviction of suspects. The CPS is in sole charge of the prosecution to ensure the independence of the investigation and that the prosecution of intellectual property offenses is not undermined.

Art, antiques, and cultural property crime – which includes theft, fraud, looting, and trafficking across police force, state, and international borders – is a burgeoning criminal activity. A recent FBI report estimates losses up to $6 billion annually. Investigation can equally cross borders, and police forces worldwide use teams of specialist investigators and advisers and share information from specific databases of stolen property to deal with such crimes. This type of crime can sometimes involve ransom demands or approaches to insurance companies for "rewards" to return unique items such as valuable paintings and other works of art. This may involve a settlement being made which is outside the control of the investigator.

Let us now turn to case studies which illustrate some of the main moral issues arising for investigators from property crime in general, and fraud and cyber crime in particular. These issues include the great harm potentially caused to the victims of property crime (and, therefore, the need for appropriate prioritization by investigation agencies), the moral obligation of work colleagues, other organizations in an industry, and so on to report to the relevant authorities their ongoing suspicions of serious crime (and, therefore, the need for investigation agencies to establish relationships of cooperation, trust, etc.), and the moral obligation of oversight of investigation agencies to ensure that they are independent, vigilant, thorough, and proactive in relation to their monitoring activities, investigation of complaints, and other responsibilities. A further moral issue pertains to the punishment and, in particular, the fining of large corporations, such as HSBC, Barclays, J. P. Morgan, and so on, who have been investigated and found to be guilty of, say, criminal negligence. Typically, these fines are paid by the corporation rather than by individual managers and are, therefore, in effect paid by the shareholders. Yet it is the shareholders who are the victims of the crimes for which the corporations are being fined! So the shareholders are twice victimized and the offenders – at least in so as they are senior managers – receive no punishment. This is a "criminal justice" process that is hardly likely to encourage high-quality, successful investigations of corporate criminals at senior levels, let alone ensure that justice is done to victims or that would-be offenders are deterred.[9]

6.4   Case Studies

Case Study 6.4.1   Madoff's Ponzi Scheme and the Global Financial Crisis

Bernard L Madoff ran the biggest Ponzi scheme in history, operating it for 30 years and causing cash losses of $19.5bn. Shortly after the scheme collapsed and Madoff confessed in 2008, evidence began to surface that, for years, major banks had suspected he was a fraud. None of them reported their suspicions to the authorities, and several banks decided to make money from him without, of course, risking any of their own funds. Theories about his fraud varied. Some thought he might have access to insider information. But quite a few thought he was running a Ponzi scheme. Goldman Sachs executives paid a visit to Madoff to see if they should recommend him to clients. A partner later recalled: "Madoff refused to let them do any due diligence on the funds and when asked about the firm's investment strategy they couldn't understand it. Goldman not only blacklisted Madoff in the asset management division but banned its brokerage from trading with the firm too."

UBS headquarters forbade investing any bank or client money in Madoff accounts, but created or worked with several Madoff feeder funds. A memo to one of these in 2005 contained the following, in large boldface type: "Not to do: ever enter into a direct contact with Bernard Madoff!!!"

JPMorgan Chase had more evidence, because it served as Madoff's primary banker for more than 20 years. The lawsuit filed by the Madoff bankruptcy trustee against JPMorgan Chase makes astonishing reading. More than a dozen senior JPMorgan Chase bankers discussed a long list of suspicions.

The Securities and Exchanges Commission has been deservedly criticized for not following up on years of complaints about Madoff, many of which came from a Boston investigator, Harry Markopolos, whom they treated as a crank. But suppose a senior executive at Goldman Sachs, UBS, or JPMorgan Chase had called the SEC and said: "You really need to take a close look at Bernard Madoff. He must be working a scam."

But not a single bank that had suspicions about Madoff made such a call. Instead, they assumed he was probably a crook, but either just left him alone or were happy to make money from him.

(Extract from Charles Ferguson (2012) www.guardian.co.uk, Sunday, May 20)

Case Study 6.4.2   Cyber Theft and State Crime

On the outskirts of Shanghai, in a run-down neighborhood dominated by a 12-story white office tower, sits a People's Liberation Army base for China's growing corps of cyber-warriors.

The building off Datong Road, surrounded by restaurants, massage parlors and a wine importer, is the headquarters of P.L.A. Unit 61398. A growing body of digital forensic evidence – confirmed by American

(Continued)

intelligence officials who say they have tapped into the activity of the army unit for years – leaves little doubt that an overwhelming percentage of the attacks on American corporations, organizations and government agencies originate in and around the white tower.

An unusually detailed 60 page study to be released Tuesday by Mandiant, an American computer security firm, tracks for the first time individual members of the most sophisticated of the Chinese hacking groups – known to many of its victims in the United States as "Comment Crew" or "Shanghai Group" – to the doorstep of the military unit's headquarters. The firm was not able to place the hackers inside the 12-story building, but makes a case there is no other plausible explanation for why so many attacks come out of one comparatively small area.

"Either they are coming from inside Unit 61398," said Kevin Mandia, the founder and chief executive of Mandiant, in an interview last week, "or the people who run the most-controlled, most-monitored Internet networks in the world are clueless about thousands of people generating attacks from this one neighborhood."

(Extract from David Sanger et al. (2013) *New York Times* February 18)

Case Study 6.4.3   Cyberheist

British police have helped to smash a criminal network that hijacked 5m PCs and stole £300m from banks including HSBC in one of the world's biggest "cyberheists."

Thousands of Britons may have had money taken from their accounts by the Ukraine-based gang, which infected PCs in more than 80 countries with so-called Citadelmalware.

In a process known as "keylogging," the malware used malicious code, hidden in innocent-looking emails, to monitor the user's keystrokes and send information such as account names and passwords to the criminals, allowing them to access the account.

British detectives from the National Cyber Crime Unit (NCCU) in London – part of the new National Crime Agency – have been working with the FBI on an investigation codenamed Operation Puzzled. So far they have shut down 10 of the "command and control" servers used to control the network of infected computers, three of them in Britain.

Two more UK-based servers are in the process of being shut down, police said yesterday.

"The NCCU believe this criminal network was targeting thousands of UK citizens although at this stage it is not possible to estimate what the financial impact may have been," a spokesman for the unit said this weekend.

In a separate operation last week, four people were charged after the arrests of 12 men suspected of being involved in an attempt to steal millions of pounds by hijacking a computer in a Santander branch in London.

However, this is dwarfed by the scale of the Ukrainian network, which had already stolen £300m from personal and business bank accounts in Britain and elsewhere.

Microsoft announced in June that it had helped the FBI take down more than 1,000 Citadel networks used to control the malware-infected PCs, but this is the first time Britain's role has been disclosed.

The company alleged that Citadel is controlled by a boss known as Aquabox who sells malware kits on the Internet.

(Extract from David Leppart (2013) *The Sunday Times* September 15)

6.5   Fraud

Fraud can be loosely defined as theft involving deception.[10] Frauds can be perpetrated in so many different ways – fraudsters are innovative, they move with the times, for instance, using the Internet and technology (e.g., credit card skimmers).

As with homicide, robbery, and sexual assault, fraud is a specialized area of investigation, and its investigators should be trained accordingly. Fraudsters can be highly educated, charismatic, and manipulative, like Bernie Madoff (see Case Study 6.4.1 above). Fraudsters build trust with their victims, show concern and offer help, before finding a weakness (often greed) which they then exploit. It is important that investigators are capable and skilled to handle such criminals, the complex legal and financial aspects of the case, and the media impact it may create.

As the Bernie Madoff Ponzi scheme illustrates, while there might be one principal offender, there are often multiple collaborators, for instance, those within Madoff's organization who assisted the scheme in various ways. Accordingly, there may well be collective, and not simply individual, moral responsibility (see Chapter 7, Section 7.6 for an analysis of collective responsibility). Moreover, the circle of those who have collective moral responsibility for the fraud itself may have implicated others for lesser, connected moral transgressions. For example, certain members of the relevant regulatory agency may be collectively morally responsible for failing to investigate those who perpetrated the fraud.[11]

The scale of fraud is enormous. For example, fraud is estimated to have cost the UK economy more than £30 billion in 2011. Moreover, there is now an extremely wide range of frauds and, in the case of cyber fraud, new forms are constantly evolving.[12] Moreover, it turns out (see Case Study 6.4.2) that an enormous amount of cyber crime, including cyber theft, is actually conducted by governments or with the collusion of governments, notably the Chinese government. In some authoritarian regimes, such as China, the boundaries between private and public sector agencies, and between commerce and law enforcement, are porous or even nonexistent. Accordingly, the state engages in cyber theft on behalf of its commercial enterprises (which in China are largely state-owned).

Cyber criminals are invading homes and offices across the world, not by burglary, but by breaking into laptops, personal computers, and wireless devices.[13] This is computer hacking, the use of malicious software inserted into computer systems that undertake activity inside the system to corrupt it or to extract personal data to rob the individual or company. This activity has an enormous impact on personal, corporate, and even nations' finances – costing billions of dollars/pounds in stolen information, money, and the disruption and repairing of systems. It can also be life-threatening, since the disruption can disable hospitals and emergency services. Moreover, identifying and prosecuting cyber criminals can be extremely difficult, given that they are often operating in cyberspace and based overseas.

As stated above, fraud can be loosely defined as theft involving deception; as such, it involves not only the violation of individual property rights but also the breach of the basic moral principle not to deceive. However, the scale of fraud, nationally and globally, is such that it has a further untoward moral consequence; it is does great damage to economic and other institutions.

Nor is the problem simply one of the fraudsters themselves; for those who are defrauded are also often implicated. When investigating frauds, investigators can find that financial institutions (banks, credit unions, mortgage providers, insurance companies, etc.) are reluctant to disclose fraudulent activities. The financial cost to these institutions is enormous and only a fraction of the crimes are investigated to a conclusion by their own investigators or by other agencies such as the police, the FBI in the United States, the Serious Fraud Office (SFO) in the United Kingdom and the Australian Crime Commission (ACC) in Australia. Investigators also find that, when requesting details pursuant to a search warrant from a lawful authority, precision is required in drafting their submission: the investigator only gets what is asked for. To be less than precise means returning for another warrant; exploratory searches of financial databases, known as "fishing expeditions," where investigators want to conduct nonspecific searches seeking information or intelligence, are not permitted – so as to avoid collateral intrusion and breach of privacy.

As we saw above, failure to report crime or otherwise assist in criminal investigations is morally problematic; this is all the more so in the case of fraud, given its magnitude.

The moral upshot of this situation is that there is now a moral imperative on the part of governments and law enforcement agencies to mobilize resources and develop strategies and tactics to combat what amounts to a serious national and global criminal threat (including, as we saw above, from other governments). Moreover, it is likely that the threat is such that there is a need to engage in a degree of institutional design, including by: (i) accelerating the process of embedding the intelligence-based policing model and extending it to new and emerging areas of fraud; (ii) establishing wider and deeper national and international inter-agency links with police and non-police agencies alike; (iii) developing and funding specialist technical units (e.g., forensic computer accountants); (iv) rethinking regulatory arrangements in the financial and other sectors in the light of the failure of "victim" organizations to adequately respond to fraud; (v) introducing fraud-awareness-raising programs for police, financial and other institutions, and the public at large.

There is some evidence that governments and law enforcement agencies are rising to the challenge. Cyber crime has been identified in the United Kingdom's National Security Risk Assessment as a "tier one" threat alongside international terrorism, an international military crisis, and a major accident or natural hazard requiring a national response. To meet the threat, the government has granted £30m over four years to improve national capability to investigate and combat cyber crime. Three new units across England have been set up to work alongside the Metropolitan Police Centre e-crime Unit (PCeU) that was established in October 2008 as part of the National e-Crime Programme.

In the United States, the FBI has a Cyber Division at FBI Headquarters, tasked to address cyber crime in a coordinated and cohesive manner. Specially trained cyber squads at FBI headquarters and in each of its 56 field offices are staffed with agents and analysts who investigate computer intrusions, theft of intellectual property and personal information, child pornography and exploitation, and online fraud. It has set up Cyber Action Teams that are equipped to travel around the world at a moment's notice to assist in computer intrusion cases. These teams will work aggressively, searching data on the Internet and covertly gathering information to combat cyber criminals. The process places great emphasis on gathering intelligence to help identify the cyber crimes that are most dangerous to the security and economy of the United States.

Throughout the United States there are 93 Computer Crimes Task Forces, fully equipped with state-of-the-art technology to combine with the resources of federal, state, and local counterparts, working in partnership on cyber crime. The Financial Intelligence Center keeps focus on the entire picture of financial crimes and provides tactical analysis of financial intelligence data, identifies potential criminal enterprises, and is used to support investigations and identify emerging economic threats.

The FBI has a major national focus on health care fraud and mortgage fraud and, in recent years, has substantially increased resources in these areas. Its agents and analysts use intelligence, surveillance, computer analysis, and undercover operations to identify emerging trends and to find the key players behind large-scale mortgage fraud and other financial crimes. They work closely with other agencies and the private sector to detect fraud and recover money. In 2011 this combined work in health care fraud returned $4.1 billion dollars to the US Treasury, to Medicare, and to other victims of fraud. These activities will take investigators right into the private lives of claimants and detailed examination of their personal and financial activities in an effort to catch and prosecute the key players in the larger frauds. These intelligence-based activities involving, as they do, integrating and accessing databases, surveillance, and undercover operations give rise to a raft of interrelated privacy concerns, which are discussed in Chapter 10.

The FBI has increased the number of forensic accountants to 250 working on financial investigations and in 2010 it began placing agents at the Securities and Exchange Commission (SEC) to better understand securities fraud and identify trends more quickly, so providing intelligence to their field investigators.

This collaborative approach is being adopted globally. Police forces in the United Kingdom, Australia, and elsewhere have reconfigured their crime and fraud departments to establish electronic crime specialisms for intelligence gathering, cyber crime, investment scams, asset confiscation, and forensic accounting. In London, a leading global financial center, the City of London Police Economic Crime Directorate (ECD) maintains strong working partnerships with the major financial institutions, representative bodies and other law enforcement agencies. A vital part of ECD's work is in forging and developing working relationships with outside bodies, building understanding and trust between individuals, and encouraging a partnership approach to tackling fraud. The ECD works globally and with multiple agencies in relation to mass-marketing fraud. The police are only one of several agencies investigating mass-marketing fraud. Other agencies in the United Kingdom are the Financial Services Authority, Trading Standards services, the Office of Fair Trading, and the National Crime Agency.

It is essential that the investigator is aware of the rules of evidence before starting the investigation and forensic examination of the equipment where digital evidence may be stored. The investigator needs to have highly specialized technical knowledge in order to successfully examine and glean evidence from digital storage. The evidence collected will be in an intangible form, that is, electronic in composition, and it must be presented to a court in compliance with the rules of evidence for the respective country.

In such investigations (and other complex inquiries) it is likely the investigator will have an investigative plan detailing the policy and procedure that will be followed throughout the investigation; search of the premises, seizure of evidence, storage, technical examination, interview plans, and case preparation. Investigation of cyber crime may involve investigators acting in "undercover" roles relevant to the investigation that is being carried out.

In cyber crime cases great care must be taken when seizing digital evidence. The investigator must ensure that all physical evidence such as the computers, hard drives, printers, telephones, and documents is collected – and ensure also that the suspect does not have access to this evidence. For their part, technicians must be careful to avoid any electronic "ambushes" or destructive software/programs within the seized equipment.

In some jurisdictions physical evidence generated by a computer, such as a computer printout, may be considered hearsay – the original evidence being held to be in an electronic form in the computer. Moreover, as we saw in Chapter 2, arguably hearsay evidence is derivative evidence and so is not "Best Evidence" suitable for presentation as such in a court of law. In other jurisdictions, however, such physical evidence, if assessed as forensically sound and a digitally perfect copy of the original electronic material, can be regarded as "Best Evidence" by the courts.[14]

Notes

1 See Stuart P. Green (2006) *Lying, Cheating and Stealing: A Moral Theory of White Collar Crime*, Oxford: Oxford University Press, for a useful set of analyses of the various kinds of property crime. Regarding theft, in particular, see Green's (2012) *13 Ways to Steal a Bicycle: Theft Law in the Information Age*, Cambridge, MA.: Harvard University Press.

2 See, for example, Jeremy Waldron (1988) *The Right to Private Property*, Oxford: Oxford University Press.

3 This is not to say that there are not serious problems of political legitimacy and institutional corruption in many, perhaps most, liberal democracies such as, for example, in the United States, where evidently the moral and legal right to hold the highest office in the land, that of US President, is dependent on access to great wealth for campaign purposes and access to great wealth is in

turn dependent on a willingness to further the interests of the large corporations who provide the campaign funds in question. See Lawrence Lessig (2011) *Republic, Lost: How Money Corrupts Congress and a Plan to Stop it*, New York: Twelve.

4   See, for example, Seumas Miller (2011) Global financial institutions, ethics and market fundamentalism, in N. Dobos, C. Barry, and T. Pogge (eds) *The Global Financial Crisis: Ethical Issues*, Basingstoke: Palgrave, pp. 24–51.

5   See Seumas Miller (2013) The LIBOR scandal: Culture, corruption and collective action problems in the global banking sector, in G. Gilligan and J. O'Brien (eds) *Regulating Culture: Integrity, Risk and Accountability in Capital Markets*, Oxford: Hart Publishing.

6   For elaboration on the practicalities of property investigation, see Michael F. Brown (2001), Chapter 10, Robbery, burglary and stealing investigations. On business investigations see Iain MacNeil, Keith Wotherspoon, and Kathryn Taylor (1998) *Business Investigations*, Bristol: Jordan Publishing.

7   For example, Beecher-Monas (2007), Wells and Olson (2003), and Michael J. Saks (2008) Explaining the tension between the Supreme Court's embrace of validity as the touchstone of admissibility of expert testimony and lower courts' (seeming) rejection of same, *Episteme*, October, pp. 329–331.

8   See Live Leak (2011) UK: Householder who stabbed burglar to death faces no further charges, http://www.liveleak.com/view?i=a84_1311344668 (accessed January 14, 2014).

9   Andrew Ross Sorkin (1913) The victims in J P Morgan settlement, *International Herald Tribune*, September 25, p. 22.

10 For a general introduction to fraud and its investigation see, Geoffrey Smith, Mark Button, Les Johnson, and Kwabena Frimpong (eds) (2011) *Studying Fraud as White Collar Crime*, London: Palgrave Macmillan. For analysis of the crime of fraud see Green (2006), Chapter 13, Fraud. For an elaboration of the practicalities of fraud investigation, see Joseph T. Wells (1992) *Fraud Examination: Investigative and Audit Procedures*, New York: Quorum Books.

11 Those who culpably (and collectively) failed to investigate are not collectively responsible for the fraud *per se*.

12 We note that there are definitional issues arising from the use of the term "cyber crime." Specifically, some so-called cyber crimes are simply traditional crimes (e.g., theft, fraud) involving the use of computers and the like. However, the recent developments in communication and information technology have arguably given rise to new forms of crime not adequately described by traditional definitions, for instance, computer hacking.

13 Peter Grabosky, Russell G. Smith, and Gillian Dempsey (2001) *Electronic Theft: Unlawful Acquisition in Cyberspace*, Cambridge: Cambridge University Press.

14 See ACPO Guide Electronic Evidence (2012), http://www.acpo.police.uk/documents/crime/2011/201110-cba-digital-evidence-v5.pdf; http://afentis.com/expert-witness/forensic-articles/acpo-guide-electronic-evidence/.

7

Terrorism

7.1 Terrorism

Roughly speaking, terrorism is a political or military strategy that:

1. Consists in intentionally killing, maiming, torturing, or otherwise seriously harming, or threatening to seriously harm, civilians;
2. Is a means of terrorizing, individually and/or collectively, the members of some social or political group in order to achieve political or military purposes;
3. Relies on the killings – or other serious harms inflicted – receiving a high degree of publicity, at least to the extent necessary to engender widespread fear in the target political or social group.[1]

By being a violation of some of the most basic moral rights of citizens, notably the right to life, terrorism is, or ought to be, a crime (see Chapter 1). However, by virtue of its tactics and the fact that it is often an attack on the State as such, terrorism poses special ethical problems for investigators. One question is whether or not an investigation of terrorists and their acts of terrorism should be entirely assimilated to criminal investigations, both in terms of allowable investigative methods and in terms of whether or not terrorists ought to enjoy the full panoply of moral and legal rights accorded to ordinary criminals and to the same degree, for example, so-called criminal procedural rights such as the right not to be detained for lengthy period without being charged and tried.[2] This problem is

Investigative Ethics: Ethics for Police Detectives and Criminal Investigators, First Edition.
Seumas Miller and Ian A. Gordon.
© 2014 Seumas Miller and Ian A. Gordon. Published 2014 by John Wiley & Sons, Ltd.

exacerbated by the essentially preventive – as opposed to reactive – function of many terrorist investigations; the point of the investigation is to prevent a terrorist attack rather than determine who performed it after the fact (see Chapter 1, Section 1.5). For another thing, the investigation of terrorists often involves transjurisdictional issues; these are obviously legal in character in the first instance, but often there is an underlying moral issue, for example, when an Australian citizen is being held for interrogation by US authorities and, as such, is subject to US laws governing investigation and interrogation.

A further issue concerns the insulation of ordinary citizens from the (possibly legitimate) infringements of the rights of persons suspected of terrorism. In wartime civilians are, in theory, a separate category from combatants, and the rules of engagement with enemy combatants or the investigation of combatants suspected, for example, of war crimes do not pertain to noncombatants. However, terrorists typically operate within the "civilian" community, and so the investigation of those suspected of terrorism is, for all intents and purposes, an investigation of ordinary citizens. Accordingly, in the context of investigations of terrorist acts, it is morally problematic to suspend or reduce the legal rights of terrorists, through, for example, longer than normal periods of detention without trial, without simultaneously suspending or reducing the same rights of ordinary citizens. After all, in the context of an investigation, terrorists and ordinary citizens are in both cases simply ordinary citizens who are suspected, but not convicted, of terrorism.

The problem arises in a particularly acute form prior to the detention of suspects and arises in large part because of the dangers to ordinary citizens posed by terrorists – or at least by terrorists who are not in detention. Of course, in general the investigation of the crimes of dangerous persons raises important ethical issues not necessarily in play in other investigations and arises because of the threat to life and limb that these persons pose for those around them. Some of these issues were discussed in Chapter 5 in relation to serial killers. However, the problem is greater in the case of terrorists, since they are typically an organized group who target large numbers of people and do so indiscriminately; it is most evident in the case of suicide bombers.

The specific moral problem that arises in the investigation of suicide bombers arises from four considerations that do not normally obtain *jointly*: (i) the "suspect" has not yet committed the offense – there can be no such thing as a serial suicide bomber; (ii) the suspect may well be walking around with a bomb which can be triggered instantly killing him/herself, the investigating officer(s), and others in the vicinity; (iii) the suicide bomber is intent on killing him/herself as well as others and, therefore, the normal self-interested motive to live cannot be appealed to; (iv) the option of warning is not available since this will cause the terrorist to trigger the bomb. Accordingly, the option of detaining the dangerous suspect – as opposed to using lethal force – is ruled out at a certain point in the investigation of suicide bombers, notwithstanding that they have not committed the offense and might not even be in possession of a bomb.

On the model of terrorism-as-crime in the context of the well-ordered liberal democratic state, whereas terrorist acts should be treated as ordinary, albeit very serious, crimes, nonetheless, terrorist acts have additional destabilizing features that might reasonably call for a somewhat different mix of law enforcement tactics and strategies than those deployed against ordinary crime. The question is whether these tactics and strategies reasonably ought to involve an extension of police powers and, in particular, additional constraints – additional, that is, to the ones already in place to protect citizens from one another and from external threats – on the human, civil, and political rights that are constitutive of the status of a citizen in a well-ordered liberal democratic state. It needs to be stressed that these moral and legal rights are quite fundamental to liberal democracy; a polity in which they are not respected is not a liberal democracy. On the other hand, it also needs to be stressed that none of these rights are absolute, and none exist without some constraints, for instance, the right to self-defense is a constraint on the right to life of attackers. Therefore, it is very much a matter of determining whether or not the current threat posed by terrorism morally justifies additional constraints and, if so, which ones. To reiterate, the context in question is that of a well-ordered liberal democracy at peace. Doubtless, matters are somewhat different in theaters of war or under a state of emergency. Here we note the importance of not confusing these different contexts and blurring the distinction, for example, between what is an appropriate police power of detention of suspects under a state of emergency, as opposed to normal peacetime conditions.

Some of the fundamental moral and legal rights in question include the right to freedom of speech and thought (infringed by laws against sedition), the right to freedom of action (infringed by laws enabling preventive detention and/or prolonged periods of detention without being charged with an offense and brought to trial), the right not to self-incriminate (infringed by laws curtailing right to silence), the right to privacy (infringed by laws enabling intrusive surveillance), the right not to be tortured (infringed by legalized torture warrants), and the right to life (infringed by laws enabling the shooting of fleeing suspects).

A number of these rights are in play in the investigation of terrorists by police during peacetime, including the right to privacy, the right not to be tortured, the right to freedom of action, and the right to life. We give detailed consideration to privacy rights in Chapter 10 and to the right not to be tortured in Chapter 12. Here we focus on the right to freedom of action and the right to life. The former is infringed by prolonged periods of detention without trial.

7.2   Detention without Trial

Infringements of the human right to freedom of action include laws enabling preventive detention of suspects and detention of suspects for prolonged periods without their being charged and tried.

The cornerstone of liberal democracy is individual freedom and, aside from freedom of thought and speech, the most fundamental freedom, or set of freedoms, is freedom of action. Freedom of action includes freedom of bodily movement, freedom to associate and form relationships with others, freedom to buy and sell, freedom to plan and implement projects, including one's career, and so on. It is self-evident that detention and imprisonment strike at the very heart of individual freedom. For this reason imprisonment ought to be reserved only for serious crimes and in circumstances in which the suspect is guilty beyond reasonable doubt. Moreover, for the same reason detention for prolonged periods without trial is morally unacceptable.

At this point a tendency has developed to invoke the notion of trade-offs and a balance between individual rights and security considerations; this is especially the case in relation to antiterrorist legislation.[3]

Here there are two crucial questions. First, whether or not there is, in fact, a need for a trade-off and, specifically, a trading down of particular individual rights. Arguably, privacy can be traded down to a significant degree, but not freedom of action, albeit there are limits to this argument given that freedom depends in part on privacy (see Chapter 10). Or perhaps we can increase security by spending more money (and time) on, for example, airport security, surveillance of at-risk installations, and border controls without any significant diminution of existing privacy rights or existing rights to freedom. Second, in so far as there is a need for balancing and to trade off, what is to be put on the scales, and what is to be traded off against what?

With respect to one side of the scale, what proponents have in mind is perhaps clear enough: individual freedom is on the scales and is to be traded down. However, it is the other side of the scales that is unclear. Notions of national security or community safety are far too general and vague to be helpful here. There is a need for more precise and differentiated notions. Indeed, as far as the notion of community safety is concerned, this presumably largely consists in the human rights to life and other aspects of personal security; so the other side of the scales consists in an individual right after all, namely, the right to personal security. As is often the case, balancing rights to freedom and rights to personal security – if this is what has to be done – is a complex matter; sometimes the latter will trump the former, for example, searching luggage for bombs at airport security points, and there are contexts in which the former will trump the latter, for example, British soldiers going to war against Hitler's Nazi forces.

However, it is by no means clear that there is a need for a trade-off between fundamental rights to individual freedom and rights to personal security in well-ordered liberal democratic states at peace. For one thing, security actually consists in large part in the provision of the conditions for the exercise of individual freedom. National security and law and order in liberal democratic polities, as Miller has argued elsewhere,[4] largely consist in, or are heavily dependent on, respect for human and other moral rights, especially rights to personal security and property rights. Without respect for personal security and property rights, there is no law and order in a liberal democracy and, therefore, the exercise of individual liberty is difficult, if not impossible.

For another thing, the trade-off can be, and ought to be, a trade-off between the rights of offenders and suspected offenders on the one hand, and the rights of innocent people on the other. It is not as if what are to be traded down are the rights to, say, life and liberty of innocent civilians. I take it that the proposition is not that police and other security personnel ought to be empowered to shoot to kill, or indefinitely detain, *innocent* people in order to protect the rights of other innocent people. Unfortunately, some recent antiterrorist legislation trades down the rights of people known to be innocent. Consider, for example, the right to silence. In Australia, recent antiterrorist legislation (ASIO Bill (No 2)) permits ASIO (Australian Security Intelligence Organisation) to detain and question persons who are not even suspects, if it is believed these innocents could provide relevant information.[5]

However, the main intellectual – as opposed to political – problem concerns the rights of suspects. Suspects are, by definition, not identical to those who have been tried and found guilty of a crime. So, unlike those who have been tried and found guilty, suspects continue to be presumed to be innocent and, as a consequence, cannot be, or ought not to be, detained for lengthy periods, or otherwise subjected to restrictions or harm. Rather, suspects who are arrested must either be charged and brought to a speedy trial, or released following a brief period of interrogation. Moreover, suspects who are subjected to detention and interrogation ought to be afforded appropriate rights to protection such as the right to an attorney.

This is not to say that there might not be a need to calibrate, for example, periods of detention without trial in the context of changing circumstances, including the current threat of terrorism in the United States, United Kingdom, and elsewhere. Thus, it may be that terrorist suspects ought to be able to be detained for weeks rather than days in the context of the need to extract evidence from encrypted communications on seized computers. In the United Kingdom there has been a controversy in relation to whether or not to extend the period of detention without charge for terror suspects from, for example, 28 days to 42 days.[6] But such calibration must not be assimilated to a circumstance in which a terrorist suspect can be detained indefinitely without trial (including by the device of ongoing renewal of a detention order) as is currently the case with non-British citizens in the United Kingdom, where there is currently provision for indefinite detention of suspects without bringing them to trial, if they do not have British citizenship and expelling them is judged to present a real risk of their being tortured.[7]

A procedure that is closely related to detention without trial is the so-called control orders introduced in the United Kingdom under the 2005 terrorism legislation. These control orders (now rescinded) enabled terrorist suspects to be restricted in various ways, including in respect of travel (domestic and/or foreign) and communications (e.g., use of Internet), and/ or by the requirement to report regularly to the police. As is the case with detention without trial, control orders are an infringement of central aspects of the human right to freedom; and, again as in the case of detained terrorist suspects, those under control orders should either be prosecuted or allowed to enjoy their human right to freedom.

Preventive detention is yet another counterterrorist measure that infringes individual freedom. India, in particular, is well known for the use of its laws enabling this procedure. Preventive detention is morally problematic in that, at least in principle, it does not necessarily pertain to those suspected of a past or present crime – let alone tried and convicted of a crime – but to those suspected of being likely to commit a *future* crime; that is, persons are to be detained, notwithstanding the fact that the crime for which they are being detained has not been committed and is not in the process of being committed. Here it is important to distinguish between: (a) someone suspected of having already committed a crime – this first crime is in the present or past – as a precursor to committing a second crime in the future, for instance, conspiring in the present to commit a murder in the future; and (b) someone who is not suspected of any present (or past) crime, but only of being likely to commit a future crime – for instance, someone who is not suspected of any past or present crime, such as the crime of conspiracy to murder, but who is, nevertheless, believed to be likely to commit a murder in the future. At least in principle, preventive detention might pertain to a person in the situation described in (b), and not just to a person in the situation described in (a). As such, preventive detention infringes the basic moral principle that a person should not be detained, or otherwise penalized, for a crime that he or she is known not to have committed or to be in the process of committing. Accordingly, preventive detention cannot be morally justified under normal circumstances, and ought not to be a standing police power.

Notwithstanding the above, preventive detention for limited periods might be morally justified in some emergency situations. For example, in the context of ongoing, large-scale, caste-based and communal violence of the sort experienced in Bihar and Gujarat in India in recent years, preventive detention for limited periods of persons highly likely to incite massed crowds to violence might be morally justified. However, this is a moral justification for preventive detention of select individuals for a limited period and only in the context of a well-founded, and lawfully decreed, state of emergency. By contrast, preventive detention is not justified in well-ordered liberal democratic settings in which there is no emergency, as in most parts of most contemporary liberal democratic states. Moreover, preventive detention under a state of emergency should be subject to stringent accountability processes, including judicial oversight.

Notwithstanding the above, there is a circumstance in which preventive detention is morally (and legally) justified for lengthy periods, namely, in war. Prisoners of war are detained until the cessations of hostilities. Accordingly, in so far as terrorists can be assimilated to combatants fighting a war, then the path is open to their detention for as long as the armed conflict in question persists.[8] Some terrorist groups, for example, Al Qaeda in Afghanistan, are organized armed groups engaged in armed conflict in de facto theaters of war. Presumably, therefore, they are combatants and can be treated as such, albeit they are also criminals by virtue of, for example, targeting innocent civilians. However, other terrorist groups are not engaged in armed conflict in theaters of war and, therefore, cannot be assimilated to combatants. This suggests that, in some contexts, such as well-ordered liberal democratic states, terrorists should be treated as ordinary criminals and the law enforcement framework should be applied; however, in other contexts, such as de facto theaters of war, terrorists should be treated as combatants and the terrorism-as-war framework should be applied.[9]

Earlier we raised the issue of trading down of the rights of, especially, terrorist suspects. One illicit way in which the scales on the right hand side (the security side) are being weighed down with a consequent trading down of the rights of suspects, is by the broadening of the scope of antiterrorist legislation so as to embrace not simply actual specific acts of terrorism or actual membership of terrorist organizations, but also *threatened* acts of terrorism and also the consequences of actual acts of terrorism in terms of the *fear* that they might produce. In some jurisdictions[10] terrorism includes the (possibly indirect and distant) *threat* of bombings and like actions, and therefore brings with it actions that have the potential to cause harm, for example, undertaking terrorist training; moreover, some antiterrorism laws also focus on the motivation to intimidate and therefore bring into play the intentional causing of the *fear* of harm, as opposed to harm itself. There are other ways of widening of laws against terrorism, such as associating with a terrorist, and new crimes (or the resuscitation of ones in disuse), such as sedition. Here, as elsewhere, there is a need to analyze each of these elements on a piecemeal basis. Undergoing terrorist training, for example, manifests a high degree of culpability and, in the context of an increasing terrorist threat, warrants severe penalties. On the other hand, whether or not an action intentionally or otherwise caused fear is arguably so indeterminate a matter as to lead to abuse in the application of any laws enacted to eliminate or reduce such fear-causing actions.

Let us now turn to a consideration of a number of case studies which illustrate some of the moral problems arising from terrorist actions and attempts to combat specific terrorist tactics, notably suicide bombers. We begin with the 9/11 attack.

7.3 Case Studies

Case Study 7.3.1   9/11

At 8:46 on the morning of September 11, 2001, the United States became a nation transformed. An airliner traveling at hundreds of miles per hour and carrying some 10,000 gallons of jet fuel ploughed into the North Tower of the World Trade Center in Lower Manhattan. At 9:03, a second airliner hit the South Tower. Fire and smoke billowed upward. Steel, glass, ash, and bodies fell below. The Twin Towers, where up to 50,000 people worked each day, both collapsed less than 90 minutes later.

At 9:37 that same morning, a third airliner slammed into the western face of the Pentagon. At 10:03, a fourth airliner crashed in a field in southern Pennsylvania. It had been aimed at the United States Capitol or the White House, and was forced down by heroic passengers armed with the knowledge that America was under attack.

More than 2,600 people died at the World Trade Center; 125 died on the four planes. The death toll surpassed that at Pearl Harbor in December 1941. This immeasurable pain was inflicted by 19 young Arabs acting at the behest of Islamist extremists headquartered in distant Afghanistan. Some had been in the United States for more than a year, mixing with the rest of the population. Though four had training as pilots, most were not well educated. Most spoke English poorly, some hardly at all. In groups of four or five, carrying with them only small knives, box cutters, and cans of Mace or pepper spray, they had hijacked the four planes and turned them into deadly guided missiles.

The 9/11 attacks were a shock, but they should not have come as a surprise. Islamist extremists had given plenty of warning that they meant to kill Americans indiscriminately and in large numbers. Although Usama Bin Ladin himself would not emerge as a signal threat until the late 1990s, the threat of Islamist terrorism grew over the decade . . .

Until 1997, the U.S. intelligence community viewed Bin Ladin as a financier of terrorism, not as a terrorist leader. In February 1998, Usama Bin Ladin and four others issued a self-styled fatwa, publicly declaring that it was God's decree that every Muslim should try his utmost to kill any American, military or civilian, anywhere in the world, because of American "occupation" of Islam's holy places and aggression against Muslims.

In August 1998, Bin Ladin's group, al Qaeda, carried out near-simultaneous truck bomb attacks on the U.S. embassies in Nairobi, Kenya, and Dar es Salaam, Tanzania. The attacks killed 224 people, including 12 Americans, and wounded thousands more.

In December 1999, Jordanian police foiled a plot to bomb hotels and other sites frequented by American tourists, and a U.S. Customs agent arrested Ahmed Ressam at the U.S. Canadian border as he was smuggling in explosives intended for an attack on Los Angeles International Airport.

In October 2000, an al Qaeda team in Aden, Yemen, used a motor-boat filled with explosives to blow a hole in the side of a destroyer, the USS *Cole*, almost sinking the vessel and killing 17 American sailors.

The 9/11 attacks on the World Trade Center and the Pentagon were far more elaborate, precise, and destructive than any of these earlier assaults. But by September 2001, the executive branch of the U.S. government, the Congress, the news media, and the American public had received clear warning that Islamist terrorists meant to kill Americans in high numbers.

From the time of the first World Trade Center attack in 1993, FBI and Department of Justice leadership in Washington and New York became increasingly concerned about the terrorist threat from Islamist extremists to U.S. interests, both at home and abroad.

(Continued)

Throughout the 1990s, the FBI's counterterrorism efforts against international terrorist organizations included both intelligence and criminal investigations. The FBI's approach to investigations was case-specific, decentralized, and geared toward prosecution. Significant FBI resources were devoted to after-the-fact investigations of major terrorist attacks, resulting in several prosecutions.

The FBI attempted several reform efforts aimed at strengthening its ability to prevent such attacks, but these reform efforts failed to implement organization-wide institutional change. On September 11, 2001, the FBI was limited in several areas critical to an effective preventive counterterrorism strategy. Those working counterterrorism matters did so despite limited intelligence collection and strategic analysis capabilities, a limited capacity to share information both internally and externally, insufficient training, perceived legal barriers to sharing information, and inadequate resources.

There were opportunities for intelligence and law enforcement to exploit al Qaeda's travel vulnerabilities. Considered collectively, the 9/11 hijackers

- included known al Qaeda operatives who could have been watch-listed;
- presented passports manipulated in a fraudulent manner;
- presented passports with suspicious indicators of extremism;
- made detectable false statements on visa applications;
- made false statements to border officials to gain entry into the United States; and
- violated immigration laws while in the United States.

(Extract from the Executive Summary of *9/11 Commission of Inquiry*)

Case Study 7.3.2   The Jean Charles De Menezes Shooting

Following the terrorist attacks in New York and Washington on 11 September 2001, the UK police service examined its strategy to combat the increased threat of 'suicide terrorist' bombing. A working party was formed to research the phenomenon of suicide terrorism across the world and to suggest the tactics that the police in the

United Kingdom could deploy to counter this threat. Extensive work followed which involved research and visits to other countries, liaison with government departments and expert legal advice, resulting in a policy drawn up by the Association of Chief Police Officers (ACPO) and shared with all forces in the United Kingdom.

There has been a significant worldwide increase in terrorist attacks by suicide terrorist bombers and responses to the threat are not clear cut as there is no definitive profile of a suicide bomber in terms of age, sex or ethnicity. The research by the working party highlighted the problems of identifying such threats and then neutralising them. The plan 'Operation Kratos' was created as a result and encompassed a range of tactics used to defend against the threat from suicide terrorist bombers. Operation Kratos was adopted as part of the national firearms tactics in UK police forces.[11]

On 7 July 2005 suicide bombers detonated explosives in London with devastating effects. On 21 July 2005 there were further failed attempts to detonate bombs in London and suspects were identified. The following day, during a pre-planned police surveillance operation (Operation Theseus) linked to the attempted bombings, Jean Charles de Menezes was shot in the head at close range by armed police officers whilst on a train at Stockwell Underground Station. It is now known that his identity was mistaken for that of a failed suicide bomber. It was not conclusively established whether or not the armed officers gave any warning to Mr de Menezes.

The details of tactics for Kratos are contained in Part 2 of the Manual, access to which is restricted. Following the incident in London, however, the Metropolitan Police Authority (MPA) published a number of reports on the incident. One of the MPA reports includes a description of Operation Kratos:[12]

There are three separate plans under the generic title of Operation Kratos:

- Operation Andromeda is designed to deal with the spontaneous sighting by a member of the public of a suspected suicide bomber.
- Operation Beach is where there is an intelligence-led covert operation to locate and arrest persons suspected of involvement in acts of terrorism.
- Operation Clydesdale is where intelligence has been received about a suicide attack on a pre-planned event.

(*Continued*)

The aim of the operation is to: identify, locate, contain and neutralise the threat posed. The options for all three operations range from an unarmed stop of the suspect by uniformed officers, through to the deployment of armed police officers. These options involve a range of tactics that have remained confidential to avoid giving information to terrorist groups. It has become clear however that 'neutralising the threat' may involve shooting dead a suspected suicide bomber without warning.

Following the events in London on 7 July 2005, suicide terrorist bombers unsuccessfully attempted on 21 July to explode devices on three underground trains and a bus. The UK threat level for terrorism was at Level 1 'Critical' – the highest it had ever been and there was enormous pressure on the MPS [Metropolitan Police Service] to protect the public and arrest suspects. The MPS began a major operation to locate those suspects and prevent further similar acts; the Gold commander for the firearms operation (Operation Theseus 2) was Commander John McDowall. Information was received that Hussain Osman and Abdi Omar, could have been involved and a possible address at 21 Scotia Road was identified. A surveillance operation began at Scotia Road, which is a multi occupancy building. The Gold commander's strategy included:[13]

To control the premises at Scotia Road through covert surveillance, follow any person leaving the premises until it was felt safe to challenge them and then stop them.

The Gold commander considered that an Operation Kratos situation could develop and appointed a Designated Senior Officer (DSO) – Commander Cressida Dick. He also appointed two Silver commanders, a Detective Chief Inspector for the firearms operation and a Detective Superintendent for the operations room (Room 1600) to provide a link with SO13 – the MPS Anti Terrorism Branch, which provided an intelligence feed to the DSO.

'DSO'[14] was a new term to the Command terminology and, since the Stockwell incident, it has been renamed 'DSO-SILVER'. This officer is in command of the tactical operation (Kratos) and, if necessary, may order a firearms officer to shoot a suspect.

When Kratos was introduced into UK policing there was some confusion as to whether the DSO was a Gold or Silver commander in a Kratos operation. That said, it is very clear from the Stockwell One

Report that Commander Dick, as DSO, considered herself in command of the firearms operation with the responsibility to achieve the strategic aims set by the Gold commander. Commander Dick was trained as a DSO and had considerable experience commanding firearms operations involving life-threatening situations. She was in operational command of the firearms operation and the Silver Firearms commander was apparently working as her ground commander. Both the DSO and the Silver Firearms commander had firearms tactical advisers working with them (Trojan 80 and Trojan 84 respectively). The DSO had a loggist who recorded her verbal decisions and their rationale. The DSO transcribed them into her Decision Log, some hours later. A specialist tactical firearms team (CO19) was assigned to the operation.

As she had been given a wrong location, the DSO missed the first 25 minutes of the Gold commander's briefing to the Silver commanders and their firearms advisers. The DSO requested and was given a second briefing by the Gold commander and he later gave her a written intelligence update.

Trojan 84 initially briefed CO19; they were told about the command structure in place, that a DSO had been appointed and that they should trust the intelligence being provided. The Silver firearms commander further briefed CO19. This was a comprehensive intelligence briefing, encompassing all knowledge on incidents and including a link to the actual bombings on 7 July 2005. He described the individuals involved in the bombings as being 'deadly and determined' and 'up for it'. CO19 was told that any subject coming from the flats would be allowed to 'run' and that an interception would take place as soon as possible away from the address so as not to compromise it. These briefings were not recorded, which was justified by time constraints. CO19 was instructed to move to a holding point near Scotia Road.

The address at Scotia Road had a communal doorway. At 9.33–9.34 a.m., Jean Charles de Menezes came out of the doorway and was seen by surveillance officers to walk to a bus stop and board a Number 2 bus. He was kept under surveillance and remained on the bus until Brixton Road, where he got off. It appeared that he had the intention of using the underground at Brixton Station. The station was closed due to a security alert, so he walked back to the bus stop and actually boarded the bus he had left. This behaviour

(Continued)

apparently raised a question with surveillance officers as to whether he was using anti-surveillance techniques. He travelled on the bus to a stop near Stockwell Station.

Room 1600 did not have equipment to record radio and telephone conversations coming into the room. It was occupied by about 20 people and described as 'noisy'. The inquiry report details conversation between the surveillance team members about identification of Mr de Menezes as the suspect Mr Osman.[15] There was no positive identification. The terms 'good possible likeness', 'could not positively identify' were used, with one staff member saying that he 'did not believe the person was identical to Osman'.

It is apparent from the inquiry report that this uncertainty was not made clear to the DSO and Silver firearms commanders. CO19 officers and those in Room 1600 stated that they were made aware that Mr de Menezes was acting nervously or was twitchy.[16] The Silver firearms commander, who was with CO19 at the holding point, heard on the surveillance radio that Mr de Menezes had been identified as the suspect, which was also heard by Trojan 84 and the CO19 team leader. The DSO stated that she was informed, 'it is him, the man is off the bus. They think it is him and he is very, very jumpy.' This is recorded within her loggist's notes.

As the bus was nearing the station, the officers directing the operation formed the view that he was likely to be the suspect, Hussain Osman. CO19 was directed to get behind the suspect but had to travel from the holding point. Mr de Menezes got off the bus at Stockwell and walked towards the station. In the belief that Mr de Menezes had been positively identified as Mr Osman and, following consultation with her firearms adviser Trojan 80, the DSO decided that Mr de Menezes could not be allowed to enter the Stockwell Underground Station. The order to stop him was therefore given by the DSO. There is no evidence that the DSO gave an order to shoot Mr de Menezes.[17]

The CO19 team was not yet in place at the underground station and it was not clear who had been designated to carry out the stop order. The surveillance team members were armed but not trained for such interventions. The order was directed to them but due to the arrival of CO19 outside the station, the DSO countermanded the order and specified that CO19 should stop Mr de Menezes. By this time, however, he had gone into the station still followed by the surveillance team; CO19 ran into the station in pursuit, but they were two minutes behind Mr de Menezes.

It follows from the inquiry report[18] that all CO19 officers believed they were dealing with a person who had been identified as a suspect terrorist bomber. The firearms officers, however, had different perceptions of what was meant by the order 'to stop Mr de Menezes'. Some believed that the threat required nonlethal intervention, others that even shooting him may be necessary to protect the public and police officers on the underground train.

Mr de Menezes boarded the train and sat in a carriage with other passengers and three members of the surveillance team. Two CO19 officers entered the carriage and a surveillance officer pointed to Mr de Menezes. Accounts differ on this point, but it is believed that Mr de Menezes stood up and faced the arriving police officers. He was grabbed around the waist by one of the nearby surveillance officers (Ivor) who believed he was about to detonate a bomb and pushed back into his seat. The CO19 officers stated that they felt they had to act immediately to prevent loss of life to the people on the train. They tackled Mr de Menezes and both fired a number of shots into his head killing him. The time between Mr de Menezes leaving Scotia Road and his death was 33 minutes.

The question arises – on the evidence available – did the officers (including the commanders) use 'force which is no more than absolutely necessary'? On 12 December 2008 the inquest[19] held into the death of Mr de Menezes returned an open verdict. The jury declined to bring a verdict of lawful killing. The coroner had previously concluded that a verdict of unlawful killing was not justified so it was unavailable to the jury. There was criticism in the media of the coroner's decision to withhold the verdict 'unlawful killing' from the jury.

The IPCC has reviewed its original decision in the light of the inquest into Mr de Menezes' death. On 2 October 2009 it reported that it would stand by its decision not to recommend disciplinary actions against the MPS officers involved in the fatal shooting of Mr de Menezes.

(Extract from Ian Gordon and Seumas Miller (2012) The Fatal Police Shooting of Jean Charles de Menezes: Is Anyone Responsible' in Simon Bronitt, Miriam Gani, and Saskia Hufnagel (eds), *Shooting to Kill: Socio-legal Perspectives on the Use of Lethal Force*, Hart, pp. 215–239)

Case Study 7.3.3   The Killing on the Rock (Gibraltar)

In March 1988, based on intelligence received, the UK Government believed that the PIRA[20] planned to use a car bomb to kill band members of the Royal Anglian Regiment that would assemble for a parade in Gibraltar. Spanish Security Officers were monitoring three suspects – Danny McCann, Sean Savage and Mairead Farrell – who had met up in Spain. The Government had tasked a Special Forces team (SAS) to the operation.

On 5 March Savage parked a white Renault car in the busy town area; it is now believed this was to ensure a parking space prior to the parade. He then met up with Farrell and McCann who had crossed into Gibraltar from Spain; all were under surveillance and were seen to be paying close attention to the parked vehicle before moving from the area. An army explosives expert then made a visual examination of the vehicle but no suspicious elements were seen in or on the vehicle.

The identities of the three suspects were confirmed; the operations commander decided that the car probably contained a bomb. The local police commander (UK control) handed control to the SAS commander to arrest the suspects. The SAS team was informed that the suspects had already placed their bomb and were ready to detonate it.

The three suspects had split up, Farrell and McCann were together, Savage was further down the road. As the SAS teams moved in it appeared McCann was alerted to their presence, he is alleged to have made an 'aggressive' movement with his hand towards a bag, the SAS trooper thought it to be a movement for a weapon or detonator and fired a number of shots killing McCann. After McCann was killed, it was claimed that Farrell made a move towards her handbag and she also was shot and killed. Another SAS trooper present also fired shots at both persons virtually simultaneously.

Savage who was a short distance away saw this action and ran away. Other members of the SAS team pursued and caught up with him; they alleged he was challenged; he ignored it and went to reach inside his jacket. He was shot between 16 and 18 times. McCann was shot five times, Farrell eight times and all three were subsequently found to be unarmed without any kind of remote trigger. There was no bomb in the white Renault car parked in Gibraltar by Savage.

The Spanish police later found a car in Marbella containing materials for a bomb, including 64 kg of Semtex; keys found in Farrell's handbag identified the car.

This was a turbulent and murderous period in Northern Ireland. Following the deaths in Gibraltar, at their funeral in Belfast on the 16 March, a UDA[21] gunman, Michael Stone, fired shots and lobbed grenades into the crowd, killing three and wounding many others. On 19 March at the same cemetery, the crowd attending the burial of Kevin Brady, one of Stone's victims, stopped a car containing two UK soldiers, who were not in uniform, stripped and beat them before they were shot dead by IRA gunmen.

Then on 18 September 1990, the IRA attempted to assassinate Air Chief Marshal Sir Peter Terry in retaliation for his part in Operation Flavius; he had been Governor of Gibraltar at the time and had authorised the use of the SAS. A gunman shot through a window at his home hitting him at least nine times and injuring his wife. He survived but with extensive injuries.

In 1995, the European Court of Human Rights (McCann et al. v. UK) ruled by a majority verdict ten votes to nine that:

> The Court is not persuaded that the killing of the three terrorists constituted the use of force which was no more than absolutely necessary in defence of persons from unlawful violence within the meaning of Article 2 paragraph 2 (a) (art. 2-2-a) of the Convention.

Therefore there had been a breach of the above article of the European Convention on Human Rights in relation to the deprivation of life. As a newspaper columnist[22] later wrote:

> The European court of human rights may have got the balance right when in 1995 it ruled that Britain had breached the convention by excessive use of force, while at the same time denying any claims for damages or costs, as the three had been engaged in an act of terrorism.

7.4 Collective Actions and Omissions

The above case studies exemplify moral problems confronting law enforcement agencies in relation to terrorism. The 9/11 case study illustrates the ease with which a terrorist group can perpetrate a terrorist attack and the consequent difficulties facing law enforcement agencies seeking to prevent a terrorist attack, particularly if they are relatively underprepared for it. On the other hand, the de Menezes and the Gibraltar case studies illustrate the difficulties facing law enforcement agencies seeking to prevent a terrorist attack, even when they are well prepared for it. Further comparisons could be drawn between the Gibraltar incident and the shooting of Jean Paul de Menezes; both occurred following surveillance and questionable intelligence gathering and assessment. However, unlike De Menezes, McCann, Savage, and Farrell had a bomb in a car in Spain ready to be used. So, while the use of deadly force may not have been necessary, no one has ever denied the intention of those three to kill and maim.

Note that in the 9/11 and de Menezes cases the failure of law enforcement agencies and their personnel are clearly *collective* failures (as opposed to possibly morally unacceptable successes, as in the Gibraltar case study). So it was not simply a matter of a single individual making a mistake or otherwise failing to do their duty. Moreover, there is no suggestion in the 9/11 or de Menezes case studies that any individual officer or group of officers intentionally did the wrong thing. For the most part in these two case studies, and certainly in the de Menezes scenario, law enforcement personnel were both well intentioned and conscientious in their actions. Nevertheless, in both cases there was a collective failure which had profoundly tragic consequences. We note that it was at bottom a case of mistaken identity and, therefore, it was an epistemic failure; a failure of knowledge. As such, it goes to the heart of the investigative role, as we have conceived of it (see Chapter 2). For reasons of space in what follows we focus attention on the de Menezes case study only.[23]

Jean Charles de Menezes was an innocent person wrongly suspected by police of being a terrorist suicide bomber who was intentionally killed by police in the belief that he was a mortal threat to the passengers in the London underground station where he was shot dead. The ethical issues to be addressed in this chapter concern the individual and/or collective *moral* responsibility, if any, for the killing of an innocent person.

While the events that terminated in Mr de Menezes' death involved a number of what might at this point be referred to as mistakes or errors of judgment on the part of police, we will focus on just three: (i) the failure of the surveillance team in relation to determining whether or not Mr de Menezes was the terrorist suspect Hussain Osman (an epistemic failure) and, in particular, clearly communicating to Commander Dick that Mr de Menezes was or was not Mr Osman, or that they did not know or were otherwise uncertain of their subject's identity; (ii) the failure on the part of Commander Dick to see to it that Mr de Menezes was challenged and stopped at some point after leaving Scotia Road, but prior to his entering the underground railway station, that is, at a location which would not have compromised the surveillance operation at Scotia Road, and in a manner that might not have required killing him (he being at most a threat to himself, the arresting officers and, perhaps, one or two passersby); (iii) the failure on the part of the two officers who shot Mr de Menezes each to provide himself with adequate grounds for believing – an epistemic task – that they were shooting dead a suicide bomber who was at the time in question a mortal threat to the train passengers; after all, the person shot dead was merely a suspected suicide bomber and one in relation to whom the firearms officers had no clear evidence that he was carrying a bomb – because the operation had not been declared by Commander Dick to be a Kratos operation and they did not at any point perceive a bomb or were otherwise provided with good evidence that the suspect was carrying a bomb. In referring to these failures as mistakes or – especially in the case of Commander Dick and the firearms officers – errors of judgment, we are not implying any specific moral failing on the part of the police; whether or not there was a moral failure is a matter to be determined. Here we simply note that, by virtue of their failures being, in large part, epistemic – failures to acquire knowledge – the police officers in question are not necessarily absolved of all moral responsibility for the outcome. As was argued in Chapter 2, Section 2.5, investigators and other police officers can be morally blameworthy for their epistemic failures (and morally praiseworthy for their epistemic successes) when the knowledge in question is morally significant – which was obviously the case here.

That said, and as stated above, we should stress that there was no intention to kill an innocent person; indeed, police actions were carried out with the intention to save innocent lives. Moreover, obviously the police did not foresee that an innocent life would be taken.

A related ethical issue concerns Kratos as a mode of police operations. Is Kratos an ethically sustainable operational policy? If not, then a question arises in relation to the moral responsibility of those who put the policy in place for any untoward consequences that might emanate from its application on the ground. In relation to the ethical acceptability of Kratos, suppose that the police shot dead a person under the same circumstances as they shot Mr de Menezes, except that the person turned out to be Mr Osman; would their actions have been justified if, for example, Mr Osman was *not* carrying a bomb with him at the time? Mr Osman was, after all, only a suspected suicide bomber; otherwise, why was the plan to "let him run" upon leaving Scotia Road? At no point was any good evidence provided that the person under surveillance was actually carrying a bomb. Is it therefore ethically justifiable for police to shoot dead a suspect without warning, when the suspect is in a crowded location and they have good evidence that he is a suicide bomber, but they do not know whether he has a bomb on him at the time? And if shooting dead a person under these circumstances is not permissible under Kratos, because it is not permissible under the relevant criminal laws, is it, nevertheless, not likely that under Kratos police will end up shooting suspect suicide bombers under these circumstances? Indeed, on one construal of events – a construal that is, admittedly at odds with the testimony of the police and not found by the coroner to be correct by the epistemic standard of being beyond reasonable doubt – this is exactly what happened in the case of the shooting of Mr de Menezes. The firearms officers, rightly or wrongly, reasonably or unreasonably, believed the situation was a de facto Kratos operation and, therefore, did not give Mr de Menezes any warning, did not afford him the opportunity to be arrested without the use of force, and for his part Mr de Menezes did not fail to comply with any instruction from the police.

7.5   Concept of Moral Responsibility

We first need to distinguish some different senses of responsibility.[24] Sometimes to say that someone is responsible for an action is to say that the person had a reason, or reasons, to perform some action, then formed an intention to perform that action (or not to perform it), and finally acted (or refrained from acting) on that intention, and did so on the basis of that reason (or those reasons). Note that an important category of reasons for actions are ends, goals, or purposes; an agent's reason for performing an action is often that the action realizes an agent's goal. Moreover, it is assumed that in the course of all this the agent brought about or caused the action, at least in the sense that the mental state or states that constituted his reason for performing the action was or were causally efficacious (in the right way), and that his resulting intention was causally efficacious (in the right way).

We will dub this sense of being responsible for an action "natural responsibility." This sense of being responsible is relevant to the actions of the firearms officer in shooting Mr de Menezes, in that they intentionally performed an action of shooting Mr de Menezes dead and did so for the reason that they believed him to be a suicide bomber.

As was argued in Chapter 2, Section 2.5, a person can be responsible for their epistemic actions, including deciding to investigate some matter, making inferences from one belief to another, and making a judgment with respect to the truth of some matter. Criminal investigators deciding to investigate a particular person, making inferences on the basis of evidence, and making a judgment with respect to whether someone committed a crime are all instances of such epistemic "action," which terminates in beliefs, statements – including formal statements (Statements) – and the like.

On other occasions, what is meant by the phrase "being responsible for an action" is that the person in question occupies a certain institutional role and that the occupant of that role is the person who has the institutionally determined duty to decide what is to be done in relation to certain matters – including what is to be investigated or what is, in fact, the case in relation to some requirement for knowledge – and to see to it that it does happen (or see to it that the required knowledge in question is acquired and, perhaps, communicated to others). Thus, the members of the surveillance team had the responsibility to identify Mr Osman, video-record anyone leaving the premises, and communicate information in a clear and precise manner to the control room, irrespective of whether or not they did so, or even contemplated doing so. Clearly, they failed in respect of their institutional responsibility with regard to this essentially epistemic task.

A third sense of "being responsible" for an action is a species of our second sense. If the matters in respect of which the occupant of an institutional role has an institutionally determined duty to decide what is to be done include ordering other agents to perform, or not to perform, certain actions (including acquiring certain knowledge), then the occupant of the role is responsible for those actions performed by those other agents. We say of such a person that he or she is responsible for the actions of other persons in virtue of being the person in authority over them. Thus, as the person in authority, Commander Dick had a responsibility to see to it that the police on the ground interdicted Mr de Menezes before he entered the underground station. Her failure in this respect was a failure to discharge her institutional responsibility as the person in authority.

The fourth sense of responsibility is, in fact, the sense that we are principally concerned with here, namely, moral responsibility. Roughly speaking, an agent is held to be morally responsible for an action or omission – including an epistemic act or omission – if the agent was responsible for that action or omission in one of our first three senses of responsibility, and that action is morally significant.

An action or omission – including an epistemic act or omission – can be morally significant in a number of ways. The action or omission could be intrinsically morally wrong, as in the case of a rights violation. Or the action or omission might have moral significance by virtue of the end that it was performed to serve or the foreseen or reasonably foreseeable outcome that it actually had, for example, the killing of an innocent person, as in the case of Mr de Menezes.

We can now make the following preliminary claim concerning moral responsibility – note that we will use the term action or omission to include epistemic acts and omissions:

1. If an agent is responsible for an action or omission (or foreseen or reasonably foreseeable outcome of that action or omission) in the first, second, or third sense of being responsible, and the action, omission or

outcome is morally significant, then – other things being equal – the agent is morally responsible for that action, omission or outcome, and – again, other things being equal – ought to attract moral praise or blame and (possibly) punishment or reward for it.

Here the "other things being equal" clauses are intended to be cashed in terms of capacity for morally responsible action, for example, suppose the agent was a psychopath, or in terms of exculpatory conditions either by way of justification or excuse. Thus, other things might not be equal if, for example, the agent was coerced, or there was some overriding moral justification for performing what would otherwise have been a morally wrong action. Note also that, *contra* some accounts of moral responsibility, we are distinguishing this notion from that of blameworthiness/praiseworthiness.

Let us first consider the surveillance officer or officers who failed in their institutional responsibility by not clearly communicating whether or not Mr de Menezes was Mr Osman or whether they were uncertain in this regard. Given the moral stakes, that is, the possibility of loss of innocent life (whether the life of an innocent person mistakenly identified as a suicide bomber or the lives of innocent Londoners caught in a bomb blast), and the fact that the members of a surveillance team can reasonably be expected to provide clear communications in relation to their subjects, then they can be held morally responsible for their failure to provide a clear communication, albeit there might be mitigating circumstances, for example, confusion, lack of resources.

Now consider Commander Dick. Again, given the moral stakes and the existence of a plan (namely, to stop any suspected suicide bomber before they got to an underground train station or similar locale) that she could reasonably have been expected to adhere to, she can be held morally responsible for failing to see to it that Mr de Menezes was interdicted prior to going into the underground, albeit there might be mitigating circumstances.

Of course, in making these claims regarding moral responsibility for a variety of failures, we are not claiming that the surveillance team or Commander Dick is morally responsible for Mr de Menezes' death.

What of the firearms officers? The justification for killing Mr de Menezes available to the firearms officers was that they believed him to be a suicide bomber and they shot him to protect the lives of the train passengers and their own lives.

It seems clear that the coroner was correct to argue that it was not a case of unlawful killing, because it cannot be shown beyond reasonable doubt that the two officers did not believe that the man they shot was a suicide bomber who was a mortal threat to the lives of the passengers and themselves.

However, the jury in reaching an open verdict rather than a verdict of lawful killing did so on the grounds that, on the balance of probabilities, it was not clear that the two police officers believed that they were shooting a suicide bomber who was a deadly threat at the time of the shooting. Moreover, even if they did believe that this was the case, there remain further questions from a moral, if not a legal, perspective. This is, in part, because of the nature of individual moral responsibility when it comes to taking the life of another human being.

Police officers need to exercise authority on a daily basis; they have institutional responsibilities in the sense explained above.

Historically, policing in the United Kingdom and Australia has made use of a distinctive notion of authority, so-called original authority. In relation to the concept of original authority, we need to distinguish compliance with laws from obedience to the directives of men and women, especially one's superiors. Thus, according to the law, an investigating officer must not prosecute a fellow police officer if the latter is self-evidently innocent. On the other hand, the investigator might be ordered to do so by his superior officer. Now, individual police officers are held to be responsible to the law as well as to their superiors in the police service. However, their primary responsibility is to the law. So, a police officer should disobey a directive from a superior officer that is clearly unlawful. And yet, the admittedly controversial doctrine of original authority does not end here. It implies further that there are at least some situations in which police officers have a right to disobey a superior's otherwise *lawful* command, if obeying it would prevent them from discharging their own obligations to the law.[25]

According to the doctrine of original authority, there are at least some actions, including the decision to arrest or not arrest (at least in some contexts) or to shoot or not shoot, which are ultimately matters for the decision of the individual officer, and decisions for which he or she is, or might be, individually legally liable.[26] The contexts in question are ones in which the action of arresting a given person would prevent the police officer from discharging his obligations to the law, and (in this instance) his obligation to keep the peace, in particular. If this is indeed the legal situation, then it reflects a commitment to the ethical notion of professional autonomy. Police are being held to be akin to members of professional groups such as doctors. In the case of a surgeon, for example, it is up to the surgeon – and not the surgeon's employer – to decide whether or not to operate on a patient who might suffer complications if operated on.

In some tension with this understanding of the legal situation in UK policing, we note that it was the Commissioner of the Police of the Metropolis, in his capacity as the employer, who was fined for an offense under the Health and Safety at Work Act for failing to provide for the health, safety, and welfare of Mr de Menezes. At any rate, our concern is with morality not legality.

Let us now consider the actions of the two firearms officers who shot dead Mr de Menezes. The first point is that it was the moral responsibility of the two police officers to decide whether or not to shoot Mr de Menezes, irrespective of whether they had been ordered to do so; and, evidently, this is reflected in the law. (See above on this point.) The second point is that they had not been ordered to do so; the situation had not been declared to be a Kratos operation. So, for better or worse, individual moral responsibility can, in principle, be sheeted home to the two firearms officers for killing an innocent person depending, of course, on the facts of the case.

What of exculpatory conditions? Their justification was that they believed that Mr de Menezes was a suicide bomber. Even supposing this to be true – and the jury did not accept that on the balance of probabilities – there remains the question of the justification for that belief. Did they have sufficient evidence to warrant that belief? It seems that they did not, especially given that good and decisive evidence is required in the case where the taking of another human life is concerned.

However, there is another important moral consideration in play here. The firearms officers had a moral obligation to protect the lives of innocent train passengers. If they had failed to shoot the suspect, and he had turned out to be Mr Osman carrying a bomb, then in all probability there would have been a far greater loss of life. This consideration has considerable moral weight and does so notwithstanding the inadequacy of the evidence for their belief (or judgment) that Mr de Menezes was Mr Osman and a mortal threat at the time. So, whatever the legal situation, and whatever any past failure to satisfy themselves with regard to the identity of Mr de Menezes, at the point of decision whether or not to shoot him, the firearms officers confronted what was in effect a moral dilemma: (i) shoot dead a person they believe is highly likely to be a suicide bomber about to detonate a bomb; of course, if he turns out not to have a bomb then they will have killed an innocent person; (ii) refrain from shooting him; of course, if he turns out to be a suicide bomber about to detonate a bomb then numerous innocent passengers and the police officers themselves will be killed. In these circumstances it is difficult not to view the "other things being equal" as having application. Arguably, there was not a good and decisive reason in favor of either course of action. Rather, at the point of decision great risks attached to each of the available options; there was a moral balancing act to be performed, and a split second decision to be made. In these circumstances the firearms officers might be held to be morally responsible for the death of an innocent person, but they surely cannot be held to be morally *culpable* for what they did; they were morally responsible, but not morally blameworthy.

7.6 Collective Moral Responsibility

Above we distinguished four senses of responsibility, including moral responsibility. Let us now consider collective moral responsibility.

As is the case with individual responsibility, we can distinguish four senses of collective responsibility, including in relation to epistemic actions and omissions. In the first instance we will do so in relation to joint actions.[27]

Agents who perform a joint action are responsible for that action in the first sense of collective responsibility. Accordingly, to say that they are collectively responsible for the action is just to say that they performed the joint action. That is, they each had a collective end, each intentionally performed their contributory action, and each did so because each believed the other would perform his contributory action, and that therefore the collective end would be realized.

In the case of the members of the surveillance team, the joint action in question was an epistemic action; it was a joint action the point or purpose of which was knowledge, for example, knowledge of the identity of those entering and leaving Scotia Road. So, the individual members of the surveillance team performed the joint (epistemic) action of surveilling Scotia Road.

It is important to note here that each agent is individually (naturally) responsible for performing his contributory action, and responsible by virtue of the fact that he intentionally performed this action, and the action was not intentionally performed by anyone else. Of course, the other agents (or agent) *believe* that he is performing, or is going to perform, the contributory action in question. But mere possession of such a belief is not sufficient for the ascription of responsibility to *the believer* for performing the individual action in question. So what are the agents *collectively* (naturally) responsible for? The agents are *collectively* (naturally) responsible for the realization of the (collective) *end* which results from their contributory actions. Consider two agents jointly killing someone in a crowded setting, one by grabbing him and holding him fast, the other by shooting him in the head. Each is individually (naturally) responsible for his own action, and the two agents are collectively (naturally) responsible for bringing it about that the person is dead, given that the actions of both were necessary.

Again, if the occupants of an institutional role (or roles) have an institutionally determined obligation to perform some joint action, then those individuals are collectively responsible for its performance, in our second sense of collective responsibility. Here there is a *joint* institutional obligation to realize the collective end of the joint action in question. In addition, there is a set of derived *individual* obligations; each of the participating individuals has an individual obligation to perform his or her contributory action. (The derivation of these individual obligations relies on the fact that if everyone performs his or her contributory action then it is probable that the collective end will be realized.)

There is a third sense of collective responsibility that might be thought to correspond to the third sense of individual responsibility. The third sense of individual responsibility concerns those in authority. Suppose the members of the Cabinet of country A (consisting of the Prime Minister and his or her Cabinet ministers) or the members of the relevant police authority, collectively decide to exercise their institutionally determined right to introduce a counter terrorism measure, for example, Kratos. The Cabinet and/or the relevant police authority (say, ACPO) is then collectively responsible for this policy and, potentially, for the untoward consequences of its implementation.

There are a couple of things to keep in mind here. First, the notion of responsibility in question is, at least in the first instance, institutional – as opposed to moral – responsibility.

Second, the "decisions" of committees, as opposed to the individual decisions of the members of committees, need to be analyzed in terms of the notion of what has been termed and analyzed by Miller elsewhere, namely, a joint institutional mechanism.[28] By the lights of that account, the "decision" of the Cabinet, and also perhaps of ACPO, can be analyzed as follows. At one level each member of the Cabinet or ACPO voted for or against Kratos. Let us assume some voted in the affirmative and others in the negative. But at another level each member of the Cabinet or ACPO (or both) agreed to abide by the outcome of the vote; each voted having as a collective end that the outcome with a majority of the votes in its favor would be realized. Accordingly, the members of the Cabinet and/or of ACPO were jointly institutionally responsible for the policy change, that is, Cabinet and/or ACPO were collectively institutionally responsible for the change.

What of the fourth sense of collective responsibility, collective *moral* responsibility? Collective moral responsibility is a species of joint responsibility. Accordingly, each agent is individually morally responsible, but conditionally on the others being individually morally responsible. There is interdependence in respect of moral responsibility. This account of collective moral responsibility arises naturally out of the account of joint actions. It also parallels the account given of individual moral responsibility.

Thus we can make our second preliminary claim about moral responsibility – again bearing in mind that the joint actions in question include joint epistemic actions, such as that of the surveillance team:

2.   If agents are collectively responsible for a joint action or omission (or the realization of a foreseen or reasonably foreseeable outcome of that

action or omission), in the first or second or third senses of collective responsibility, and if the joint action, omission or outcome is morally significant then – other things being equal – the agents are collectively morally responsible for that action, omission, or outcome, and – other things being equal – ought to attract moral praise or blame, and (possibly) punishment or reward for bringing about the outcome.

As is the case with the parallel account of individual moral responsibility, there are crucial "other things being equal" clauses to provide for the possibilities that the agents in question either lack the requisite moral capacities – and so cannot be held morally responsible – or are possessed of moral capacities but in the circumstances in question have an excuse or justification for their joint actions and omissions, and for the outcomes of such actions and omissions.

Note that there can be cases where there the morally significant collective end of a joint action is realized, yet one or more individuals fails to successfully perform their individual action, and cases where the morally significant collective end of a joint action is not realized, yet one or more individuals successfully perform their individual action. In the former kind of case, assuming the individual (or minority) has the collective end (and presumably, therefore, did not intentionally fail to perform their contributory action), the individual shares in the collective moral responsibility for the realization of the end, notwithstanding their individual failure in relation to their contributory action. In the latter kind of case, again assuming the individual has the collective end, the individual shares in the collective moral responsibility for the failure to realize the end, notwithstanding their individual success in relation to their contributory action.[29]

In the light of our account of collective moral responsibility, what sense can we now make of the police killing of Jean Charles de Menezes?

The first point is that, as noted already, collective moral responsibility for an outcome is consistent with individual moral responsibility for individual actions that are in part constitutive of some joint action, omission, or outcome. As we have seen, the individual members of the surveillance team were collectively (jointly) morally responsible for failing to clearly communicate to the control room whether or not Mr de Menezes was Mr Osman – or that they were uncertain in this regard. Moreover, Commander Dick is morally responsible for failing to see to it that Mr de Menezes was stopped prior to his entering the underground station. Finally, the two firearms officers were collectively (jointly) morally responsible for failing to provide themselves with good and decisive evidence for the proposition that Mr de Menezes was a suicide bomber and a mortal threat to the train passengers. Here we stress that these failures all had mitigating factors, especially, no doubt, the failures of the firearms officers.

The second point is that each of these failures was a necessary condition for the outcome, that is, the outcome that may be described as the killing of an innocent person. This second point gives rise to the question as to whether the surveillance team, Commander Dick, and the firearms officers are collectively morally responsible for that outcome, albeit none individually intended the outcome and none individually foresaw the outcome. We suggest that, notwithstanding that the failure of each was a necessary condition for the outcome, this causal chain was not accompanied by a collective end (so there was no joint action or joint intentional omission). Moreover, the members of the group did not, as a group, foresee the outcome; indeed, not even one of these individuals foresaw the outcome.

Could the members of the group reasonably have foreseen that the consequences of their actions would be the killing by police of an innocent person, bearing in mind that they ought to have had, as part of their collective end, to avoid taking innocent life? Surely not all of them could reasonably have foreseen this outcome – for example, not the members of the surveillance team. Accordingly, the police were not collectively morally responsible for the death of an innocent person, Jean Charles de Menezes.

In Case Study 7.3.2 it was mentioned that the Metropolitan Police as a corporate entity were found to have committed a criminal offense under the Health and Safety Act and fined £175,000 (plus court costs). If a criminal offense implies a moral offense, then perhaps there is some acceptably weaker notion of collective moral responsibility that might be provided to underpin the guilty verdict of the criminal court. On the other hand, the fact that the penalty is a small fine for a large organization such as the London Metropolitan Police with a multi-billion pound budget suggests that the notion of criminal offense in play here is an attenuated one.

Notes

1   For detailed discussion of the definition of terrorism see Seumas Miller (2009) *Terrorism and Counter-terrorism: Ethics and Liberal Democracy*, Oxford: Blackwell, Chapter 2, and Igor Primoratz (2013) *Terrorism: A Philosophical Investigation*, Cambridge: Polity Press, Chapter 1. For an introduction to the investigation of terrorism see, Thomas R. O'Connor (2009) *Bringing Terrorists to Justice: Investigation and Adjudication*, Delhi: Indo-American Books.

2   For recent developments in Australia in particular, see J. Hocking (2004) *Terror Laws*, Sydney: UNSW Press.

3   See, for example, what Philip Ruddock, the former Australian Attorney General, had to say about this. He is quoted in S. Bottomley, and S. Bronitt (2006) *Law in Context* (3rd edn), Sydney: Federation Press, p. 412.

4   Seumas Miller and John Blackler (2005), Chapter 1.

5 A. Lynch and G. Williams (2006) *What Price Security? Taking Stock of Australia's Anti-terror Laws*, Sydney: UNSW Press, pp. 33–34.

6 See BBC (British Broadcasting Corporation), Smith plans 42-day terror limit, http://news.bbc.co.uk/1/hi/uk_politics/7130072.stm.

7 Sections 21 to 32 of the Anti-Terrorism, Crime and Security Emergency Bill 2001 (United Kingdom Government, 2001) now allow detention without trial where the option of deportation is not available. Article 3 of the European Convention on Human Rights to which the United Kingdom is a signatory forbids torture and inhuman treatment. See D. Haubrich (2003) September 11, anti-terror laws and civil liberties: Britain, France and Germany compared. *Government and Opposition* 38.1, p. 15.

8 See Miller (2009), Chapter 4 and also Don E. Scheid (2010) Indefinite detention of mega-terrorists, *Criminal Justice Ethics*, 29.1, pp. 1–28.

9 For detailed argument on this issue see Miller (2009), Chapters 4 and 5.

10 See Bottomley and Bronitt (2006), p. 402.

11 A summary of the development of Kratos is contained in Independent Police Complaints Commission (IPCC) (2007) *Stockwell One: Investigation into the shooting of Jean Charles de Menezes at Stockwell underground station* (February 2007), s 9, paras 9.1–9.19, 40–44, http://policeauthority.org/metropolitan/downloads/scrutinites/stockwell/ipcc-one.pdf.

12 Metropolitan Police Authority (MPA) (2005) *Suicide Terrorism Report*, No 13 (27 October 2005), http://policeauthority.org/Metropolitan/committees/mpa/2005/051027/13/index.html (accessed 14 January 2014).

13 See IPCC (2007), n 7, 24.

14 See MPA (2005), n 11. Owing to the extreme nature of the risk to the public, a very robust command structure has been designed and implemented. Specially trained ACPO officers, acting as the "Designated Senior Officer" (DSO), will command these operations. It is the DSO who will give the order to a firearms officer to shoot.

15 IPCC (2007) n 7, paras 12.1–12.17, pp. 53–57.

16 IPCC (2007) n 7, para. 12.17, p. 57.

17 IPCC (2007) n 7, para. 12.37, p. 61.

18 IPCC (2007) n 7, para 12.27, p. 59 and para 12.36, p. 61.

19 IPPC (2007) n 7, para 9.14, p. 43.

20 Provisional Irish Republican Army – a republican terrorist group.

21 Ulster Defence Association – a loyalist terrorist group.

22 Ian Jack (2008) *The Guardian*, Saturday, March 8, 2008.

23 The material in this section is drawn from Ian Gordon and Seumas Miller (2012) The fatal police shooting of Jean Charles de Menezes: Is anyone responsible? in Simon Bronitt, Miriam Gani, and Saskia Hufnagel (eds), *Shooting to Kill: Socio-legal Perspectives on the Use of Lethal Force*, Oxford: Hart, pp. 215–239.

24 See Miller (2010a), Chapter 4, Collective moral responsibility, and Miller (2006) Collective moral responsibility: An individualist account, in Peter A. French (ed.) *Midwest Studies in Philosophy*, 30, pp. 176–193.

25 Relevant legal cases here are the "Blackburn cases," principally *R v Metropolitan Police Commissioner; Ex parte Blackburn* [1968] 2 QB 118, cited in K. Bryett,

A. Harrison, and J. Shaw (1994) *An Introduction to Policing: The Role and Function of Police in Australia*, vol. II, Sydney: Butterworths, 43, in which Lord Denning considered the Commissioner of the London Metropolitan Police "to be answerable to the law and to the law alone" in response to a demand for *mandamus* from a plaintiff seeking to get the courts to require police intervention, and *Fisher v Oldham Corporation* [1930] 2 KB 364, cited as above at 42, in which the court found the police service was not vicariously liable in virtue of the original authority of the office of constable. Concerning the exercise of original authority in decisions to arrest, in some jurisdictions proceeding by summons has increased significantly and officers do not possess original authority in respect of any part of the summons process. To this extent their original authority has diminished. See Miller and Blackler (2005), Chapter 2.

26   A concept very close to original authority is sometimes referred to as a species of discretionary power, namely the concept of a discretionary decision that cannot be overridden or reversed by another official. See R. Dworkin (1977) *Taking Rights Seriously*, Cambridge, MA: Harvard University Press, 1977, p. 32. Here we need to distinguish a decision that cannot, as a matter of fact, be overridden, for example, the use of deadly force by a lone officer in the field, and a decision that cannot be overridden as a matter of law. Only the latter can be referred to as a species of authority.

27   For detailed accounts of the notion of joint action in play here see Miller (1992), (1995), and (2001a), Chapter 2.

28   See Miller (2001a), Chapter 5 and (2010a), Chapter 1.

29   It is consistent with the above that, if an individual (or minority) *culpably* failed to realize their individual end, yet knew that the collective end would, nevertheless, be realized, then that individual does *not* share in the collective moral responsibility of the successful outcome since, for one thing, the individual did not, in fact, have the collective end. It is also consistent with the above that if an individual (or minority) *culpably* failed to realize their individual end in the knowledge that, as a consequence of this culpable failure of theirs, the collective end would not be realized, then the individual (i) does not have the collective end and (ii) is individually morally responsible for the collective failure to realize the collective end. So there is no collective moral responsibility for the failure.

8

Police Corruption

8.1 Corruption

Providing an acceptable definition of corruption has proved to be an elusive goal.[1] Many of the available definitions are in terms of the abuse of power on the part of public officials, for instance, "Corruption is the abuse of power by a public official for private gain." Doubtless, the abuse of public offices for private gain is corruption. But what of so-called noble cause corruption – corruption undertaken for the public good? Consider the police officer who fabricates evidence to secure the conviction of a known drug dealer. And what of private citizens who lie when they give testimony in court and, thereby, corrupt the judicial process?

Failure to provide a theoretical account of the concept of corruption might lead one to simply identify corruption with specific legal and/or moral offenses, such as (say) bribery.

However, paradigmatic cases of corruption include police fabrication of evidence, perjury, abuse of authority, fraudulent use of travel funds by politicians, stuffing ballot boxes with false voting papers to win an election, falsifying experimental results to enhance one's academic status, and so on. So the list of legal and/or moral offenses is going to be a very long one, indeed, indeterminately lengthy. In any case, naming a set of offenses that might be regarded as instances of corruption does not obviate the need for a theoretical, or quasi-theoretical, account of the concept of corruption.

Investigative Ethics: Ethics for Police Detectives and Criminal Investigators, First Edition.
Seumas Miller and Ian A. Gordon.
© 2014 Seumas Miller and Ian A. Gordon. Published 2014 by John Wiley & Sons, Ltd.

Corruption is fundamentally a moral, as opposed to a legal, phenomenon. While many corrupt acts are unlawful – or ought to be unlawful – this is not necessarily the case. For example, historically in many jurisdictions bribery has not been unlawful. Moreover, evidently not all acts of immorality are acts of corruption; corruption, it seems, is only one species of immorality. Consider a suicide bomber who murders innocent children. Surely this is not an act of corruption, since neither the victim nor the perpetrator remains alive, let alone in a state of corruption. Rather it is a human rights violation and, as such, serves to illustrate the distinction between human rights violations and corruption. This is, of course, not to say that human rights violations might not on occasion also be acts of corruption, for instance, a leader who unjustly and unlawfully incarcerates his or her political opponent (a human rights violation) might also be corrupting the political process. See also Case Study 8.2.1 below, which involves both human rights violations and abuses of police authority.

We conclude that corrupt actions are merely one species of immoral actions, albeit an important species. What further features do corrupt actions possess? Here we restrict ourselves to cases of institutional corruption. More specifically, what further features do corrupt actions possess which warrant, at least in some cases, their being criminalized and, therefore, the appropriate subject of criminal investigations?

Institutional corruption, whether it is bribery, abuse of authority, fabrication of evidence, or some other species of corruption typically does institutional damage by undermining an institutional process or purpose.

However, the undermining of institutional processes and/or purposes is not a sufficient condition for institutional corruption. Consider internal affairs investigators in some large jurisdiction who, as a result of cutbacks in funding, become less numerous and progressively less well trained in the context of a gradually increasing workload of cases. As a consequence, there may well be a diminution over the years in the quality of the investigations of these investigators, and so the police investigative processes are to an extent undermined. This is corrosion, but it is not necessarily corruption, notwithstanding the institutional damage that is being done.

Evidently, an act or policy might undermine an institutional process or purpose without the person who performed it intending this effect, foreseeing this effect, or even being in a position such that they should have foreseen this effect. Such an act may well be an act of corrosion, but it would not necessarily be an act of corruption. Consider our internal affairs example again. Neither the government and other officials responsible for resourcing and training the investigators, nor the investigators themselves, might intend or foresee this institutional harm; indeed, perhaps no-one could reasonably have foreseen the harmful effects of these shortcomings in training and failure to respond to increased workloads – or if they did, could have done nothing about it. So this is corrosion, but not corruption.

Because persons who perform corrupt actions do so intentionally or knowingly – or at least such persons should have known the corrupting effect that their actions would have – these persons are blameworthy, generally speaking. This is one respect in which corruption is different from corrosion.

If an action is corrupt, then it corrupts something or someone – so corruption is not only a moral concept, it is a *causal* or quasi-causal concept. Moreover, if an act is an act of institutional corruption then it has a corrupting effect on an institution and, specifically, on an institutional process, purpose, or person.

However, arguably an infringement of a specific law or institutional rule does not in and of itself constitute an act of corruption. In order to do so, any such infringement needs to have an institutional *effect*, for example, to defeat the institutional purpose of the rule, or to subvert the institutional process governed by the rule. Considered in itself, the offense of, say, lying is an infringement of a law, rule, and/or a moral principle. However, the offense is only an act of institutional corruption – given corruption is causal in nature – if it has some effect, for example, it is performed in a courtroom setting and thereby subverts the judicial process.

In the light of this account of corruption let us return to our earlier question concerning the criminalization of corruption.

Some acts of corruption might not be sufficiently serious to count as crimes, such as minor conflicts of interest in the allocation of workloads. However, many acts of corruption, at least when taken in aggregate, constitute a serious threat to central institutions. Consider in this connection widespread vote rigging in elections.

In the area of policing, corruption by police officers often constitutes a rights violation in addition to undermining the institution of the law and its processes. Consider the fabrication of evidence later used against a defendant in a criminal trial. In such instances the moral right of the defendant to a fair trial has been violated.

So, while the investigation of police corruption is not necessarily the investigation of serious moral rights violations which are also crimes, it often is. Moreover, the investigation of those acts of corruption that are not in themselves rights violations typically involves moral rights violations indirectly. For such acts, being acts of serious corruption, undermine central institutions and, in particular, the institution of the police. However, as was argued in Chapter 1, the institution of the police has as its fundamental purpose the protection of justifiably enforceable, legally enshrined moral rights. Accordingly, police corruption, even when it does not directly involve the violation of moral rights, nevertheless violates them indirectly via undermining the processes and/or purposes of the institution of the police. Let us now turn to some case studies to concretize these and other issues to be dealt with later on in this chapter.

8.2 Case Studies

Case Study 8.2.1 The Rampart Scandal

In 1998 a LAPD officer, Rafael Perez, was arrested for stealing a large quantity of cocaine from a police evidence locker, its value was $80,000. At the ensuing trial Perez pleaded guilty to the theft and did a deal with prosecutors; in return for a five-year prison sentence and an amnesty from further prosecution, he would give information about fellow officers who were implicated in unlawful activities. Perez had been a member of the Community Resources Against Street Hoodlums (CRASH) anti-gang unit of the Los Angeles Police, which was based in the Rampart Division of the Force. Within a very short time Perez implicated over 70 of his former colleagues in a range of criminal activity ranging from unprovoked shootings, framing suspects, perjury, and so on.

Perez admitted that he and his partner, Nino Durden, had shot, framed and then given false evidence against Javier Ovando – a gang member who had been convicted of assaulting the officers and sentenced to 23 years imprisonment. The shooting had also left Ovando paralysed. At a later court hearing the conviction was overturned and he successfully sued Los Angeles City Authority and received $15m. The disclosures by Perez appeared to identify widespread police corruption in CRASH. The disclosures led to investigations into falsifying evidence and perjury: the eventual outcome was that 106 convictions were overturned. It is believed that subsequent legal actions against Los Angeles City led to around 140 lawsuits being settled, with payments in excess of $125m in settlements. Rampart became the largest example of police corruption in the US.

During the investigation of Perez and his disclosures, which involved numerous interviews, the investigators began to question whether Perez was in fact telling the truth. He failed lie detector tests and made mistakes when testifying in court. Out of 58 officers who were put before Internal Administrative Boards, based on evidence gleaned from the interviews with Perez, only 24 were found to have committed misconduct. A view emerged that Perez was following his own agenda, where his allegations may be directed against former colleagues who he disliked. When Perez was sentenced he made a statement to the court in which he apologized and tried to explain his actions:

In the Rampart CRASH unit things began to change. The lines between right and wrong became fuzzy and indistinct. The "us" against "them" ethos of the overzealous cop began to consume me and the ends seemed to justify the means. We vaguely sensed we were doing the wrong things for the right reasons. Time and again, I stepped over that line. Once crossed, I hurdled over it again and again, landing with both feet, sometimes on innocent persons . . . My job became an intoxicant that I lusted after.[2]

The following is an interview with Detective Mike Hohan, L.A.P.D. Detective, Principal investigator on the Rampart Corruption Task Force:[3]

Q. What did he say about how widespread this putting cases on people was within CRASH?
A. He said it went throughout the city; that, based on his comments, I believe it was something like 95 percent of all the specialized CRASH units or specialized units in the city did this type of activity.
Q. Has that borne out, by the way?
A. No.
Q. What has borne out?
A. What has borne out is that there are a number of irregularities in cases that developed out of Rampart CRASH. Some of them may rise to the level of criminal conduct. Others rise to the level of administrative misconduct. And others appear to be completely correct.
Q. Is it 20 percent, 30 percent, 60 percent?
A. I couldn't say precisely. What I can say is that we reviewed approximately 2500 arrest reports. And I believe that, out of those, we found approximately 100 that were questionable. . . .
Q. I never quite got what he meant by being "in the loop." He begins to describe to you all, "Well, there were some cops who were actually out there involved, and then there were others who were in the loop." What does he mean by that?
A. You might say it's the classic tale of corruption, in the sense that an officer that was in the loop was somebody that knew about the activity that was going on, had participated in some level of the activity, and, because of that, they had him. They had something on him, so the officer couldn't tell anybody about what

(*Continued*)

happened. So you had this. And within this group of people in the loop, you had some people that were proactive. They went out and they did these things. And you had other people that acquiesced. They knew what happened, but because they were either there or witnessed it, they couldn't do anything about it.

Q. How wide was this loop as Perez described it?

A. When he described it, he named quite a few CRASH officers and former CRASH officers that he alleged were in the loop.

Q. And what did you find?

A. We found that officers were involved in misconduct, but again, not to the level I think that Rafael Perez has indicated.

Case Study 8.2.2   Corrupt Colleague

Information from a source states a police officer has told an organized crime gang that a local criminal, Jones, is a registered police informant for the Serious Crime Squad. There is no supporting intelligence and the original source had heard it from someone else. The information indicates the officer is called Boysie and he works in a drug squad.

An officer called Boyd has the nickname Boysie – he was a detective constable on the force drug squad but is now working as a local field intelligence officer on a protracted national enquiry on importation of firearms for hire to criminals. The officer's personal record shows that he is in the process of divorce from his wife, and it is common knowledge in the enquiry team where he works that the divorce is quite acrimonious due to Boysie "playing around." Boysie is regarded as a capable detective although he has been known to cut corners and, whilst in drug squad, his Inspector suspected that Boysie did not register all his informants, but had no proof. That belief was not recorded anywhere.

The local Commander reports this matter to the Professional Standards Dept (PSD). In a PSD briefing, an officer says that Boysie is friendly with Detective Inspector Smith, who is on the Serious Crime Squad. They regularly go clubbing in the City. He also says that Boysie has just bought a new car – a Mercedes sports car, which Boysie claims was paid for by his share of the house sale. Boysie's personal record does not show any change of address.

The original source (a registered informant) was tasked to get information about the disclosure of Jones' name. He learned that a criminal, Wright, had been arrested by Boysie for dealing cocaine but, in return for information on other dealers, Boysie had released Wright for insufficient evidence. Boysie had kept the drugs and it was known in the clubs that he used cocaine. Wright continued to give Boysie information and this was known by Allan, the main player in the organized crime gang and Wright's cousin.

A week later a probationer police constable tells his supervisor that he has seen another police officer in a pub with some criminals. He was in the pub (in another town) with relatives and saw Boysie in company with a woman and two other men (he recognized Boysie from a drugs talk given to his probationer class). In their shift briefing yesterday on target criminals, he recognized one, Allan, as one of the men with Boysie. The supervisor reports the matter to the Commander who arranges for PSD to interview the constable. PSD show him a photo of Wright and he identifies him as the other man in the pub.

Case Study 8.2.3   Noble Cause Corruption

A young officer, Joe, seeks advice from the police chaplain. Joe is working with an experienced detective, Mick. Mick is also Joe's brother-in-law and looked up to by Joe as a good detective who gets results. Joe and Mick are working on a case involving a known drug dealer and pedophile. Joe describes his problem as follows:

"Father – he has got a mile of form, including getting kids hooked on drugs, physical and sexual assault on minors, and more. Anyway, surveillance informed Mick that the drug dealer had just made a buy. As me and Mick approached the drug dealer's penthouse flat we saw a window fly open – the dealer sticks his head out and flings a parcel out onto the street. It was full of heroin. When we entered the premises, we found no drugs inside. Mick thought it would be more of a sure thing if we found the evidence in the flat rather than on the street. The defence could hardly deny possession. Last night Mick tells me that he was interviewed and signed a statement that we both found the parcel of heroin under the sink in the flat. He said all I had to do was to go along with the story in court and everything will be sweet, no worries. What should I do Father – perjury is a serious criminal offence?"

(Case study provided by Father Jim Boland, NSW Police Service)

8.3   Causes of Police Corruption

Recent commissions of inquiry into police corruption, including the Mollen Commission into the New York Police Department, the Rampart Commission into the Los Angeles Police Department, and the Royal Commission into the NSW Police Service, have uncovered corruption of a profoundly disturbing kind. Police officers have been involved in perjury, fabricating evidence, protecting pederast rings, taking drug money, and selling drugs. In South Africa, police have been involved in murder, armed robbery, and rape, as well as theft, fraud, fabrication of evidence, and the like. High levels of police corruption have been a persistent historical tendency in police services throughout the world. Corruption in policing is neither new nor especially surprising. Indeed, a number of causes of police corruption have been identified.[4]

As discussed in previous chapters, in order to do their job effectively, police have been given a number of rights and powers – such as the right to use coercive force in ways forbidden to others, and the power to do so – and wide discretion in the exercise of these rights and powers. Police have many opportunities to abuse these powers; to harass the innocent with threats or trivial charges, to turn a blind eye to serious crime, and so on.

They also face considerable temptations to avail themselves of these opportunities. They may be offered material inducements, such as the offer of money or favors in return for protection, or dropping of charges, for example. They may be tempted by the opportunity to express some personal prejudice against (say) a particular racial group. Or they may be influenced by the chance to avoid what we could think of as the costs of police work. After all, a lot of conscientious police work is unpleasant – dangerous, or tedious, or time-consuming. The temptation to take short-cuts to avoid these costs, or to seek benefits to offset these costs, is considerable.

A further contributing factor to police corruption is the inescapable use by police officers of what in normal circumstances would be regarded as morally unacceptable activity. The use of coercive force is in itself harmful; indeed, potentially lethal. Accordingly, in normal circumstances it is morally unacceptable. So it would be morally wrong, for example, for a private citizen to forcibly take someone to his house for questioning. Similarly, locking someone up deprives them of their liberty, and is therefore considered in itself morally wrong. Again, deception, including telling lies, is under normal circumstances morally wrong. Intrusive surveillance is in itself morally wrong – it is an infringement of privacy. And the same can be said of various other methods used in policing.

Coercion, depriving someone of their liberty, deception, and so on are harmful methods; they are activities which, considered in themselves and under normal circumstances, are morally wrong. Therefore, they stand in need of special justification. In relation to policing, there is a special justification. These harmful and normally immoral methods are on occasion necessary in order to realize the fundamental end of policing, namely the protection of justifiably enforceable, legally enshrined moral rights. However, the fundamental point that needs to be made here is that the use of these harmful methods – albeit methods that in the right circumstances are both lawful and morally justifiable – can have a corrupting influence on police officers. A police officer can begin by engaging in the morally justifiable activity of telling lies to criminals, cultivating informants to get them to betray their criminal associates, and engaging in elaborate schemes of deception as an undercover agent, and end up engaging in the morally unjustifiable activity of telling lies and deceiving innocent members of the public or his fellow officers. A police officer can begin by engaging in the morally justifiable and lawful activity of deploying coercive force to arrest violent offenders resisting arrest, and end up engaging in the morally unjustified and unlawful activity of beating up suspects to secure a conviction.

It might be suggested that such methods could be wholly abandoned in favor of the morally unproblematic methods already heavily relied upon, such as rational discourse, appeal to moral sentiment, reliance on upright citizens for information, and so on. Doubtless, in many instances morally problematic methods could be replaced. And, certainly, overuse of these methods is a sign of bad police work, and perhaps of the partial breakdown of the police–community trust so necessary to police work. However, the point is that the morally problematic methods could not be replaced in *all* areas of police work, even if in some. For one thing, the violations of moral rights that the police exist to protect are sometimes violations perpetrated by persons who are unmoved by rationality, appeal to moral sentiment, and so on. Indeed, such persons, far from being moved by well-intentioned police overtures, may seek to influence or corrupt police officers for the purpose of preventing them from doing their moral and lawful duty. For another thing, the relevant members of the community may, for one reason or another, be unwilling or unable to provide the necessary information or evidence, and police may need to rely on persons of bad character, or methods such as intrusive surveillance.

So, unfortunately, harmful methods, which are in normal circumstances considered to be immoral, are on occasion necessary in order to realize the fundamental end of policing, namely the protection of moral rights.

The paradox whereby police necessarily use methods which are normally morally wrong to secure morally worthy ends sets up a dangerous moral dynamic. The danger is that police will come to think that the ends always justify the means; to come to accept the inevitability and the desirability of so-called "noble cause corruption" (see Case Study 8.2.3, Noble Cause Corruption above).[5] From noble cause corruption, they can in turn graduate to straightforward corruption; corruption motivated by greed and personal gain.

Further, as a matter of sociological fact, police display a high degree of group identification and solidarity. In many ways, such solidarity is a good thing: without it, effective policing would be impossible. But it can also contribute to police corruption. Police who refrain from acting against their corrupt colleagues out of a sense of loyalty are often compromised by this failure, and ripe for more active involvement in corrupt schemes (see Case Study 8.2.1, The Rampart Scandal, above).

A particularly significant contributing factor to police corruption is the widespread use in contemporary societies of illegal drugs such as heroin, cocaine, and Ecstasy (again, see Case Studies 8.2.1 and 8.2.3 above.) Police officers, especially detectives, are called on to enforce anti-drug laws in circumstances that have the following features: (i) there are large amounts of money, and a willingness on the part of drug users, and especially drug dealers, to bribe police; (ii) there are no complainants – the "victims" are not persons who would come to the police and report that they have been the victim of a criminal act; (iii) corrupt police officers can accept bribes or steal drugs or drug money with relative impunity, given (ii); (iv) there is a feeling in some sectors of the community that drug addiction is not so much a crime as a medical condition or perhaps a lifestyle choice (at least in the case of so-called recreational users), and that therefore drug taking should not be regarded as a crime; (v) young police officers typically share the attitudes of their peers outside policing, and thus may regard the use of illegal drugs as a relatively minor offense; and (vi) police officers who are especially vulnerable, such as young police officers or those working in drug investigations, may out of fear turn a blind eye to drugs, or even succumb to drug taking themselves, and thereby enter the spiral of corruption which moves from moral vulnerability to moral compromise, and thence to corrupt activities.[6]

Let us now list some of the general conditions which contribute to police corruption. These conditions include: (i) the necessity at times for police officers to deploy harmful methods, such as coercion and deception, which are normally regarded as immoral; (ii) the high levels of discretionary authority and power exercised by police officers in circumstances in which close supervision is not possible; (iii) the ongoing interaction between police officers and corrupt persons who have an interest in compromising and corrupting police; (iv) the necessity for police officers to make discretionary ethical judgments[7] in morally ambiguous situations; and (v) the operation of police officers in an environment in which there is widespread use of illegal drugs and large amounts of drug money.

In addition to these causes of police corruption, there are some less obvious ones.

First, lack of competence can be a contributor to, and even a species of, corruption. Normally, we do not think that incompetence is morally blameworthy, even where it contributes to a bad outcome, since someone cannot be blamed for not bringing about what they did not have the capacity to bring about. However, we can blame people for failing to act to equip themselves with necessary skills or knowledge when they have been provided with the opportunity. For example, a police officer who, out of laziness or indifference, fails to acquaint himself sufficiently with certain aspects of the law, and then through ignorance of the law proceeds to make unlawful arrests, is engaging in a form of corrupt activity. His actions are wrongful, and the reason that he is performing those actions is self-interest, or at least self-indulgence.

We can also blame people for continuing in a job when they know they do not possess, and cannot acquire, the necessary skills or aptitude for it. This kind of moral failure is illustrated by a police officer who continues in the job knowing that he is too fearful to make arrests which he should have been making. Weakness is a moral failing, and he is weak. But weakness is not in itself corruption. What makes such a police officer corrupt is that, even though he knows he is weak, and therefore lacking in the ability to adequately function as a police officer, he continues in the job for reasons of self-interest.

Second, police can count as corrupt even where they use their expertise for the achievement of the right ends, when they do so by making use of bad means. The officer who "verbals" someone he knows to be guilty of violent crime, in order to secure the conviction which would otherwise be impossible, achieves such good ends as the punishment of the guilty, as well as the protection and reassurance of the public. These are ends which police should try to achieve, indeed ends which are partially constitutive of their role. As we have already said, this kind of corruption is known as "noble cause corruption."

8.4 Combating Police Corruption

The above case study, The Rampart Scandal, illustrates not only the extent and diversity of police corruption in a major US police force, but also a number of the difficulties associated with the investigation of police corruption, including the reliability of informants, the fact that many potential witnesses may themselves be compromised, and so on.

In looking at options for promoting integrity and combating ethical failure by police officers, it is very easy to look and opt for some kind of "magic bullet" solution, such as increasing penalties or giving more intrusive powers to investigative agencies.[8] And it is easy to adopt such measures without considering the full array of implications associated with their employment, not only including their demonstrable (as opposed to hoped for) benefits but also their costs in terms of resources, damage to an ethico-professional ethos, and so on. Which of these favored measures has been tested and, as a consequence, is *known* to work? Under what conditions? What unanticipated side-effects have they been known to have? What is more, such "magic bullet" solutions are often offered in relative ignorance of both the actual nature and causes of the problems that they are supposed to address. The truth is often in the detail.

Consider the integrity testing of police officers. Does this practice actually reduce police corruption? Or does it rather increase levels of distrust between, say, management cops and street cops and, thereby, compound the problem of the so-called "blue wall of silence" whereby street cops (in particular) protect their corrupt colleagues?

Perhaps random integrity testing in relation to minor ethical misconduct is problematic in this respect, whereas targeted integrity testing in relation to serious forms of corruption is much less so because it is widely accepted by police officers. The findings of a recent empirical attitudinal study of Victoria Police officers seem to confirm that this is the case.[9]

In attempting to determine the causes of unethical professional practices, there are a number of preliminary questions that need to be addressed. One set of questions pertains to the precise nature of the unethical practice at issue, and the context in which it occurs. What practices are involved? Minor gratuity taking? Theft from burgled premises? Excessive force? Fabricating evidence? What is the motivation? Is it greed? Is it a (possibly misplaced) sense of justice (noble cause corruption)? Are there, for example, some compelling practical facts that explain the practice, say, a belief that the only way to secure convictions of serious drug offenders involves the use of unlawful methods? What other pressures, such as a lack of resources, might explain the unethical practice in question? Another set of questions concerns the extent of the corruption or unethical practice. Is it sporadic or continuing, restricted to a few "rotten apples" or widespread within the police department?[10] Here, as elsewhere, rhetoric is no substitute for evidence-based conclusions, difficult though it may be to provide the latter.

A further set of problems arises in situations in which internal affairs departments may have good intelligence or even good evidence that a particular officer is corrupt but lack sufficient evidence or perhaps admissible evidence and, therefore, are not in a position to charge the officer. See the above case study, Corrupt Colleague.

The dilemma in this kind of situation is what to do with this officer? The force has two immediate options, which must be carefully risk assessed:

- It can confront the officer with the fact that there has been, let us assume, a covert inquiry, which has revealed a connection between him and a known and active criminal. Then interview him on the matter.
- It can leave him in place, without informing him of the inquiry, and continue the covert inquiry.

Each option has its own problems. The first will leave the force with an officer who, if he denies wrongdoing, can no longer be trusted – especially in the position he holds now and that which he had anticipated being promoted to. If they are unable to deal with him under internal conduct regulations, he can remain a police officer.

The second option raises the question of any impending promotion and possible job transfer; neither can be set aside without informing the officer of the reasons for such a decision. If the force, after reviewing all the facts, considers that he or she is unaware of the inquiry and so decides to continue it due to the quality of the intelligence being received, how can this be done without giving the officer some hint there is something amiss? The cancellation of a promotion coupled with his or her removal from being "preferred candidate" for any new role is highly likely to cause the officer to question what is going on. Can the force realistically make the decision to promote him or her? Can another candidate "pip them at the post" for the new role?

Integrity systems for police organizations can and do vary. However, such systems ought to have at least the following components or aspects:[11]

- An effective, streamlined complaints and discipline system;
- A comprehensive suite of stringent vetting and induction processes reflective of the different levels of risk in different areas of the organization;
- A basic code of ethics and specialized codes of practice – for example, in relation to the use of firearms – supported by ethics education in recruitment training, and ongoing professional development programs;
- Adequate welfare support systems, for example, in relation to drug and alcohol abuse and psychological injury;
- Intelligence gathering, risk management, and early warning systems for at-risk officers, for example, officers with high levels of complaints;
- Internal investigations, that is, the police organization takes a high degree of responsibility for its own unethical officers;
- Proactive anticorruption intervention systems, for example, targeted integrity testing;
- Ethical leadership, for example, promoting police who give priority to the collective ends definitive of the organization rather than their own career ambitions; and

- External oversight by an independent, well-resourced body with investigative powers.

As the foregoing points suggest, a key element in an integrity system for police organizations is an organization-wide, intelligence-based, ethics risk-assessment process. This involves good intelligence and an organization-wide ethics risk-assessment plan and – based on good intelligence and the risk-assessment plan – the identification of corruption/rights violations/ ethical misconduct risks in the police organization.

Ethical risks in a contemporary police organization might include risks in many, if not most, of the following areas:

- Data security, notably electronic data;
- Drug investigations (see discussion above);
- Excessive use of force;
- Informant management, given that most informants are themselves criminals (see Chapter 9);
- Infiltration by organized crime.

Other areas of concern in many police organizations are the ethical risks stemming from: severe stress among police officers and the inability of managers to identify and respond effectively to severe stress in their subordinates; noble cause corruption, in which officers break the law to achieve good outcomes, for example, by doctoring statements and even fabricating evidence; political and/or media and/or police hierarchy pressure for results, or even actual interference in high profile investigations, thereby compromising the investigative process and (potentially) its outcome.

Once ethical risk areas have been identified, preventive countermeasures need to be put in place. These countermeasures should track the identified risks. Some countermeasures and the risks that they track include the following.

- In relation to data security: segregation of, and controlled access to, internal affairs databases; audits of database access.
- In relation to drug investigations: early warning systems, for example, profiles of at-risk officers/locations/high-risk areas; intelligence-driven targeted integrity testing of individuals/locations; audits of drug squads and forensic laboratories.
- In relation to excessive use of force: complaints-driven investigations informed by intelligence, for example, a high number of complaints of excessive use of force.
- In relation to informant management: accountability mechanisms such as documentation naming the informant, ensuring that a police officer

with an informant has a supervisor who meets with the officer and the informant, having a supervisor who monitors the police officer's dealings with the informant, and recording all payments (including electronic transfers), to prevent theft and other abuses.

- In relation to infiltration by organized crime: stringent and constantly updated vetting procedures (especially for officers in sensitive areas), ensuring adequate supervision of all officers, and monitoring and utilization of intelligence databases (including criminal associations).
- In relation to stress: ensuring adequate supervision of all officers; introduction of stress management tools.
- In relation to all of the above: ongoing ethics training based on identified risks in specific roles.

Having discussed integrity systems for police organizations in general terms, we turn now to an historically important challenge that faces police organizations, namely, the investigation of police corrupting and the problem it faces in the form of police culture, the so-called "blue wall of silence."

8.5 Investigation of Police Corruption

Police culture is not necessarily a pervasive and monolithic social force that is the dominant determinant of the attitudes and actions of police officers in all police organizations. Many of the classic features of police culture are principally features of police serving in large, metropolitan, bureaucratic, and hierarchical organizations. Moreover, between and within even these organizations there are significant attitudinal and behavioral differences in respect of police corruption. We further suggest that police culture is in large part a rationally and morally legitimate response to the operational policing environment and, as such, cannot be, and ought not to be, jettisoned in its entirety. We now suggest that police culture, not being the pervasive, monolithic, and dominant force that it is often presented as being, is a malleable phenomenon; in principle, it can be changed and, in particular, its malignant features can be curtailed, even if they cannot be removed entirely.

Curtailment depends on a number of things, notably designing and implementing appropriate integrity systems. However, in the context of an appropriate overall integrity system, curtailment typically depends in part on adjusting the incentive structures in place so as to make compliance with the dictates of malignant features of police culture much less rational than it otherwise would be. (This is perhaps most obvious in the case of the deterrence mechanisms that are a necessary feature of most integrity systems.)

Unfortunately, in dysfunctional, corruption-riddled police organizations compliance on the part of any given police officer with the malignant features of police culture may be quite rational. This is not to say that the malignant features of police culture are an irresistible force. Far from it; these features of police culture are by no means the only important factors at work, and compliance, though rational, is not the only choice available. However, it is to say that the particular configuration of factors in play is such that these malignant features of police culture end up being the decisive factors at work. Accordingly, the challenge facing those seeking to design an appropriate integrity system is how to bring it about that these malignant features of police culture cease to be the decisive factors at work; it is not necessarily, at least in the first instance, a matter of directly removing these features.

Here we want to narrow our focus and explore, in particular, an apparently important relationship between a reluctance on the part of police to report corrupt fellow officers on the one hand, and the quality of internal affairs investigations on the other. Good, though by no means decisive, empirical evidence of this relationship has been provided in the Victoria Police study.[12] The relevant parts of the study comprise a survey of ethical attitudes, an analysis of all internal affairs corruption investigations files over a five-year period, and the conducting of some 70 focus groups of serving police officers (around 500 police officers out of a police force of 9,000). Moreover, the evidence for this relationship is further strengthened by the consideration that it has an intuitively rational structure to it.

The first point to be made here is that in well-ordered liberal democratic states, such as Australia, the majority of police officers in many, if not most, contemporary police organizations are evidently not themselves corrupt and do not engage in ongoing corrupt activities. For example, although the 1990s Wood Royal Commission into police corruption in the New South Wales (Australia) Police Force found systemic corruption, it was largely limited to groups of detectives functioning in the area of illicit drug investigations and specific local area commands in which there was an endemic drug problem, for example, the King's Cross red light area in Sydney. Moreover, evidence from the Victoria Police study indicated that the majority of police officers in Victoria Police and, presumably, similar police organizations, strongly desire to rid their organization of corruption and criminality. A further finding of the Victoria Police study was that the majority of police officers believe that they morally (and not simply legally) ought to report/provide evidence in relation to the minority of corrupt colleagues.

Notwithstanding this belief that they ought to report and provide evidence in relation to their corrupt colleagues, most police officers are apparently unwilling to report their corrupt colleagues; this was a further finding of the Victoria Police study. How can this be so?

Certainly, there is nothing illogical or even atypical in this. People often have moral beliefs that they are unwilling to act on, notably when it is not in their self-interest to do so or when there are other felt moral considerations in play, such as feelings of loyalty. Unsurprisingly, it turns out that the attitudes and, therefore, the culture of Victoria Police are a complex and differentiated phenomenon: evidently, there is a strong and widespread belief that corrupt police morally ought to be reported – including because it is unlawful not to do so – but there is a contrary feeling that it is or might be disloyal to do so. This contrary feeling is an attitudinal barrier to reporting corrupt fellow officers, especially at the lower end of corruption, or in relation to noble cause corruption. In the context of our attempt here at explication of the rational structure underlying police action (or, at least, inaction) this attitudinal barrier can usefully be thought of as a presumption against reporting corrupt colleagues. Considered on its own, this presumption might well be overridden by the belief among police that police corruption (at least in its more serious forms) ought to be reported. However, there is a third consideration in play, namely, the irrationality of reporting corrupt colleagues. Evidently, this third consideration is the decisive one. Let us explain.

According to the empirical evidence provided in the Victoria Police study, one important aspect (we do not say it is the only important aspect) of the rational structure of the situation is as follows:

Conclusion (c): Police officers (junior and senior) are reluctant to provide evidence in relation to corrupt officers because (for the reason that):

Premise (a): Police *believe* that internal investigations are unlikely to result in convictions and/or termination and that they are, in any case, often management-driven witchhunts of innocent police or of police who have, at most, engaged in minor ethical misconduct;

Premise (b): If honest police officers report/provide evidence in relation to corrupt officers and those officers are exonerated and remain in the force, then the police culture is such that their own careers will suffer from the stigma of having sided with a punitive management/internal affairs department and "ratted on" their colleagues (colleagues who, after all, have been exonerated and, therefore, are presumably innocent or at least widely believed to have been innocent or at most guilty of only a minor infraction).

Of course, the fact that their exonerated colleagues are widely believed to be innocent, or at most guilty of only a minor infraction, is a function in large part of police culture. The loyalty of fellow police officers ("one's brothers") surely demands a strong presumption in favor of one's innocence or, at the very least, a presumption in favor of the offense in question being an understandable breach of a legal or ethical principle. (The breach may be regarded as understandable because the principle in question is a minor one or because the circumstances were such that compliance was not unproblematic or some such.)

Notice, however – to return to the rational structure of (a) and (b) therefore (c) above – that police culture (the "blue wall of silence") gets traction here only on the assumption that police believe that internal investigations are unlikely to result in convictions and/or termination of corrupt officers, and that there will be, as a consequence, a widespread view that the officers investigated were not guilty of any serious offense, but merely the victims of a punitive management/internal affairs department.

The widespread belief of police in many police organizations that internal investigations are unlikely to result in convictions and/or termination of corrupt officers is not without rational foundation. Historically, internal investigations in many, if not most, large metropolitan police organizations – including, until recently, Victoria Police – have, as a matter of *fact* (and not simply of officers' beliefs), had relatively little success; certainly, they have typically resulted in low rates of conviction and/or termination of officers under investigation. Moreover, again historically, in many, if not most, large metropolitan police organizations, police who inform on other police are as a matter of fact ostracized, if not subjected to harassment, by their colleagues, and in many cases their careers have been ruined. So police officers' beliefs in this respect are well founded.

The lack of success of internal police investigations is, of course, in part dependent on the reluctance of police officers to provide evidence regarding their corrupt colleagues. There are also the challenges for investigators presented by corrupt officers who themselves have expertise in investigative techniques. However, there has also been a reluctance on the part of police to become internal investigators; police solidarity has often made investigating allegations of corruption against one's fellow officers unattractive, especially relative to investigating alleged offenders who are not police officers. At any rate, for these and other reasons, historically in many police organizations internal investigators have not had a good record. In recent years these attitudes, at least in modern police organizations in liberal democracies, have undergone a change for the better and, as a consequence, there are many committed and highly competent internal investigators. Yet the problem of corruption persists in many police organizations, doubtless in part because of the "blue wall of silence," but also at times because internal investigations have been less effective than they should have been.

One of the flaws to be found in many internal investigations is a breach of confidentiality that has compromised the investigation. Such breaches of confidentiality are themselves acts of corruption, and yet they have often taken place with impunity. But, again, this is reflective of the malignant features of police culture; a culture of being reluctant to ensure that suspected corrupt police are brought to book, whether those police are the ones who engaged in the original act of corruption or those who sort to protect them by engaging in the secondary act of corruption, for example, a breach of confidentiality.

So there is a vicious circle in operation: the "blue wall of silence" undercuts the efficacy of internal investigations, which, in turn, reinforces the "blue wall of silence." However, the point we want to stress here is that – in some police services – it would be irrational of police officers to report, or provide evidence in relation to, their corrupt colleagues. For, on the one hand, they reasonably believe that this will not result in the conviction/termination of these corrupt officers and, on the other hand, they reasonably believe that it will ruin their own careers. Moreover, the irrationality of reporting corrupt colleagues is, we suggest, the decisive factor in determining their action (or at least inaction). They believe that it is morally wrong not to report their corrupt colleagues (at least in serious cases), feelings of loyalty notwithstanding; however, they believe that no good will come of it but only harm to themselves.

What is the way out of this impasse? There is a need for the following countermeasures. First, internal affairs departments ought to investigate only criminal matters and serious disciplinary matters that warrant termination. (And perhaps the difficulty of terminating police also needs to be looked at, for example, by recourse to Loss of Commissioner Confidence provisions, although there are procedural rights issues in this area.)[13] Other ethical misconduct ought to be regarded as a management/remedial issue. The latter is important partly as a means of reducing the possibility that initial minor ethical lapses on the part of new recruits will come to be regarded, by the offending officers themselves as well as others, as fatal moral compromises that forever impugn their integrity and prevent them from ever reporting the serious ethical misconduct of their corrupt colleagues.

Second, the rate of internal investigations convictions/terminations needs to be improved to a high level of success. In the first instance (that is, in the context of a reluctance on the part of officers to inform on their corrupt colleagues), this can be partly achieved by:

1. Increasing the quality of internal investigations (for example, by head-hunting high-quality investigators), increasing data security measures (for example, the use of "sterile corridors," the stringent vetting of IA

personnel, including administrative staff), audits of investigations, and adequate resourcing of IA departments;
2. The use of well-resourced proactive anticorruption strategies, for example, targeted integrity tests, intrusive surveillance methods that do not rely heavily on the willingness of police to provide evidence regarding corrupt colleagues; and
3. Recourse to well-resourced external oversight bodies with an independent investigative capacity, especially in relation to serious corruption in the upper echelons of a police organization.

Third, the stigma attached to being an internal investigator and to reporting, or providing evidence against, corrupt police needs to be reduced by:

1. Normalizing the role of internal investigator, for example, by making two years as an internal investigator mandatory for all police investigators seeking promotion to senior investigative positions;
2. Instituting measures to protect (physically and career-wise) those who provide evidence against corrupt colleagues, for example, the implementation of internal witness protection programs and transparent promotion processes; and
3. Introducing ongoing tailor-made ethics education programs that sensitively and squarely address the issues of police culture, internal affairs investigations, and professional reporting.

In short, it needs to become rational, and not simply legally and ethically mandated, for police officers to report, and provide evidence in relation to, their corrupt colleagues. Given that most police officers are not themselves corrupt and believe that they morally ought to report or provide evidence in relation to their corrupt colleagues, they will do so – or at least are more likely to do so – if conditions are created under which it will be rational for them to do so; that is, if it works for them and brings rewards rather than punishment. These conditions will include the following:

A reasonable number, and a high rate, of convictions/terminations of corrupt police officers as a result of a well-resourced, high quality, internal investigations department focused only on criminal and serious disciplinary matters, and operating in the context of:

1. the normalization of the role of internal investigator (consistent with the maintenance of high standards of investigation); and
2. the felt duty on the part of most police to report/provide intelligence/ evidence regarding criminal/corrupt colleagues in knowledge that if they do:
   (i) the persons in question are likely to be convicted/terminated; and
   (ii) they themselves will suffer no harm or adverse career consequences.

These specific conditions are consistent with, and conducive to, a functional and defensible police culture – one in which loyalty is felt to be owed to police officers who embody the ideals and legitimate ends of policing, but not to corrupt colleagues. Such a functional police culture is likely, in turn, to facilitate the emergence of these specific conditions.

Naturally, these recommendations in relation to internal investigations and professional reporting are only one piece in the puzzle; we are not suggesting that they constitute a panacea. Indeed, we earlier elaborated a detailed set of key elements of an integrity system for police organizations. More generally, we are suggesting that, in combating police corruption, more attention needs to be paid to the rational structure underlying individual police decision making and the ways in which it might be adjusted (and, in a sense, less emphasis placed on police culture as a stand-alone determining factor). However, the rational structure in question is not the familiar one of rational self-interested actors unmoved by morality or by irrational (or nonrational) social forces; police are clearly moved by a complex mix of individual self-interest, moral beliefs, and cultural factors.[14] Combating corruption in policing, as elsewhere, involves in part unearthing this rational structure and devising ways to adjust it so that self-interest, moral beliefs, and cultural factors work together to promote ethical conduct and reduce corruption rather than the reverse.

Notes

1 Material in this section is derived from Seumas Miller (2011b) Corruption, *Stanford Encyclopedia of Philosophy* (on-line journal: www.plato.stanford.edu). See also Seumas Miller, Peter Roberts, and Edward Spence (2005) *Corruption and Anti-Corruption: A Study in Applied Philosophy*, Saddle River, NJ: Prentice Hall, and Miller (2010a), Chapter 5.

2 See Jeremiah Marquez (2005) LAPD: Ramparts scandal: L.A. police corruption settlements estimated to reach \$70 million, http://injusticebusters.org/index.htm/LAPD.htm.

3 See Frontline (n.d.) *Rampart Scandal*, http://www.pbs.org/wgbh/pages/frontline/shows/lapd/scandal/credibility.html.

4 See Seumas Miller (1998b) Corruption and anti-corruption in the profession of policing, *Professional Ethics*, 6.3–4, pp. 83–106, and Miller and Blackler (2005), Chapter 5.

5 On noble cause corruption in policing, see Edwin Delattre (1994) *Character and Cops: Ethics in Policing* (2nd edn), Washington, DC: AEI Press, and Seumas Miller (2004) Noble cause corruption revisited in P. Villiers and R. Adlam (eds), *A Safe, Just and Tolerant Society: Police Virtue Rediscovered*, Winchester, UK: Waterside Press, pp. 105–118.

6 In relation to such a slippery slope in policing see Lawrence W. Sherman (1985) Becoming bent, in Frederick Elliston and Michael Feldberg (eds) *Moral Issues in Police Work*, Totowa, NJ: Rowman and Allanheld, pp. 253–266.

7   We take it that a discretionary ethical judgment is a judgment in which the officer exercises his discretionary authority to make an ethically informed judgment.

8   Material in this and following section is derived from Seumas Miller (2010c) Integrity systems and professional reporting in police organisations, *Criminal Justice Ethics*, 29.3, pp. 241–257.

9   Seumas Miller, Steve Curry, Ian Gordon, John Blackler, and Tim Prenzler (2008) *An Integrity System for Victoria Police: Volume 2*, Australian Research Council Linkage grant funded report for Victoria Police, Canberra: Centre for Applied Philosophy and Public Ethics.

10 Miller and Blackler (2005), Chapter 5.

11 Seumas Miller and Tim Prenzler (2008) *An Integrity System for Victoria Police: Volume 1*, Australian Research Council Linkage grant funded report for Victoria Police, Canberra: Centre for Applied Philosophy and Public Ethics.

12 Miller et al. (2008).

13 Loss of Commissioner Confidence provisions exist in a number of Australian police services, including Victoria Police and New South Wales Police.

14 We do not mean to imply that these three categories are mutually exclusive.

9

Informants and Internal Witnesses

In Chapters 1–4 of this book we discussed a number of central issues to do with the normative framework within which criminal investigations take place, namely, the relationship between the criminal law and morality, the epistemic role of investigators, evidence and intelligence in criminal investigations, and investigative independence. In Chapters 5 and 6 we discussed (respectively) the investigation of crimes against the person and the investigation of property crimes. In Chapters 7 and 8 we narrowed our focus somewhat and looked at (respectively) the investigation of terrorism and police corruption. In the remaining four chapters we discuss four areas of criminal investigations that have historically given rise to moral problems in a particularly acute form; indeed, each has, at times, involved serious rights violations by investigators who have been overzealous (to say the least) in their pursuit of their investigative ends. Perhaps the most dramatic examples of this are to be found in the use of the so-called "third degree" in police interviews (see Chapter 12, Section 12.4). Nor are the moral problems in this area necessarily generated by the investigators or other police officers; far from it. As will become evident from the discussion below, the lives of witnesses can be threatened by those whom they testify against, including drug syndicates and the like, and informants are often criminals who, at times, provide information to investigators for the purpose of advancing their own criminal interests. In short, the moral (or, at least, immoral) actors in these areas are various, the kinds of moral rights violations are multiple, and the solutions to the moral problems that can arise are not necessarily obvious or easy to implement satisfactorily.

Investigative Ethics: Ethics for Police Detectives and Criminal Investigators, First Edition.
Seumas Miller and Ian A. Gordon.
© 2014 Seumas Miller and Ian A. Gordon. Published 2014 by John Wiley & Sons, Ltd.

In the light of our favored normative theory of policing, and associated normative theory of criminal investigations, in terms of the protection of justifiably enforceable, legally enshrined moral rights, it is important that we address at least some of the central moral problems in these areas. The areas in question are: informants and internal witnesses (this chapter); surveillance and monitoring (Chapter 10); undercover operations and entrapment (Chapter 11); and interviewing (Chapter 12).

9.1 Evidence, Reliability, and Credibility

Victims of crime, witnesses to crime, covert informants, and offenders themselves provide information which can constitute evidence and/or intelligence. Here we need to distinguish information that may further a criminal investigation in some way or other, be it intelligence or evidence understood in a general sense, and information that is admissible as evidence in a court of law. The latter may, of course, take the form of records, for example, of telephone calls, and other documentation. However, a critically important form of evidence is that provided by witnesses and, in particular, independent witnesses, that is, persons who have no special interest in the outcome of a trial other than that the truth be revealed and justice be served. Independent witnesses do not include victims and offenders for obvious reasons.

Statements made by witnesses can be thought of as having evidential weight by virtue of the content of the statement considered on its own and/or by virtue of the fact that the witness has made the statement. The latter goes to the reliability of the witness *per se*; if a witness is considered reliable then the statement made by that witness will be considered to be *prima facie* true, considered independently of its content. The former goes to the credibility of the content of the statement made; even if the witness is considered to be reliable, if the content of the statement made is regarded as incredible then the statement might not be considered to be *prima facie* true. Suppose, for example, that Jones claims that he saw the suspect (a small, elderly, frail woman) beat up the victim (a big, physically strong young man) and that Jones is regarded as an upright, responsible adult with normal vision and so on. On the one hand, Jones is regarded as a reliable witness and hence what he states ought to be taken as *prima facie* true; on the other hand, the content of his statement considered on its own merits – and independently of who stated it – might reasonably be taken to be *prima facie* false or, at least, extremely doubtful.

In general, the reliability of a witness is twofold: moral and epistemic. A witness is morally reliable if they are unlikely to tell lies or otherwise engage in deception. A witness might be morally unreliable if they are of bad character, for instance, a criminal, or not independent by virtue of having some interest in the matter at hand, which is likely to cause them to be insincere in their statements or otherwise engage in deception, for example, if they are the alleged offender or the spouse of the alleged offender.

A witness is epistemically reliable if they have the perceptual, rational, or other knowledge-acquiring capacities relevant to the matter at hand (or, at least, have these capacities to the necessary degree); that is, they are unlikely to make an error (as opposed to being insincere). Thus someone with poor eyesight might not make a reliable eyewitness.

In the light of the above discussion of evidential weight and witness reliability, we can now make use of a general distinction between the reliability of the witness and the credibility of the statements made by the witness, albeit these are connected. Other things being equal, statements made by (morally and epistemically) reliable witnesses have greater credibility than those made by unreliable witnesses.

We have distinguished between the (epistemic and moral) reliability of the witness and the credibility of the content of the witness' report considered independently of the reliability of the witness. A further distinction pertains to the reliability of the specific mode of epistemic access. Perception is one mode of epistemic access, logical inference is another, testimony is a third; and there are more fine-grained distinctions within these generic modes of access. Thus there are various forms of perceptual epistemic access, for example, sight and touch, some of which might be considered more reliable than some others, at least in relation to certain evidential matters. Consider a stick in water which appears to be bent to the eye but straight to one's touch. Evidently, touch is a more reliable mode of epistemic access in relation to the shape of solid physical objects.

Moreover, multiple modes of access are typically involved in the evidence of witnesses, if only because a witness's report, their testimony (first mode of access), itself depends on what they have witnessed by means of (say) perception (second mode of access).

These three considerations, namely, the reliability of the witness, the reliability of the mode of epistemic access, and the credibility of the content of the report (considered independently of the witness and the mode of access), determine the epistemic weight that ought to be accorded to a witness's report. Moreover, sometimes the reliability of the witness is a decisive factor, sometimes the mode of epistemic access, and sometimes the credibility of the content.

Consider the following scenario in relation to an important and pervasive mode of epistemic access: testimony. Assume C and B are equally reliable witnesses. Assume further that the content of what C says, for instance, that B said such and such, might be regarded as just as likely to be true as the content of what B said, for instance, that B saw A commit an assault. However, in respect of the substantive matter in question, namely, whether or not A committed an assault, B's statement might be regarded as having greater evidential weight than C's statement by virtue of B's statement being an eyewitness report as opposed to hearsay. One reason for thinking this, at least in our example, is that C's hearsay evidence is indirect and, indeed, reliant on B's direct eyewitness evidence. Of course, we only have B's word that he saw A commit the assault and, to this extent, B's evidence is, strictly speaking, not direct evidence but only direct testimonial evidence of his direct experiential evidence (his seeing the crime being committed). However, C's evidence, although also testimonial, is even more indirect in that it is evidence, in the first instance, of what B said, not of what B saw and, therefore, twice removed from the direct evidence, namely, B's experiential evidence.[1]

This is not to say that hearsay does not have some evidential weight (in the general sense of evidence, as opposed to the special sense of evidence admissible in a court of law). Indeed, potentially at least, hearsay has considerable evidential weight; perhaps even greater weight in some instances than direct testimonial evidence. Consider the evidence of a priest, A, that B confessed to A that B raped and killed a child, C. (Let us assume that the priest in the church in question believes that his vow of secrecy should be broken in the circumstances in question.)

If B is a devout believer and yet also a known pedophile seeking to avoid punishment for his heinous crime, this hearsay evidence of the priest might even be considered weightier than eye-witness D's claim that he saw E (and not B) kill C, supposing D to be a somewhat unreliable witness (say, one of doubtful character and with poor eyesight).

In general, hearsay evidence is not admissible in common law courts of law on the grounds of unreliability; roughly speaking, that the person who made the original statement is not available for his/her claims to be tested in court. (This is, of course, not the case with the above example of the reported confession.) The issue of whether hearsay evidence ought, in fact, to be admissible in courts of law is a controversial one. We will not engage in further discussion of this issue here.

The functionality of the criminal justice system as a whole is heavily dependent on witnesses:

> Without witnesses, the rudiments of prosecution, such as identifying the accused and establishing the requisite nexus between the accused and the crime, would become insurmountable obstacles to conviction, and the criminal justice system would cease to function.[2]

Accordingly, there is a stringent moral requirement on the part of witnesses to tell the truth. In the first place, this is because there is a general moral norm to tell the truth, and witnesses, along with the rest of us, morally ought to tell the truth, that is, to avoid both insincerity and error. In the second place, there is a great deal more at stake, morally speaking, in the case of the statements of witnesses than is typically the case in ordinary conversations. As we have seen, what is at stake includes: justice in the form of redress for the victim and punishment for the offender; the protection of other potential victims; and the community's interest in justice and in the integrity of its criminal justice institutions. In the third place, witnesses generally promise or swear to tell the truth thereby adding to the strength of the obligation, if not its substance.

An additional important moral consideration in play in relation to information and evidence provided by witnesses and informants is secrecy or, at least, professional confidentiality.

9.2 Professional Confidentiality

What is professional confidentiality, and what is the relation between privacy and professional confidentiality?

It is agreed on all hands that privacy is an important moral right. Moreover, there is a close relationship between privacy and professional confidentiality. Indeed, there is at least one central kind of case in which confidentiality derives from the right to privacy.

There are circumstances under which a professional's knowledge concerning a client's inner self or intimate relations is in the client's interest. A doctor or psychologist should know about a patient's bodily sensations or mental states, in so far as this is necessary for successful treatment, and in so far as the patient has consented to be treated. Similarly, a police investigator might need to know various personal and private details about a victim of (say) child abuse, if the crime is to be established and the offender apprehended and successfully prosecuted. This need to know for the benefit of the client is one ground for a principle of confidentiality. Such information, while available to the doctor or psychologist, social worker or police officer, would still be unavailable to others. Moreover, the need for professional confidentiality might be given additional moral weight by being: (i) the subject of a promise on the part of the professional to the client not to disclose the sort of information in question to others, and (ii) enshrined in the law so that the professional has a legal duty not to disclose this information to others. Accordingly, for the occupant of the professional role to disclose this information concerning their client to unauthorized third parties would constitute a moral and legal breach of confidentiality.

Although clients have a (derived) right to confidentiality, there are circumstances under which a psychologist or police officer or other professional may disclose confidential information concerning their client, notwithstanding the fact that it is not in the client's interest, or at least notwithstanding the fact that the client has not given his or her informed consent. Such cases include ones in which the client is seriously harming, or is likely to seriously harm, some third party, and cases in which the client is seriously harming, or is likely to seriously harm, himself or herself and is not able to give informed consent. In short, there are sometimes countervailing moral rights to the right to confidentially, including the right not to be seriously harmed and the right to life. Consider our above example of an unconvicted serial pedophile/murderer who discloses his past crimes, and an intention to commit a further murder, to his psychologist. Evidently the murderer's right to professional confidentiality – a right in turn based on a right to privacy – is overridden by greater moral considerations, namely, the right to life of the person the murderer intends to kill.[3]

A further point here concerns breaches of confidentiality. As far as possible, any breach of confidentiality should be contained. Such containment amounts to a requirement of confidentiality. In the above-described murderer/psychologist scenario, the psychologist is morally obliged to breach the confidentiality of her relationship with the murderer by going to the police. However, the information provided to the police ought now be the object of a further confidentiality requirement, at least until the investigation has been completed.

So the right to professional confidentiality, like the right to privacy, is a nonabsolute right. The principle of confidentiality can be overridden under certain circumstances by other moral considerations, including ones that are enshrined in the law. These include the rights of third parties at risk from clients.

Thus far we have been concerned with a species of professional confidentiality that derives from the right to privacy of clients, victims, and others. However, there are grounds other than privacy for the professional confidentiality. In policing, as we noted in Chapter 3, there is an imperative not to compromise investigations by disclosing confidential information. The duty to keep confidences so as not to compromise investigations is based on a number of different considerations. It is, in the first instance, based on the epistemic requirements of an investigation; without such confidences, and the assurance thereof, intelligence and evidence may not become available in the first place or, if available, it may cease to be useful if offenders come to be aware that it is in the possession of investigators, as with information regarding a planned crime. The duty to keep confidences is also in part based on the ultimate moral purpose of ensuring that offenders do not escape justice, for example, a tip-off to an offender can undermine an entire police investigation of that person. It is also in part based on the need to ensure that witnesses and/or informants are protected. Maintaining the confidentiality of informants is important to protect them from harm. In the United States, however, a web site called 'whosarat.com' reveals the identities of informants and their law enforcement agents.

Through the site's database, visitors can contribute information about local police, federal agents, and police informants. This type of disclosure puts the lives of informants at risk.

Notwithstanding the inherent moral rights of informants and witnesses to be protected, and the epistemic, including secrecy, requirements of investigators, the ultimate and central moral basis for the principle of confidentiality in the context of police investigations is the moral rights of victims, or potential victims. If confidentiality in criminal investigations is breached, then citizens can have no guarantee that their rights – their legally enshrined, justifiably enforceable moral rights – will be protected; rather, offenders will be able to offend with impunity.[4]

This completes our general characterization of confidentiality. We have suggested that the notions of privacy and confidentiality need to be kept separate. We claim that professional confidentiality sometimes derives from the more fundamental right to privacy, and sometimes derives from other moral rights, especially rights that directly or indirectly protect persons from various forms of criminal activity. Let us now look at two specific areas of policing in which confidentiality is of the utmost importance, namely informants and witnesses. We note that terminology in this area can be confusing and the boundaries between different categories of informant and witness are somewhat vague. At any rate, by informants we do not mean civic-minded members of the public who from time to time provide investigators with useful information but whose relation with investigators is informal, ad hoc, and not based on a desire to be remunerated or an untoward motivation such as revenge. By witnesses we mean persons who provide admissible evidence, as opposed to (so to speak) mere information or intelligence.

In order to illustrate some of the moral issues that arise for witnesses and the use of informants by criminal investigators let us consider the following two case studies.

9.3 Case Studies

Case Study 9.3.1 RUC Informants

In 2007 The Police Ombudsman for Northern Ireland reported[5] on the investigation of a series of complaints about conduct of officers in the then Royal Ulster Constabulary (RUC) relating to the murder of Raymond McCord Jnr. in November 1997. His father, Raymond McCord, complained that over a number of years police officers had

(Continued)

acted to protect informants from being fully accountable to the law. The initial investigation raised concerns over other incidents including murders, attempted murders, and drug dealing.

In a long and complex investigation the Police Ombudsman found police intelligence systems held information, graded as "reliable and probably true," which was also corroborated by other sources which linked police informants to: the murders of 10 people and 72 instances of other crime, including 10 attempted murders; 10 "punishment" shootings, 13 punishment attacks, a bomb attack in Monaghan, 17 instances of drug dealing, and other criminality including criminal damage, extortion, and intimidation.

The investigators identified less significant and reliable intelligence that may link an informant (1) and his associates to an additional five murders. Informant 1 was believed to have received nearly £80 000 in payments over the period investigated, which included incentive payments.

The investigation revealed that certain officers in the Special Branch section of the Force took steps to ensure certain informants, linked to a terrorist organization (the Ulster Volunteer Force (UVF)), were protected from the law; including where it was known those informants had committed crimes. Sometimes informants were even accompanied by Special Branch officers during interviews with other police officers investigating their crimes, to ensure the informants did not incriminate themselves. This intervention went as far as blocking the legitimate searches of premises for weapons.

The investigation by the Police Ombudsman was hampered by the fact that many documents were missing, lost, or destroyed and this was considered to be a deliberate ploy by senior police officers to avoid being held to account for their actions. In effect, the Ombudsman thought there was a culture in the RUC of subservience to the Special Branch and this allowed some informants to commit serious crimes, without the Criminal Investigation Department having the ability to effectively investigate those offenses and bring the offenders to justice.

The report led to a change in handling informants in what is now the Police Service of Northern Ireland (PSNI).

Case Study 9.3.2 "Leaking" Witness Protection Information

A deputy U.S. marshal was convicted Tuesday of violating the secrecy of the federal government's witness protection program by leaking information about a key witness cooperating in a Chicago mob investigation. Deputy marshal John Ambrose stared straight ahead as jurors returned the verdict after almost three days of deliberation. He was acquitted of two charges of lying to federal agents, and sentencing was set for Sept. 9. Defense attorney Francis Lipuma promised an appeal. "This is far from over, we're going to keep up the good fight," the attorney said.

Ambrose, a veteran fugitive hunter with a sterling record until now, is the only person in the 39-year history of the ultrasecret Witness Security Program to deliberately violate its security safeguards. "This is a real tragedy for federal law enforcement and for Deputy Marshal John Ambrose," said Gary S. Shapiro, first assistant U.S. attorney.

The program was established to protect witnesses against mobsters and terrorists who would want to silence them with threats or violence, and Shapiro said the government's ability to get such witnesses to testify depends on their feeling safe from retaliation.

FBI agents first realized there was a leak in the program when they heard two mobsters in a prison visitors room talking about a mole in federal law enforcement. Witnesses including U.S. Attorney Patrick Fitzgerald and the head of the FBI's Chicago office, Robert Grant, testified that, when they confronted Ambrose with evidence he had leaked witness security information, he admitted doing so.

Lipuma argued Ambrose was an innocent man who may have "shot his mouth off" in boasting about his job to a family friend but never betrayed his oath as a lawman. Prosecutors said the person Ambrose told had known mob ties and the secrets made their way to a reputed mob boss. The protected witness whom the leak involved, Nicholas Calabrese, was the only so-called made member of the Chicago Outfit, as this city's organized crime family calls itself, to switch sides and tell what he knew about mob murders, prosecutors said. Calabrese admitted to taking part in 14 murders himself.

Ambrose was twice assigned to guard Calabrese at a so-called safe site. His testimony in the government's landmark Operation Family

(Continued)

Secrets investigation ultimately sent three mob bosses to prison for life. Prosecutors have not alleged that Ambrose endangered Calabrese's life but said passing the information effectively delivered it to the mob.

(NBC News (2009), copyright Associated Press www.nbcnews.com/id/30463996/#.UvbZ7nk0iao)

9.4   Informants

Informants are an important source of information for law enforcement agencies, especially in areas such as drug dealing and corruption where there is no direct victim as such, or in relation to other hard-to-reach groups where it is difficult to find voluntary information, for example, terrorist groups. Following the Twin Towers incident in 2001 the subsequent enquiry was critical of the CIA and its lack of informants.

According to Skolnick (1994), "without a network of informants – usually victims, sometimes police – narcotics police cannot operate."[6]

On the other hand, informants are something of a double-edged sword. Some researchers have questioned the benefits of informants in terms of crime reduction,[7] and they can have a corrupting effect on police. The case study described above (9.3.1, RUC Informants) graphically illustrates the risks that can attach to the use of informants.[8]

Snout, grass, stoolie, and so on, are the slang terms for someone who gives information to the police and will be paid money or given some consideration for informing. Not all informers, however, deserve such impliedly derogatory terms; many people volunteer information or will readily give information in response to questions from investigators. However, as noted above, our concern here is not with information provided by ordinary citizens on an ad hoc basis.

Following a surge of organized crime in the 1970s, the term "super-grass" began to appear in newspaper reports on criminal trials. It reflected the change within the UK police service to engage with informants, mainly criminals themselves, who were prepared to give information and then testify in court against high-level criminals and gangs.[9]

Typically, informants are members or associates of the criminal element. And they inform on other criminals, or provide information to police, for a multiplicity of reasons; though primarily for their own advantage. Accordingly, the information provided is not necessarily accurate.

Such advantages might be thought – at least by the informant – to include the police refraining from investigating offenses he or she has already committed, or even turning a blind eye to present and future offenses, as, for example, the so-called "license to deal" given to informants who are themselves drug dealers in order to catch "bigger fish."[10] Sometimes the informant, in effect, might be coerced by the police officer; noncooperation might lead to arrest and conviction for past offenses hitherto ignored. This is morally undesirable from the perspective of the moral rights of the informant. At other times, the relationship between (say) a detective and his informant can become one in which the detective is manipulated by the informant. In some extreme cases the informants have become de facto handlers and the police handler the informant. Organized crime, for example, has a vested interest in corrupting police officers and one favored way of doing so is for a criminal to become a police informant, and for the police officer to begin to feed information to his "informant" in return for financial rewards made available by the organized crime bosses.[11]

As with surveillance and undercover operations, the use of informants gives rise to privacy concerns (see Chapters 10 and 11), albeit these might be at one remove from the police themselves. Accordingly, if an informant infringes (as opposed to violates) the privacy rights of a suspect then there should be a reasonable suspicion of serious wrongdoing and the infringement should be otherwise justified.[12] There is also the potential risk to the life and/or limb of the informant, if the suspect discovers that they are an informant. Additional risks that attach to the use of informants in the absence of an appropriate accountability system are as follows:

- There is no management or official documentation of meetings and, therefore, what transpires – for example, what was promised by the officer and by the informant – is open to challenge.
- There is no corroboration that the actual payment to the informant was made or in what form, for example, that of drugs or reciprocal information, and, as a consequence, the arrangement is open to abuse by officers – some officers have, for example, taken a share of the payment intended for the informant.
- There is no control over the venue and timing of the meetings and, therefore, there is a physical risk to both officer and informant.
- The secrecy of the identity of the informant means that general tasking of informants by and on behalf of other officers cannot easily be done.
- In the pressure to get to the target of an investigation, officers may be tempted to promise large money payments or favorable prosecutorial or judicial outcomes to informants. Unfortunately, in some instances they have been unable to keep these promises. Informants may, indeed, receive a reduced sentence for substantial assistance, but what qualifies as substantial assistance is determined subjectively by a judge, not the

investigator. Oftentimes, this subjectivity can lead to too much leniency, or not enough.

• There is the risk of compromise in a court case where the informant makes allegations against an officer to protect himself or herself.

It follows that, if the relationship between police handler and informant is secretive – the police organization has no knowledge of it – then such problems are unlikely to be resolved, and the relationship is likely to be very damaging, not only to the detective, but to police operations.

Some informants might not be prepared to provide information unless confidentiality is guaranteed. On one view, the relationship between police officers and their informants is one of trust on a par with that between professionals and their clients. Even if this is so, the requirements for confidentiality between police and police informants are obviously different. For one thing, the reason for confidentiality in the case of informants might have more to do with the possible harm that might come to the informant from those he or she is informing about, rather than from the informant's basic right to privacy.

In this context, there is obviously a need for stringent accountability mechanisms, including that the informant be named in documentation, that a police officer with an informant has a supervisor who meets with the officer and the informant, that the supervisor monitors the police officer's dealings with the informant, and that all payments are recorded (including electronic transfers to prevent theft).

The first consideration that ought to inform informant management systems is that informants realize their essentially epistemic purpose in relation to the provision of intelligence and evidence. So, there needs to be active identification of informants and their opportunities, and informants need to be regularly assessed in relation to their actual or potential contribution to intelligence/evidence requirements. Questions here include: whether or not they are living in, or able to inform on, priority locations and are actually providing information that meets the intelligence requirement; the quantity and quality of the intelligence provided; whether they can benefit other agencies within the police force.

The United Kingdom[13] has succinctly described what is required for managing informants or, in its broader definition, covert human intelligence sources (CHIS): "the assessment, cultivation, recruitment and running of covert human intelligence sources is a skilled business, demanding the highest standards of integrity. It should be conducted by experienced, properly trained officers, working in a secure environment to the clear requirements of an informed and supportive management."

Informants encompass a broad range of persons who may provide intelligence and/or evidence; persons giving it for personal rewards of some sort, but also undercover officers and those who act as test purchasers, for instance, in drugs investigations. It can apply to a police officer who has confidentially reported corrupt or unethical behavior by a colleague, and is then asked to get more information from that colleague. In many jurisdictions the officer must be registered as an informant otherwise the intrusion may be unlawful.

The grounds for authorizing the use of an informant include the following, each of which potentially, directly or indirectly, involves moral rights not to be harmed or suffer needs-based deprivations:

- in the interests of national security
- for the purpose of preventing or detecting crime or of preventing disorder
- in the interests of public safety
- for the purpose of protecting public health.

The use of the source should be proportionate with detailed records being kept and available for scrutiny by an oversight body.

So the use of informants is not restricted to police and extends to other investigators. For example, security services, revenue and customs officers in the United Kingdom and elsewhere make extensive use of informants. It is common practice to recruit persons who come to police attention for suitability as an informant – in particular, if they are involved in criminal activity or members of target groups or organizations, for example, protest groups, gangs, hard-to-reach communities, and so on. Persons specifically trained for the task usually conduct this latter type of recruitment.

Informant management should satisfy the following requirements:

- an officer responsible for day-to-day actions with the informant and his or her welfare
- an officer with general oversight of the use made of the informant
- maintenance of a record of the use made of the informant
- any document liable to disclose the identity of the informant will only be available to persons where absolutely necessary.

Investigations involving covert operations typically generate large amounts of information, which ought to be recorded on the intelligence system of the relevant police service. The information in question includes the tactics used and the people involved in any given covert operation. So there is a risk that this information becomes available to persons who ought not to have access to it. Accordingly, systems must be in place to minimize this risk, while ensuring that the information remains accessible to those authorized to access it.

Investigations involving covert operational teams may acquire information which is not related to the operation or the investigation of which the operation is a part – collateral information. An important moral question arises here as to limits that ought to be placed on the recording, storage, and accessing of such "collateral" information. On the one hand, some of this information may be potentially useful intelligence in relation to other investigations. On the other hand, such potentially useful information may infringe the privacy and/or confidentially rights of individuals or organizations (see Chapter 10).

Let us assume that acquiring, or at least retaining, the potentially useful information in question does infringe the privacy and/or confidentiality rights of some individual or organization and, therefore, that *prima facie* it ought not to be recorded and stored for future access. By assumption, the acquisition and retention of the information in question is not morally justified by virtue of serving the purposes of the (presumably morally legitimate) investigation during the course of which it was acquired. However, its retention might be morally justified if it demonstrably served the purposes of some other *extant* investigation, or if it otherwise pertained to a person or organization subject to reasonable suspicion of criminal activity (and if its acquisition/retention met the other moral constraints on information acquisition/retention in that investigation or in respect of that person/organization, e.g., proportionality). On the other hand, the retention of the information would not be morally justified by the mere fact that it was judged to be potentially useful in relation to some unspecified future investigation of an individual or organization in relation to which there was no reasonable suspicion of criminal activity.

The management of informants ideally involves the use of trained staff tasked for recruitment of informants in line with the intelligence priorities for the organization rather than the motives of would-be informants seeking personal benefits (e.g., sentence reduction, revenge, etc). The use of informants for anticorruption work requires some additional expertise over and above that for standard criminal investigations.

Notwithstanding the need for such accountability mechanisms, they do generate problems of their own. Some police would argue that it is now virtually impossible to "run gigs" effectively. More generally, there is considerable risk attached to being an informant and the consequent need for strict confidentiality. Unfortunately, concern for their personal safety, and hence for confidentiality, can cause would-be informants not to remain or become such, if there is to be documentation revealing their identity and if persons other than their immediate handler are to be made aware of their identity and disclosures.

Safety measures, including monitoring of the informant–handler relationship, and strict confidentiality protection for informants and their disclosures, need to be buttressed by rigorous training in informant management, and maximization of the utility of intelligence provided by informants, for example, by means of a central (protected) data source. Some authors have suggested the use of ethics committees to test and quality-assure informant handling proposals, and random integrity testing in relation to the use of informants, given the various risks, such as corruption.[14] A further issue is whether an outside person, such as a magistrate, ought to approve and supervise informants, as happens in Belgium and Netherlands.[15]

Notwithstanding these problems with informants and with the accountability systems put in place to deal with them, in times of increasing police workloads, informants have also been recognized as one of the most cost-effective ways of solving crime. It has been suggested by some authorities that police, *both* uniformed police and detectives, should make more use of informants.

9.5 Witness Protection

As noted above, the combating of police corruption in particular is heavily dependent on witnesses. The importance of protecting witnesses was graphically illustrated in Victoria in 2004 when key witnesses to serious crimes, Terence and Christine Hodson, were murdered in their own home, and part of the prosecution case in relation to these serious crimes collapsed as a consequence.[16] As is their right, the Hodsons had opted not to accept the full protection afforded by the Victoria Police witness protection program. The above case study, "Leaking" Witness Protection Information, illustrates the potential difficulties of maintaining confidentiality and, thereby, providing protection to witnesses. At the end of the day, the professional integrity of police officers themselves is critical.

According to Slate[17] almost all protected witnesses have serious criminal records. Moreover, the main criterion for entry in the United States' Federal Witness Protection Program is the danger that attaches to the witness, or his or her family, as a consequence of giving testimony.

Police who give testimony against other police are often referred to as internal witnesses. The development of internal witness support programs and support units is reflective of a professionalizing police management's acknowledgment not only of the importance of ensuring witnesses are able to give evidence without fear of the consequences, but also of the strength of the police culture – and management's increasing capacity to come to terms with the aberrant aspects of that culture.

A thumbnail sketch of police culture suggests it is based on: (i) police officers' social isolation within society, and (ii) their apprehension of physical danger. The product of that culture is (iii) a solidaristic mindset anchored by the expectation of mutual support in time of danger. The group loyalty this engenders, less "mateship" than survival instinct, anathematizes those failing to support the mutuality of the occupational ethic.

As we saw in Chapter 8 on the investigation of police corruption, the punitive instinct of many a police service's paramilitary command structure, and resultant worker distrust in management, has long since added police management to the felt dangers against which the workforce has sought to protect itself. Corruption may parasitically flourish in a setting in which a perceived need for group integrity and a situationally apathetic, sometimes complicit police management militate against malfeasance being denounced; a situation in which police accusing other police of corruption may be victimized by their peers for "breaking ranks," and/or by police management for "making trouble."

Management's ill-advised response has been at times the denunciation of all aspects of police culture, a reaction as invalid as denouncing parenthood on the basis of the incidence of incest. This counterproductive approach served only to reinforce unthinking worker solidarity behind which corruption sheltered. When that finally became clear, management changed tack. The problem was not that of invoking good men and women to denounce corruption, the problem was worker empowerment – making it *possible* for the police workforce to denounce corruption.

Witness protection programs exist on a spectrum sometimes categorized in terms of level 1 (life-threatening), level 2 (case-specific) and level 3 (community-wide).[18] Level 1 witnesses need to be relocated and provided with a new identity. Before doing so there is a need for: a determination that the evidence to be provided by the witness is crucial and relates to very serious crimes; an assessment of the level of threat to the witness; an assessment of the suitability of the witness (including psychological and other testing, for instance, in relation to substance abuse); and the drawing up of a clear and detailed memorandum of understanding. Witness protection personnel need to be trained appropriately, and the roles of those assisting people in the program – as opposed to those determining their possible noncompliance with the requirements of the program and, as a consequence, removing them from it – need to be clearly separated. It goes without saying that strict confidentiality and security of information are at a premium in relation to such witness protection programs. Level 1 witnesses include the so-called "supergrasses" involved in the fight against organized crime, for example, the Mafia in the United States and Italy, and former members of terrorist groups such as the IRA in the United Kingdom and Northern Ireland in the 1970s and 1980s.[19]

Many of these Level 1 witnesses are themselves criminals who have been offered indemnity in return for acting as witnesses for the prosecution case against their former criminal colleagues. This gives rise to important questions in relation to their credibility. Is the testimony of such criminals to be believed? Hence the importance of corroborating evidence, for example, videotaped interviews or the testimony of other witnesses. It is also important to ensure that such witnesses are not being rewarded, since this can impugn their credibility. Here there are fine distinctions in play between being rewarded and being indemnified (without being rewarded). Again, entrants into such a witness protection program must understand that, for example, any breach of security on their part may lead to their removal from the program and termination of their indemnification, that is, they will be charged for the offenses against which they had originally been indemnified.

Level 2 witnesses are witnesses subject to verbal threats, stalking, or the like, but who are not facing a threat to life or limb. They may need protection in the form of enhanced home security, personal electronic warning devices, and so on.

Level 3 witnesses have received no direct threat, but feel at risk. They might simply need the reassurance of knowing that they will not find themselves alone with the accused in, say, a courthouse room, and that police have informed the accused that they are not to approach the witness or his/her domicile. Protections for Levels 2 and 3 are determined on a case by case basis.

In the context of the notoriously solidaristic police culture, internal witnesses in police organizations pose special problems. These problems are above and beyond the general issue of legal protections against defamation or breaching official secrets legislation; by and large, a duty to report misconduct deals with these problems, albeit there is a residual need for legal protection for internal witnesses – including so-called "whistleblowers" acting in good faith and in the possession of the facts – in the small number of cases where all official channels have been exhausted, including external oversight agencies, such as an ombudsman, and there is a need to go public, for instance, to the media. These additional protections pertain to victimization, not only on the part of those who are the subject of allegations by internal witnesses, but also managers seeking to "bury" the problem. Here there are a range of policies that should be in place:[20]

- making victimization of internal witnesses a criminal offense;
- establishing an external oversight body to whom complaints of victimization can be made and who can monitor the quality of internal processes in relation to internal witnesses, for example, an ombudsman;
- appropriate training of managers in relation to such internal investigations;
- penalties, such as loss of command, for managers who fail adequately to investigate cases of victimization;

- an appropriately high-level authority in relation to any decision to make internal witnesses undergo psychological testing, and (in appropriate cases) a recognition/reward system for internal witnesses whose claims/ evidence are upheld/vindicated.

An illustrative example of a particular witness support program is that developed by the New South Wales Police in 1995 in the context of the Royal Commission into Corruption in the NSW Police Service. The Royal Commission, in its final report, expressed itself satisfied with the 1995 Internal Witness Support Program (IWSP), whose operations it described in the following terms:

6.13 In broad summary, where a person now qualifies as an internal witness, the procedures applicable and the support available involve the following:

- the commander of the IWSU [Internal Witness Support Unit] is notified of each internal police complaint. Once a complainant is assessed as being an internal witness, the file is allocated to a case officer within the Unit;
- the case officer seeks further information so that a full assessment can be made of the complainant's suitability for assistance under the program;
- the commander of the IWSU sends a report to the Executive Director, Human Resources, notifying the complainant's status under the program. Staff are not placed in the program without their consent;
- the case officer asks the witness to nominate a mentor and a support officer. The mentor is a senior officer available to provide support and positive reinforcement to the witness. The support officer provides support to the witness at the work location. In cases where the witness desires support to be provided solely by the IWSU, a case officer within the Unit assumes the role;
- the proposed mentor and support officer are briefed about the program and provided with briefing notes by the IWSU case officer. They are encouraged to make an informed choice about whether they are willing to take on the role;
- support officers and mentors submit 'command line file notes' directly to the IWSU case officer;
- the IWSU maintains a computer file on all registrants. The computer system used within the IWSU is secure and confidential;
- each file is reviewed periodically, at which time the case officer makes personal contact with the witness; and
- there are also regular reviews to ensure that the Unit is tailoring its response on a needs basis.[21]

Notwithstanding the progress that has been made in this area, and the good report card provided by the Royal Commission, we are entitled to harbor a degree of skepticism in relation to the success of witness support programs. The basis for such skepticism is located in the continued strength of the dysfunctional aspects of police culture, and the poor track record of police organizations in their duty to protect police who report their corrupt colleagues. No matter how well-designed institutional arrangements such as the IWSP might be, they rely on the integrity of those who comprise them – the members of a suborganization within a police service organization – and also on the willingness to trust the members of the IWSP, or other like suborganizations, on the part of those who might have reason to seek their assistance. But it is precisely the lack of a sufficiency of integrity and trust that has undermined anticorruption programs in police organizations in the past.

Indeed, such are the problems with witness protection programs that some have suggested that admission to witness protection programs should not be at the discretion of the police.[22] At any rate, the adequacy of witness protection programs is also, in part, a matter of whether or not witnesses are in fact protected. It is also a matter of their felt level of security; this can be gauged by questionnaires. In addition, there are other measures, for example, the extent and quality of the physical security protections afforded level 2 witnesses. Ombudsman reports and audits are a further source of information in regard to the adequacy of witness protection programs.

Notes

1 See C. A. J. Coady (1992) *Testimony*, Oxford: Oxford University Press on these matters.
2 See N. R. Fyfe (2001) *Protecting Intimidated Witnesses*, Aldershot: Ashgate, p. 1.
3 Alternatively, the client's right to confidentiality is not breached in this case; rather, the right never extended so far as to include nondisclosure of serious criminal offenses. See Seumas Miller, M. Collingridge, and J. Bowles (2001) Privacy and confidentiality in social work, *Australian Social Work*, 54.2, pp. 3–14.
4 This is, of course, not to say that the privacy rights of witnesses and innocent third parties do not generate an entitlement that their disclosures be kept confidential consistent with the requirement to bring offenders to justice (and ensure the innocent are not convicted).
5 Police Ombudsman for Northern Ireland (2007) *Operation Ballast: investigation into the circumstances surrounding the murder of Raymond McCord Jnr.*
6 J. H. Skolnick (1994) *Justice without Trial: Law Enforcement in a Democratic Society*, New York: Macmillan, p. 117.
7 C. Dunnighan and C. Norris (2002) The detective, the snout and the audit commission: The real costs in using informants, *Howard Journal of Criminal Justice*, 38.1, pp. 67–86.

8   For a useful discussion of the ethical issues that the use of informers gives rise to see Clive Harfield (2012) Police informers and professional ethics, *Criminal Justice Ethics*, June, pp. 1–23.

9   For a UK- focused discussion of informants and informant management practices and legal requirements see Clive Harfield and Karen Harfield (2010) *Covert Investigation* (3rd edn), Oxford: Oxford University Press, Chapter 9.

10   See R. Billingsley, T. Nemitz, and P. Bean (eds) (2001) *Informers: Policing, Policy and Practice*, Cullompton, Devon: Willan Publishing, Chapter 1.

11   See Billingsley et al. (2001), Chapter 2.

12   See Harfield (2012).

13   See Association of Chief Police Officers (ACPO) *Manual of Standards for Covert Human Intelligence Sources* (CHIS) – a restricted document.

14   See ACPO Manual of Standards, pp. 63–64.

15   P. Gill (2000) *Rounding up the Usual Suspects? Developments in Contemporary Law Enforcement Intelligence*, Aldershot: Ashgate, p. 183.

16   Office of Police integrity (2005) *Review of Victoria Police Witness Protection Program*, Melbourne: Office of Police Integrity.

17   Risdon N. Slate (1997) The Federal Witness Protection Program: Its evolution and continuing growing pains, *Criminal Justice Ethics*, Summer 1997, pp. 20–34.

18   Slate (1997), pp. 8–9.

19   S. Greer (2001) Where the grass is greener?: Supergrasses in comparative perspective, in R. Billingsley, T. Nemitz, and P. Bean (eds) *Informers: Policing, Policy and Practice*, Cullompton, Devon: Willan Publishing.

20   Commonwealth Ombudsman (1997) *Professional Reporting and Internal Witness Protection in the Australian Federal Police*, Canberra: Commonwealth Ombudsman.

21   James Wood (1997) *Final Report of the Royal Commission into the NSW Police Service, Vol. II: Reform*, Sydney: Government of New South Wales, pp. 400–401.

22   Fyfe (2001), p. 65.

10

Surveillance and Monitoring

In this book we have argued that, normatively speaking, the primary role of criminal investigators is an epistemic or knowledge-aiming role in the ultimate service of the protection of legally enshrined, justifiably enforceable moral rights. However, we have also seen that a distinctive feature of policing is its unavoidable and routine use of harmful methods, such as coercion and deception, which are considered to be morally unacceptable in ordinary circumstances. In this chapter our focus is on an important moral right in play in policing contexts, namely the right to privacy. We consider a number of moral issues that arise as a result of the use by police of methods that infringe the right to privacy and also breach moral principles related to privacy, such as the moral requirement not to deceive.[1] The methods in question come under the general heading of surveillance and monitoring. We note that to infringe a moral right is not necessarily to violate that right. Violation of a moral right is unjustified infringement of it.[2]

10.1 Moral Right to Privacy

Many people feel seriously diminished by the disclosure of personal information, even when it is accurate and they are not damaged professionally or socially. Small wonder that more than sixty years ago a prominent Boston lawyer who became one of our greatest jurists, Louis D. Brandeis, characterized the rights of privacy as "the most comprehensive of rights and the one most valued by civilized men." The thought was echoed by the late, great William O. Douglas, who said, "The right to be left alone is the beginning of all freedom."[3]

Investigative Ethics: Ethics for Police Detectives and Criminal Investigators, First Edition.
Seumas Miller and Ian A. Gordon.
© 2014 Seumas Miller and Ian A. Gordon. Published 2014 by John Wiley & Sons, Ltd.

Brandeis et al. are surely correct in holding that privacy is an important moral value. However, the notion of privacy has proven to be a difficult one to explicate adequately. Nevertheless, there are a number of general points that can be made.[4]

First, privacy is a moral right that a person has in relation to other persons with respect to: (i) the possession of information about him/herself by other persons, or (ii) the observation/perceiving of him/herself – including tactile interference, such as body searches – by other persons. The range of matters regarded as private in this basic sense embraces much of what could be referred to as a person's "inner self." This inner self comprises a person's unexpressed thoughts, feelings, bodily sensations, and imaginings. But it may also comprise elements or aspects of a person's body: roughly speaking, those elements or aspects that are not normally perceptually accessible to others in public spaces. This inner self is the core of the sphere that is subject to an individual person's autonomous decision making. Here, the inner self stands in contrast with the outer self; the self that is necessarily present to others or that a person chooses to make known or to present to others.[5] A person's autonomy with respect to this inner self is not primarily de facto autonomy, although a person does have a degree of de facto autonomy with respect to (say) what they are thinking. Rather, it is a moral right to autonomy in respect of their inner self.

Second, a person's moral right to autonomy in respect of their inner self – the right to privacy – derives from the fact that a person's inner self in large part comprises their personal identity; it is in large part who they are. (Naturally, a person's identity is also in part constituted by their outer or public self.) Moreover, a person's inner self is in part constituted by their autonomy with respect to their inner self; their ability, albeit limited, to decide what to think and feel – to decide, albeit within limits, who they are. More than anything else, it is the moral value of personal identity – including autonomy – that explains the moral repugnance of violations of privacy. The more intrusive and sustained these violations are, the more repugnant they are; and the more they involve an attempt to change – as opposed to merely passively observe – elements of one's personal identity, the more morally repugnant they are. Hence our deep moral aversion to thought control. Like unjustified attempts to restrict our movement, thought control is a violation of our autonomy; but at a deeper level it is an assault on our personal identity, including our autonomy – an assault on who we are.

Third, while closely related, the right to autonomy is not the same thing as the right to privacy. For one thing, a person has a right to autonomous decision making in relation to a range of issues outside the sphere of the inner self; the right to autonomy embraces much of a person's decision making in the public sphere. However, the right to autonomy and the right to privacy are conceptually connected. Roughly speaking, the notion of privacy delimits an area, namely, the inner self; however, the moral right to decide what to think and do is the right to autonomy, and the moral right to decide *who to exclude and who not to*, is an element of the right to autonomy. So the right to privacy consists of the right to exclude others (right to autonomy) from the inner self (the private sphere).

Fourth, a person's intimate relationship with another person gives rise to a zone of interpersonal privacy from which third parties are excluded. For example, a married couple has a right to engage in intimate sexual acts in their home unobserved by others. Such zones of interpersonal privacy or intimacy typically exist between members of families, for example, parents and children, friends, and lovers. Moreover, such intimacy is regarded as a moral good. Certainly the development of interpersonal relations with emotional depth requires, and is in part constituted by, intimacy. However, intimacy can be morally problematic as in the case of exploitative sexual relationships, for instance, an investigator who forms a sexual relationship merely to gain information on a suspect.

Fifth, certain facts pertaining to objects a person owns, or monies a person earns, are held to be private simply in virtue of the right to ownership. Ownership appears to confer the right not to disclose, or have disclosed, information concerning the thing owned. Or at least there is a presumption in favor of nondisclosure, including nondisclosure to, or by, government departments; a presumption that can be overridden to a limited extent by, for example, the public interest in tax gathering, or in tracking the proceeds of a crime.

Sixth, certain facts pertaining to a person's various public roles and practices, including one's voting decisions, are regarded as private.[6] These kinds of facts are apparently regarded as private in part in virtue of the potential, should they be disclosed, of undermining the capacity of the person to autonomously function in these public roles, or to fairly compete in these practices. If others know how a person votes, the person's right to freely support a particular candidate might be undermined. If business competitors have full access to a person's business plans at every stage, or to the details of products under development – as opposed to access to what businesses are legally required to disclose to the market or what they might choose to disclose – then they will gain an unfair advantage over the person. If a would-be employer knows a job applicant's sexual preferences, then the employer might unfairly discriminate against the job applicant by not hiring them because of their sexual preferences.

Seventh, and more generally, a measure of privacy is necessary simply in order for a person to pursue his or her projects, whatever those projects might be. For one thing, reflection is necessary for planning, and reflection requires a degree of freedom from the intrusions of others, that is, a degree of privacy. For another, knowledge of someone else's plans can enable those plans to be thwarted. *Autonomy* – including the exercise of autonomy in the public sphere – requires a measure of privacy.

Eighth, the sphere of an individual's privacy can be widened to include other individuals who stand in a professional relationship to the first individual. Here, part of the sphere of an individual's privacy, for example, the bodily states of a sick person, is widened to include another person, such as the person's doctor, and the result is a *confidential* relationship. An analogous point can be made in relation to lawyers and their clients, and in relation to police and the victims of crimes who are also witnesses to those crimes.

Ninth, the data owned, and "actions" performed, by organizations and groups – including businesses and government agencies – or by individual persons in their capacity as members of organizations or groups, may also be regarded as private, or at least confidential. For example, a business company needs a measure of confidentiality in relation to its plans and products under development, if it is to be able to compete on equal terms in the marketplace. Again, law enforcement agencies must retain confidential information in relation to the activities of criminal organizations, if they are to successfully investigate those organizations.

Tenth, the notion that privacy is an absolute right that cannot be overridden under any circumstances is unsustainable. The rights to privacy of some individuals, and the right to confidentiality of members of some organizations, will in some cases be overridden by the rights of other individuals and other members of organizations to be protected by the law enforcement agencies from rights violations, including murder, rape, grievous bodily harm, pedophilia, and armed robbery.

Let us now turn to some case studies that display some of the privacy and confidentiality issues that arise in criminal investigations.

10.2　Case Studies

Case Study 10.2.1　US Patriot Act

Minutes before midnight on May 26, President Obama, in France, by a species of teleportable pen signed into law a four-year extension of the Patriot Act: the central domestic support of the security apparatus devised by the Bush administration, after the bombings of 11 September 2001 and the "anthrax letters" a week later. . . . The Patriot Act controls secret investigations. . . .

Obama promised, in the Democratic primaries of 2008, to filibuster against a proposed amnesty for telecoms firms that illegally co-operated with a request by the Office of the Vice President to divulge information about their customers. The conduct of the telecoms firms was a violation of the Foreign Intelligence Surveillance Act (FISA), which forbade eavesdropping on Americans without judicial oversight. But in July 2008, once Obama had secured the Democratic nomination, this became the first promise on which he reneged. . . .

Three elements of the Patriot Act have drawn persistent challenge. First, the "lone wolf" provision, which allows the intelligence bureaucracy to launch and sustain surveillance of a person who has not been linked to any foreign power. Thanks to a second provision, the "roving wiretap," a target of surveillance may remain a target even when he shifts his means of communication by a change of phone, postal address, email, or other medium: no reapplication for a warrant is required, and no demonstration of probable cause. Finally, the "'business records provision" enables the searchers empowered by the Patriot Act to get a court order under FISA to seize "tangible things" such as personal papers and records (the definition of relevant objects is elastic); and it denies a judge discretion to limit such a warrant to specific and designated items.

(Extract from David Bromwich (2011) 'Obama, Bush and the Patriot Act.' Blog posted at *Huff Post Politics* on May 30, 2011)

Case Study 10.2.2   Encryption

Investigators have cracked the encryption key for a laptop drive owned by a Colorado woman accused of real-estate fraud – rendering a judge's controversial order to make her hand over the passphrase or stand in contempt of court irrelevant. The government seized the Toshiba laptop from Ramona Fricosu back in 2010 and successfully asked the court to compel her to either type the key into the computer or turn over a plain-text version of the data held on her machine.

Her lawyer's argument that compelling her to hand over encryption keys would violate her Fifth Amendment rights against self-incrimination was rejected. Prosecutors offered Fricosu limited immunity in this case without going so far as promising they wouldn't use information on the computer against her. The Electronic Frontier Foundation filed a brief supporting the defense in the case, arguing

(Continued)

that Fricosu was being forced to become a witness against herself. District Judge Robert Blackburn refused to suspend his decision for the time it would take to convene an appeal. The regional 10th U.S. Circuit Court of Appeals refused to review his decision.

Fricosu was left with the stark choice of either coughing up her encryption keys by the end of February or risking a spell behind bars for contempt of court. Philip Dubois, Fricosu's attorney, claimed that his client had forgotten the encryption passphrase.

However, the Feds handed the plain-text contents of the laptop to Dubois on Wednesday. It seems more than likely that the authorities had come across the right passphrase without Fricosu's forced assistance.

This was the first appellant court to rule on the balance between Fifth Amendment rights against compelled self-incrimination and the public interest in allowing police to potentially unearth evidence in criminal cases involved encrypted computers and storage devices. However the ruling is not binding in other regions, especially in the absence of a Supreme Court ruling on the issue.

The US Fifth Amendment holds that no one "shall be compelled in any criminal case to be a witness against himself." Supreme Court rulings have previously ruled that a criminal suspect can be compelled to turn over a key to a safe possibly containing incriminating evidence, but is not obliged to supply the combination of a safe to investigators.

(Extract from John Leyden (2012) Feds unlock suspect's encrypted drive, avoid Constitution meltdown: Digital age plays havoc with 5th Amendment. Posted in *Law*, March 1, 2012 14:01 GMT, *Free whitepaper – A Vision for the Data Centre*)

Case Study 10.2.3   Degrees of Privacy

People will expect more privacy when at home than when talking in a public place. If a suspect is seen using a mobile phone, but appears to have no regular contract with a telephone company, or if he travels by taxi or hire car whilst leaving his own vehicle at home, a reasonable analysis may well be that he is covering his tracks, and taking deliberate steps to hide his business from the police. However frustrating for the investigator it may be, this alone cannot justify more intrusive methods. In no country is it against the law to hide one's affairs from the police. Has the effort been wasted though? The answer is "no." Although the police are not entitled to assume that his secrecy has a criminal motive, the information may be considered alongside other information to form a reasonable conclusion which would justify further action.

Imagine now that a surveillance team have successfully followed the subject into a restaurant where he meets two other men. The conversation is guarded and only partly overheard, but the team recognise slang words and phrases which they recognise to be connected to the drugs trade. One of the men pays by credit card and enquiries into that reveal that he pays for a meal for two or three people at that restaurant regularly. If the restaurant staff confirm that he usually books a table, there would probably be justification for seeking to anticipate the next meeting, and placing some sort of listening device at the table, where the suspects are not entitled to expect a very high degree of privacy. If at the next meeting one of the men is heard to say that they should not talk there, but only at home, there might well now be some justification for seeking to intrude into the subject's conversations, in his own home. The previous observations should be able to clarify which rooms people meet and talk in. If at that meeting drug dealing is clearly discussed and the subject says that he will telephone a third party, that evidence might then justify seeking to intercept mobile phone calls, provided only the phone he is using can be identified and targeted. If technical reasons mean that there is a real risk of intercepting and listening to other innocent people's phone calls, then the interception might not be justified.

(Extract from Bob Denmark, *Ethical Investigation: A Practical Guide for Police Officers*, London: UK Foreign and Commonwealth Office, Chapter 7, available at http://www.jeiruegas.com/docs/Ethical%20Investigation%20 Bob%20Denmark.pdf)

Case Study 10.2.4   Home Searches and Thermal Imaging

Federal agents could not see inside Danny Lee Kyllo's home. Nor did they have a search warrant to enter the premises. But they did have an infrared camera that used thermal imaging technology, enabling

(Continued)

them to identify suspected heat lamps growing 100 marijuana plants. They used the images to get a warrant, leading to Kyllo's arrest and conviction.

The Supreme Court today, in Kyllo vs. U.S., ruled that authorities scanning a home with an infrared camera without a warrant constituted an unreasonable search barred by the Fourth Amendment. It did so, the court said, because the device is not in general use by the public, so Kyllo had an expectation of privacy, and because the imaging provided by the camera revealed details about Kyllo's home "that would previously have been unknowable without physical intrusion." "I think this is an important ruling because a lot of people, including myself, were concerned that the court would just say the technology is fine as long as you're detecting something outside [of the home], such as heat emissions," said Sherry Colb, a professor at Rutgers Law School. "That would be a great cause for concern," she said, referring to a footnote in the ruling that observes there are technologies being developed that might allow authorities to see through an opaque wall.

Detective Larry Wilson of the Plano, Texas, police force, said it has been common for police to use thermal imaging on houses without first obtaining a warrant, and that will change.

But he says the police in his department and others he's trained around the country have been instructed not to use the devices without having first obtained probable cause through other means. So he says the ruling should not greatly affect current police use of infrared cameras on homes. "Whenever we're doing an indoor grow operation investigation we've already established the necessary probable cause prior to doing the thermal imaging," said Wilson. "Now the only step that's going to be added is to get an affidavit and get a judge to do that and issue a warrant." Thermal imaging is not precise enough itself to provide probable cause, he added. "The way that the imager is utilized is left open to interpretation," he said. "You can't say that the heat you're looking at that's being emitted from the house through vents or whatever for sure that it's being produced from once source or another."

(Extract from David Rupp (2012) Supreme Court rules on police using infrared, *ABC News*, June 11, http://abcnews.go.com/US/story?id=93127&page=1)

10.3   The Right to Privacy and Criminal Investigations

As we saw above, privacy is an important moral right. However, the right to privacy is not absolute; the right to privacy can be overridden under certain circumstances. Indeed, in some instances the right to privacy of an individual is overridden by other rights or interests of that same individual, for instance, a self-harming suspect under video surveillance in a police cell or a suspect in an interview room with a police officer.[7]

On the other hand, since privacy is a moral right, infringements of it ought to be kept to a minimum, for example, by restricting access to personal information required for a criminal investigation to relevant members of the investigative team, and the justification of such infringements as are necessary ought to be spelled out clearly and in reasonable detail (see below).

Moreover, there are degrees of privacy (see Case Study 10.2.3 above) and since privacy pertains to one's home or other environs (e.g., one's workspace) as well as to one's person (see Case Study 10.2.4 above), what is or is not an acceptable infringement of privacy is not necessarily clear cut. The use of thermal imaging in relation to the contents of one's house (Case Study 10.2.4) is a case in point.

This raises the important question as to the baseline or threshold of privacy below which infringements should not be tolerated unless consented to or justified on the basis on reasonable suspicion in the context of an investigation of a serious crime. What is this baseline, or rather baselines, given the various modes of access to persons, their homes, and so on? This is a difficult and complex question, which we cannot pursue here. However, we do note that it is partly a factual issue: namely, what does the community regard as acceptable?; partly a normative issue, namely, what *ought* the community regard as acceptable? We suggest that the answer to the latter depends in part on the answer to the former and that, in any case, the answer to the latter set of questions is in large part context-dependent – for example, it depends on the security risks that might be minimized by infringing privacy.

It is important to distinguish infringements of privacy conceived of as one-off events involving the privacy of a single individual or group on an occasion or during the course of a single investigation (e.g., a wiretap of a suspect), from more generalized conditions of surveillance or monitoring (e.g., thousands of CCTV cameras in the city of London). Perhaps the use of any given CCTV camera taken on its own is morally unproblematic because none are especially intrusive but that in aggregate the extent of surveillance is regarded as morally unacceptable.[8]

Further, it is important to keep in mind that, in circumstances in which the right to privacy and (say) security stand in some tension, nevertheless, the relationship is not necessarily an inverse one; so an increase in security does not necessarily require a commensurate reduction in privacy. For example, access to the footage in CCTV cameras in public spaces might be allowed only under certain restrictive conditions such as in the event of a crime having taken place.[9]

Nevertheless, in relation to the accessing of data and/or intercepting of communications by law enforcement agencies, a balance often has to be struck between the rights of citizens – including suspects – to privacy and confidentiality on the one hand, and the rights of actual and potential victims to protection from serious crime on the other. Moreover, the state of technology at a given point in time to some extent determines the possibility of striking the appropriate balance at that time.

For example, the current availability to the general public of very secure computer systems and of high-level encryption products makes accessing data and/or intercepting communications on the Internet by law enforcement agencies extremely difficult and expensive, if not impossible in practice (see above Case Study 10.2.2, Encryption). This issue needs to be addressed in a manner that both satisfies privacy concerns and does not unduly inhibit law enforcement agencies.

One way not to proceed at this point is for law enforcement agencies (and their superiors) to take matters into their own hands and ignore the privacy concerns of the community. As we saw in Chapter 3, based on documents provided by Edward J. Snowden, the NSA has since 2000 or thereabouts been covertly collaborating with technology companies in the United States to build entry points into their products to enable the NSA to access messages before they are encrypted. Given this possibility was widely discussed and abandoned by government in the face of public opposition in the 1990s, the practice cannot be regarded as legitimate. Moreover, the covert nature of this practice gives rise to accountability concerns, even if the notion of such access were to be otherwise morally and legally acceptable: if the public does not know about it, including how – or even if – it is appropriately authorized, how can they be assured it is carried out in a lawful and morally justifiable manner?

Naturally, even if these concerns were addressed, there remains the prior moral issue of whether such pre-encryption access should be allowed to law enforcement agencies (assuming it had sufficient community support and was subject to appropriate accountability mechanisms). As we have seen, the right to privacy is not absolute and there are occasions on which it will be overridden by other more weighty moral considerations. On these occasions there needs to be a means to access encrypted communications by law enforcement agencies (before or after the encryption takes place). Accordingly, if the method of pre-encryption access discussed above is not the answer, then another needs to be found, albeit one consistent with the relevant moral principles and subject to appropriate accountability mechanisms. We return to this general issue in the next section.

In striking the above-mentioned balance between privacy and security, whether it is in relation to communications by telephone or by some other means, a number of principles need to be kept in mind.[10]

First, because such accessing and/or intercepting are, by definition, an infringement of the right to privacy, the presumption must be against their use. This presumption can be overridden by other very weighty moral considerations – especially the need to protect other moral rights – or by exceptional circumstances, such as might obtain in wartime. But the presumption cannot be overridden by a blanket appeal to the common good or to the general need for security.

Second, the benefits of such accessing and/or intercepting must offset the likely costs, including the costs in terms of the erosion in public trust.

Third, the accessing and/or interception in question must be in relation to serious crimes.

Fourth, there must be at least a reasonable suspicion or reasonable belief or probable cause[11] that the person whose privacy is to be infringed has committed, or intends to commit, a serious crime – or is otherwise implicated in a serious crime – and that the resulting information is likely to substantially further the investigation under way in relation to that crime. The more intrusive and sustained the infringement of the right to privacy, the more serious the crime in question needs to be (principle of proportionality) and the higher the standard of evidence that ought to be required that the person whose right to privacy is to be infringed is implicated in this crime.

Fifth, there must be no feasible alternative method of gathering the information that does not involve an infringement of privacy.

Sixth, the law enforcement officials must be subject to stringent accountability requirements, including the issuing of warrants in circumstances in which the justification provided is independently adjudicated.

Seventh, those whose privacy has been infringed must be informed that it has been infringed at the earliest time consistent with not compromising the investigation, or connected investigations.

It is sometimes suggested that infringements of privacy are not morally wrong if the person whose privacy is invaded does not know about it, and if there are no harmful consequences. However, we have argued that persons have a *moral right* to privacy. Therefore, an unauthorized invasion of that privacy is a *prima facie* moral wrong, irrespective of whether the person knows his/her privacy has been invaded, and irrespective of the harmful consequences. The point is simply that the "invader" is in possession of information, or has made observations, which he or she does not have a right to possess or to make; indeed, he or she has acquired that information, or made those observations, in violation of the privacy rights of another person. If a person steals someone else's property, then the thief has committed a wrong, notwithstanding the fact that the victim might never notice that the item has gone missing; there is a perpetrator and a victim, even though the victim is unaware that they are a victim.

As noted in Chapter 3, an increasingly important issue in relation to privacy is the integration and sharing of different sets of information available to different government – including law enforcement – agencies. This is morally problematic in that, as we have seen, there is a presumption against the gathering of information on citizens by government officials, including law enforcement personnel.

10.4 Privacy, Criminal Investigations, and Encryption

Notwithstanding the above discussion of the status of the right to privacy and the need to protect that right from unjustified infringements, there is a perception among many operational detectives that legal rules have gone too far in preserving the rights of suspects, to the extent that they have become a major impediment to effective investigation. One of the alleged reasons for this is the advent of new technologies – including the new information and communication technologies – and their exploitation by criminals (including, as it turns out, nation-states engaged in cyber-crime – see Chapter 6, Case Study 6.4.2).

Nor are these complaints without their theoretical backers. Amitai Etzioni argues that the prevailing concern to protect individual privacy in relation to the Internet, in particular, is misguided, and that public safety and public health are being put at risk by policies driven by strong commitments to individual privacy.[12] As always, there is a need to balance individual rights against the public good and, according to Etzioni, the balance has shifted too much in favor of individual rights. Given the sustained theoretical nature of Etzioni's discussion of these matters, we will consider his view in some detail.

Our concern here is with encryption. In the course of examining this issue, we will offer a critique and adjustment to the general communitarian conception of the right to privacy that he offers. It should be said at the outset that we are by no means completely at odds with Etzioni. Nevertheless, in our view his position is seriously deficient in a number of respects.

In essence, encryption is a complex code that protects the secrecy of electronic communications. Moreover, as already noted, some of these codes (hyper-encryption) are very difficult, if not impossible, to crack. There has been an enormous increase in the use of encryption technologies, including the use of hyper-encryption.

There are obviously considerable benefits that accrue to business, government and individuals from the use of encryption, including the safeguarding of confidentiality and privacy. Unfortunately, hyper-encryption also affords opportunities for criminals to protect their communications, and thereby thwart the efforts of law enforcement agencies to apprehend criminals and protect ordinary citizens.

Accordingly, the question becomes: Should public authorities have the capability to decipher encrypted messages?;[13] and, relatedly, should authorities have the power to require suspects to decrypt encrypted messages under certain circumstances, supposing the authorities cannot, or cannot without great difficulty, decrypt them? (See Case Study, 10.2.2 Encryption, above).

Etzioni argues that authorities should have the capability to decipher encrypted messages – and, presumably, to require that suspects do so under certain conditions – on the grounds that the threats to public safety posed by the new encryption technologies outweigh the right to privacy of those using encryption. Citing D. E. Denning and W. E. Baugh,[14] Etzioni lists threats posed by encryption to law enforcement, public safety and national security.[15] The items on this list can be classified into three relevant categories of threat: (i) encryption can make it impossible to obtain necessary *evidence*; (ii) encryption can frustrate communications intercepts in relation to the *known or suspected criminal activity* of individuals and organizations, and (iii) encryption can hinder *intelligence-gathering*. Etzioni also mentions that encryption can lead to *greater infringements of privacy* than would otherwise have occurred, as when, for example, investigators opt for intrusive audio and visual surveillance when they are unable to intercept email messages. However, even if true, this does not of itself justify infringements of privacy, but only lesser, rather than greater, infringements of privacy. For this reason we will disregard it in our discussion below.

By Etzioni's lights, privacy ought to be infringed only if there is "a well documented and macroscopic threat to the common good, not merely a hypothetical danger."[16] Notwithstanding the low probability (and indeed hypothetical nature) of some macroscopic dangers posed by encryption, Etzioni judges the capability to decipher is warranted by virtue of the high disutility of the macroscopic dangers, were they to occur. For example, biological terrorism is perhaps improbable, but it has a very high disutility. Moreover, privacy ought to be infringed only by a given method if this method is likely to secure the end for which it is being used, and if there is no other nonintrusive, or less intrusive, method.

In the case of encryption, public key recovery is the means to avert macroscopic dangers: "A key recovery system is a backup system for encryption keys that enables the encrypted data to be deciphered, even if the primary keys are destroyed. Public key recovery involves placing a key with public authorities."[17] In this connection, Etzioni discusses the practical question as to whether or not strong encryption products might be available from sources outside the jurisdiction of the public authority in question. He points out that such outside sources might themselves have a backup key, and, even if they did not, the consumer might not be aware whether or not the sources have such a backup key. Moreover, as Etzioni notes,[18] even if criminals could use their own specialized systems, the use of such systems would point law enforcement agencies toward where the criminals were concentrated. (And such use would restrict the lines of criminal communication in relation to other nonsecure systems.) At any rate, for the purposes of argument, we are going to accept Etzioni's claim that public key recovery, if introduced, would be of considerable assistance to law enforcement agencies in particular, and that there is no alternative (and less intrusive) means. Accordingly, the question of whether or not to introduce a public key recovery system resolves itself into a theoretical question concerning the balance to be struck between the individual right to privacy on the one hand, and the need for public safety on the other.

Etzioni concludes that public safety overrides individual privacy, and does so by virtue of the necessity for the use of a public key recovery system to deal with the significant macroscopic public safety problem posed by hyper-encryption. Moreover, Etzioni suggests that the introduction of a public key recovery system is simply an extension to computer technology of prevailing accepted law enforcement powers in relation to older technologies, for example, telephone interception.[19]

There are a number of problems with Etzioni's arguments and his overall conception. Let us now turn to these.

Etzioni tends to run together a variety of different public agencies under the umbrella term "public authorities." This is potentially confusing, since different public agencies have very different responsibilities, and presumably, therefore, very different needs in terms of access to information. Accordingly, we will be concerned in what follows only with law enforcement agencies and, especially, criminal investigation agencies.

We have already argued that criminal investigation powers in contemporary liberal democracies in relation to telephone interception are acceptable if they are constrained by the principles that we set out above – the interception in question is in relation to a serious crime, there is reasonable suspicion that the person whose privacy is to be infringed is implicated in the crime, and it is probable that the resulting information is likely to substantially further the investigation in relation to that crime. Moreover, we accept that these (suitably constrained) powers in relation to telephone interception are analogous to possession on the part of criminal investigation agencies of the ability to decipher encrypted messages. It follows that, if a public key recovery system is necessary for criminal investigation agencies to have the ability to decipher encrypted messages, then – other things being equal – a public key recovery system ought to be established. However, it also follows that the exercise of the resulting ability to decipher encrypted messages ought to be constrained by the same principles that constrain telephone interception.

In fact, Etzioni seems to accept something like the above set of principles or conditions.[20] At any rate, let us now return to the above-mentioned three categories of threat that, according to Etzioni, justify the possession on the part of criminal investigation agencies of the ability to decipher encrypted messages. The first category consists of encrypted messages that are needed for evidence. Assume that the evidence pertains to serious crimes, and that there are reasonable grounds for thinking that this is so. There is still a problem, namely, that the person whose privacy is to be infringed might be someone other than a suspect, and other than a person seeking to aid or protect a suspect. The person might be a complete innocent, and be known by the investigators to be such. Naturally, such an innocent person might be prevailed upon to consent to furnish the necessary evidence. But in that case there would be no infringement of privacy. At any rate, the general point is that the first category of threats does not conform to the above-mentioned conditions, and Etzioni has not made out an adequate case for their inclusion.

The second category, namely encrypted messages sent by persons known or reasonably suspected to be involved in criminal activity, are of a kind that comply with the above set of requirements, or could be made to do so. Accordingly, they do not present a problem for Etzioni. What of the third category?

These are encrypted messages that might facilitate intelligence-gathering purposes. Obviously, this category of threats does not necessarily conform to all, or indeed any, of the above requirements. In particular, this category does not conform to the requirement that the person about whom the intelligence is being gathered, and whose privacy is being infringed, is reasonably suspected of some serious crime. Moreover, intelligence gathering is by definition at times speculative and hunch-driven, rather than strongly evidence-based. Accordingly, Etzioni has not made out an adequate case for the inclusion of this third category.

We conclude that Etzioni has made out a case for criminal investigation agencies having the capability to decipher encrypted messages under very restricted conditions; roughly speaking, the conditions under which they currently have the capability to access or intercept messages that are not encrypted. However, these conditions would not justify the interception or accessing of at least two of the general categories of encrypted messages that Etzioni believes ought to be able to be accessed by criminal investigation agencies.

It might be argued that Etzioni has presented more powerful arguments than we have allowed. In particular, he has the general argument of the need to ensure public safety. While this is one of the main general justifications offered by Etzioni for infringement of individual privacy, it is in our view unacceptable.

First, the benefits of such general practices must offset the costs, including the costs in terms of the erosion in public trust. As the East European experience under communism has taught us, high levels of surveillance, intelligence gathering, and detailed record keeping are inconsistent with an open, free society based on trust between public bodies and private citizens. Etzioni has not, in our view, offered convincing support for the proposition that the level of infringement of privacy that he advocates would not ultimately have too high a cost, but since in principle he might be able to, let us set this argument aside.

Second – and most important – since accessing and/or intercepting are by definition an infringement of privacy, the presumption must be against their use. That presumption can be overridden in particular cases or by exceptional circumstances, such as in wartime, but not by a *blanket* appeal to the common good or to the general need for public safety. Here we come to the nub of what is problematic about Etzioni's communitarianism. Let us deal with this issue in greater detail.

We are in full agreement with Etzioni that privacy is not an absolute right that cannot be overridden under any circumstances, whether it is privacy on the Internet or on any other communication or information system. The rights to privacy of some individuals, and the rights to confidentiality of members of some organizations, will in some cases be overridden by other moral considerations. For example, the rights to privacy of some individuals and/or confidentiality rights of members of organizations can *in some instances* be overridden by certain moral rights of other individuals, such as the right to life, the right not to be assaulted, or the right to autonomy. Consider, in this connection, the communications of violent drug-dealers, pedophiles, and terrorists. Consider also programmers who devise and release destructive viruses and worms that infiltrate strategic government and economic computer systems via the Internet. All these communicators have an interest in sophisticated forms of encryption. Accordingly, law enforcement agencies have a legitimate need of access to "plain text" versions of encrypted communications for the purposes of tracking down such persons.

Further, we agree with Etzioni – and Miller has argued as much elsewhere[21] – that, in relation to accessing of data and/or intercepting of communications on the Internet by criminal investigation agencies, a balance has to be struck between rights to privacy and confidentiality on the one hand, and the rights to protection from serious crime on the other. Moreover, the state of technology at any point in time to some extent determines the possibility of striking a balance. Perhaps the current availability to the general public of very secure computer systems and of high-level encryption products has shifted the balance too much in favor of rights to privacy and confidentiality. If so, then, arguably, recourse to public key recovery systems is needed to redress this imbalance.

However, the crucial question in the striking of this balance concerns what is to be put on the scales. Etzioni opts for public safety as against individual moral rights. *Contra* Etzioni, we suggest that public safety is too general and amorphous a notion. What is called for in its place is a more precise and differentiated notion. In the first place, we need to specify a set of individual moral rights that override the individual right to privacy (at least in general). These would include the right to life, and the right not to suffer grievous bodily harm. Accordingly – in the first place – we have individual moral rights being put in the balance against individual moral rights, and not – as Etzioni holds – a public good being put in the balance against an individual moral right.

In the second place, there is a restricted range of specific public goods, such as the integrity of government computer systems, which might under certain circumstances tip the scales against the individual right to privacy. However, two points are important to note here. First, there is a presumption in favor of the individual right to privacy in such cases. Second, the crucial consideration that might offset this presumption is the direct, or indirect, infringement of individual moral rights (albeit in some cases jointly held rights) that might result from threats to these public goods. For example, individual citizens have a right to be protected from (say) terrorism. But in that case, the communications of those who break into government computer systems, and do so for the ultimate purpose of putting the lives of citizens at risk to terrorists, are no longer protected by the moral right to privacy.

We have been arguing against Etzioni's communitarian account of the balance to be struck between the right of individuals to privacy and the need for public safety. We have proffered instead an individualist rights-based account, and suggested in effect that individual rights to privacy can be infringed, but only by virtue of threats to other more important individual moral rights. But there is a further dimension of Etzioni's account that is deficient in our view, namely his account of the right to privacy. Let us now turn to this issue.

Etzioni distinguishes between two sorts of privacy, informational privacy and decisional privacy (the right to control one's own acts).[22] In fact, as he himself points out, the latter seems to be a species of autonomy, rather than privacy. At any rate, our concern is with his account of privacy, not autonomy.

According to Etzioni, privacy is a contingent notion, dependent on socio-historical context, yet in our time in need of reconceptualization. In so far as this does not constitute a rejection of the notion of a residual common core element of privacy that exists in all socio-historical contexts, this is innocuous enough. If Etzioni means to reject any such common core element, then his account becomes incoherent; if there is no common core, then he cannot literally be speaking of the same thing from one context to another.

In fact, most of Etzioni's arguments are not really to do with reconceptualizing the notion of privacy, but rather with shifting, indeed increasing, restrictions on individual privacy in the light of his concerns about public health and public safety. However, Etzioni does make some communitarian claims about the concept of privacy. The main one of these is: "Privacy thus is a societal license that exempts a category of acts (including thoughts and emotions) from communal, public and governmental scrutiny."[23] As a corollary to this, Etzioni claims:

> privacy encompasses behaviours that members of a particular social entity are positively expected, by prevailing social mores or laws, to carry out so as not to be readily scrutinizable. For instance, defecating is expected or required to take place out of sight in many societies.[24]

In all this, Etzioni confuses two very different kinds of claim. The first kind of claim concerns the various socio-historical conditions which gave rise to the concept or concepts of privacy, and which currently sustain a conception of privacy in (say) contemporary American society. The second kind of claim concerns the (moral) normative nature and morally acceptable restrictions on privacy. If we interpret Etzioni's above-quoted statements as making the first kind of claim, then they are more or less acceptable. They are more or less plausible accounts of the socio-historical character of the concept(s) of privacy. However, if we interpret the statements as making the second kind of claim, then they are unacceptable. For, thus interpreted, Etzioni is suggesting that an individual's moral right to privacy is somehow conferred on the individual by the society to which he or she belongs. That is, the individual only has a particular right in so far as the *society decides* that the individual has that right; today you can have a right to life, but tomorrow perhaps you cannot. This is an incoherent conception of moral rights, and one that opens the door to authoritarianism or perhaps even totalitarianism.

Elsewhere, Etzioni claims that his conception of the right to privacy rests squarely on the legal conception contained in the Fourth Amendment.[25] Once again, this is an unacceptable and dangerous move. Moral notions, including privacy, ground legal conceptions, and not vice versa. Once we accept the proposition that moral notions ought to be grounded in legal ones, then the way is clear to simply change the law, and thereby claim to have changed morality. But this is incoherent; lawyers, judges, and politicians cannot make morality up. Rather we can – if we are lucky – cause them to reflect morality in the laws that they make and apply.

Notes

1   For a recent account of the various methods, see Harfield and Harfield (2012).
2   We could further distinguish between a violation of a right which was, nevertheless, justified, all things considered, as opposed to an infringement of a right which was not a violation of a right (but only an infringement).
3   See Arthur Miller (1982) *Miller's Court*, New York: Houghton Mifflin.
4   An earlier version of the material in this section appeared in Seumas Miller (1997a) Privacy and the Internet, *Australian Computer Journal*, 29.1, pp. 12–16, and an earlier one still in Seumas Miller (1996) *Issues in Police Ethics*, Wagga Wagga: Keon.
5   See Thomas Nagel (2002), Concealment and exposure, in his *Concealment and Exposure and Other Essays*, Oxford: Oxford University Press.
6   See Stanley I. Benn, *A Theory of Freedom*, Cambridge: Cambridge University Press, 1988, p. 289.
7   Richard D. Emery (1998) Cameras in the station house, *Criminal Justice Ethics*, 17.1, pp. 43–44.
8   For a recent discussion of these and related issues see Tom Sorell (2011) Preventative policing, surveillance, and European counter-terrorism, *Criminal Justice Ethics*, April, pp. 1–22.
9   Benjamin J Goold (2002) Privacy rights and public spaces: CCTV and the problem of the "unobservable observer," *Criminal Justice Ethics*, Winter/Spring, p. 23.
10   Earlier versions of the material in this section appeared in Miller (1997a) and in Miller and Blackler (2005) Chapter 4.
11   These various cognate notions of reasonable suspicion, reasonable belief, and probable cause (used in US jurisdictions) are somewhat vague, but arguably delineate different thresholds: reasonable suspicion, for example, seems weaker than reasonable belief and probable cause. Fortunately, there is no need to pursue these issues here, other than to note that a degree of vagueness does not entail complete indeterminacy.
12   Amitai Etzioni (1999) *The Limits of Privacy*, New York: Basic Books. An earlier version of the material in this section appeared in Seumas Miller (1999) Privacy, encryption and the Internet, in A. D'Atri, A. Marturano, S. Rogerson, and T. Ward Bynum (eds), *Proceedings of the 4th ETHICOMP International Conference on the Social and Ethical Impacts of Information and Communication Technologies* (CD format), Rome, pp. 1–11, and in Miller and Blackler (2005), Chapter 4.
13   See Etzioni (1999), p. 77.

14   D. E. Denning and W. E. Baugh (1997) *Encryption and Evolving Technologies as Tools of Organized Crime and Terrorism*, Washington, DC: US Working Group on Organized Crime, National Strategy Information Centre.

15   See Etzioni (1999), pp. 78–80.

16   See Etzioni (1999), p. 12.

17   See Etzioni (1999), p. 81.

18   See Etzioni (1999), p. 86.

19   See Etzioni (1999), pp. 91–94.

20   See Etzioni (1999), p. 92.

21   See Miller (1997a).

22   See Etzioni (1999), p. 15.

23   See Etzioni (1999), p. 196.

24   See Etzioni (1999), p. 196.

25   See Etzioni (1999), p. 203.

11

Undercover Operations and Entrapment

This chapter consists of a discussion of one of the covert methods of criminal investigations that have historically given rise to moral problems in a particularly acute form, namely, undercover operations, including the setting of traps or "sting" operations.[1] This discussion of the moral problems posed by undercover operations takes place in the context of our favored normative theory of policing as the protection of justifiably enforceable, legally enshrined moral rights and, in particular, our normative account of the role of the criminal investigator as essentially an epistemic or knowledge-aiming role. Undercover operations are quintessential *epistemic* policing methods since they are principally aimed at gathering intelligence and evidence. In the first instance, this intelligence and evidence gathering is in the service of knowledge of the who, what, where, when, how, and why of criminal activity; but the ultimate purpose it serves, or ought to serve, is the protection of legally enshrined moral rights by way of facilitating the conviction and punishment of serious criminal offenders. However, as our discussion of entrapment in Section 11.3 below makes clear, some undercover operations, so-called "stings" in particular, can, on occasion, if not carefully conducted in accordance with the appropriate moral principles and laws, violate the moral rights of suspects and, indeed, even actually facilitate rather than combat criminal activity. One of the tasks we have set ourselves in this chapter is to elaborate the conditions under which such traps or stings are, at least in principle, morally justifiable.

Investigative Ethics: Ethics for Police Detectives and Criminal Investigators, First Edition.
Seumas Miller and Ian A. Gordon.
© 2014 Seumas Miller and Ian A. Gordon. Published 2014 by John Wiley & Sons, Ltd.

11.1   The Ethics of Covert Operations

In the context of a believed failure to stem crime, especially in the case of organized crime, police have turned from a reliance on complainants to various kinds of covert operations. Such operations include undercover investigations and various forms of trapping. Covert operations invariably involve deception of one sort or another, and deception is morally problematic.[2] Deception is part and parcel of undercover work in particular.

Deception can exist in relation to a personal relationship, and not simply in respect of some particular action. However, deception in policing seems inevitable and, in any case, does not necessarily involve an infringement of moral rights. In some circumstances lying is an infringement of a moral right. For example, lying about the accused in a court of law may be an infringement of the moral right of the accused. But, outside such special contexts as a court of law, lying to someone, or simply failing to make known something to him/her, is not *per se* generally regarded as of the same high degree of moral wrongness as, say, assaulting or killing a person. Naturally, consequences can make a difference. The moral wrongness of lying about a person's whereabouts taken on its own might be relatively slight. However, if the consequences of this lie put the person's life at risk, then the moral seriousness of the lie increases dramatically.

It might seem that, on the above analysis, police use of deception, at least in the investigative phase, is justified. While deception is inherently wrong, it is justified by the good consequences that flow from its use. Unfortunately, this argument is not as compelling as it might seem. For, while the consequences are sometime good, this is not necessarily or always the case. Police can deceive criminals to serve their purposes, but they can also be used by such people. And the danger is that the police end up engaging in a game of deception and counterdeception that they ultimately lose. Moreover, the police can develop a habit of deception that they find difficult to shrug off; so they start by deceiving criminals and end by deceiving one another and members of the public. Moreover, the widespread practice of deception is corrosive of trust not only within an organization such as the police, but also between police and members of the public. The erosion of trust between police and other police, and between police and the public that they serve, can ultimately undermine the ends of law enforcement itself. For, at the end of the day, individual police rely on one another to enforce the law, and they also rely on the community. Abridgement of this policy of building trust for the short-term investigatory advantages that deception may confer – as in the setting of traps or "sting" operations – can come to pose a far greater danger for a democratic society, and for policing than the criminal behaviors against which they are directed (see Section 11.3 below).

And there are specific forms of corruption that are extremely morally problematic. Of the notion of the state implicating itself in "sting" activities such as those directed against the vice industry, Gary Marx wrote:

> State sponsored deception, of course, raises all the ethical issues generally associated with deception. It also raises some issues that are unique to the state as the symbolic repository of societal values (for example, the need to avoid setting bad examples) . . . Propriety and the symbolic importance of a pristine government image may militate against certain extreme activities . . . Betrayal involving another's body adds an additional troubling element.[3]

Hypothetically, we can only generalize that a police organization, as a moral exemplar and an organ of ethical government, bears a responsibility for the deployment of its employees. The impropriety of, for example, setting a police departmental employee to work as a prostitute in a brothel in order to secure evidence against corrupt police officers involved in the vice trade, cannot be justified in the light of a successful prosecutorial outcome. The point to be made here is that the deceptive activity had an additional moral problematic character; it was not just deception, it was engaging in prostitution.

Perhaps such inherently morally problematic activities on the part of undercover operatives are avoidable. However, almost inevitably, many undercover operations give rise to a different kind of moral problem, namely, betrayal.

As noted in Chapter 10, a person's intimate relationship with another person gives rise to a zone of interpersonal privacy from which others are excluded; moreover, such intimacy is typically viewed as a moral good. However, as also noted in Chapter 10, intimacy can be morally problematic. Consider the predatory intimacy that might obtain in an exploitative sexual relationship (see Case Study 11.2.2, Undercover Officers and Political Activists, below), or the betrayal of trust that results when an undercover operative finally "shops" an offender that he has "befriended."

The moral dangers attendant upon undercover operations involving, as they do, the breach of moral principles, for example, not to deceive or betray, demand that we provide a principled account of the difference between the justifiable use of normally immoral methods and forms of corruption (or otherwise immoral behavior) that are motivated by good ends but are not morally acceptable. That is, that we provide a principled account of the difference between morally justified use of covert methods, notably undercover operations, and so-called noble cause corruption.

We did so in Chapter 1, in effect. There we argued that, when police officers act in accordance with the legally enshrined moral principles governing the use of harmful methods, they achieve three things. They do what is morally right; their actions are lawful; and they act in accordance with the will of the community.

It might be argued – and seems to have been argued by Andrew Alexandra[4] – that recourse to the notion of the use of harmful methods in accordance with communally sanctioned objective moral principles does not remove the theoretical problem posed by noble cause corruption, and specifically the alleged (by Alexandra) immorality of even the lawful use of harmful methods by police. To be sure, a suspect who is guilty of a serious crime has not been treated immorally if he is lawfully – and not unreasonably – harmed by being coerced, deceived, surveilled, or betrayed by an undercover operative.[5] But Alexandra asks: What if he is innocent? In *that* case, harmful methods have been lawfully used, but their use is immoral, suggests Alexandra. Let us respond to this argument.

Importantly, the person harmed needs to be a suspect, that is to say that there is, or should be, some form of evidence that he is guilty. Nevertheless, sometimes persons reasonably suspected of committing crimes are in fact innocent. However, innocent persons wrongly suspected of crimes are not harmed by the police *in the knowledge* that they are innocent. So we do not have intentional harming of persons known to be innocent. Rather, we have intentional harming of persons thought likely to be guilty; and we have unintended harming of the innocent as a by-product of police work. Troublesome as this is, it does not put immorality at the core of the police function, as Alexandra seems to suggest. There are some police methods that do involve knowingly harming those known to be innocent, for instance, intrusive surveillance of a criminal engaged in sexual activity with a woman known not to be a criminal. In such cases the harm, while foreseen, is presumably not intended. Moreover, elaborate steps should be taken to avoid or minimize harming the innocent and, if the harm is both serious and unavoidable, then perhaps these methods ought not to be deployed.

11.2　Case Studies

Case Study 11.2.1　Chook Fowler and "Crotch-Cam"

One can scarcely imagine the effect the videotape, played on June 5th, 1995, at the Royal Commission into New South Wales Police Corruption, had upon 30-year police veteran, Detective Inspector Graham "Chook" Fowler – though we are aware of the devastating effect it was subsequently to have on public confidence in the police. Fowler, who had headed the Kings Cross and the City of Sydney detectives, had been called as a witness, and was being questioned by Queen's Counsel Gary Crooke, assisting the Royal Commissioner Justice James Wood. Twenty-five times, in the course of his examination, Fowler had denied being corrupt. Crooke then asked Fowler to watch the television monitor in front of him, saying, "One thing that I would ask you to consider is that this video is produced effectively for your consideration by the people of New South Wales and by all honest police." As the 22-minute video began showing scenes of Detective Inspector Fowler allegedly talking openly about protection rackets, he began to fidget and frown in the witness box. The video allegedly showed Fowler exchanging money with policeman, Trevor Haken, who had been working undercover with the Commission for nine months.[6]

Filmed by a mini-video camera hidden under the dashboard in Haken's car, and later released to the media, excerpts were run on TV news broadcasts, establishing corruption as endemic amongst the state's detectives. The NSW Police Service suspended Fowler from duty that day. Detective Sergeant Trevor David Haken, who also appeared on the videotape, gave evidence before the Royal Commission against corrupt fellow officers and criminals. Haken's evidence was the touchstone, the critical turning point in the Commission's investigations, and revealed he had been a corrupt officer who had been "turned." Of the beginnings of his involvement with the Royal Commission, Haken's wife said, "There was nothing unusual about the two plain-clothes police officers who came to the door that Saturday morning, August 20th, 1994. They said they had a summons for him [Haken], so I got him and they went out the front . . . He came in and said he had to go to court. I've never seen anyone look so grey."

Haken had finally been caught out. The NSW Crime Commission had enough evidence to put him in jail for years . . . Shortly afterwards the Crime Commission evidence was handed over to the recently formed Police Royal Commission.[7]

The [*Sydney Morning*] *Herald* subsequently learned that it was the State Crime Commission which held the key which the Royal Commission used to unlock the door to police corruption. The Crime Commission handed over material about Trevor Haken which apparently allowed the Royal Commission to force him to "roll over" and become a "supergrass" for the State.[8]

(*Continued*)

Perhaps it was professional pride after being exposed as a fraud, but Haken took to the role of undercover investigator with relish, taking ever-greater risks and gathering valuable information for the Royal Commission.[9]

The existence of 80 taped conversations such as those involving Fowler was revealed; Haken indicated he had collected and distributed $AU26,180 in bribes during this period. By August 22nd, Haken had named 24 persons as corrupt,[10] with newspapers suggesting he might name as many as 200.[11] The toll of police named – or "stung" – by Haken soon included acting Chief of Staff, Chief Superintendent Bob Lysaught, and acting Commander of the Fraud Enforcement Agency, Detective Superintendent Brian Meredith.

It is clear that not merely Haken's confession of past wrongdoings, but his ongoing and active collaboration with the Royal Commission, had provided the major break the Commission needed to penetrate the solidaristic detective cohort. Contradicting suggestions Haken's cooperation with the Royal Commission had been coerced, on August 24th, 1995, counsel assisting the Royal Commission made things plain:

> Mr. Agius was at pains yesterday to point out that Haken was not threatened, and Haken agreed with him that he had never asked what the Royal Commission might have on him. From that day [September 2nd, 1994], Haken, armed with his secret recording device and the mobile recording studio in his car, was extraordinarily busy. . . On June 5th [1995], Haken's undercover role ended when he stepped into the witness box for the first time. Only the day before, in a military-style operation, his family had been taken from their home at Mt. Kuring-gai to parts unknown.[12]

Haken, with his wife and children, disappeared from their home of 20 years into the witness protection scheme; it would seem Witsec, the Australian Federal Police program, moved the separated Jayne Haken and her children to the United States – the Hakens' marriage had not survived the stresses his activities imposed upon it. Although his police career was finished, Haken remained an asset of NSW's Director of Public Prosecutions, and he was involved as a principal witness in a number of further criminal prosecutions arising from the Royal Commission.

(Extract from John Blackler's prepared case study in John Blackler and Seumas Miller (2000) *Police Ethics (vol. 2): Case Studies for Police Investigators*, Wagga Wagga: Charles Sturt University and NSW Police Service, pp. 259–261)

Case Study 11.2.2 Undercover Officers and Political Activists

Journalist Rob Evans writing in the *Guardian* said: "Undercover police officers had long-term sexual relationships with political activists and joined them at family gatherings and on holidays to make their targets 'emotionally dependent' on them, according to papers submitted to the high court."[13]

He was describing a case where the Metropolitan Police Service was seeking to move the proceedings to a hearing behind the closed doors of the Investigative Powers Tribunal; a little-known tribunal that usually deals with complaints about MI5. The police claimed that the Tribunal had been specifically set up to consider allegations of unjustifiable surveillance by the State. The police said they may not be able to defend the case due to a policy of neither confirming nor denying the identity of undercover police officers.

This was the first civil action following publicity about undercover police activity, over many years, against political campaigners. It appeared that most of the claimants had long-term and serious relationships with undercover police officers, one lasting nearly six years. One claimant was a man who became a close personal friend with an undercover officer, who later had a sexual relationship with his girlfriend. Reference was made to one woman who had a child with an undercover officer, who then left her when his undercover deployment ended.

Lawyers said none of the women involved would have entered these intimate relationships had they known the men were undercover police officers. They claimed the actions of the officers had caused "serious emotional and psychiatric harm" during their intelligence gathering; which "raised questions about the extent to which covert police powers have been used to invade personal, psychological and bodily integrity of members of the public."

The publicity led to the collapse of other criminal cases and the quashing of convictions.

Case Study 11.2.3 FBI Undercover

In 2009, over a period of months, William Masso, a New York City Police Department (NYPD) officer, met with a confidential informant (CI) who was working for the Federal Bureau of Investigation. Masso expressed his interest in obtaining and selling cigarettes and other contraband. The FBI directed the CI to supply Masso with alleged stolen cigarettes, which were then sold by Masso. In 2010 Masso agreed to help the CI's boss, who was an undercover agent, to transport and sell stolen goods and recruited other persons, including serving police officers, to assist in that role.

Between September 2010 and October 2011, the FBI supplied Masso and his coconspirators with goods they were led to believe had been stolen including three M-16 rifles, one shotgun, 16 handguns, 12 slot machines, thousands of cigarettes, and counterfeit merchandise, which they transported across state lines. The total "street" value of the goods was around $1m. Masso was on active duty when he committed the offenses and was assisted by other police officers both active and retired and other persons who were not police officers. Following his arrest Masso pled guilty to four counts of conspiracy in relation to the articles transported. Eight of his codefendants later submitted guilty pleas. To carry out this scheme the defendants were prepared to use their police credentials and knowledge, where Masso actually put his police jacket conspicuously on display when transporting the goods. If they were stopped, the police officers involved had agreed to say they were police officers working off-duty to deliver items another person had purchased at an auction.

(FBI press release, http://www.fbi.gov/newyork/press-releases/2012/former-nypd-officer-who-led-conspiracy-to-distribute-firearms-and-stolen-goods-sentenced-in-manhattan-federal-court-to-57-months-in-prison)

11.3 Traps or "Stings"

Many undercover operations might be considered to be entrapment in the ordinary common sense meaning of that term, that is,. to *trap* someone.[14] This sense of entrapment is to be distinguished from legal definitions of the term, especially US definitions, in which entrapment is a legal defense.[15] Consider Case Study, 11.2.1 Chook Fowler and "Crotch-cam," above, in which Trevor Haken traps or entraps Chook Fowler.

Clearly the infringement of the right to privacy is a central feature of undercover operations in which a police officer establishes a relationship and gains the trust of an offender. Indeed, important questions arise here as to the morally admissible nature and extent of such relationships. It is one thing to establish friendly relations; it is another to establish a sexual relationship.

In some undercover operations, police, in effect, act as observers, albeit *inside*-observers. The offenders commit the offenses that they commit independently of the actions of the undercover operatives. However, often undercover operatives interact with offenders in such a way as to make a difference to whether or not, or when, where, or how, an offense is committed. This was the case with Chook Fowler in Chook Fowler and "Crotch-cam"; Haken was not simply an observer, he was also an active participant. This is a trap or "sting" in our target sense of the term. Consider the following scenario.[16]

Detective James McLaughlin of Keene, New Hampshire, United States, poses as a young boy in chat-rooms on the Internet. He looks for adults who are seeking sex with underage boys. He does so for the purpose of providing evidence to secure criminal convictions. In one case, Detective McLaughlin arrested a 47-year-old British marine insurance expert named Philip Simon Rankin. After a long series of email communications, during which a "relationship" was established, McLaughlin and Rankin agreed to meet in a restaurant in Keene, Rankin doing so in the belief that he was going to be meeting a 14-year-old boy.

We are using the term "trap" to refer to a proactive law enforcement strategy used in many jurisdictions in preference to reactive strategies, such as complaints investigations. Traps make use of undercover operatives posing as drug buyers, prostitutes, or criminals. It can involve the building of lengthy interpersonal relationships. The most important consideration in favor of traps or stings is evidenced in Chook Fowler and "Crotch-cam." Corruption in the NSW Police was systemic, and evidently the only way to bring corrupt police to justice was by way of a trap involving "turned" corrupt police officers operating undercover. Only such officers would be trusted by corrupt fellow officers, and only a managed trap scenario would enable reliable evidence, such as videotapes, to be obtained.

Traps can be random or targeted. Targeted traps focus on a specific person (or persons) who is/are reasonably believed to be involved in crime. Random traps are not directed at any specific person. For example, a police officer posing as a prostitute on a street corner in order to trap clients is engaged in random entrapment.

Traps or stings raise a number of ethical issues, including: (i) deception; (ii) the infringement of privacy; (iii) uncertainty in relation to the moral culpability of the offender, that is, the offender was "tricked" into doing what he or she otherwise would not have done; and (iv) impropriety of law enforcement agents, since they might be creating crimes that otherwise would not exist.

Accordingly, questions arise as to the moral and legal limits that ought to be placed on traps. The options here range from banning all forms of trapping, to allowing certain kinds of traps in relation to a narrowly circumscribed set of crimes. Here there are at least two relevant preliminary considerations. First, many serious crimes, such as murder, rape, and grievous bodily harm, do not lend themselves to traps. After all, trapping must involve the actual commission of a crime, and presumably allowing someone to be murdered in order to convict the murderer is morally unacceptable. On the other hand, some related crimes, such as conspiracy to commit murder, might be suitable for traps. Second, given the morally problematic nature of trapping, it should only be used sparingly, and presumably only in relation to serious crimes. So, random or targeted traps of petty thieves are morally problematic. On the other hand, targeted trapping of pedophiles is morally justified.

Let us briefly consider deception in relation to entrapment. If a suspect is to be trapped, he or she will need to be deceived. However, such deception will occur at the investigatory stage of police work. Evidently, when deception occurs at the investigatory stage – as opposed to the testimonial stage – it may well be morally justifiable.[17] Thus lying to a murderer to enable an arrest may be morally justified, whereas lying in court is not morally justified.

Let us now turn to privacy issues. Infringement of privacy in trapping scenarios is morally justifiable under certain conditions. As we have argued above, privacy is not an absolute right, whether privacy on the telephone, the car phone, the Internet, or on any other communication or information system. The rights to privacy of some individuals, and the right to confidentiality of members of some organizations, will in some cases be overridden by the rights of other individuals and other members of organizations to be protected by the law enforcement agencies from the perpetrators of serious crimes such as murder, child pornography, armed robbery, and fraud.

As we have already argued, infringements of privacy by law enforcement officials are morally justifiable if certain conditions are met. These conditions include the following: (i) there is reasonable suspicion that the person whose privacy is to be infringed intends to commit a serious crime; (ii) the methods in question are effective; and (iii) there is no alternative nonintrusive, or less intrusive, method of investigation.

Arguably, trapping is required – or is far more effective than reactive methods, such as investigating complaints – in relation to certain crimes. The crimes in question include ones that do not involve a complainant, for instance, drug-dealing, or areas such as organized crime, where offenses might be difficult to prove because offenders are well organized, well funded, and/or highly secretive. But in relation to certain kinds of offense and offender, arguably traps do better on a cost/benefit analysis than reliance on informers, or on undercover operatives who observe but do not trap. Informers often provide unreliable information, and often fail to provide evidence of the guilt of those they implicate in crimes. Undercover operations are resource intensive and their outcomes uncertain. This is especially so when undercover operatives simply wait for a suspect to create the opportunity to commit a crime, and then hope to gather evidence in relation to the crime when it does happen. By contrast, traps involve stage-managing a crime at a time and place chosen by police; so there is an assurance that the crime will be recorded and the offender convicted. (See Case Studies 11.2.1 and 11.2.3 above.)

If persons who have been trapped are justifiably to be convicted, then they must have committed a crime. However, even if they have performed a criminal act, there might be important reasons not to convict them. Specifically, they might have been the victims of morally unjustified traps. What tests ought to be applied to determine whether someone was the victim of morally unjustified trap (entrapment in the legal sense in the United States)? In the United States, two legal tests to determine whether someone has been entrapped have been proposed; the subjective test and the objective test. However, only the subjective test is actually in used.[18] Note that in the sense in question in the legal environment of the United States, entrapment is necessarily unlawful; by definition, it involves proactive policing practices that fail (in particular) the subjective test. While our concerns in this book are not with the law, let alone specific jurisdictions, the subjective and objective tests raise important ethical and philosophical issues that are of interest in their own right. Accordingly, we discuss these tests, and the conditions associated with them, at some length.

The subjective test asks whether the suspect has a disposition to commit crimes of the kind in question. Theoretically, but not necessarily or indeed actually, in law we might establish the existence of a disposition on the basis of his or her past behavior, for example, past criminal convictions. Evidently, the point of this test is to ensure that the person entrapped has the requisite degree of culpability; an important motivating reason for using this test is the concern that, without it, the police might induce an intention or inclination to commit a crime that was otherwise absent.[19]

The objective test asks whether or not the State has acted improperly by virtue of instigating the crime. This resolves itself into two issues. The first issue is whether or not the contribution of the police to the creation of the opportunity to commit the crime is excessive. For example, suppose an undercover police officer supplies a person with the raw materials and the equipment to manufacture heroin, and suppose that the raw materials and equipment are not available to the person from any other source(s). The second issue is whether or not the inducement offered to commit the crime was unreasonable (too strong), for instance, offering someone a million dollars to engage in illicit sex.[20]

One problem for the subjective test is how to provide evidence of a disposition. This problem is heightened in legal contexts in which knowledge of past crimes and convictions is not normally allowed to be used in determining guilt in relation to a current crime. A further possible problem for the subjective test is that it does not rule out strong inducements. Police officers might abuse the system by offering inducements that are too strong, and yet conviction would follow if the suspects had strong dispositions to commit the crime.[21] A related problem arises from the fact that a disposition to commit a crime is not equivalent to an intention to commit that crime. Suppose someone has a disposition to commit a crime. However, knowing that he has this disposition, he puts himself in a context in which there is no opportunity to commit the crime. Consider a heroin addict who wants to avoid taking heroin and decides to live in a heroin-free area or a pedophile who wants to avoid the crime of pedophilia by ensuring that he is never in the company of children. Now, assume a police officer presents the heroin addict with heroin, or the pedophile with what he (the pedophile) believes is an opportunity to engage in sex with a child. These examples show that the mere presence of a disposition is not sufficient for morally justified trapping; so the subjective test – at least as described above – would have to be strengthened.

A possible problem for the objective test is that it protects some people who should be found guilty.[22] Suppose strong inducements are used in cases of suspects with strong dispositions to commit the crime, and suppose these suspects are in fact guilty of this kind of crime. Such inducements will be ruled out by the objective test, and yet the guilty persons in question will go free. On the other hand, it is far more preferable that some of the guilty go free than that some of the innocent are convicted. So this objection is relatively weak. A stronger objection is that the objective test – in so far as it involves random testing – amounts to the government engaging in integrity testing of its citizens. This is surely unacceptable; governments have no right to convict a citizen merely because the citizen fails to resist an inducement to commit a crime, even if it is an inducement that they ought to have resisted. As Dworkin points out, "To encourage the commission of a crime in the absence of any reason to believe the individual is already engaged in a course of action is to be a tester of virtue, not a detector of crime."[23] Moreover, the objective test is not a particularly effective test of virtue. For someone who lacked the disposition to commit that kind of crime, or indeed crimes in general, might nevertheless fail the objective test on a single occasion.

What might be acceptable is targeted integrity testing of individuals reasonably suspected of committing the crime that is the subject of the test. Moreover, random integrity testing of certain categories of public servants, such as police or politicians, in relation to a circumscribed set of crimes might be acceptable under certain conditions. For example, suppose bribe-taking is rife in a specific government department, and all other measures have failed to curtail it; perhaps random integrity testing is now warranted. The general moral justification for this is that such public servants need to have a certain standard of integrity in relation to specific kinds of inducement, and they voluntarily accept a public office on the basis that they meet that standard. Accordingly, their integrity might reasonably be open to testing, especially if it is made clear to them before they accept the public office that their integrity might be subjected to a test.

There is a general objection to trapping, and this objection apparently stands irrespective of whether the subjective test or the objective test is applied. This is the objection that traps involve the creation of crime, rather than the detecting or preventing of crime that would have existed independently of trapping.[24] If this objection is sustained then, evidently, trapping should be abandoned. But is this objection sustained?

In order to assist our deliberations, consider the following.[25] Suppose a person, A, forms an intention to commit the one-off crime of stealing $5,000 of drug money. Person A believes the money was abandoned by his drug-dealing neighbor, B, in the garden outside B's house when B was arrested by the police, and that his crime will go undetected. Suppose that, unknown to A, this money was in fact confiscated by the police. However, the police decide not to remove the money, but rather to leave it with the purpose of trapping A, who they suspect might be tempted by the prospect of such "easy money," notwithstanding his general compliance with the law. A goes to steal the money and is caught red-handed.

Notice that if the objective test is applied, the police are entitled to engage in this kind of trapping. In the first place, the inducement, $5,000, is of a kind that the normal citizen could reasonably be expected to resist. In the second place, it was the drug-dealer who created the opportunity for theft; all the police did was fail to remove this opportunity. On the other hand, this kind of trap is ruled out by the subjective test; for A does not have a disposition to steal.

Given the nature of this one-off opportunity, and A's general disposition to comply with the law, A would probably not have committed any crime if the police had not trapped him. The reason is that he would never have been afforded the opportunity to commit the only sort of opportunistic crime that he is capable of committing. Yet, given that he believed that the opportunity had arisen, he formed the intention to commit the crime. We suggest that the mere possession of an intention – in a context of police provision of opportunity – is not sufficient to justify trapping. The reason is not that A is not culpable; clearly A is guilty of an act of theft. Rather, the reason is that trapping under these conditions involves the creation of crime, rather than the detecting or preventing of crime that would have existed independently of the trap.

Let us take another look at our scenario, but this time let us assume that, unbeknown to the police, A has a disposition to commit opportunistic acts of theft of large amounts of money, if they are left lying around and A believes he will escape detection. But let us further assume that there are no such opportunities. While A hopes for such opportunities, and tells his friends he is waiting for such opportunities, none have been or are ever likely to be forthcoming. As it happens, a one-off opportunity does come, and A is entrapped. As before, the objective test does not rule out this kind of trap. Moreover, the subjective test does not rule out this kind of trap either; for A has a disposition to engage in opportunistic theft of large amounts of money.

Notwithstanding the existence of A's disposition to engage in opportunistic theft of large amounts of money, it still remains the case that A would not have committed any crime if the police had not trapped him. The reason is that he would never have been afforded the opportunity to commit the only sort of opportunistic crime that he is disposed to commit. Accordingly, we suggest that the possession of a disposition and an intention – in a context of police provision of opportunity – is not sufficient to justify trapping. The reason is that trapping under these conditions involves the creation of crime, rather than the detecting or preventing of crime that would have existed independently of the trap.

As a corollary to the above, we conclude that neither passing the subjective test nor passing the objective test (nor passing both tests) is sufficient to justify trapping. Needless to say, this does not show that trapping is not justified under certain circumstances.

Walter Sinnott Armstrong[26] argues that trapping on the Internet is dissimilar to other forms of traps by virtue of being: (i) less intrusive, since there are not so many innocent people involved as (say) posing as a drug-dealer at a university campus; (ii) less dangerous to police; and (iii) less abuse-prone, since the evidence is there for all to see.

However, the general problems with trapping also afflict trapping on the Internet. Traps, whether on the Internet or not, face the general objection that they involve the creation of crime. Moreover, the above-mentioned objections to the objective and the subjective tests remain. On the other hand, specific forms of trapping, for instance, targeted traps and random traps of certain categories of public officer, might well be justifiable.

Let us bring this chapter to a close by attempting to detail the general conditions under which the trapping of ordinary citizens might be morally permissible.[27] In so doing, we will try to accommodate the various objections made above to traps, and to the subjective and objective tests.

First, there are a number of such general conditions, such as the condition that the method of trapping is the only feasible method available to law enforcement agencies in relation to a certain type of offense, and that the offense type is a serious one. This condition reflects the general presumption against trapping.

Second, the trap should be a targeted trapping of a person (or group) who is/are reasonably suspected of engaging in crimes of the relevant kind. This condition rules out testing the virtue of citizens.

Third, the suspect is ordinarily presented with, or typically creates, the kind of opportunity that they are to be afforded in the entrapment scenario. This condition in large part rules out police creation of crime.

Fourth, the inducement offered to the suspect is: (i) of a kind that is typically available to the suspect, and (ii) such that an ordinary citizen would reasonably be expected to resist it.[28] This condition rules out excessive inducements, and therefore one way in which crime might be created by the police.

Fifth, the person not only has a disposition to commit the type of crime in relation to which they are to be trapped, but also a standing intention to commit that type of crime. This condition not only protects those with inoperative inclinations to crime, but also those with a fleeting intention to commit a one-off crime – an intention not underpinned by any disposition to criminal activity. Evidence of a disposition to commit a type of crime might consist of an uninterrupted pattern of past crimes of that type, and no evidence of any change in attitude or circumstance. Evidence of a standing intention to commit that type of crime might be verbal and/or evidence of current detailed planning activities, and/or attempts to provide the means to commit such crimes.

Notes

1　See Harfield and Harfield (2012).
2　See John Kleinig (1996) *Ethics of Policing*, New York: Cambridge University Press, Chapter 7.
3　See Gary T. Marx (1992) Under-the-covers undercover investigations: Some reflections on the state's use of sex and deception in law enforcement, *Criminal Justice Ethics*, 11.2, Winter–Spring, pp. 13–24. See also Gary T. Marx (1988) *Undercover: Police Surveillance in America*, Berkeley, CA: University of California Press, and Cyrille Fijnaut and Gary T. Marx (eds) (1995) *Undercover: Police Surveillance in Comparative Perspective*, The Hague: Kluwer, 1995. For a more recent UK-focused study see Harfield and Harfield (2012), Chapter 9.

4   See Andrew Alexandra (2000) Dirty Harry and dirty hands, in Tony Coady, Steve James, Seumas Miller, and Michael O'Keefe (eds) (2000), *Violence and Police Culture*, Melbourne: Melbourne University Press. But see Seumas Miller (2004) Noble cause corruption in policing revisited, in P. Villiers and R. Adlam (eds) *A Safe, Just and Tolerant Society: Police Virtue Rediscovered*, Winchester: Waterside Press, pp. 105–118.

5   We are assuming here that the law appropriately tracks reason-based ethical principles.

6   See *Daily Telegraph-Mirror* (Sydney newspaper), June 6, 1995, p. 1.

7   See *Sydney Morning Herald*, "Spectrum," March 8, 1997, p. 6.

8   See *Sydney Morning Herald*, July 15, 1995, p. 5.

9   See *Sydney Morning Herald*, "Spectrum," March 8, 1997, p. 6.

10   See *Sydney Morning Herald*, August 22, 1995, p. 1.

11   See *Sydney Morning Herald*, August 19, 1995, pp. 25–26.

12   See *Sydney Morning Herald*, August 25, 1995, p. 1.

13   See *The Guardian*, November 21, 2012.

14   The material in this section is taken from Miller and Blackler (2005), Chapter 6. An earlier version appeared in Miller (1996).

15   For a useful overview of the legal and ethical issues raised by current forms of entrapment and the application of contemporary republican normative theory to these issues, see Simon Bronitt and Declan Roche (2000) Between rhetoric and reality: Socio-legal and republican perspectives on entrapment, *International Journal of Evidence and Proof*, 4, pp. 77–106.

16   This is taken from Walter Sinnott-Armstrong (1999) Entrapment in the Net? *Ethics and Information Technology*, 1, p. 95.

17   See Jerome Skolnick (1982) Deception by police, *Criminal Justice Ethics*, 1.2, Summer/Fall, pp. 40–54.

18   For useful discussions of these tests and the issues that they raise, see Gerald Dworkin (1988) *The Theory and Practice of Autonomy*, Cambridge: Cambridge University Press, Chapter 9, and Kleinig (1996), Chapter 8.

19   See Dworkin (1988), p. 134, and Kleinig (1996), p. 153.

20   See Dworkin (1988), p. 135, and Kleinig (1996), p. 154.

21   See Sinnott-Armstrong (1999), p. 99.

22   See Sinnott-Armstrong (1999), p. 99.

23   See Dworkin (1988), p. 144.

24   See Dworkin (1988), p. 136.

25   See Dworkin (1988), p. 140, for a contrary view.

26   See Sinnott-Armstrong (1999).

27   See Dworkin (1988), p. 144, for a reasonably similar set of conditions to this. See also Kleinig (1998), p. 158.

28   Or – in the case of tests for personnel in high-risk occupations – "such that a person in that role would reasonably be expected to resist it."

12

Interviewing

In this book we have argued that, normatively speaking, the primary role of criminal investigators is an epistemic or knowledge-aiming role in the ultimate service of the protection of legally enshrined, justifiably enforceable moral rights. Moreover, we have discussed the enabling conditions for the successful conduct of this role, such as investigative independence, and a number of the central moral problems that arise for criminal investigators when they use harmful or otherwise morally problematic methods, such as intrusive surveillance or undercover operatives. In this final chapter we consider the ethical issues that arise for what is one of the most important activities undertaken by criminal investigators, namely, interviewing. Interviewing victims, witnesses, and suspects is a central aspect of the epistemic role of the criminal investigator and is crucial to the success of a criminal investigation. Accordingly, it is of the utmost importance that best practice is followed, both in terms of the outcome – relevant knowledge – and also of compliance with moral constraints and other standards. Unfortunately, violations of the moral rights of interviewees have taken place, including in liberal democratic states in the very recent past.

12.1 Interviews

Interviews that are professionally undertaken and quality assured are likely to yield the required benefits.[1] In particular, they can:

Investigative Ethics: Ethics for Police Detectives and Criminal Investigators, First Edition.
Seumas Miller and Ian A. Gordon.
© 2014 Seumas Miller and Ian A. Gordon. Published 2014 by John Wiley & Sons, Ltd.

- provide direction to an investigation and yield critical intelligence and evidence, thereby facilitating a prosecution or, alternatively, the early release of an innocent person;
- provide weighty evidence in support of the prosecution case, thereby saving time, money, and other resources;
- increase public confidence in the police service, notably the confidence of witnesses and victims of crime.

Conversely, failure to professionally undertake and quality-assure interviews can have adverse consequences in terms of noncompliance with legislation and moral rights leading to injustices to suspects and punishment of officers, failure to gather critical informational evidence/intelligence leading to unsolved crime, lack of credibility within the police organization, and loss of public confidence.[2] A high-profile example of this was the so-called Birmingham Six case in the United Kingdom in the 1970s (see Case Study 2.2.1, The Birmingham Six, in Chapter 2).

In that case six men were convicted of bombing public houses in Birmingham, killing 21 people. Their confessions were a key piece of evidence. In 1991 the "Birmingham Six" won their freedom after a new inquiry in which discrepancies were found in the police interview record of one of the men. It seemed that the police had fabricated documentary evidence against the six. The Director of Public Prosecutions could no longer rely on either the forensic or the police evidence that convicted them in 1975. The Court of Appeal heard the case at the beginning of 1991 and quashed their convictions.

Following cases such as that of the Birmingham Six, the Guildford Four and, in particular, the murder of seven-year-old Nikki Allen and the subsequent police investigation in 1993,[3] the United Kingdom was obliged to address the core function of interviewing by police officers. The "PEACE" Investigative Interview Training package was introduced in 1993; "PEACE" is a mnemonic for a five-step approach to investigative interviewing in the UK police service:[4]

- Planning and Preparation – what to consider when planning for an interview;
- Engage and Explain – how to cope with the special features of getting an interview started and establishing the ground rules;
- Account, Clarification, and Challenge – obtaining the interviewee's account, clarifying this, and, where necessary, challenging it;
- Closure – the considerations before closing an interview;
- Evaluation – asking questions about what was achieved during the interview and how it fits into the whole investigation. Evaluation also includes the development of an interviewer's skill level, through assessment (self, peer, and manager) and feedback.

The training process for PEACE has now developed into "tiers" to manage the different skills levels required for interviews from basic to specialist investigation, such as of children and vulnerable people, through to serious and complex crime. It includes a requirement for supervisors to assess interviews to ensure compliance with PEACE. The outcome is more emphasis on the "investigation" with interviewers being required to try to obtain information that will assist in the investigative process.

The gathering of information from a well-prepared victim and witness interview will contribute significantly to the investigation. An effective interview of a suspect will commit them to an account of events that may include an admission. In the admission, the suspect may detail how the offense was committed and thus the investigation can be focused. The value of a properly obtained admission can prove the *mens rea* of the offense beyond doubt.

Research suggests effective interviewers are those who:

- have personal integrity and a good grasp of the moral principles and rights in play;
- have a knowledge of the psychology of interviewing and scientific experimentation;
- have received a thorough experience in a wide range of practical techniques to draw on in interviews as appropriate;
- have had the opportunity for substantial practice in a learning environment; and
- are supervised and given feedback on their real-life interviews.

Investigative interviewing is arguably the major fact-finding method police officers have at their disposal when investigating crime. Indeed, eyewitness testimony and confessions – forms of evidence relying on police interviews – are considered among the most persuasive forms of evidence.

At the outset officers need to appreciate the contribution made by the interview to the success of an investigation. They should also understand that every interview can potentially generate intelligence that can be used not only in the specific investigation but also in other policing activities. Interviewers should make sure they get as much information as possible and do not close the interview prematurely.

As a general principle, success in an interview relies on the cooperation of victims, witnesses, and the community. It should not be approached as an essentially adversarial encounter in which something is to be done to the interviewee – be they victim, witness, or suspect – by the interviewing officer. Rather the interviewer should treat interviewees, including suspects, with respect and be open-minded and impartial.

Naturally, in the case of suspects it might transpire that the suspect is not going to cooperate and, indeed, is attempting to thwart the attempt of the investigator to unearth the truth. If this is the case, then the encounter is more realistically framed as competitive rather than a cooperative. Nevertheless, communication, even competitive communication, presupposes a degree of cooperation, including with conversational norms, such as truth-telling and trust. The suspect at least purports to be telling the truth, even if he is not doing so and even if the interviewer does not believe he is doing so. Naturally, if the competitive dimension reaches a certain threshold of intensity, then the communicative exchange will break down and presumably nothing, or very little, will be learned from the suspect.

The competitive dimension of at least some interviews involves the use of strategies and tactics on the part of both interviewer and interviewee. One strategy on the part of the interviewer might be that of being straight-forward and honest, albeit focused on getting to the truth, and, therefore, being logical in his or her thinking and questioning; an alternative might be to use at least a degree of deception and even coercion, notwithstanding the morally problematic character of these practices.[5]

Police also need to appreciate the many reasons why witnesses and suspects may not be cooperative in interviews, including fear of embarrassment, retaliation, loss to themselves, legal proceedings, harming someone else, self-disclosure, and fear of restitution.[6]

Nor is the interviewing of suspects, in particular, a waste of time. A large proportion of suspects readily make admissions, including confessions. On the other hand, police must be aware of why some people will make false confessions. These occur in different ways and for different reasons, including dispositional (e.g., age, personality characteristics, intellectual impairment, etc.) and situational (e.g., isolation, confrontation minimization) factors.

It should be kept in mind that the vast majority of suspects who admit to wrongdoing do so early in the interview. Despite the best efforts of the interviewer, few suspects change their story once they have denied wrongdoing.

If offenders believe they have been treated well, they are less likely to form a negative view of police or to communicate a negative view of police to others.

Unfortunately, the history of police interviewing of suspects, in particular, is replete with violations of suspect's rights, including torture (the "third degree"). As a consequence, some miscarriages of justice have resulted from police malpractice. On the other hand, in interviewing – as elsewhere in policing – there are gray moral areas and it is not always obvious what course of action ought to be taken.

12.2 Case Studies

Case Study 12.2.1 Confession

DETECTIVE SERGEANT WRIGHT:	We're going to find the truth eventually Jim [Smith], why don't you tell your side of it now? (*Long pause*)
DCI MEADOWS:	That's right, the truth is bound to come out. (*Long pause*)
DC FLEMING:	We know what's happened, Jim, we just want to hear it from you.
SMITH:	I thought about telling you on the way down, but I'm frightened for the family. I daren't talk.
DCI MEADOWS:	Jimmy, we can look after your family, tell us what's frightening you.
SMITH:	I daren't.
DS WRIGHT:	Come on, Jimmy, did you kill Martin?
SMITH:	No.
DCI MEADOWS:	You were there? (*Long pause*)
DCI MEADOWS:	You were there, weren't you?
SMITH:	Aye, but I never killed him, I nearly fucking died myself with shock.
DCI MEADOWS:	Who killed him then (*Long pause*)
DCI MEADOWS:	Come on, Jimmy, you've started now.
SMITH:	Andrew.
DCI MEADOWS:	How did he do it?
SMITH:	He shot him in the head.
DCI MEADOWS:	Where?
SMITH:	In the head.
DCI MEADOWS:	No, where was he when he shot him?
SMITH:	In Andrew's Jag.
DCI MEADOWS:	You're shaking, son, do you want a cup of tea or something?
SMITH:	Some water please.

Detective Constable Fleming left the room and returned with a cup of water drunk by Smith and then refilled by DC Fleming. The conversation continued.

(*Continued*)

DCI MEADOWS:	Is that better?
SMITH:	Aye.
DCI MEADOWS:	Do you want a cigarette or anything?
SMITH:	Please.
DS WRIGHT:	(*Passing his cigarettes and lighter to the front of the table*) Help yourself when you want one, Jimmy.
DCI MEADOWS:	Calm yourself down and start from the beginning.
SMITH:	Andrew had to kill Martin or he might have been next.
DCI MEADOWS:	Are you sure you didn't shoot him?
SMITH:	It was Andrew. Christ, he would kill me if he could hear me now.

(Extract from R. Hall (1981) *Greed: The "Mr Asia" Connection*, Sydney: Pan, pp. 175–176)

Case Study 12.2.2   The Beating

Height of the antipodean summer, mercury at the century-mark, the noonday sun softened the bitumen beneath the tyres of her little Hyundai sedan to the consistency of putty. Her three-year-old son, quiet at last, snuffled in his sleep on the back seat. He had a summer cold and wailed like a banshee in the supermarket, forcing her to cut short her shopping. Her car needed petrol. Her tot was asleep on the back seat. She poured 20 litres into the tank; thumbing notes from her purse, harried and distracted, her keys dangled from the ignition.

Whilst she was in the service station a man drove off in her car. Police wound back the service station's closed-circuit TV camera, saw what appeared to be a heavy-set Pacific Islander with a blonde-streaked Afro entering her car. "Don't panic," a police constable advised the mother, "as soon as he sees your little boy in the back he will abandon the car." He did; police arrived at the railway station before the car thief did and arrested him after a struggle when he vaulted over the station barrier.

In the police truck on the way to the police station: "Where did you leave the Hyundai?" Denial instead of dissimulation: "It wasn't me." It was – property stolen from the car was found in his pockets. In the detectives' office: "Its been 20 minutes since you took the car. Little tin box like that car – it will heat up like an oven under this sun. Another 20 minutes and the child's dead or brain damaged. Where did you dump the car?" Again: "It wasn't me."

Appeals to decency, to reason, to self-interest: "It's not too late; tell us where you left the car and you will only be charged with take-and-use. That's just a six month extension of your recognizance." Threats: "If the child dies, I will charge you with manslaughter!" Sneering, defiant and belligerent; he made no secret of his contempt for the police. Part-way through his umpteenth, "It wasn't me," a questioner clipped him across the ear as if he were a child, an insult calculated to bring the Islander to his feet to fight. There a body punch elicited a roar of pain, but he fought back until he lapsed into semi-consciousness under a rain of blows. He quite enjoyed handing out a bit of biffo, but now, kneeling on hands and knees in his own urine, in pain he had never known, he finally realized the beating would go on until he told the police where he had abandoned the child and the car.

The police officers' statements in the prosecution brief made no mention of the beating; the location of the stolen vehicle and the infant inside it was portrayed as having been volunteered by the defendant. The defendant's counsel availed himself of this falsehood in his plea in mitigation. When found, the stolen child was dehydrated, too weak to cry; there were ice packs and dehydration in the casualty ward but no long-time prognosis on brain damage.

(Case Study provided by John Blackler, a former New South Wales police officer.)

12.3 Interviews and Suspects' Moral Rights

Suspects only ought to be held in custody for a good (morally justifiable) reason, for example, on the grounds that they are likely to be guilty of some crime and are awaiting trial.

As we saw in early chapters, suspects have moral and legal rights, and indeed in many cases precisely the same rights as ordinary citizens who are not suspects. Naturally, there are some rights that ordinary citizens possess that are suspended in the case of suspects. For example, the right to freely move around might be suspended in the case of a violent offender. Indeed, to be arrested is by definition to have one's right to various freedoms suspended. But there are other rights, such as the right to life and the right not to be assaulted, which are not suspended.

A further fundamental right that is not suspended, indeed, that comes into play when a suspect is questioned by police – or by prosecutors – is the right not to incriminate himself or herself. This right is related to another right, namely the right to silence.[7] However, the right to silence can be abridged in relation to the crimes of others. A person can be morally required to answer questions in relation to the crimes of other persons. So the right not to incriminate oneself is more fundamental than the right to silence. Indeed, the right to silence is apparently derived from the right not to incriminate oneself. A person has a right to silence in order to protect himself or herself from self-incrimination. (The right not to incriminate oneself is also extended to a person who is held to be so close to oneself as to be in part constitutive of oneself. So a person has a right not to incriminate his or her spouse.)

On one view, the right not to incriminate oneself is related to the right to self-defense. The notion appears to be that, no matter how heinous a crime a person may have committed, the person always retains the moral right to protect their own life. So, on this view, a convicted murderer is morally entitled to try to prevent his or her executioner from performing the execution, even up to the last moment.[8]

If this right to self-defense is the basis for the right not to incriminate oneself, and indirectly, therefore, the basis for the right to silence, then this might explain why the right to silence can be abridged in circumstances in which the suspect is granted immunity from prosecution. A suspect's right to silence can be abridged, but only, it might be argued, in circumstances under which they cannot be prosecuted, and hence punished, for the crime in question. Here, as elsewhere, abridgment of the right to silence presumably consists in the suspect being liable to criminal sanctions (e.g., for contempt of court) or at least suffering an adverse inference being drawn with respect to their guilt, if they fail to speak in court.

On this view of a foundational, so to speak, right to self-defense the right is inalienable and not able to be suspended. Relatedly – the argument goes – a person always retains the moral right not to incriminate himself or herself. Even if a person has committed a heinous crime, the person retains the right not to (in effect) speak against himself or herself and facilitate his or her own conviction (and in the case of jurisdictions retaining capital punishment, retains the right not to, in effect, bring about his or her own death.)

Note that the right to silence is, after all, a right and not a duty; one can incriminate oneself if one so chooses; on occasion an offender can be more willing to incriminate himself than the police or magistrate are to convict him. Note also that the right to silence is consistent with investigators offering inducements (within reason) to suspects to break their silence. Naturally, coercing, including torturing, suspects in order to break their silence would not be consistent with respecting a suspect's right to silence. (See discussion below and see Case Study 12.2.2, The Beating, above.)

Suspects who are held in the custody of the police are in the care of the police. So, in fact, they have some rights in relation to the police that ordinary citizens not being held by the police do not have. For example, the police are obliged to provide food, water, toilet facilities, and so on to someone they are holding in custody.

Interviewing of suspects is sometimes regarded by police as a means to secure a confession, and thereby a conviction. If an offender confesses to a crime, then there is, in theory, a far greater probability that he or she is guilty. Indeed confessional evidence plays a large part in the presentation of many police prosecutions. "Investigation by confession" is very bad police work; it can be a "short cut" for police who have neither the training, the ability, or, due to pressure of work, the time to follow other avenues of inquiry. But the larger forensic reality is that, even in the most thoroughly investigated crimes, absence of some form of admission of guilt markedly decreases the chances of police securing a conviction. Moreover, magistrates, judges, and juries arguably need the reassurance of a confession, being unwilling to convict in its absence. This is, of course, not to say that physical evidence is always superior to a confession. Physical evidence can be faked, just as confessions can be false.

From the fact that someone has confessed, it does not follow that they are guilty. Moreover, while extracting a confession, and thereby ensuring a conviction, might be as a matter of fact the goal of many police interviewers, it is not the purpose that justifies interviewing. The primary justification for interviewing is rather to elicit the truth – we do not dispute that interviewing has, and ought to have, other purposes, for example, to gather testimonial evidence (part of the means to the truth, as argued in Chapter 2). Moreover, the truth may well be that the person being questioned did not in fact commit the crime, even though the police interrogators believe that he or she did commit it, at least initially.

It has been disputed that eliciting the truth – or at least knowledge, in the sense of justified true stated belief (see Chapter 2) – is the primary purpose. Rather, it is held, the purpose is to obtain a suspect's, witness's, or informant's account of what happened in order that the court can determine the truth.[9] But here there is an ambiguity between the truth in the sense of what actually took place and the interviewee's beliefs with respect to what took place. Naturally, in the first instance it is the truth with respect to what the interviewee *believes* that is the aim. There is, of course, a further issue, namely, whether or not those beliefs are true ones; after all, the interviewee, although sincere, could be mistaken. However, if the interviewee is lying, that is, saying what they believe to be false, then it is, we suggest, an aim of the investigator to determine that this is the case by, for example, testing such claims for consistency and against other evidence and doing so in the context of the interview. Moreover, the truth with respect to what the interviewee believes is itself evidence in the service of the larger aim of the investigator, namely, to determine the truth with respect to the who, what, where, when, how, and why of the crime.

A further issue pertains to failure to disclose the truth, as opposed to saying what is false. As already noted, suspects, in particular, have a right to silence derived (arguably) from a right not to self-incriminate. However, exercising one's right to silence is not the same thing as telling lies.

There are learnable effective questioning techniques. Importantly, these techniques do not involve the use of coercion or deception. Use of coercion and deception might yield confessions – especially in the already intimidating circumstance of being held in custody and questioned by police – but they are morally dubious techniques. For one thing – as we have seen in earlier chapters – coercion and deception are in themselves morally harmful. For another, as we saw above, coercion violates the suspect's right to silence, and the right not to incriminate oneself. The use of deception is less obviously a violation of a suspect's right; indeed, some instances of deception might be justifiable.[10] However, some are presumably not. For example, if a suspect who is in fact innocent is lied to by an investigator and told that DNA evidence proves his presence at the crime scene, then he might plead guilty and plea-bargain as his best option, notwithstanding that he knows he is innocent.

Moreover the use of deception and coercion tends to go hand in hand with the presupposition that that the point of interviewing a suspect is to get him or her to confess and thereby secure a conviction. Multiple dangers attach to police treating interrogations as simply a device to get a suspect to confess, notably the conviction of the innocent.

Effective questioning is based on a number of principles. One of the most important of these is that the questioning should be undertaken on the assumption that the purpose of the interrogation is to discover the truth, and the truth will be forthcoming if a process of reasoning is set in motion. This process of reasoning consists of the provision of rational answers to questions, and the provision of further questions that are rational in the light of the questions given.

Another useful principle in the case of interviewing suspects is that the questioning can often take place in the context of an understanding of the moral dimension of the institutional device of confession. Case Study 12.2.1 above, Confession, illustrates the moral context in which suspects admissions and confessions are often made.

Suspects often confess; why so? Confession consists of: (i) the painful confrontation of an individual with his or her moral failings, including crimes; (ii) truthful communication or expression of those moral failings to another person, including possibly a police officer; (iii) feelings of guilt or shame in respect of those moral failings; (iv) desire on the part of the individual to purify or purge themselves by making known their moral failing or crime, and possibly refrain from such wrongdoing in the future, trying to make amends for past wrongdoing and even seeking reconciliation with the victim.[11]

So confession is a powerful social device which presupposes that: (i) the moral worth of an individual is something that the individual believes and feels to be very important to himself or herself, and (ii) the moral approval of others is very important to an individual. The effectiveness of questioning techniques in respect of suspects can sometimes depend on the recognition of this moral dimension of confession, and, indeed, trade on it. Naturally, it might not work in the case of hardened criminals; on the other hand, even hardened criminals can succumb.

We seek to explain the ubiquity of confession in western religious-legal practice by claiming that confession serves certain fundamental functions within a society. For example, the confession of the guilty absolves judges of the responsibility for the administration of their punishment; confession is a method of asserting fundamental values of a society, which at the same time restores the guilty to the boundaries of normal society; confession defines what it is to be human, in that the guilty show normal psychological reactions to humility, shame, and repentance; confession is an important aspect of social control, since it is a method of linking the interior conscience with the exterior public order. It is along these lines that we want to establish both the importance for sociology of the analysis of confession, and the importance for society of an ubiquitous remedial institution, a ritual of social inclusion. In arguing that confession has important social consequences or functions, we are not necessarily arguing that confession uniformly has positive, congenial, remedial functions.

Confession may symbolically restore people to society whilst, at the same time, committing them to mental institutions, prison, or the gallows. Confession may also be false or extorted. The "compulsion to confess" may not be the outcome of an isolated, guilty self, but of the subtle social pressures brought to bear on a suspect. As the Royal Commission on Criminal Justice[12] demonstrated, it is, in practice, extremely difficult for suspects to exercise their legal "right to silence." Even the innocent under the pressure of determined interrogation, when police officers play upon their weaker points of character, will talk volubly.

Confession lies at the sensitive intersection between the interior freedom of individual conscience and the external requirements of public order. Confession is a social activity shot through with contradictions between spontaneity and compulsion, between disinterested confessions and confessions as part of "bargain justice," between moral consensus and political force.

12.4   Torture

Unfortunately, the so-called "war on terror" appears to have given impetus to a revival in western liberal democracies of the practice of torture in the service of intelligence gathering, as opposed to the extraction of confessions.[13] The torture by US military police of Iraqi civilians held in Abu Ghraib prison in Iraq during the insurgency period following the US-led attack on Saddam Hussein's regime in 2003 is perhaps the most high-profile recent example of this.

During this period hundreds of US soldiers were being killed by improvised explosive devices, suicide bombers, and so on. Understandably, the Americans were desperate to find out who was killing their troops. Large numbers of Iraqi civilians who happened to be in the vicinity of hostile actions were rounded up and detained, many of them in the Abu Ghraib prison. Inevitably, most of those detained were innocent of any wrongdoing, and of no intelligence value. (The Americans themselves estimated that up to 90% of those detained were in this category.) Military police in the prison accepted that they could – and should – help interrogators from Military Intelligence by "loosening up" prisoners. Police drew on a range of techniques that had been refined in the "war on terror," including not simply the infliction of pain, but also psychological disorientation and humiliation. The photos that revealed the sexual humiliation and physical savagery that the military police used to create "unpleasant or intolerable situations" for the detainees shocked the world. The military police that were identified in the photos were charged with criminal misconduct.

The first thing to be noted about torture is that it is an infringement of human rights. Aside from the extreme pain involved, torture is also an infringement of individual autonomy. Indeed, its main purpose is to "break down" the victim so that he or she becomes a nonautonomous and compliant instrument serving the purposes of the torturer. Accordingly, torture of suspects, whether by police or the military, is a human rights violation and as such outlawed in most liberal democracies (a notable exception being Israel).

Notwithstanding the fact that torture is a human rights violation, could there be some, admittedly highly unusual, circumstance in which it was morally justified? Here the so-called "ticking bomb" scenario is salient (see also Case Study 12.2.2, The Beating). Assume the following conditions obtain. First, a bomb has been planted and is about to explode, unless the person about to be tortured discloses its whereabouts. Second, the person to be tortured is not an innocent person, rather he is the one who planted the bomb and is refusing to make known its whereabouts precisely because he wants it to explode and kill a large number of innocent people. Third, the form of torture to be used, while extremely painful, is not such that it will permanently physically or psychologically impair the person to be tortured. Four, it is known with a high degree of certainty that using torture on this person at this time will succeed, and it is also known that there is no other way of discovering the whereabouts of the bomb.

The first point to be made in relation to this example is that it is not the kind of situation that security forces *routinely* face. Even in the context of the so-called "war on terror," such cases only arise very occasionally, if at all, given the high degree of improbability that all four conditions would be satisfied. At best, they illustrate the requirement to infringe moral principles for the sake of the greater good in some highly unusual emergencies.

The second point to be made is that torture, in this highly unusual situation, may well be morally justified. The justification is akin to that in play in the case of self-defense or killing in defense of the lives of others. For the person who is to be tortured has planted the bomb and is preventing his captors from finding and defusing it. In this respect, he is not importantly different from another bomber who is physically preventing a bomb disposal unit from entering the premises where he has planted the ticking bomb. In that circumstance, members of the bomb disposal unit would be morally justified in, for example, shooting the bomber to enable them to enter the premises and defuse the bomb. In short, the person about to be tortured is in the process of attempting to commit murder. Is not torture morally justified if it is the only way to prevent the person to be tortured from committing murder?

Now consider the case study, The Beating. In this case study torture of the car thief seems morally justifiable. Consider the following points: (i) The police reasonably believe that torturing the car thief will probably save an innocent life; (ii) the police know that there is no other way to save the life; (iii) the threat to life is imminent; (iv) the baby is innocent; (v) the car thief is known not to be an innocent – his action is known to have caused the threat to the baby, and he is refusing to allow the baby's life to be saved.

Some commentators on scenarios of this kind are reluctant to concede that the police are morally entitled – let alone morally obliged – to torture the offender. How could these commentators justify their position?

Someone might claim that torture is an absolute moral wrong. On this view, there simply are no real or imaginable circumstances in which torture could be morally justified.

This is a hard view to sustain, not least because we have already seen that being tortured is not necessarily worse than being killed, and torturing someone not necessarily morally worse than intentionally killing him. Naturally, someone might hold that intentional killing is an absolute moral wrong, that is, intentionally killing anyone – no matter how guilty – is never morally justified. This view is consistent with holding that torture is an absolute moral wrong, in other words, torturing anyone – no matter how guilty – is never morally justified. However, the price of consistency is very high. The view that intentional killing is an absolute moral wrong is a very implausible one. It would rule out, for example, killing in self-defense. Let us, therefore, set it aside and continue with the view that torture, but not intentional killing, is an absolute moral wrong.

For those who hold that killing is not an absolute moral wrong, it is very difficult to see how torture could be an absolute moral wrong, given that killing is sometimes morally worse than torture. In particular, it is difficult to see how torturing (but not killing) the guilty terrorist and saving the lives of thousands could be morally worse than refraining from torturing him and allowing him to murder thousands – torturing the terrorist is a temporary infringement of his autonomy, whereas his detonating of the nuclear device is a permanent violation of the autonomy of thousands.

We have seen that there are likely to exist, in the real world, one-off emergency situations in which torture is, all things considered, the morally best action to perform. It may seem to follow that institutional arrangements should be in place to facilitate torture in such situations. However, it is perfectly consistent to oppose any legalization or institutionalization of torture. For the view that torture is morally justified in some extreme emergencies is compatible with the view that torture ought not to be legalized and institutionalized.

Most of the theorists who oppose the legalization and institutionalization of torture also (at least implicitly) reject the possibility, let alone actuality, of one-off emergencies in which torture is morally justified. The argument has been put that there are, or could well be, such one-off extreme emergencies in which torture is morally justified. So the first task here is to demonstrate that these two claims are not inconsistent. Specifically, it needs to be shown that it does not follow from the fact that torture is in some extreme emergencies morally justified, that torture ought to be legalized, or otherwise institutionalized. So the claim is that it is just a mistake to assume that what morality requires or permits in a given situation must be identical with what the law requires or permits in that situation. This calls for some explanation.

The law in particular and social institutions more generally are blunt instruments. They are designed to deal with recurring situations confronted by numerous institutional actors over relatively long periods of time. Laws abstract away from differences between situations across space and time, and differences between institutional actors across space and time. The law, therefore, consists of a set of generalizations to which the particular situation must be made to fit. Hence, if you exceed the speed limit you are liable for a fine, even though you were only 10 kph above the speed limit, you have a superior car, you are a superior driver, there was no other traffic on the road, the road conditions were perfect, and therefore the chances of you having an accident were actually less than would be the case for most other people most of the time driving at or under the speed limit.[14]

By contrast with the law, morality is a sharp instrument. Morality can be, and typically ought to be, made to apply to a given situation in all its particularity. (This is, of course, not to say that there are not recurring moral situations in respect of which the same moral judgment should be made, nor is it to say that morality does not need to help itself to generalizations.) Accordingly, what might be, all things considered, the morally best action for an agent to perform in some one-off (i.e., non-recurring) situation might not be an action that should be made lawful. Consider the real-life example of the five sailors on a raft in the middle of the ocean and without food. Four of them decide to eat the fifth – the cabin boy – in order to survive.[15] This is a case of both murder and cannibalism. Was it morally justifiable to kill and eat the boy, given the alternative was the death of all five sailors? Perhaps not, considering that the cabin boy was entirely innocent. However, arguably it was morally excusable, and indeed the sailors, although convicted of murder and cannibalism, had their sentence commuted in recognition of this. But there was no suggestion that the laws against murder and cannibalism admit of an exception in such an extreme case; the sailors were convicted and sentenced for murder and cannibalism. Again, consider an exceptionless law against desertion from the battlefield in time of war. Perhaps a soldier is morally justifiable in deserting his fellow soldiers, given that he learns of the more morally pressing need for him to care for his wife who has contracted some life-threatening disease back home. However, the law against desertion will not, and should not, be changed to allow desertion in such cases.

So the law and morality not only can and do come apart; indeed, sometimes they *ought* to come apart. This is the first point. The second point pertains to the nature of the subinstitution of torture within the larger military, police, and correctional institutions.[16]

So what can be said of the likely institutional fit between military, police, and correctional institutions on the one hand, and the subinstitution of torture on the other? The role structure of this subinstitution consists of torturers, torturer trainers, medical personnel who assist torturers, and the like.

It would be a massive understatement to say that historically the subinstitution of torture – whether in a lawful or unlawful form – has been no stranger to military, police, and correctional institutions. Moreover, the practice of torture is endemic in many military, police, and correctional institutions in the world today, including democracies such as India and Israel. It is only in recent times, and with great difficulty, that torture in Australian prisons and police services, for example, has been largely eliminated, or at least very significantly reduced. The Australian, British,

American, and like cases are important not only because they illustrate that torture can be endemic to liberal democratic institutions, but also because they demonstrate that liberal democratic institutions are able – given the political will, suitable re-education and training, stringent accountability mechanisms, and so forth – to successfully combat a culture of torture.

Further, there is now a great deal of empirical evidence that, in institutional environments in which torture is routinely practiced, it has a massive impact on other practices and on moral attitudes. For example, in police organizations in which torture is routinely used the quality of investigations tends to be low. Careful marshalling of evidence is replaced by beating up suspects. Again, police in organizations in which offenders are routinely tortured do not, unsurprisingly, tend to develop respect for the moral rights of offenders, suspects, or even witnesses. And there is this further point. The prevalence of torture in numerous military, police, and correctional institutions throughout the world has taken place notwithstanding that, for the most part, it has been both unlawful and opposed by the citizenry.

Clearly should the legalized subinstitution of torture be integrated into any of these institutions it would be very difficult to remove and would, even in liberal democracies, have a major impact on the direction, culture, and practices of these institutions. Again, this is what the historical and comparative empirical evidence tells, notwithstanding the initial and even continuing aversion of many, perhaps most, of the individuals in these institutions to torture as such. Consider the Israeli case. Limited forms of torture were legal in Israel prior to 1999, but illegal post-1999. However, evidently torture has by no means been eradicated since 1999. According to the Public Committee against Torture, reporting on the period between September 2001 and April 2003: "The affidavits and testimonies taken by attorneys and fieldworkers . . . support the conclusions . . . violence, painful tying, humiliations and many other forms of ill-treatment, including detention under inhuman conditions, are a matter of course . . . The bodies which are supposed to keep the GSS [General Security Service] under scrutiny and ensure that interrogations are conducted lawfully act, instead, as rubber-stamps for decisions by the GSS . . . The State Prosecutor's Office transfers the interrogees' complaints to a GSS agent for investigation and it is little wonder that it has not found in even a single case that GSS agents tortured a Palestinian "unnecessarily".[17]

For a liberal democracy to legalize and institutionalize it, that is, to weave the practice of torture into the very fabric of liberal democratic institutions, would be both an inherent contradiction – torture being an extreme assault on individual autonomy – and, given what we know about the practice of torture in military, police, and correctional institutions, highly damaging to those liberal democratic institutions. It would be equivalent to a liberal democracy legalizing and institutionalizing slavery on the grounds, say, of economic necessity. Legalized and institutionalized slavery is inconsistent with liberal democracy, as is legalized and institutionalized torture. So if legalized and institutionalized slavery and/or legalized and institutionalized torture are necessary because morally required, then liberal democracy is not possible in anything other than an attenuated form. But, of course, neither legalized/institutionalized slavery nor legalized/institutionalized torture is morally required, quite the contrary. At best, torture is morally justified in some one-off emergencies – just as murder and cannibalism might be morally excusable in a one-off emergency on the high seas, or desertion from the field of battle might be morally justifiable given a one-off emergency back home – but absolutely nothing follows as far as the legalization/institutionalization of torture is concerned.

A final point here concerns the proposition that, absent legalized/institutional torture, *unlawful* endemic torture in the security agencies of contemporary liberal democracies confronting terrorism is inevitable. The implication here is that, unless legalized, torture will become endemic in these agencies. It has already been argued that the legalization/institutionalization of torture would be profoundly damaging to liberal democratic institutions. Assume this is correct; it does not follow from this that a torture culture will not come to exist in those agencies in the context of torture being unlawful. Nor does it follow that an unlawful torture culture, indeed an unlawful subinstitution of torture, is inevitable. Here there is a tendency to use the kind of argument that is plausible in relation to, say, the prohibition of alcohol. It is better to legalize alcohol, because then it can be contained and controlled. This form of argument used in relation to torture is spurious. Consuming alcohol to excess is not morally equivalent to torture, and we do not legalize the use of alcohol in emergency situations only. Legalizing the use of torture in extreme emergencies would be much more akin to legalizing perjury in extreme situations. As with torture – and unlike alcohol – perjury is only morally justified in some extreme one-off situations.[18] However, no one is seriously considering legalizing perjury in one-off extreme situations (at least to our knowledge), and with good reason – to do so would strike at the very heart of the legal system.

Notes

1 For a relatively comprehensive account of the issues and contexts in criminal justice interviews see Tom Williamson (ed.) (2006) *Investigative Interviewing: Rights, Research and Regulation*, Cullompton, Devon: Willan Publishing.
2 See John Baldwin (1993) Police interview techniques: Establishing truth or proof? *British Journal of Criminology*, 33.3, pp. 325–352.

3   See Malcolm Pithers (1993), available at http://www.independent.co.uk/
     news/uk/uproar-after-acquittal-in-nikki-allen-murder-case-not-guilty-verdict
     -ends-sixweek-trial-in-which-judge-refused-to-admit-alleged-confession-on
     -interview-tape-as-evidence-1505896.html.
4   See National Policing Improvement Agency (2009) *National Investigative Interview-
     ing Strategy*, http://www.acpo.police.uk/documents/crime/2009/200901CRINSI01
     .pdf (accessed January 15, 2014).
5   See Fred E. Inbau, John E. Reid, Joseph P. Buckley, and Brian C. Jayne (2001)
     Criminal Interrogations and Confessions (4th edn), Gaithersburg, MD: Aspen
     Press. Among other things, these authors differentiate between interviewing and
     interrogating with the latter having an assumptive and coercive character, for
     example, "We know you did it . . ."
6   On these issues see Gisl Gudjonsson (1992) *The Psychology of Interrogations,
     Confessions, and Testimony*, New York: Wiley, Chapter 4.
7   See David Morgan and Geoffrey Stephenson (eds) (1994) *Suspicion and Silence:
     The Right to Silence in Criminal Investigations*, London: Blackstone Press.
8   For criticisms see Michael Skerker (2010) *An Ethics of Interrogation*, Chicago:
     University of Chicago Press, Chapter 4.
9   See Peter Stelfox (2009) *Criminal Investigation: An Introduction to Principles
     and Practice*, Cullompton, Devon: Willan Publishing, p. 118.
10   Jerome H. Skolnick and Richard A. Leo (1992) The ethics of deceptive inter-
     rogation, *Criminal Justice Ethics*, Winter/Spring, pp. 3–11.
11   See M. Hepworth and Bryan Turner (1982) *Confession: Studies in Deviance
     and Religion*, London: Routledge and Kegan Paul, and Seumas Miller and
     John Blackler (2000) Restorative justice: Retribution, confession, and shame,
     in J. Braithwaite and H. Strang (eds) *Restorative Justice: From Philosophy to
     Practice*, Aldershot: Ashgate, pp.77–93.
12   See Royal Commission on Criminal Justice (1993) *Report*, http://www
     .official-documents.gov.uk/document/cm22/2263/2263.pdf (accessed January
     15, 2014).
13   The material in this section is derived from Seumas Miller (2011c) Torture, in
     Stanford Encylopedia of Philosophy, available at www.plato.stanford.edu. See
     also Miller (2009b), Chapter 7 and (2005) Is torture ever morally justifiable?,
     International Journal of Applied Philosophy, 19.2, pp. 179–192.
14   F. Schauer (2003) *Profiles, Probabilities and Stereotypes*, Cambridge, MA:
     Belknap Press argues this thesis in relation to laws and uses the speed limit as
     an example. Arguably, Schauer goes too far in his account of laws, and is insist-
     ing that the law is blunter than it needs to be. However, that does not affect
     what is being said here.
15   Andrew Alexandra reminded me of this example.
16   For an account of social institutions see Miller (2010a).
17   Public Committee against Torture in Israel (2003) *Back to a Routine of Torture:
     Torture and Ill-treatment of Palestinian Detainees during Arrest, Detention
     and Interrogation (September 2001 – April 2003)*, Jerusalem: Public Committee
     against Torture in Israel.
18   For a real-life example, see Miller and Blackler (2005), p. 129.

References

Alexandra, Andrew (2000) Dirty Harry and dirty hands, in Tony Coady, Steve James, Seumas Miller, and Michael O'Keefe (eds), *Violence and Police Culture*, Melbourne: Melbourne University Press.

Alexandra, Andrew, and Seumas Miller (1996) Needs, moral self-consciousness and professional roles, *Professional Ethics*, 5.1–2, pp. 43–61.

Alexandra, Andrew, and Seumas Miller (2009) *Ethics in Practice: Moral Theory and the Professions*, Sydney: UNSW Press.

Alexandra, Andrew, and Seumas Miller (2010) *Integrity Systems for Occupations*, Aldershot: Ashgate.

Allen, Christopher (2008) *Practical Guide to Evidence*, London: Routledge-Cavendish.

Anechiarico, Frank, and James B. Jacobs (1996) *The Pursuit of Absolute Integrity: How Corruption Control Makes Government Ineffective*, Chicago: University of Chicago Press.

Association of Chief Police Officers (ACPO) (2012) *ACPO Good Practice Guide for Digital Evidence*, http://www.acpo.police.uk/documents/crime/2011/201110 -cba-digital-evidence-v5.pdf (accessed January 14, 2013).

Association of Chief Police Officers (ACPO) (n.d.) *Manual of Standards for Covert Human Intelligence Sources* (CHIS). A restricted document.

Ayling, J., P. Grabosky and C. Shearing (2009) *Lengthening the Arm of the Law: Enhancing Police Resources in the 21st Century*, Cambridge: Cambridge University Press.

Baldwin, John (1993) Police interview techniques: Establishing truth or proof? *British Journal of Criminology*, 33.3, pp. 325–352.

Ball, James (2013) Verizon court order: telephone call metadata and what it can show, *The Guardian*, Friday, June 6, 2013, http://www.theguardian

Investigative Ethics: Ethics for Police Detectives and Criminal Investigators, First Edition.
Seumas Miller and Ian A. Gordon.
© 2014 Seumas Miller and Ian A. Gordon. Published 2014 by John Wiley & Sons, Ltd.

.com/world/2013/jun/06/phone-call-metadata-information-authorities (accessed October 8, 2013).

BBC (British Broadcasting Corporation), Smith plans 42-day terror limit, December 6, 2007, http://news.bbc.co.uk/1/hi/uk_politics/7130072.stm (accessed September 27, 2013).

Beecher-Monas, Erica (2007) *Evaluating Scientific Evidence: An Interdisciplinary Framework for Intellectual Due Process*, Cambridge: Cambridge University Press.

Belgian Privacy Commission, *Opinion on the Transfer of Personal Data by SCRL SWIFT Following the UST (OFAC) Subpoenas*, https://www.aclu.org/files/images/asset_upload_file96_26942.pdf (accessed January 14, 2013).

Benn, S. I. (1998) *A Theory of Freedom*, Cambridge: Cambridge University Press.

Bichard, M. (2004) *Bichard Inquiry Report*, dera.ioe.ac.uk/6394/1/report.pdf.

Bilefsky, Dan (2006) Data transfer broke rules, report says, *New York Times*, September 28, 2006.

Billingsley, R., T. Nemitz, and P. Bean (eds) (2001) *Informers: Policing, Policy and Practice*, Cullompton, Devon: Willan Publishing.

Bittner, Egon (1980) *The Functions of the Police in Modern Society*, Cambridge, MA: Oelgeschlager, Gunn, and Hain.

Blackler, John, and Seumas Miller (2000a) *Police Ethics (vol. 1): Case Studies in Street Policing*, Wagga Wagga: Charles Sturt University and NSW Police Service.

Blackler, John, and Seumas Miller (2000b), *Police Ethics (vol. 2): Case Studies for Police Investigators*, Wagga Wagga: Charles Sturt University and NSW Police Service.

Blackler, John, and Seumas Miller (2000c), *Police Ethics (vol. 3): Case Studies for Police Managers*, Wagga Wagga: Charles Sturt University and NSW Police Service, 2000.

Bottomley, S., and S. Bronitt (2006) *Law in Context* (3rd edn), Sydney: Federation Press.

Brandl, Steven G., and David E. Barlow (eds) (1996) *Classics of Policing*, Cincinnati, OH: Anderson Publishing Co.

Bronitt, Simon, and Declan Roche (2000) Between rhetoric and reality: Socio-legal and republican perspectives on entrapment, *International Journal of Evidence and Proof*, 4, pp. 77–106.

Bromwich, David (2011) Obama, Bush, and the Patriot Act, *The Huffington Post*, May 30, 2011, http://www.huffingtonpost.com/david-bromwich/patriot-act -obama-_b_868831.html (accessed October 8, 2013).

Brown, Malcolm, and Paul Wilson (1992) *Justice and Nightmares; Success and Failures of Forensic Science in Australian and New Zealand*, Kensington, NSW: University of New South Wales Press.

Brown, Michael F. (2001) *Criminal Investigation: Law and Practice* (2nd edn), Boston: Butterworth and Heineman.

Brown, W. (ed.) (1995) *Australian Crime*, Sydney: Book Company International.

Bryett, Keith, Arch Harrison, and John Shaw (1994) *An Introduction to Policing*, vol. 2, Sydney: Butterworths.

Coady, C. A. J. (1992) *Testimony*, Oxford: Oxford University Press.

Cohen, Stanley (1985) *Visions of Social Control: Crime, Punishment and Classification*, Cambridge: Polity Press.

Commonwealth Ombudsman (1997) *Professional Reporting and Internal Witness Protection in the Australian Federal Police*, Canberra: Commonwealth Ombudsman.

Conlon, Gerry (1991) *Proved Innocent: The Story of Gerry Conlon and the Guildford Four*, London: Penguin.

Critchley, T. A. (1967) *A History of Police in England and Wales 900–1966*, London: Constable.

Damaska, M. (1975) Structures of authority and comparative criminal procedure, *Yale Law Journal*, 80, http://digitalcommons.law.yale.edu/fss_papers/1590 (accessed January 13, 2014).

Davis, Frank (1990) *Blackburn; A Forensic Disaster*, Sydney: Harry the Hat Publications.

Davis, Michael (1998) Conflicts of interest, in Ruth F. Chadwick (ed.), *Encyclopaedia of Applied Ethics*, London: Academic Press, vol. 1, A–D, p. 590.

Dawid, Philip (2008) Statistics and the law, in Andrew Bell, John Swenson-Wright, and Karin Tybjerg (eds), *Evidence*, Cambridge: Cambridge University Press.

Denmark, Bob (n.d.) *Ethical Investigation: A Practical Guide for Police Officers*, UK Foreign and Commonwealth Office, http://www.jeiruegas.com/docs/Ethical%20Investigation%20Bob%20Denmark.pdf (accessed October 8, 2013).

Denning, D. E., and W. E. Baugh (1997) *Encryption and Evolving Technologies as Tools of Organized Crime and Terrorism*, Washington DC: US Working Group on Organized Crime, National Strategy Information Centre.

Delattre, Edwin (1994) *Character and Cops: Ethics in Policing* (2nd edn), Washington DC: AEI Press, 1994.

Devlin, Patrick (1968) *The Enforcement of Morals*, Oxford: Oxford University Press.

Dunnighan, C., and C. Norris (2002) The detective, the snout and the audit commission: The real costs in using informants, *Howard Journal of Criminal Justice*, 38.1, pp. 67–86.

Dworkin, Gerald (1988) *The Theory and Practice of Autonomy*, Cambridge: Cambridge University Press.

Dworkin, Ronald (1977) *Taking Rights Seriously*, Cambridge, MA: Harvard University Press.

Dworkin, Ronald (1998) *Law's Empire*, Oxford: Hart Publishing.

Emery, Richard D. (1998) Cameras in the station house, *Criminal Justice Ethics* 17.1, pp. 43–44.

Ericson, Richard V. (1981) *Making Crime: Detectives at Work*, Toronto: Butterworths.

Eterno, John, A. and Eli B. Silverman (2012) *The Crime Numbers Game: Management by Manipulation*, Boca Raton: CRC Press.

Etzioni, Amitai (1999) *The Limits of Privacy*, New York: Basic Books.

Ewing, A. C. (1953) *Ethics*, London: Macmillan.

FBI (Federal Bureau of Investigation) (2012) A mother's worst nightmare: fusion center key in rescue of abducted infant, January 17, 2012, http://www.fbi.gov/

news/stories/2012/january/fusion_011712/fusion_011712 (accessed September 27, 2013).

Feinberg, Joel (1987) *Harm to Others: The Moral Limits of the Criminal Law*, Oxford: Oxford University Press.

Ferguson, Charles (2012) Heist of the century: Wall Street's role in the financial crisis, *The Guardian*, Monday, May 21, 2012, http://www.theguardian.com/business/2012/may/20/wall-street-role-financial-crisis (accessed October 8, 2013).

Fijnaut, Cyrille, and Gary T. Marx (eds) (1995) *Undercover: Police Surveillance in Comparative Perspective*, The Hague: Kluwer.

Flood, Brian, and Roger Gaspar (2009) Strategic aspects of the UK National Intelligence Model, in Jerry H. Ratcliffe (ed.) *Strategic Thinking in Criminal Intelligence*, Sydney: Federation Press, pp. 47–65.

Frontline (n.d.) Rampart Scandal, *Frontline*, http://www.pbs.org/wgbh/pages/frontline/shows/lapd/scandal/credibility.html (accessed September 27, 2103).

Fyfe, N. R. (2001) *Protecting Intimidated Witnesses*, Aldershot: Ashgate.

Gert, Bernard (2004) *Common Morality: Deciding What to Do*, Oxford: Oxford University Press.

Gettier, Edmund (1963) Is justified true belief knowledge? *Analysis*, 23, pp. 121–123.

Gill, P. (2000) *Rounding up the Usual Suspects?: Developments in Contemporary Law Enforcement Intelligence*, Aldershot: Ashgate.

Goldstein, Herman (1990) *Problem-Oriented Policing*, New York: McGraw-Hill.

Goldstein, Herman (1996) Team policing, in Steven G. Brandl and David E. Barlow (eds), *Classics of Policing*, Cincinnati, OH: Anderson Publishing Co.

Goold, Benjamin J. (2002) Privacy rights and public spaces: CCTV and the problem of the "unobservable observer," *Criminal Justice Ethics*, Winter/Spring, pp. 21–27.

Gordon, Ian, and Seumas Miller (2012) The fatal police shooting of Jean Charles de Menezes: Is anyone responsible? in Simon Bronitt, Miriam Gani, and Saskia Hufnagel (eds), *Shooting to Kill: Socio-legal Perspectives on the Use of Lethal Force*, Oxford: Hart, pp. 215–239.

Grabosky, Peter, Russell G. Smith, and Gillian Dempsey (2001) *Electronic Theft: Unlawful Acquisition in Cyberspace*, Cambridge: Cambridge University Press.

Green, Stuart P. (2006) *Lying, Cheating and Stealing: A Moral Theory of White Collar Crime*, Oxford: Oxford University Press.

Green, Stuart, P. (2012) *13 Ways to Steal a Bicycle: Theft Law in the Information Age*, Cambridge, MA: Harvard University Press.

Greer, S. (2001) Where the grass is greener? Supergrasses in comparative perspective, in R. Billingsley, T. Nemitz, and P. Bean (eds), *Informers: Policing, Policy and Practice*, Cullompton, Devon: Willan Publishing, pp. 123–140.

Grice, Paul (1968) Utterer's meaning, sentence meaning and word meaning, *Foundations of Language*, 4.3, pp. 225–242.

Guardian (n.d.), BAE Files, www.guardian.co.uk/baefiles (accessed September 27, 2013).

Gudjonsson, Gisl (1992) *The Psychology of Interrogations, Confessions and Testimony*, New York: Wiley.

Hall, Kristin (2012) On operations of Tennessee's fusion center, *Associated Press*, http://blogs.knoxnews.com/humphrey/2012/02/on-operations-of-tennessees-fu.html (accessed September 27, 2013).

Hall, Richard (1981) *Greed: The "Mr. Asia" Connection*, Sydney: Pan Books.

Harfield, Clive (2012) Police informers and professional ethics, *Criminal Justice Ethics*, June, pp. 1–23.

Harfield, Clive, and Karen Harfield (2012) *Covert Investigation* (3rd edn), Oxford: Oxford University Press.

Harre, Rom, and E. H. Madden (1975) *Causal Powers*, Oxford: Blackwell.

Haubrich, D. (2003) September 11, anti-terror laws and civil liberties: Britain, France and Germany compared. *Government and Opposition* 38.1, pp. 3–28.

Hepworth, M., and Bryan Turner (1982) *Confession: Studies in Deviance and Religion*, London: Routledge and Kegan Paul.

Higgins, Oliver (2009) The theory and practice of intelligence collection, in Jerry H. Ratcliffe (ed.), *Strategic Thinking in Criminal Intelligence*, Sydney: Federation Press, pp. 85–107.

Hocking, J. (2004) *Terror Laws*, Sydney: University of New South Wales Press.

Inbau, Fred E., John E. Reid, Joseph P. Buckley, and Brian C. Jayne (2001) *Criminal Interrogations and Confessions* (4th edn), Gaithersburg, MD: Aspen Press.

Independent Police Complaints Commission (IPCC) (2007) *Stockwell One: Investigation into the shooting of Jean Charles de Menezes at Stockwell underground station* (February 2007) s 9, paras 9.1–9.19, 40–44, http://policeauthority.org/metropolitan/downloads/scrutinites/stockwell/ipcc-one.pdf (accessed January 14, 2014).

Jabbra J. G., and O. P. Dwivedi (1988) *Public Service Accountability: A Comparative Perspective*, West Hartford, CT: Kumarian Press.

Jack, Ian (2008) My silence about the terrorists was only partly cowardice, *The Guardian*, Saturday, March 8, 2008, http://cain.ulst.ac.uk/victims/docs/newspapers/guardian/jack_gu_080308.pdf (accessed September 27, 2013).

Jackall, Robert (1996) Response to McCoy, in John Kleinig (ed.), *Handled with Discretion: Ethical Issues in Police Decision Making*, Lanham, MD: Rowman and Littlefield, pp. 179–182.

Jackall, Robert (1997) *Wild Cowboys; Urban Marauders and the Forces of Order*, Cambridge, MA: Harvard University Press.

Jackall, Robert (2005) *Street Stories: The World of Police Detectives*, Cambridge, MA: Harvard University Press.

Johnston, Les (1992) *The Rebirth of Private Policing*, London: Routledge.

Kappeler, Victor E., Richard D. Sluder, and Geoffrey P. Alpert (1994) *Forces of Deviance; Understanding the Dark Side of Policing*, Prospects Heights, IL: Waveland Press.

Kleinig, John (1996) *The Ethics of Policing*, Cambridge: Cambridge University Press.

Kleinig, John, Peter Mameli, Seumas Miller, Douglas Salane, and Edwina Schwartz (2011) *Security and Privacy: Global Standards for Ethical Identity Management in Contemporary Liberal Democratic States*, Canberra: ANU e-Press.

Leaver, Alan (1997) *Investigating Crime*, Sydney: Law Book Company.

Leigh, David, and Rob Evans (n.d.) BAE Files, *The Guardian*, www.guardian.co.uk/baefiles (accessed October 8, 2013).

Leppard, David (2013) Police smash £300m bank cyberheist gang, *The Sunday Times*, Sunday, September 15, 2013, http://www.thesundaytimes.co.uk/sto/news/uk_news/National/article1314019.ece (accessed October 8, 2013).

Lessig, Lawrence (2011) *Republic, Lost: How Money Corrupts Congress and a Plan to Stop it*, New York: Twelve, Hachette Book Group.

Leyden, John (2012) Feds unlock suspect's encrypted drive, avoid Constitution meltdown: Digital age plays havoc with 5th Amendment, *The Register*, March 1, http://www.theregister.co.uk/2012/03/01/forced_decryption_ruling_moot/ (accessed October 8, 2013).

Lichtblau, Eric, and James Risen (2006) Bank data is sifted by U.S. in secret to block terror, *New York Times*, June 23, 2006, A1.

Live Leak (2011) UK: Householder who stabbed burglar to death faces no further charges, http://www.liveleak.com/view?i=a84_1311344668 (accessed January 14, 2014)

Lusher, Edwin (1981) *Report of the Commission to Inquire into New South Wales Police Administration*, Sydney: NSW Government Printer.

Lustgarten, Laurence (1986) *The Governance of Police*, London: Sweet and Maxwell.

Lynch, A., and G. Williams (2006) *What Price Security? Taking Stock of Australia's Anti-terror Laws*, Sydney: UNSW Press.

MacNeil, Iain, Keith Wotherspoon, and Kathryn Taylor (1998) *Business Investigations*, Bristol: Jordan Publishing.

Marquez, Jeremiah (2005) LAPD: Ramparts scandal: L.A. police corruption settlements estimated to reach $70 million, *Associated Press*, March 31, 2005, http://injusticebusters.org/index.htm/LAPD.htm (accessed September 27, 2013).

Marx, Gary T. (1988) *Undercover: Police Surveillance in America*, Berkeley, CA: University of California Press.

Marx, Gary T. (1992) Under-the-covers undercover investigations: Some reflections on the state's use of sex and deception in law enforcement, *Criminal Justice Ethics*, 11.2, Winter–Spring, pp. 13–24.

McCoy, Candace (1996) Police, prosecutors and discretion in investigation, in John Kleinig (ed.), *Handled with Discretion: Ethical Issues in Police Decision Making*, Lanham, MD: Rowman and Littlefield, pp. 159–178.

Metropolitan Police Authority (MPA) (2005) *Suicide Terrorism Report*, 13 (October 27, 2005), http://policeauthority.org/Metropolitan/committees/mpa/2005/051027/13/index.html (accessed October 8, 2013).

Miller, Arthur (1982) *Miller's Court*, New York: Houghton Mifflin.

Miller, Claire Cain, Secret court ruling put tech companies in data bind, *New York Times*, June 13, 2013.

Miller, Seumas (1992) Joint action, *Philosophical Papers*, 21.3, pp. 275–299.

Miller, Seumas (1995) Intentions, ends and joint action, *Philosophical Papers*, 34.1, pp. 51–67.

Miller, Seumas (1996) *Issues in Police Ethics*, Wagga Wagga: Keon.

Miller, Seumas (1997) Privacy and the Internet, *Australian Computer Journal*, 29.1, pp. 12–16.

Miller, Seumas (1998a) Authority, discretion and accountability: The case of policing, in C. Sampford, N. Preston, and C Bois (eds), *Public Sector Ethics: Finding and Implementing Values*, London: Routledge, pp. 37–53.

Miller, Seumas (1998b) Corruption and anti-corruption in the profession of policing, *Professional Ethics*, 6.3–4, pp. 83–106.

Miller, Seumas (1999) Privacy, encryption and the Internet, in A. D'Atri, A. Marturano, S. Rogerson, and T. Ward Bynum (eds), *Proceedings of the 4th ETHICOMP International Conference on the Social and Ethical Impacts of Information and Communication Technologies* (CD format), Rome, pp. 1–11.

Miller, Seumas (2001a) *Social Action: A Teleological Account*, New York: Cambridge University Press.

Miller, Seumas (2001b) Collective responsibility, *Public Affairs Quarterly*, 15.1, pp. 65–82.

Miller, Seumas (2003) Individual autonomy and sociality, in F. Schmitt (ed.), *Socialising Metaphysics: The Nature of Social Reality*, Lanham, MD: Rowman and Littlefield, pp. 269–300.

Miller, Seumas (2004) Noble cause corruption in policing revisited, in P. Villiers and R. Adlam (eds), *A Safe, Just and Tolerant Society: Police Virtue Rediscovered*, Winchester, UK: Waterside Press, pp. 105–118.

Miller, Seumas (2005) Is torture ever morally justifiable? *International Journal of Applied Philosophy*, 19.2, pp. 179–192.

Miller, Seumas (2006) Collective moral responsibility: An individualist account, in Peter A. French (ed.), *Midwest Studies in Philosophy*, 30, pp. 176–193.

Miller, Seumas (2008) Collective responsibility and information and communication technology, in J. van den Hoven and J. Weckert (eds), *Moral Philosophy and Information Technology*, New York: Cambridge University Press, pp. 226–250.

Miller, Seumas (2009a) Research in applied ethics: Problems and perspectives, *Philosophia*, 37.2, pp. 185–201.

Miller, Seumas (2009b) *Terrorism and Counter-terrorism: Ethics and Liberal Democracy*, New York: Wiley-Blackwell.

Miller, Seumas (2010a) *The Moral Foundations of Social Institutions: A Philosophical Study*, New York: Cambridge University Press.

Miller, Seumas (2010b) What makes a good internal affairs investigation? *Criminal Justice Ethics*, 29.1, pp. 30–41.

Miller, Seumas (2010c) Integrity systems and professional reporting in police organisations, *Criminal Justice Ethics*, 29.3, pp. 241–257.

Miller, Seumas (2011a) Global financial institutions, ethics and market fundamentalism, in Ned Dobos, Christian Barry, and Thomas Pogge (eds), *The Global Financial Crisis: Ethical Issues*, Basingstoke: Palgrave, pp. 24–51.

Miller, Seumas (2011b) Corruption, in Edward N. Zalta (ed.), *The Stanford Encyclopedia of Philosophy* (Spring 2011 edn), http://plato.stanford.edu/archives/spr2011/entries/corruption/ (accessed September 27, 2013).

Miller, Seumas (2011c) Torture, in Edward N. Zalta (ed.), *The Stanford Encyclopedia of Philosophy* (Summer 2011 edn), http://plato.stanford.edu/archives/sum2011/entries/torture/ (accessed September 27, 2013).

Miller, Seumas (2013) The LIBOR scandal: Culture, corruption and collective action problems in the global banking sector, in G. Gilligan and J. O'Brien (eds), *Regulating Culture: Integrity, Risk and Accountability in Capital Markets*, Oxford: Hart Publishing.

Miller, Seumas (2013) *Analysis of Focus Groups and In-depth Interviews of NSW Police Officers*, Report for NSW Police.

Miller, Seumas (2014) Police detectives, criminal investigations and moral responsibility, *Criminal Justice Ethics*, 33.

Miller, Seumas, David Biles, Tracey Green, and Jerry Ratcliffe (2001) *Report on Drug-related Complaints against the NSW Police*, Australian Research Council-funded SPIRT Grant.

Miller, Seumas, and John Blackler (1995) *Police Ethics*, Wagga Wagga: Keon Press.

Miller, Seumas, and John Blackler (2000) Restorative justice: Retribution, confession and shame, in J. Braithwaite and H. Strang (eds), *Restorative Justice: From Philosophy to Practice*, Aldershot: Ashgate.

Miller, Seumas, and John Blackler (2005) *Ethical Issues in Policing*, Aldershot: Ashgate.

Miller, Seumas, John Blackler, and Andrew Alexandra (2006) *Police Ethics* (2nd edn), Sydney: Allen and Unwin.

Miller, Seumas, M. Collingridge, and J. Bowles (2001) Privacy and confidentiality in social work, *Australian Social Work*, 54.2, pp. 3–14.

Miller, Seumas, Steve Curry, Ian Gordon, John Blackler, and Tim Prenzler (2008) *An Integrity System for Victoria Police*: vol. 2, Australian Research Council Linkage grant funded report for Victoria Police, Canberra: Centre for Applied Philosophy and Public Ethics.

Miller, Seumas, and Tim Prenzler (2008) *An Integrity System for Victoria Police*: vol. 1, Australian Research Council Linkage grant funded report for Victoria Police, Canberra: Centre for Applied Philosophy and Public Ethics.

Miller, Seumas, Peter Roberts, and Edward Spence (2005) *Corruption and Anti-corruption: A Study in Applied Philosophy*, Saddle River, NJ: Prentice Hall.

Moore, Michael S. (2009) *Causation and Responsibility: An Essay in Law, Morals and Metaphysics*, Oxford: Oxford University Press.

Morgan, David, and Geoffrey Stephenson (eds) (1994) *Suspicion and Silence: The Right to Silence in Criminal Investigations*, London: Blackstone Press.

Nagel, Thomas (2002) Concealment and exposure, in *Concealment and Exposure and other Essays*, Oxford: Oxford University Press.

Nagel, Thomas (1997) *The Last Word*, Oxford: Oxford University Press.

National Centre for Policing Excellence (2005) *Guidance on the National Intelligence Model*, http://whereismydata.files.wordpress.com/2009/01/national-intelligence-model-20051.pdf (accessed October 8, 2013).

National Commission on Terrorist Attacks upon the United States (2004) Executive summary, in *9/11 Commission of Inquiry*, http://www.9-11commission.gov/report/ (accessed October 8, 2013).

National Policing Improvement Agency (2009) *National Investigative Interviewing Strategy*, http://www.acpo.police.uk/documents/crime/2009/200901CRINSI01.pdf (accessed January 15, 2014).

NBC News (2009) U.S. marshal guilty of leaking secrets to mob, *Associated Press*, April 28, 2009, http://www.nbcnews.com/id/30463996/ns/us_news-crime_and_courts/t/us-marshal-guilty-leaking-secrets-mob/#.UlOFCYYnoko (accessed October 8, 2013).

Neyroud, Peter, and Alan Beckley (2001) *Policing, Ethics and Human Rights*, Cullompton, Devon: Willan Publishing.

Nickel, James W. (2007) *Making Sense of Human Rights* (2nd edn), Oxford: Wiley-Blackwell Publishing.

Nicholson, N. (1979) *The Yorkshire Ripper*, London: Star.

Nickell, Joe, and John F. Fischer (1999) *Crime Science: Methods of Forensic Detection*, Lexington, KN: University of Kentucky Press.

O'Connor, Thomas R. (2009) *Bringing Terrorists to Justice: Investigation and Adjudication*, Delhi: Indo-American Books.

Office of Police Integrity (2005) *Review of Victoria Police Witness Protection Program*, Melbourne: Office of Police Integrity.

Packer, H. L. (1964) Two models of criminal process, *University of Pennsylvania Law Review*, 113, November, pp. 1–68.

Paton, H. J. (1948) *The Moral Law*, translation and analysis of Immanuel Kant's *Groundwork of the Metaphysic of Morals*, London: Hutchinson.

Perlroth, Nicole, Jeff Larson, and Scott Shane (2013) Files show N.S.A. foiling encryption, *International Herald Tribune* September 7th, 2013, page. 1.

Pitcher, George, (ed.) (1964) *Truth*, Saddle River, NJ: Prentice Hall.

Pithers, Malcolm (1993) Uproar after acquittal in Nikki Allen murder case: Not guilty verdict ends six-week trial in which judge refused to admit alleged confession on interview tape as evidence, *The Independent*, November 22, 1993, http://www.independent.co.uk/news/uk/uproar-after-acquittal-in-nikki-allen -murder-case-not-guilty-verdict-ends-sixweek-trial-in-which-judge-refused-to -admit-alleged-confession-on-interview-tape-as-evidence-1505896.html (accessed September 27, 2013).

Police Ombudsman for Northern Ireland (2007) *Operation Ballast: investigation into the circumstances surrounding the murder of Raymond McCord Jnr.*

Primoratz, Igor (2013) *Terrorism: A Philosophical Investigation*, Cambridge: Polity Press.

Public Committee against Torture in Israel (2003) *Back to a Routine of Torture: Torture and Ill-treatment of Palestinian Detainees during Arrest, Detention and Interrogation (September 2001 – April 2003)*, Jerusalem: Public Committee against Torture in Israel.

Rashid, Ahmed (2001) *Taliban: The Story of the Afghan Warlords*, London: Pan Books.

Ratcliffe, Jerry H. (ed.) (2009) *Strategic Thinking in Criminal Intelligence*, Sydney: Federation Press.

Ratcliffe, Jerry, David Biles, Tracey Green, and Seumas Miller (2005) Drug related complaints against police: Some findings from a New South Wales study, *Policing: An International Journal of Police Strategies and Management*, 28.1, pp. 69–83.

Real Life Crimes (1993) *Peter Sutcliffe; the Yorkshire Ripper*, Real Life Crimes 5, London: Midsummer Books.

Royal Commission on Criminal Justice (1993) *Report*, http://www.official-documents.gov.uk/document/cm22/2263/2263.pdf (accessed January 15, 2014).

Royaume de la Belgique Commission de la Protection de la Vie Privée (2006) *Summary of the Opinion on the Transfer of Personal Data by SCRL SWIFT*

Following the UST (OFAC) Subpoenas, https://www.aclu.org/files/images/asset_upload_file96_26942.pdf (accessed October 8, 2013).

Rupp, David, Supreme Court rules on police using infrared, *ABC News*, 11 June, 2012, http://abcnews.go.com/US/story?id=93127&page=1 (accessed October 8, 2013).

Saks, Michael J. (2008) Explaining the tension between the Supreme Court's embrace of validity as the touchstone of admissibility of expert testimony and lower courts' (seeming) rejection of same, *Episteme*, 5.3, pp. 329–342.

Sanger, David, David Barboza and Nicole Perlroth, Chinese army unit is seen as tied to hacking against U.S., *The New York Times*, February 18, 2013, http://www.nytimes.com/2013/02/19/technology/chinas-army-is-seen-as-tied-to-hacking-against-us.html?pagewanted=all (accessed October 8, 2013).

Scarman, Leslie, *The Scarman Report The Brixton Disorders 10-12 April 1981: Report of an Inquiry*, London: Pelican Books, 1982.

Schauer, Frederik (2003) *Profiles, Probabilities and Stereotypes*, Cambridge, MA: Belknap Press.

Scheffler, Samuel (ed.) (1988) *Consequentialism and its Critics*, Oxford: Oxford University Press.

Scheid, Don E. (2010) Indefinite detention of mega-terrorists, *Criminal Justice Ethics*, 29.1, pp. 1–28.

Sherman, Lawrence W. (1985) Becoming bent, in Frederick Elliston and Michael Feldberg (eds), *Moral Issues in Police Work*, Totowa, NJ: Rowman and Allanheld, pp. 253–266.

Shue, Henry (1984) *Basic Rights*, Princeton, NJ: Princeton University Press.

Sinnott-Armstrong, Walter (1999) Entrapment in the Net?, *Ethics and Information Technology*, 1.2, pp. 95–104.

Sinnott-Armstrong, Walter, Adina Roskies, Teneille Brown, and Emily Murphy (2008) Brain images as legal evidence, *Episteme*, 5, pp. 359–373.

Skerker, Michael (2010) *An Ethics of Interrogation*, Chicago: University of Chicago Press.

Skolnick, Jerome (1977) *Justice without Trial; Law Enforcement in Democratic Society* (2nd edn), New York: Macmillan.

Skolnick, Jerome (1982) Deception by police, *Criminal Justice Ethics*, 1.2, Summer/Fall, pp. 40–54.

Skolnick, Jerome (1994) *Justice without Trial: Law Enforcement in a Democratic Society* (3rd edn), New York: Macmillan.

Skolnick, Jerome H., and Richard A. Leo (1992) The ethics of deceptive interrogation, *Criminal Justice Ethics*, Winter/Spring, 3–12.

Slate, Risdon N. (1997) The Federal Witness Protection Program: Its evolution and continuing growing pains, *Criminal Justice Ethics*, Summer, pp. 20–34.

Smith, Geoffrey, Mark Button, Les Johnson, and Kwabena Frimpong (eds) (2011) *Studying Fraud as White Collar Crime*, London: Palgrave Macmillan.

Sorell, Tom (2011) Preventative policing, surveillance, and European counter-terrorism, *Criminal Justice Ethics*, April, pp. 1–22.

Sorkin, Andrew Ross (1913) The victims in J P Morgan settlement, *International Herald Tribune*, September 25, p. 22.

Stelfox, Peter (2009) *Criminal Investigation: An Introduction to Principles and Practice*, Cullompton, Devon: Willan Publishing, 2009.

The Royal Commission on the Police (1962) *The Royal Commission on the Police: Final report Cmnd. 1728*: London: HM Stationery Office.

Transparency International UK (2012) *Benchmarking Police Integrity Programmes Report* – May 2012, http://www.transparency.org.uk/our-work/publications/ 10-publications/473-benchmarking-police-integrity-programmes (accessed September 27, 2013).

United Kingdom Government (2001), *Anti-Terrorism, Crime and Security Emergency Act 2001*, http://www.legislation.gov.uk/ukpga/2001/24/contents (accessed September 27, 2013).

United Kingdom Government (2003) *Sexual Offences Act 2003*, sections 1-4. See: http://www.legislation.gov.uk/ukpga/2003/42/contents (accessed September 27, 2013).

United Nations (n.d.) Article 24 of the Universal Declaration of Human Rights, http://www.un.org/en/documents/udhr/ (accessed September 27, 2013).

US v. Miller, 425 US 435 (1976), http://supreme.justia.com/cases/federal/us/425/435/, (accessed September 27, 2013).

Viswanatha, Aruna, and Brett Wolf (2012) HSBC to pay $1.9 billion US fine in money laundering case, *Reuters*, December 11, 2012, http://www.reuters .com/article/2012/12/11/us-hsbc-probe-idUSBRE8BA05M20121211 (accessed September 27, 2013).

Waldron, Jeremy (1988) *The Right to Private Property*, Oxford: Oxford University Press.

Walsh, Patrick F. (2011) *Intelligence and Intelligence Analysis*, London: Routledge.

Weiner, Tim (2013) *Enemies: A History of the FBI*, New York: Random House.

Wells, Gary, and Elizabeth Olson (2003) Eyewitness testimony, *Annual Review of Psychology*, 54, pp. 277–295.

Wells, Joseph T. (1992) *Fraud Examination: Investigative and Audit Procedures*, New York: Quorum Books.

Whitton, Evan (1988) *The Hillbilly Dictator: Australia's Police State*, Sydney: BBC Books.

Williamson, Tom (ed.) (2006) *Investigative Interviewing: Rights, Research and Regulation*, Cullompton, Devon: Willan Publishing.

Wilson, Colin, and Damon Wilson (1992) *World Famous Serial Killers*, London: Magpie.

Wood, James (1997) *Final Report of the Royal Commission into the NSW Police Service, vol. 2: Reform*, http://www.pic.nsw.gov.au/files/reports/RCPS%20 Report%20Volume%202.pdf (accessed January 15, 2014).

Writer, L., S. Barrett, and A. Bouda (1992) *Garden of Evil: The Granny Killer's Reign of Terror*, Sydney: Ironbark.

Index

Investigative Ethics: Ethics for Police Detectives and Criminal Investigators, First Edition.
Seumas Miller and Ian A. Gordon.
© 2014 Seumas Miller and Ian A. Gordon. Published 2014 by John Wiley & Sons, Ltd.

Printed and bound by CPI Group (UK) Ltd, Croydon, CR0 4YY

13/04/2025

14656563-0005